SINGULAR AND PLURAL

OXFORD STUDIES IN THE ANTHROPOLOGY OF LANGUAGE

Series editor

Laura M. Ahearn, *Rutgers University*

This series is devoted to works from a wide array of scholarly traditions that treat linguistic practices as forms of social action.

Editorial Board

Alessandro Duranti, *University of California at Los Angeles*
Paul B. Garrett, *Temple University*
Justin Richland, *The University of Chicago*

Thank You for Dying for Our Country: Commemorative Texts and Performances in Jerusalem
Chaim Noy

Singular and Plural: Ideologies of Linguistic Authority in 21st Century Catalonia
Kathryn A. Woolard

SINGULAR AND PLURAL

Ideologies of Linguistic Authority in 21st Century Catalonia

Kathryn A. Woolard

OXFORD
UNIVERSITY PRESS

OXFORD
UNIVERSITY PRESS

Oxford University Press is a department of the University of Oxford. It furthers
the University's objective of excellence in research, scholarship, and education
by publishing worldwide.Oxford is a registered trade mark of Oxford University
Press in the UK and certain other countries.

Published in the United States of America by Oxford University Press
198 Madison Avenue, New York, NY 10016, United States of America.

Library of Congress Cataloging-in-Publication Data
Names: Woolard, Kathryn Ann.
Title: Singular and plural: ideologies of linguistic authority in
21st century Catalonia / Kathryn A. Woolard.
Description: Oxford; New York: Oxford University Press, [2016] |
Series: Oxford Studies in the Anthropology of Language |
Includes bibliographical references and index.
Identifiers: LCCN 2015039517 | ISBN 978-0-19-025862-7 (pbk. : alk. paper) |
ISBN 978-0-19-025861-0 (hardcover : alk. paper) | ISBN 978-0-19-025863-4 (ebook) |
ISBN 978-0-19-060046-4 (online content)
Subjects: LCSH: Language policy—History—21st century—Spain—Catalonia. |
Ideologies—Span—Catalonia. | Catalan language—Social aspects. |
Catalans—Ethnic identity. | Catalonia (Spain)—Languages—Political aspects.
Classification: LCC P115.5.S7 W77 2016 | DDC 306.442499—dc23
LC record available at http://lccn.loc.gov/2015039517

9 8 7 6 5 4 3 2 1
Printed by Sheridan Books, Inc., United States of America

CONTENTS

PART III: *Changing Discourses of Language in Personal Life*

LIST OF FIGURES AND TABLE

Figures

Table

PREFACE

When I first began research in Catalonia in 1979, it was a place where the unusual alignments of political, economic, and linguistic forces defied stereotypical expectations about minority languages. It was also alive with aspirations for political and sociolinguistic transformations, as it returned to political autonomy after the end of the Franco regime. Catalonia has gotten all the more complex and surprising in this millennium, and once again it is alive with aspirations for political transformations, now for sovereignty. The historical layering of complexity as well as my own increased awareness of it has made this book about Catalonia in the 21st century more challenging to write than my first monograph on it was. Given this, I want to acknowledge briefly the stance I have taken here as an author and comment on how I have imagined possible readers.

It meant a lot to me when a sociolinguist told me that he found in my first book a sympathetic account of the perspectives of both of the linguistic groups in contact. I hope that readers of this new book will again find that to be true of my portrayal of individuals who generously shared their experiences and views with me. At the level of public controversies discussed in Parts I and II, it will be evident that my own sympathies are for the continued vibrant and significant use of Catalan, especially in creative patterns that do not quite fit traditions of any stripe. This book tries to give both a critical and a sympathetic view of the ideological foundations of contemporary Catalanism, with the former framed well within the latter. This is in part to redress a public record that I find imbalanced. The book is primarily addressed to an audience outside of Catalonia, especially in the United States, where Catalanist voices are rarely heard except among a relatively small circle of supporters.

While writing this book, I have found that the news about Catalonia that reaches the United States and Northern Europe is generally filtered through the perspective of the Spanish state, in part because most international reporting originates in Madrid, and in part because of the invisibility to social scientists, journalists, and lay audiences of the banal nationalism of already existing states. As a result, I often encounter systematic incomprehension of the Catalanist

movement, even at the basic factual level. A peer-reviewed political science article mischaracterizes the centralized Spanish state as federal; an anthropologist
of Latin America asks me, "What more do the Catalans want? They're already
completely autonomous," and is surprised to learn that Catalonia has more limited powers than any state in the United States. I could cite many more examples
of misconceptions that come from international newspapers of record as well as
social science.

Catalanist politics and policies rest on ideological grounds, not disinterested
objective truths, just as Spanish nationalist policies do. Thoughtful critique of
linguistic and educational policies is always in order, and that is true of Catalonia
as elsewhere. However, critical studies that demythologize the ideological foundations of minority nationalist movements often leave the implication that there
is some alternative and better non-ideological, disinterested position in our actually existing world. By default, that implicit alternative is the status quo of the
dominant state. In this case, the politicized Spanish positions from which critiques of Catalan policies are often launched go unremarked. Failure to acknowledge the dialogic nature of minority movements and to critique the positions
to which they respond leaves the nationalist underpinnings of a state like Spain
unquestioned and even strengthened. "I don't believe in any nationalisms," progressive colleagues tell me to explain their bewilderment or skepticism about the
Catalan sovereignty movement. Does that include the kind that you don't notice,
I ask; the kind that takes for granted that in Spain one should speak Spanish, but
doesn't comprehend that anyone in Catalonia or the Basque Country might be
expected to learn—or might want to learn—Catalan or Euskara? Sometimes the
response is a shrug. Sometimes it is an avowal that the return to electoral democracy after Franco made further demands from minority regions illegitimate. That
claim is increasingly hard to square with the stark contrast between Britain's
recent democratic handling of Scottish demands for independence and Spain's
absolutist refusal to even engage the question of a Catalan "right to decide." This
situation is a significant backdrop for the way I present my research here.

A further note on the place of politics in the account given in this book
is in order. I do not attempt to offer here a full account of language policymaking in autonomous Catalonia, much less of the complexities of Catalan
politics and the sovereignty movement. There are analyses wholly devoted to
these phenomena, and I give references to some of them throughout the book.
Nonetheless, the point of the now well-established study of language ideologies is to understand representations of language as socially positioned. A book
about language politics is, obviously, a book about politics, involving strategies, rhetorics, and policies of competing political organizations and actors
who are not naïve. Throughout this book I have tried to locate the discourses

I analyze in relation to electoral politics as briefly as possible without embroiling general readers in all the details of the increasingly complex Catalan political scene. I am not convinced of how successful I have been, but this is not intended as an analysis of organized party politics as such. Instead, I am interested in identifying the linguistic ideological frameworks that electoral politics draws on, and in seeing how these reflect and are reflected in other spheres of social life. To this end, the political and media texts that I discuss are taken from a wide variety, even a patchwork, of sources to illustrate discursive trends that cut across different domains. At the same time, instead of surveying the discourses on language of the full spectrum of political parties, my examples are often weighted toward particular parties because they appeared to me during my fieldwork to indicate important new discursive trends. Current events confirm for me that that view was not mistaken.

As a researcher I am equally interested in Catalonia and in language ideologies, but I realize that not all readers will share both of those interests to the same degree. I have tried to address this book to those who are not specialists in Catalonia. Catalan observers will probably not find that I say many things they did not already know, although I hope they might find something of use in the way I put it. I try to give enough background information to allow readers unfamiliar with the setting to follow my account and analysis, but I do not give an introduction to the history of Catalonia or of the language. For an abbreviated version of that, readers may see my earlier book (1989a) or a number of other sources referenced in this one. Those who are knowledgeable about Catalonia may be nonplussed at the many details that I gloss over, especially when I do not identify all the players and commentators by name in my in-text discussions. I have chosen, with apologies, to compromise on those details for the sake of the general reader, and I believe that those who are interested will find the relevant identities and other details in footnotes and in the citations I give for all sources.

I assume that most readers of this book will have at least some background in the study of the social life of language and the linguistic life of society, but I have tried to make my account accessible to readers who are not expert in sociolinguistics or linguistic anthropology by being relatively sparing with technical vocabulary. It has proven impossible to avoid a number of such terms: iconization, indexicality, intervocalic fricative, just to take a few examples from one point in the alphabet. When I introduce them, I try to give a basic definition and/or example. On a few occasions, I have resorted to telegraphing a point to specialists through the use of some technical terms. I hope these moments will not be too baffling to nonspecialists, and that all readers will find here both empirical and theoretical arguments that are worth their consideration.

ACKNOWLEDGMENTS

Over the decade that I've worked on this project, I've had many interchanges about ideas and been much influenced by the comments and the work of Catalan, American, and international colleagues. The result is an Escher-like experience. As I rewrite, reread, and occasionally newly discover published pieces I missed earlier, I keep meeting myself and some of my colleagues on the stairs going up, or is it down? Although I have tried to acknowledge these influences, bibliographic citation and prefatory thanks are inadequate to capture the deep resonance I find with the work of a number of colleagues. I take heart that this intertextuality means that we are on to something, and I hope those who might meet themselves on the stairs of this book feel the same way.

Several institutions made this research and writing possible. I did the fieldwork as a visiting researcher affiliated with the Department of Catalan Philology at the Universitat Autònoma de Barcelona, kindly sponsored by Professor Joan Argenter and supported by a fellowship from the Agència de Gestió d'Ajuts Universitaris i de Recerca de la Generalitat de Catalunya (grant # 2005PIV2-31). The Wenner-Gren Foundation provided indispensable funding for the fieldwork, and the University of California, San Diego (UCSD) contributed support for both field-work and manuscript completion. The analysis was completed and much of the writing was done when I was a resident fellow at the Netherlands Institute for Advanced Studies (NIAS), which provided me the perfect sabbatical environ-ment in its Brigadoon by the sea. Many thanks to all these institutions. All views expressed in this work are my own and not those of the funding agencies.

In carrying out the fieldwork and analysis, I had the help of more people than I can name here. My deep gratitude goes to the students and teachers who patiently let me follow and record them throughout their school day, and espe-cially to the former students who went out of their way to respond to me and bring me up to date after twenty years. There has not been space to tell all their stories in the course of this book, but all of them contributed to my understand-ing of contemporary Catalonia. I hope that those whose lives and views I do discuss and whose words I quote find that I have represented them fairly and faithfully. All personal names used in this book except those of public figures are pseudonyms, as is the name of the high school where I did my case studies. I am not able to acknowledge these indispensable people properly by name, but I hope they accept my thanks.

In Barcelona and beyond, Melissa Moyer and Susanna Fosch have been extraordinarily generous friends who have sustained me both personally and professionally and solved all kinds of problems for me. Many thanks also to Núria Guàrdia, Manel Udina, Adela Ros, and Adrianne Saltz for much support, and to Helen and Roger Bryce for providing respite.

I owe Susan Gal special thanks for the conceptual distinction that organizes this book, though she is not responsible for how far I have taken it. I'm grateful to all my fellow fellows at NIAS for creating a friendly and supportive environment, most particularly Leonie Cornips and Vincent de Rooij, who invited me to join their research group, and co-participants Peter Auer, Ad Backus, Jürgen Jaspers, Barbara Johnstone, Tanja Petrović, and Irene Stengs. For insights and collegial assistance of different kinds in different moments, my thanks to Celso Álvarez-Cáccamo, Albert Bastardas, Emili Boix,Verena Berger, Michael Berman, Marcelo Borges, Jordi Ballart, Albert Branchadell, Mary Bucholtz, José del Valle, Nicolau Dols, Joe Errington, Paja Faudree, Susan Frekko, Jonathan Friedman, John Haviland, Judit Hersko, Miyako Inoue, Misty Jaffe, Eva Jaurros-Daussà, Stewart King, Liesbeth Koenen, Maarten Mous, Michael Newman, Luci Nussbaum, Bernadette O'Rourke, Nancy Postero, Bambi Schieffelin, Miquel Simonet, Miquel Strubell, Jackie Urla, Xavier Vila, Max Wheeler, and Ana Celia Zentella. Laura Ahearn, Hallie Stebbins, and Rob Wilkinson have been encouraging and patient in the editorial process of turning this work into a book.

The Centre de Documentació de la Direcció General de Política Lingüística de la Generalitat de Catalunya was essential to the research in Part II of this book, and I thank Elena Heidepriem for her help in navigating its collection. Thanks also to Pere Mayans of the Servei d'Ensenyament del Català de la Generalitat for helping me understand the history of Catalan education policy, and to Kathy Creely, Karen Heskett, and Kirk Wang of the UCSD library for generous help with technology for producing the final manuscript. I'm grateful to artist Miquel Barceló and representative Hannah Rhadigan, cartoonist Manel Fontedevila, Josep Gisbert and Susanna Fosch again, and the artists and representatives of several organizations for facilitating permission to reproduce the illustrations in this book.

Throughout the fieldwork and again in correcting the whole manuscript, Maria Rosa Garrido Sardà has been an extraordinary research assistant who always goes an extra mile, and I am extremely grateful to her. For their work on transcription, translation, analysis, and bibliography over the years, my thanks also to Míriam Arboix, Cristina Aliagas, Vanessa Bretxa, Teresa Ciurana, Andrea

Davis, Susanna Llop, Aida Ribot Bencomo, Page Piccinini, Daniel Scarpace, Elena Vicario, and Katia Yago. A special thank you to Josep Soler Carbonell for much collegial help.

Susan DiGiacomo has been a great friend and colleague since we met doing fieldwork in Barcelona in 1979, and with this book project she's been beyond generous, giving almost every chapter of the manuscript a careful and encouraging reading and consulting on all kinds of questions. My debt to her is enormous. Joan Pujolar also provided help over the years of this project and read many chapters in manuscript. Along with Maria Rosa Garrido, they saved me from many of my embarrassing gaffes and gave me much to think about, some of which I haven't been able to reflect adequately here. The errors that remain are my own fault. Many, many thanks to Joel and Ben Sobel for living with this research project in the field and for their sympathetic support in the interminable preparation of the final manuscript. Thanks also to my father Tom Woolard for his patience as I fixed just one more thing and then another.

Finally, I thank the journals and publishers for allowing me to draw on and develop material from these earlier publications:

2007 La autoridad lingüística del español y las ideologías de la autenticidad y el anonimato. In *La lengua, ¿patria común? Ideas e ideologías del español*, ed. Jose del Valle, pp. 129–142. Madrid: Vervuert Iberoamericana.

2008 Language and identity choice in Catalonia: The interplay of contrasting ideologies of linguistic authority. In *Lengua, nación e identidad: La regulación del plurilingüismo en España y América Latina*, ed. Kirsten Süselbeck, Ulrike Mühlschlegel, Peter Masson, pp. 303–323. Madrid/Frankfurt: Iberoamericana/Vervuert.

2009 Linguistic consciousness among adolescents in Catalonia: A case study from the Barcelona urban area in longitudinal perspective. *Zeitschrift für Katalanistik* 22: 125–129.

2011 Is there linguistic life after high school? Longitudinal changes in the bilingual repertoire in metropolitan Barcelona. *Language in Society* 40 (5):617–648.

2013 Is the personal political? Chronotopes and changing stances toward Catalan language and identity. *International Journal of Bilingual Education and Bilingualism* 16 (2):210–224.

2014 What's so funny now? The strength of weak pronouns in Catalonia. (with Aida Ribot Bencomo and Josep Soler Carbonell). *Journal of Linguistic Anthropology* 23 (3) 127–141.

ABBREVIATIONS

ANC	Assemblea Nacional Catalana Catalan National Assembly
CAL	Coordinadora d'Associacions per la Llengua Catalana Coordinated Associations for the Catalan Language
C's	Ciutadans—Partido de la Ciudadanía Citizens—Party of the Citizenry
CiU	Convergència i Unió Convergence and Union (Coalition of Democratic Convergence of Catalonia and Democratic Union of Catalonia)
CT	Catalan
CS	Castilian
ERC	Esquerra Republicana de Catalunya Republican Left of Catalonia
IEC	Institut d'Estudis Catalans Institut of Catalan Studies
IRL	Institut Ramon Llull
L1	First language
L2	Second language
PP	Partido Popular Popular Party/People's Party
PSOE	Partido Socialista Obrero Español Spanish Socialist Workers' Party
PSC	Partit Socialista de Catalunya Catalan Socialist Party
TV3	TV3-Televisió de Catalunya Television of Catalonia

NOTE TO THE READER ON TERMINOLOGY AND TRANSCRIPTION

Terminology

All personal names except those of public figures are pseudonyms, as is the name of the school where I conducted the research for Part III. For public figures and scholars, I follow the common usage of giving both paternal and maternal surnames, hyphenated when that reflects their own use, as well as referring to the person within the text only by the paternal surname.

In Catalonia and the rest of Spain, "Spanish" (CS *español*, CT *espanyol*) and "Castilian" (CS *castellano*, CT *castellà*) refer to the same language. "Castilian" is the more common term and will be used in this book except where sources use the term "Spanish," which is politically significant. As here, I use the abbreviations CT for Catalan and CS for Castilian when identifying linguistic forms.

For ethnolinguistic categories, compound words are used in both Catalan and Castilian to identify speakers by their first and/or dominant language: CT *catalanoparlant, castellanoparlant*, CS *catalanohablante, castellanohablante*, the way the terms anglophone and francophone are used in Canada. Unfortunately English doesn't have equivalent forms, and terms like "Catalanspeaker" are infelicitous to the English-reading eye, so I gloss these as "Catalan speaker" and "Castilian speaker." In Catalonia the terms are usually used for social categories rather than as strictly linguistic descriptors, but there is slippage in the usage. Neither term as used in this book means that the speaker is monolingual, although as Xavier Vila (2003) has explained, self-described *castellanohablantes* often do not speak Catalan. Those of Castilian-speaking background who do speak Catalan are more likely to identify themselves as "bilingual." All "Catalan speakers" also speak Castilian, although a few of them claim not to be very comfortable in that language. Most of the individual "Castilian speakers" among the two generations of informants for this study do speak Catalan, many of them very fluently. When I wish to stress the native language of an individual, I will use the terms "first language" or "L1" Castilian or Catalan speaker in contrast to "second language" or "L2" speaker, and occasionally "native speaker" when social roots are being emphasized.

I use several terms to label political-ideological positions and actors so that the general reader can keep track of them. "Independentist" and "sovereigntist" are inelegant terms in English but are direct translations from the Catalan and the Castilian forms. "Catalanist" is a translation of *catalanista*, and advocates for the Catalan language as well as for the nation and/or sovereignty generally use that term for themselves, though perhaps not everyone to whom I apply this label in this work. I use it for both the linguistic and the political position. *Espanyolista* generally means Spanish nationalist. When writers or speakers whom I quote actually used this term, I incorporate it in my text. When I am not quoting a source and am imposing my own label, I use the term Hispanicist to identify positions that I classify as Spanish nationalist. I apply the label "Castilianist" more narrowly to advocates for the Castilian language in various debates, although their critics might call them *espanyolista*. Nobody in Catalonia calls him/herself Castilianist, and many of those to whom I apply the term would say they are not Castilianist, but rather liberal, fair-minded, normal, etc. This may be true of some of those I call Catalanist as well.

Quotations and Transcription

The originals of all Catalan and Castilian-medium quotes that appear in English in the body of the text are given in footnotes. Translations to English are my own except where indicated. In quoting from media sources, I do not use different conventions to represent the Catalan and Castilian languages, again except where noted. This is because quotations given in the media do not usually indicate the language the speaker actually used. They are routinely translated to the standard medium of the periodical or news outlet without any indication of the source language. Moreover, more than one news outlet has both Catalan and Castilian versions, and the choice between them in my corpus is not significant, so it would be misleading to mark the linguistic medium of my source.

In quotes from my own recordings of interviews and interactions (most of them appearing in Part III), short extracts from only one speaker are generally given only in English in the text; the original appears in the footnotes. Longer dialogic stretches are given in the original and the English gloss in parallel, to indicate at least some of the interactional dynamics that affected the discussion. In these transcript extracts, interviewees' turns are identified by the first initials of their pseudonyms. "KW" refers to the interviewer.

In interactional and interview extracts, the typeface distinguishes the more marked from the less marked of the two languages in that data set. Regular roman type is used for the more frequently used of the two and *italics* indicate the less frequent language. Because these were different in the interviews with the younger and older informants, the conventions I use are also different. In Chapter 7, reporting on the younger informants, Catalan is unmarked and Castilian is italicized. In Chapter 8, since Castilian was the medium of the greater part of the interviews discussed, Castilian appears in unmarked roman type and Catalan is in italics. In textual citation of lexical items in these chapters as in others, both languages are italicized without distinction.

These transcriptions of interviews and interactions, like the English glosses, are quite broad in order to be more readily accessible to readers, and they are not intended for close interactional or sociolinguistic analysis. Stumbles and hesitation phenomena are generally transcribed, but only the most salient phonological forms are represented graphically with nonstandard spelling. These are specifically deletion of intervocalic /d/ (*acabao* for *acabado* "finished") and the aspiration of /s/ in stylized Andalusian Castilian. Following Joan Pujolar (2001), I represent the emblematic aspirated form with orthographic "h"; e.g., *ehpañoleh* in place of standard Castilian *españoles* "Spaniards." In Catalan, the yodization of initial voiced palatal-alveolar fricatives is represented by orthographic "i"; e.g., *io* for *jo* ("I"), *ia* for *ja* ("already"). Although this pronunciation makes those specific words bivalent, i.e., identical in Catalan and Castilian, they are widespread and commonly accepted forms in vernacular Catalan.

Transcription Key

[words]	speech overlapping with interlocutor's, also marked in adjacent turn
(.)	short pause
(word)	uncertain transcription
(x)	unintelligible
(( ))	analyst's comment, clarification, or substitution
. . .	material omitted
:	elongation of speech segment
<u>word</u>	neither only Catalan nor Castilian: bivalent or English in original
=	latched speech, no pause
-	word breaks off

SINGULAR AND PLURAL

1 INTRODUCTION

What makes a particular language authoritative in community members' eyes and ears? What relationship to language allows a government and its institutions to be perceived as legitimate? And what entitles a speaker to use a language freely and to convince others with that use? Monolingual speakers of dominant languages rarely have to pause to consider such questions, but members of bilingual and minoritized speech communities routinely confront them, implicitly and explicitly. The answers matter because the foundations of linguistic authority are also foundations of identity, community, nation, polity, and citizenship. The subject of this book is a constellation of ongoing consequential changes in the foundations of linguistic authority and community in Catalonia, where language has long been a powerful social symbol and political issue.

Catalan language and identity have been mobile in recent years, in multiple senses: political, demographic, ideological. Politically, Catalan national identity moved into the international spotlight in September, 2012, when 1.5 million people demonstrated in the streets of Barcelona to demand what is called "the right to decide" on sovereignty for Catalonia, currently an autonomous political community within Spain.[1] The next year, even more people linked hands to form the *Via Catalana*, the "Catalan Way to Independence," stretching 480 kilometers from south to north and again capturing the attention of international news media (Televisió de Catalunya 2013a, 2013b).[2] A broad coalition from center-right to progressive left parties in the Catalan Parliament joined to call a referendum on independence for 2014 (Minder 2013). Despite the conservative Spanish government's

---

1. "Dret a decidir." For an English-medium collection of sympathetic views on the sovereignty movement from intellectuals as well as Catalan political activists, see L. Castro 2013.

2. This display of support for Catalan independence was organized by a civic group, the Assemblea Nacional Catalana (Catalan National Assembly) and modeled after the successful 1989 "Baltic Way" that had symbolically put the Baltic states on the path to independence.

FIGURE 1.1 Demonstration for Catalan independence, 2010. Photograph by Josep Renalias.

Source: Wikimedia Commons. https://commons.wikimedia.org/wiki/File:Ebullició_independentista.JPG

flat rejection of any vote as illegal and unconstitutional, 2.3 million voters turned out in November 2014 for a nonbinding citizens' consultation in which 90% supported statehood for Catalonia and 80% voted for outright independence (Generalitat de Catalunya 2014, *El País* 2014).[3] This movement had erupted publicly in 2010, in response to the Spanish Constitutional Court's curtailment of significant clauses of the revised Catalan Statute of Autonomy (Fig. 1.1). Within just a few years, Catalonia had become visibly rife with previously unthinkable possibilities, as well as apparent impossibilities given the intransigence of the Spanish government and the challenges that party politics present.

International media attributed this mobilization for Catalan independence both to the effects of the global economic crisis that began in 2008 and to Catalans' longstanding "fierce pride in a distinct culture and language" (e.g., Associated Press 2014). Economic grievances in the wake of the crisis were undoubtedly

---

3. Catalonia has a total population of about 7.5 million, of which eligible voters were estimated at roughly 5.4 million. The turnout for this nonbinding vote was low in comparison to parliamentary elections, both Spanish and Catalan, but not unlike turnout in recent elections for the European Parliament.

crucial to this 21st century surge and widening social base of Catalan nationalism. And Catalan language and identity do indeed intertwine with economic and political tensions in giving rise to the movement (Muñoz and Tormos 2012). The Catalan language has traditionally been viewed as key to the existence of the Catalan nation itself and to Catalan identity for individuals. Moreover, in the last decade autonomous Catalonia's established language policy, particularly in education, has repeatedly been challenged in Spanish government actions and in lawsuits brought in the Spanish courts, and this has aggravated sentiment for Catalan independence. With the first new wave of this relatively broad popular mobilization for independence in 2010, the official language policy of an independent Catalonia became a topic for debate in public forums, well before a date was even set for a referendum, much less the outline of an independent state sketched.

In the dominant perspective on minority nationalisms inherited from the 19th century Romantic tradition, the equation of a language, a culture, and a nation that is evoked by the international reporting on this Catalan independence movement is not surprising. However, the ethnolinguistic backdrop of the contemporary Catalan sovereignty mobilization is considerably more surprising and complex than conventional accounts of language and national identity would suggest, and those complexities motivate the research behind this book.

Demographically, a shift was already well established in late 20th century Catalonia as a result of mass labor migration to industrialized Catalonia from other parts of Spain. Roughly three-quarters of Catalans are estimated to have immigrants in the family tree who arrived since 1900 (Cabré 1999, 164).[4] The twenty-five most common surnames in Catalonia are all of Castilian origin (IDESCAT 2014). Less than one-third of the population of Catalonia now speaks Catalan as its first language. In contrast, about 55% of the adult population are first-language speakers of Castilian (the term for the Spanish language generally used in Catalonia and the rest of Spain) (IDESCAT 2013). Most of these Castilian speakers are working-class immigrants themselves or the children and grandchildren of such immigrants from other parts of Spain. In short, the autochthonous and Catalan-speaking population of Catalonia is demographically outweighed by Castilian speakers with roots in the rest of Spain,

---

4. English speakers are often confused when the term "immigrants" is used for those who moved to Catalonia from other parts of Spain, but it was the term in general use there. It indexes the significance of the historical national boundary even though no state boundary is crossed. This usage of the term was displaced by transnational immigration in the 21st century. One of my interviewees asked me in some confusion how she should refer to her parents, who had moved to Catalonia from Andalusia in that great migration, now that "immigrants" come from other countries and she could no longer use it for her family.

complicating any easy Romanticist assumption of a fiercely motivating pride in Catalan language and cultural heritage.

Despite such a demographic divide in geographical and linguistic origins, in the run-up to the November 2014 vote, polls showed that 75%–80% of the potential voters of Catalonia supported the call for the popular consultation on sovereignty. Estimates of support for independence itself varied considerably depending on the pollster and the polling question, but most showed it hovering a little below 50%.[5] These figures suggested that appreciable numbers of Spanish immigrant-descent and Castilian-speaking citizens supported the bid to hold a referendum, and a smaller but still noteworthy percentage figured among those calling for independence. Indeed, immigrant-origin and Castilian-speaking residents of Catalonia formed organizations to support the cause such as Súmate ("Join In"), and these included participants in the significant new transnational immigration as well as the earlier immigration from other parts of Spain.

Within this putatively post-national era of globalization, and especially in such a convoluted and potentially fragile ethnolinguistic context, the mobilization for national sovereignty and independence that swept Catalonia was not expected. Not only international but also Spanish and even Catalan observers and politicians were caught off guard when the movement for the "right to decide" took off so resoundingly in autumn 2012. Even many of those who participated were astonished by their own numbers.

One of the most challenging aspects for observers (in Spain as much as the rest of the world) to comprehend is how the potential for a divide along ethnolinguistic lines that coincide strongly with social class differentiation within Catalonia fits with such a broad sovereignty movement. What role do ethnolinguistic identity and the Catalan language in particular play in Catalan citizens' and leaders' views of themselves and their society? One perspective depicts Catalonia as a "divided society" with a "pronounced ethnolinguistic cleavage" and a linguistic policy that does not reflect the preferences and interests of the primarily working-class-origin Castilian-speaking population (Miley 2013). However, I ended my first book about Catalonia with a point that will be pursued in this one, and that has become all the more relevant with the sovereignty movement:

> The complexities of ethnic politics in Catalonia point out an important constraint on generalizations about the causes of ethnic conflict.... Attempts to understand the relation of class and ethnicity must consider the context of power in which conflicts take place, and in which

5. In spring 2014, a Catalan official poll showed support for independence a little below 50%, and *The Economist* reported an estimate of a majority vote, at 55% (*The Economist* 2014).

participants view them as taking place. Different interpretive contexts, such as those provided by nested political frameworks . . . not only make different aspects of experience relevant, they also change the meaning of such a constant and permeating aspect of experience as class position (Woolard 1989a, 142).

Such different interpretive contexts for understanding the politics of identity and changing meanings of social dimensions of experience will be the subjects of inquiry throughout this book.

Dominant Spanish discourses hostile to Catalan nationalism depict it and especially Catalan linguistic policy as illiberal and oppressive to Castilian speakers. Nazism and violence committed in the name of nations are rhetorical themes repeatedly invoked by Spanish critics of the Catalan sovereignty movement, as will be seen in later chapters. These inflammatory claims are consistent with the somewhat milder skepticism about minority nationalisms and language movements that is generalized across contemporary social science internationally. As the sociologist Craig Calhoun has observed, in cosmopolitan global circles today nationalism is at best considered morally illegitimate and in poor taste when it is not identified with state projects that generated horrors from Bosnia to Burundi (Calhoun 2007, 7). This skepticism stigmatizes minority nationalist and linguistic movements as exclusionary projects, despite evidence to the contrary raised repeatedly by researchers such as Jacqueline Urla (Urla 2012b) and Stephen May (May 2012).

The movement for Catalan sovereignty does not pit autochthonous Catalan-speaking "sons of the soil" against those of immigrant origin in the way that contemporary European neo-nationalist movements such as the French National Front and the Italian Northern League do, and as casual observers of Catalonia often assume to be the case. Instead, whether out of demographic pragmatism, ideological commitment, or a combination of both, Catalanists explicitly seek to recruit immigrant-descent and Castilian-speaking citizens (as well as immigrants from other linguistic groups) to the national project (Boix-Fuster 2015, Vila i Moreno 2004a).[6] The mobilization for the right to decide on sovereignty is presented by its proponents as an inclusive, broad-based (*transversal*), civic

---

6. There is xenophobia in Catalonia just as in the rest of Spain, both historically and currently in relation to transnational immigration, and it has given rise in some years to violence against immigrants. Its political expression has been relatively contained in contemporary Catalonia, and it has been marginalized by the spectrum of Catalan parliamentary parties that support sovereignty (Pardos-Prado and Molins 2009). The xenophobic party with a presence in Catalonia, Plataforma per Catalunya (PxC), is not part of the sovereignty movement and is positioned as anti-Catalanist. The conservative, anti-Catalanist Partido Popular most recently has fielded a candidate for Catalan elections whose rhetoric is widely criticized as xenophobic.

rather than ethnic, determinedly nonviolent, and even joyful effervescence of real democracy. In reference to the first post-Franco democratic Spanish elections in 1977, the anthropologist Oriol Pi-Sunyer identified the "potentially centrifugal demands of the working classes and Catalan nationalists" (Pi-Sunyer 1985, 114). That centrifugal force failed to materialize in those elections and still remained only potential more than thirty years later, consistently failing to appear in significant numbers in public actions. Despite the demography, repeated efforts to mobilize the working-class Castilian-speaking population of Catalonia against Catalan language policy and nationalism have not—or not yet—won much overt public support, but the potential remains for a politically exacerbated cleavage to open (Hierro Hernández 2013).

Beyond conjunctural economic circumstances, there are several factors that have enabled this unusual alignment in the politics of language and identity. A longstanding one is the historical legacy of the Franco dictatorship, whose suppression of workers' rights as well as of the historical nations of the Spanish periphery allied them as progressive causes against retrograde Spanish centralism. The most recent factor to come into play is the stance of the contemporary Spanish central government itself, which some liken to the intransigence of the Franco period. Many commentators call the state's response to the sovereignty movement "a factory for independentists" that produces an indignant backlash from citizens who might otherwise not have been so moved to defend Catalonia.

A third condition, which has been evolving across the decades of Catalan political autonomy, is the one that is the subject of this book: a refashioning of the ties between language and identity in Catalonia that constructs both as more open and flexible than in traditionalist visions. This is not an entirely new development, but rather a matter of shifting weight between existing discursive motifs, and of new practices that have emerged around older themes. Catalonia has long celebrated itself as a *terra de pas* ("land of passage" or frontier zone) that has mingled and absorbed different peoples over the centuries. "All those who live and work here (and who want to be) are Catalan" is a much-quoted slogan coined several decades ago by the nationalist political leader Jordi Pujol, who became president of Catalonia at the return of democratic elections in 1980. Yet many commentators saw a tension between that slogan and more restrictive visions of Catalan identity revealed in cultural policies over the decades that Pujol governed as well as in everyday interpersonal interaction. Since the turn of the millennium, however, the ideological grounding and discursive framing of the social authority of the Catalan language have been changing in both public and private life in ways that open up the possibilities of Catalan identification to a wider population. Catalonia has come to be constructed as both distinctive and diverse, as at once singular and plural. That ongoing shift and its implications for civic and interpersonal politics, linguistic practices, and national as well as personal identity, particularly for those from Castilian-speaking backgrounds, form the focus of this book. In the course of the volume we will consider how these ideological and discursive developments around language are both specific to socio-historical conditions in Catalonia and resonant with other contemporary experiences around the globe in the late modern period (Fernàndez 2008, 52).

Language Ideologies and Linguistic Authority

Questions about the grounding of linguistic authority are questions about what have come to be known in anthropology and sociolinguistics as language ideologies (or linguistic ideologies). By language ideologies we mean socially, politically, and morally loaded cultural assumptions about the way that language works in social life and about the role of particular linguistic forms in a given society (Woolard 1998). Dominant ideologies can be doxic, that is, unspoken assumptions on which ordinary people as well as elites build social action and interpret the meaning of acts and events without question. However, when there is conflict over language status and use, aspects of language ideologies rise to conscious reflection and are expressed in more explicit and contentious discursive representations of language. Both implicit language ideologies and explicit discursive forms are significant and will be addressed in this study.

The argument of this book starts with a general conceptual framework first developed in work I did in collaboration with Susan Gal and other colleagues (Gal and Woolard 2001). That framework posits that two contrasting yet interdependent ideologies of language have typically underpinned linguistic authority in the modern western world: an ideology of authenticity, which holds that a language variety is rooted in and directly expresses the essential nature of a community or a speaker, and an ideology of anonymity, which holds that a given language is a neutral vehicle of communication, belonging to no one in particular and thus equally available to all. I will further propose that, despite their apparent opposition, anonymity and authenticity share a common taproot in an ideology of sociolinguistic naturalism, the assumption that a linguistic form exists independent of willful human intervention and that it naturally and directly corresponds to a social state of affairs.

Within this framework, this book considers the evolution of ideologies and politics of language in Catalonia since it regained political autonomy within newly democratic Spain in 1979, after decades of political and linguistic repression under Franco. When autonomous Catalonia began its own policymaking again in that period, the extension of Catalan as a public language was hampered by the ideology of authenticity as well as by opposing forces that arrogated the value of publicness and anonymity to Castilian alone. In response to these constraints, under autonomy and particularly in the 21st century there has been a turn—unsteady and sometimes unconvincing, but still a turn—away from traditional authenticity-based discourses of language at both the public and personal level in Catalonia. The turn has been first toward anonymity and allied concepts such as cosmopolitanism, but historical and demographic facts do not facilitate the naturalization of Catalan linguistic authority as anonymous or rootless. Consequently, increasing challenges to sociolinguistic naturalism itself have appeared, again at both the public and the individual level. A conceptualization of linguistic authenticity as a project or goal, not based in the assumptions of naturalism, is discernable in Catalonia. The empirical chapters of this book analyze these ongoing reconceptualizations of linguistic authority and of the social meaning of Catalan language and identity at a number of different scales of social life, from electoral politics and mass media through high school classrooms and cliques to individual linguistic biographies.

Background: Catalan National and Linguistic Politics

Although focused primarily in the first decade of the 21st century, the analysis presented in this book is informed by a longitudinal perspective on the politics of language in Catalonia. I first began ethnographic research on this topic in fall 1979, when Catalonia approved the referendum that returned to it the political autonomy lost at the end of the Spanish Civil War. The first elections for a Catalan government in some forty years followed in spring 1980. In that period it seemed that I could not open a newspaper in Barcelona without finding an editorial commentary, letters to the editor, and/or the announcement of a public conference, all addressing the questions of who is Catalan, and what it means to speak—or not to speak—the Catalan language. My first book (Woolard 1989a) examined the various answers to those questions about the Catalan language and identity that were in play at both the interpersonal and electoral level in that baptismal moment of Catalan political autonomy.

Within Catalonia, and especially in the metropolitan Barcelona area where immigrant Castilian speakers were heavily concentrated, there were many question marks at the advent of autonomy in 1979 about what the new political framework would mean for use of the Catalan language. The affirmation of Catalan as part of the restoration of a just, open, and democratic society after decades of Francoist repression had received public support across a very broad social spectrum, including the leftist political parties whose base was formed by

Spanish immigrant workers. But once autonomy was established, and the value of Catalan might become practical rather than just symbolic, what would the roughly 50% of the population that did not speak Catalan actually do with the language? Would they learn it willingly, and if so, would they use it? Would the strong association of Castilian with the immigrant working class on the one hand, and of Catalan with autochthonous middle and professional classes on the other, harden and disrupt the pragmatic alliance and commitment to *convivència* (getting along together) that held publicly during the effervescent transition period in Catalonia?[7] If it became institutionalized and lost its cachet as a symbol of resistance to a rightwing dictatorship, would Catalan be perceived as imposed on an unwilling immigrant-origin population? Or, dominated itself by the global linguistic behemoth that is Spanish, might Catalan wither into a folklorized heritage like so many other minoritized languages? In short, could Catalan make the leap from tenacious minoritized language to secure public language, and if so, how?

My first study at the beginning of autonomy showed that because of the relatively high socioeconomic status of Catalan speakers compared to the preponderantly Castilian-speaking working class, Catalan itself was unusually well positioned for a minoritized language. In addition to its political cachet, Catalan carried social prestige in the eyes and ears not only of native speakers, but also among Castilian speakers in Catalonia, making it attractive as what is commonly referred to there as a "social elevator" (*ascensor social*). Such political and social connotations were expected to encourage new speakers to acquire Catalan once learning it was made feasible by the new political framework. However, actual use of the language was more socially circumscribed by the ideology of linguistic authenticity. Speaking Catalan was most often taken as a claim to *be* a certain kind of authentic Catalan, rather than just as a signal of acquired linguistic proficiency or a desire to communicate (Woolard 2003, 86). This authenticity value, while in some respects providing positive motivation, generally worked against the adoption of Catalan by non-native speakers who found they could not make good on such an identity claim, or did not wish to do so (Woolard 1991a, 59).

As a rare minoritized language that survives and makes a bid to become not just a national emblem but a principal public language in use, Catalan was in a paradoxical position. Linguistic authenticity value, a quality that contributes to language survival under conditions of subordination, can become a limiting factor when acquisition and use by a larger population is a goal (Woolard 2003, 87). I argued in my earlier work that the ideological bond between the

---

7. Brad Erickson (2011) provides an insightful analysis of the concept of *convivència*, particularly in relation to transnational immigration to Catalonia today.

Catalan language and "authentic" Catalan identity would need to be loosened if the language was to be taken up by new speakers. The linguistic challenge after autonomy was for Catalan to be transformed from a private marker of authentic ethnolinguistic identity to a more anonymous, universally available public language (Woolard 1991a, 59). The fundamental questions that this book now addresses are whether, to what degree, and in what ways that transformation has happened.

Language Politics under Catalan Political Autonomy

After autonomy was established, Catalonia set out on a process that Catalan sociolinguists dubbed "normalization" of the language. This ambiguous and sometimes controversial term, which will be explored in later chapters, meant setting language policies that would break down and redress the limits imposed on Catalan during the Franco regime, and bring about the "normal" use of Catalan across all domains of communication by all the people of Catalonia. Over the last three decades, Catalan has been transformed with uneven but nonetheless remarkable success from an institutionally marginalized language to such a public language. This has occurred primarily through an educational policy that made Catalan the principal medium of instruction in compulsory and particularly primary education since the mid-1990s.

Despite—or because of—the apparent policy successes and the apparent broad acceptance of them across the diverse community of Catalonia, linguistic fears and conflicts have continued to arise in public policy spheres. On one hand, Catalan has remained in a precarious position in judicial domains and vastly overshadowed by Castilian in commercial and popular culture spheres, even though it dominates in autonomous-community and municipal government administration and compulsory education. On the other hand, even the seemingly established position of Catalan in education has been increasingly subject to fierce political contention (Neff-van Aertselaer 2006). Repeated legal challenges to Catalan-medium instruction have been brought, many of them by what became the Spanish ruling party, the Partido Popular, and continuing court challenges have taken long, twisting paths through a politicized judiciary to contradictory court decisions that have generated further confusion and conflict.

Thus, institutional successes in disseminating knowledge of Catalan draw increased fire from partisans, especially politicians in Madrid, who profess worry that the Castilian language and its speakers are under threat in Catalonia. This opposition to Catalan policies is led from the top, often but not exclusively from outside Catalonia, and to date it has not mobilized mass displays of support among Castilian speakers in Catalonia. However, given these continuing challenges to language policy, many Catalan language activists in turn worry that the future, and for that matter the present, of Catalan is not secure. And in any case, they are not convinced that the education policies that generate so much contention have had much positive impact on actual language use among the general population.

The statistics on self-reported knowledge of Catalan are impressively high. In 2013, 94% of the population of Catalonia reportedly could understand Catalan, 82% could read it, and 80% knew how to speak it. However, extension of use is more limited. Only about 43% report that they use Catalan habitually, either alone or alongside Castilian. It is well worth noting that this represents a significant gain over the 31% who are first-language speakers of Catalan, but it falls well short of policymakers' goals (IDESCAT 2013).

Do such patterns indicate even further, more nuanced challenges? To the extent that Catalan language policy has succeeded in making Catalan an established language, might it be a victim of its own institutional success? Since compulsory education has been the main and in many cases almost the only vehicle of exposure to Catalan for young non-native speakers, is Catalan becoming "Latinized," perceived only as the distant, dry voice of the classroom and of institutional authorities to be resisted? And in yet another turn of the screw, Catalan purists worry about another possible price of success: to the degree that there *is* extension of the language to new speakers, is it associated with what such defenders perceive as further dilution of the character of the language, through increased acceptance of widespread influence from Castilian?

Over the decades of political autonomy, I have addressed these various questions about the advances and detours in the road to linguistic "normal."[8] The research at the core of this present book was conceived to give a fuller consideration of the state of the Catalan national linguistic project after over a quarter-century of political autonomy. The fieldwork that provides the principal data for empirical chapters was carried out with this goal in 2006–2007, when I spent another year in Barcelona attending political rallies and Parliament sessions, observing high school classes, interviewing students and adult informants, collecting media reports, and watching television comedy. A revised Statute of Catalan Autonomy had been approved after long and difficult political negotiations in summer 2006; paired with the Statute of 1979 it seemingly bookended a natural period of inquiry about the evolution of the sociolinguistic situation in Catalonia under political autonomy.

---

8. On the earlier periods, see for example Woolard 1986, 1987, 1989a, 1991a, 1991b, 1997a, 2003.

However, bookends can tip under the weight behind them, and that is the case here. Rather than creating closure in 2006 after its approval by the Catalan Parliament, by popular referendum, and by the Spanish legislature, the new Statute came under prolonged fire at the level of the Spanish state. Legal challenges to the approved Statute were brought by the Partido Popular (then in the political opposition and later in control of the Spanish government). The revised Statute was subject to four more years of demoralizing political and legal challenges, and ultimately to significant curtailment by the Spanish Constitutional Court in 2010, setting off the mobilization for sovereignty in backlash. A reference to Catalonia as a nation and preferential treatment for Catalan as the language of the autonomous community were among clauses the court deemed unconstitutional.[9] Even after the 2010 court ruling, central government challenges to Catalan educational language policy continued and even ratcheted higher, to the present time of writing.

When the independence movement burst into wider view in 2012, the kinds of questions about language and national identity that I first researched in 1979–1980—Who is Catalan? What does it mean to speak, or not to speak, Catalan?—were brought into the spotlight of public discussion yet again. The sociopolitical context in which such questions were raised had changed not only because of political autonomy but also because of Europeanization, globalization, transnational migration, and the trend to neoliberalism in Spain as elsewhere. For all these reasons, the terms in which answers are framed had shifted as well. Catalan commentators on the sovereignty movement now often point to 2006 as a pivotal moment when the adverse Spanish reception of the revised Statute of Autonomy closed off some paths to national accommodations, and the course was set toward the current movement. The discourses and practices around Catalan language and identity that I found in that period are given even more pressing significance now by this ensuing surge for sovereignty.

A Preview of the Arguments

New social meanings of the Catalan language as well as renewed contention over such meanings have developed in both the public sphere and individual lives in 21st century Catalonia. This book explores both social levels. What do I mean

---

9. For citizens of the United States, where the Constitution is sacrosanct in political mythology, the term "unconstitutional" may be more grievous than in Spain. The current Spanish constitution dates only to 1978 and was the outcome of negotiations among political parties including importantly the heirs of the Franco regime. It is widely viewed as a limited piece of realpolitik.

by "new social meanings"? In the final sections of this introduction, I will briefly sketch just a few examples of the kind of phenomena we will examine more closely in the following chapters, and then I will locate such phenomena in the plan of the book.

Political and cultural elites contended over language in public controversies in the period under study as they had in others. However, the arguments presented publicly hinged less and less on the value of language as an index of authenticity, and more on its value for articulating an open public sphere and a cosmopolitan community. Late modern challenges to the assumptions of nationalism and traditional authenticity are familiar from studies of other minoritized languages, and responses to these challenges elsewhere frequently have been characterized as a post-nationalist commodification of authenticity (see, e.g., Duchêne and Heller 2012, Heller 2011). The discursive challenges and solutions in Catalonia are related to these. Yet the eruption of the Catalan movement for national sovereignty obviously fits the expectation of post-nationalism only with some difficulty, and lends support to the alternate claim that the transformations of late modern society also give rise to an increase in nationalism (see Epps 2003, Pujolar 2007a on post-nationalism in relation to Catalonia). Although confronted with the discourse of post-nationalism internationally ascendant in the era, the Catalan case has been said to illustrate a postponed nationalism as much or more than post-nationalism (Vázquez Montalbán 2001). Nor did Catalan responses in the period under study here emphasize the commodification of traditional forms of authenticity in the way that has been documented elsewhere. Catalan politicians and cultural elites drew on the conventions of banal nationalism (Billig 1995) as well as an emerging discourse of cosmopolitan nationalism and what I categorize as rooted cosmopolitanism (Appiah 2005). These motifs seen in electoral campaigns and public disputes in 2006–2007 were the precursors of the rhetoric that generally prevails in the current sovereignty movement, and we will examine some emergent instances in detail.[10]

In one example of noteworthy change in the construction of language and identity at the public level, a Castilian speaker of immigrant origins named José Montilla became the president of Catalonia from 2006 to 2010. This was in itself a striking emblematic turning point for the politics of language and national belonging in Catalonia. Moreover, Montilla's linguistic (in)competence became a focus of public attention. It provoked revealing discussions and representations

---

10. The rhetoric of cosmopolitan nationalism coexists with a fervid display of Catalan national and independentist symbols unprecedented since the return to autonomy, among a much wider population than ever before. The *estelada*, the independentist version of the Catalan flag, has been especially visible in quantity and places it was not seen earlier.

of linguistic authority and linguistic form—some humorous, some cutting, many cuttingly humorous—that will be analyzed closely in the second part of this book. As a public figure, Montilla became a bridge between the spheres of the public and the individual in discussions of linguistic practices.

Turning to the level of the private individual, many first-language speakers of Castilian and most children of Spanish immigrants have learned and now use Catalan for varying purposes in daily life, as the statistics cited above suggest. For some it is habitual active use, for more it is active use in only some domains or occasions; for others it is primarily receptive competence. Accompanying and enabling these changes in lived relationships to the language is a shift in the ideo-logical grounding of linguistic authority and in discourses about language choice and use among such speakers.

Two students from a single high school but a generation apart allow a brief glimpse of the kind of changes that will be explored in the third section of this book. At age thirty-four, Rosario, daughter of working-class Andalusian immi-grants, looked back from her cosmopolitan present to the adolescent she had been when I first met her twenty years before. She described her teenaged self as wounded by rejection from Catalan schoolmates and closed off from Catalan language and identity. Now she presented herself as "totally different," speak-ing Catalan without inhibition, feeling "quite Catalan," and somewhat to her own surprise even supporting political parties that "look out a little more for Catalonia."[11]

Rosario's counterpart in the same high school twenty years later was Lola, grandchild of Andalusian immigrant workers. Lola was a rebellious student speaking Castilian with a stylized Andalusian accent and dressed in the fash-ions of a *quilla*, a slang term for working-class Spain-oriented youth style. Belying her image, Lola at sixteen, unlike Rosario as a teenager twenty years before, proudly claimed a Catalan identity. She supported independence for Catalonia, although she didn't consider herself Catalanist, "because I don't speak it. . . But I want Catalonia to be free."[12] In Lola's view, there was always social contention over something, but now it was different from when Rosario went to school:

> We don't fight anymore about who speaks Catalan and who speaks
> Castilian, now it doesn't matter. The hard feelings used to be about who

---

11. "Totalmente diferente a ahora"; "bastante catalana"; "que se preocupan un poco más por Catalunya."

12. "porque tampoco lo hablo. . .Pero . . .quiero que Ehpa- que Cataluña esté libre."

spoke Catalan and who spoke Castilian, but now the hard feelings are about other things . . .[13]

There are of course significant numbers of first-language speakers of Castilian in Catalonia who do not share the grown-up Rosario's linguistic turn toward Catalan or young Lola's Catalanist sympathies. Some Castilian speakers of similar origins find Catalanizing linguistic policy to be oppressive. We will hear that view from Rosario's classmate Josep, who would without doubt vote against Catalan sovereignty if Spain were to allow a referendum. The ethnographic research that allowed me some understanding of these individuals' views of themselves, their languages, and their community does not allow me to gauge the relative numbers of those who hold their different sympathies. That remains a question that vexes even the pollsters and quantitative social scientists who wield tools better suited to that task. Whether the Catalan sovereignty movement can recruit sufficient support from people who take the stances Rosario and Lola do, whether it can maintain its momentum despite rivalries and infighting within the parliamentary coalition and the recent emergence of new alternatives to politics as usual, whether there will ever be a vote on independence, whether there will be a reorganization of Spain into a federal state; these are all unknowns to me as to other observers. There is much more to be understood and explained about Catalan and Spanish national politics than I can begin to address in this book.[14] I have situated the questions that I do address about language within this brief overview of the contemporary Catalan sovereignty movement not because I can predict where it is headed, but because it inevitably affects the significance of the sociolinguistic observations that I am able to offer. For community members such as Lola and Rosario, new sociolinguistic solutions have emerged in everyday life that challenge traditional assumptions, and in Rosario's case challenge her own earlier ideas about limited access to the Catalan language and about its relation to her personal identity. What I hope to provide in this book is an understanding of these new, nontraditional stances toward language that are part of what enables a broader Catalan civic nationalism but that go unnoticed in many of the public commentaries on linguistic and nationalist politics in contemporary Catalonia.

---

13. "ya no nos peleamos para ver quién habla catalán y a ver quién habla castellano. Ahora ya da igual . . . Loh malos rollos antes eran de por quién hablaba catalán y por quién hablaba castellano, ahora loh malos rollos son por diferentes cosas. . . ."

14. Montserrat Guibernau's account of the historical and political context of the re-emergence of Catalan nationalism is a useful source for readers of English (Guibernau 2004). For a very recent monographic treatment of the cultural and political issues around sovereignty, see Crameri 2014.

Plan of the Book

The book is organized in three sections, each one addressing ideological foundations of linguistic authority, explicit discursive representations of language, and linguistic practices, but at different levels. Because the work ranges across several such levels of social life, my methods and evidence are of necessity eclectic.

A comment is in order on two of the analytic terms used here, ideology and discourse. There are long debates and multiple positions in social science and in anthropology in particular concerning the relationship between "ideology" and "discourse." I will not review those debates here, nor will my usage in this book reflect all of the distinctions between them that can be important to make. Often I will sweep the two terms together and not wish to emphasize the difference between them. I have written elsewhere about the multiple possible meanings of "ideology," and I deploy many of them in this work; language ideologies as I define them may be implicit or explicit, systematic or partial, hegemonic or contested (Woolard 1998). Nonetheless, I generally try to use the term ideologies to refer to what I think of metaphorically as "underlying" conceptual frames, which are instantiated in actually occurring discourses. Ideologies may saturate consciousness so thoroughly as to be doxic, hegemonic, unacknowledged, and most importantly not explicitly asserted, in which case they are identifiable only in what is unsaid (Bourdieu 1977). "Discourses of language" as I use the expression in this book will usually refer to instances in which speech, text, or other media offer actual representations of language. Of course, the relevant logic and meaning of any specific discourse will lie not just in what is literally said, but also in the interstices, presuppositions, and entailments of what is said, and so the explicit and the implicit are inextricably related.

Part I (Chapters 2–3) addresses my questions about the foundations of linguistic authority at the most general level. Chapter 2 develops a general framework for analyzing ideologies of linguistic authority, anonymity, and authenticity not only in Catalonia but also in other bilingual settings in the world, from which examples are drawn. Chapter 3 gives a broad overview of the recent situation and significance of language in Catalonia framed in terms of these linguistic ideologies and taking illustrations from a wide variety of sources in political and public discourse.

Part II (Chapters 4–6) examines public discourses and controversies about language in politics and the public sphere in Catalonia as represented in print and other media. Each of these chapters examines in some detail the construction of language choice and linguistic authority in relation to a specific public figure (Chapter 4, President Montilla) or event (Chapter 5, a municipal festival in Barcelona; Chapter 6, the promotion of Catalan culture at the Frankfurt Book Fair).

Part III (Chapters 7–8) turns to the level of the individual and of interpersonal experience. It is based on my longitudinal ethnographic study of two generations of students in one school and their linguistic practices, attitudes, and discourses. This classroom and interview research included first-language speakers of Catalan as well as of Castilian, and recent transnational immigrants as well as descendants of the earlier Spanish immigrants to Catalonia. However, the focus of the analysis I present in this book will be on the linguistic practices and identity construction of first-language Castilian speakers, rather than their Catalan-speaking or allophone immigrant classmates. The high level of transnational immigration to Catalonia since the turn of the millennium has brought significant consequences for the social climate and linguistic landscape and has been the subject of considerable social and sociolinguistic research in its own right.[15] In contrast, my concern in this book is primarily to follow out the thread of my earlier work, tracing the ethnolinguistic legacy of the decades of Spanish immigration, whose demographic weight has not receded in social or political significance. Part III investigates changes over time at the individual level through two different methods: a cohort approach, studying two different generations of students in the same high school twenty years apart (Chapter 7); and a panel study approach, following the linguistic itineraries of young adults who had participated as students in the classroom study twenty years before (Chapter 8).

Chapter 9, the conclusion, summarizes the book's arguments about Catalonia and briefly considers the relationship of some of the phenomena found there to more general trends in language ideologies and politics in other parts of the world in the late modern period.

---

15. For sociolinguistic studies on transnational immigration in Catalonia, see among others Codó 2008; Corona, Nussbaum, and Unamuno 2013; Moyer 2013; Newman, Patiño-Santos, and Trenchs-Parera 2013; Pujolar 2010; and Sabaté i Dalmau 2014.

THEORETICAL AND EMPIRICAL OVERVIEW

2 IDEOLOGIES OF LINGUISTIC AUTHORITY

AUTHENTICITY, ANONYMITY, AND NATURALISM

In the first chapter, I asked what makes a language and its speakers authoritative in the eyes and ears of members of a society. To begin to answer, I suggested that linguistic authority in modern western societies is often underpinned by one of two different ideological complexes, which in this book are called authenticity and anonymity (Gal and Woolard 2001). In this chapter I will draw on studies from a number of different settings to develop and illustrate these ideologies and their relation to each other. This framework for understanding linguistic authority generally will then be applied specifically to the Catalan situation in the rest of the book.

I sketch these two ideological complexes in broad strokes here as contrasting analytic ideal types, but they are not only that. As we will see in Catalonia, they are also interpretive categories that members of societies themselves mobilize—not always by these names, of course— in struggles to position their languages. Moreover, authenticity and anonymity are not independent from each other, but rather are to a great extent co-constituted, meaning they are defined in relation to each other as poles on an axis of linguistic differentiation (Gal 2012).

Anonymity is readily recognizable as a reflex of the universalism that is commonly traced to the Enlightenment, and authenticity is in turn an instance of the particularism that is the hallmark of the Romantic vision of social life (Geeraerts 2008). Why not just speak of universalistic and particularistic views or valorizations of language, then? I use the terms anonymity and authenticity in this discussion in part to follow the framework sketched in my earlier work with Susan Gal and adopted by others since then. More importantly, these terms capture distinct facets of the ideas of universalism and particularism as they are manifested in discourses specifically about language. They suggest the ways that languages come to sound, look, and feel to listeners, readers, and speakers, and they resonate with the ways that such social actors themselves actually describe languages.

Authenticity

Authenticity is a familiar term in studies of language and nationalist movements and sociolinguistics more generally, and in this initial discussion I use the term basically as other such studies do. That which is authentic is viewed as the genuine expression of a community or of a person's essential "Self."[1] This ideology of authenticity locates the value of a language in its relationship to a particular community. Within this logic, a speech variety must be perceived as deeply rooted in social and geographic territory in order to have value. For many European languages, these roots are in the mountain redoubts of peasant folk purity. For nonstandard varieties such as African-American Vernacular English (AAVE) in the United States, the roots are often located in the soulful streets of the inner city or the *barrio*, where real people are said to be "keeping it real."

To be considered authentic in this ideological frame, a speech variety must be very much "from somewhere" in speakers' consciousness, and thus its meaning is constituted as profoundly local. If such social and territorial roots are not discernable, a linguistic variety lacks value in this system. For example, the Corsican sociolinguist Ghjacumu Thiers reports that a disconcerted Corsican informant rejected a superordinate standard for his language precisely because it wasn't identifiably grounded in a specific region. "It's a nowhere Corsican," he complained (Thiers 1993).

The primary significance of the authentic voice is what it signals about *who* one is, rather than *what* one has to say. In the terms of linguistic anthropology and linguistic pragmatics, this signaling of identity is a form of social indexicality, in contrast to the function of semantic reference or referentiality, which concerns the propositional content of what is said. The pragmatic function of social indexicality is paramount within the ideology of authenticity. In fact, within this ideological framework, the naturalizing relationship between the linguistic form and the speaking self often goes beyond indexicality, to what in the study of linguistic ideology is called iconization (Irvine and Gal 2000). That is, the linguistic form is perceived not just to point to but additionally to depict, to be an image (or

---

1. The origins and implications of the concept(s) of authenticity more generally have been debated in an extensive literature. For an introductory view relevant to anthropology, see, among others, Appiah 2005, Handler 2001, Lindholm 2008, Taylor 1991, Trilling 1972. In the space of this book I am only able to consider authenticity with a focus on linguistic practices, and even on this topic there is a substantial literature beyond what I engage explicitly.

icon) of, the essence of the person. Such iconicity is itself the essence of linguistic authenticity. To profit from linguistic authenticity, one must sound like that kind of person who is valued as natural and authentic. (In this book, I will generally use the term [social] indexicality to encompass this kind of indexical iconicity as well, and I will only draw a distinction when it is important to emphasize the perception of a linguistic quality as actually depicting the nature of the community or speaker).

It is within this logic of authenticity that the acquisition of a second language is so often imagined to necessitate the loss of a first, so that the speaker's desired identity won't be contaminated and spoiled by linguistic traces of another identity (Mertz 1989). In some bilingual circumstances, use of a minority language is treated as exclusively about social indexicality, rather than its referential value (Trosset 1986), and indeed there are increasing numbers of examples in the literature on the commodification of authenticity that show languages used in exactly this way, for emblematic display rather than as a medium of referential communication (Pietikäinen and Kelly-Holmes 2013, Coupland 2012). Such non-referential value is often then trivialized and dismissed from the dominant language perspective. This is perfectly illustrated in Susan DiGiacomo's report that in a Spanish talk show discussion of "linguistic genocide," a well-known Spanish sociologist asserted that there are "some regions where there are two languages, one which is local, and the other which possesses communicative functions" (DiGiacomo 1999, 127).

Penelope Eckert has pointed out how traditional sociolinguists have long worked within this logic of authenticity, expecting the Authentic Speaker to be not only "locally located" but also locally oriented (Eckert 2003, 392). In the tradition of variationist sociolinguistics, and of much of anthropology as well, the Authentic Speaker, the quarry of sociolinguistic analysis, is seen as endangered by wandering beyond his or her natural habitat and being subjected to conscious, therefore unnatural social influences. This is a link between the authentic and the natural to which I will return later. Such a view is firmly in line with Anglo-American ideologies of authenticity at least since Noah Webster sought to define a distinctive national idiom. Webster wrote in 1789 that the true American English would be found "among the class of people who do not travel, nor are tempted by an intercourse with foreigners" (Webster 1967, 108).

The politics of linguistic authenticity have been transformed since Webster's time and the peak of the Romantic era of nationalism, and authenticity has become the special preserve of minority languages and speakers. These are socially constituted as "local." As Arjun Appadurai (1996) has argued influentially, locality is produced within a relationship rather than just a space, and here the relation is importantly one of power. Now, as Michael Silverstein writes, "locality is characteristically recognized as 'restrictedness' of use, and 'local' languages are always the lesser of the nameable languages" (Silverstein 1998, 405). Therefore, authenticity can have mixed effects for minoritized linguistic varieties. On the one hand, the very survival of subordinated languages and nonstandard variet-ies among native speakers under diglossic conditions often depends on their per-ceived value in authenticating a locally valued identity. But on the other hand, the same quality in turn hampers efforts to extend minoritized languages to new speakers, whether in a bid for critical mass for mere survival, or in an effort to move to a dominant position, as we will see is the case of Catalan.

If local linguistic varieties index authentic local identities, by the same logic they are off-limits to outsiders. Lack of control of such a variety can indi-cate that one does not share an essential identity. To learn such a language secondarily, through study, is a contradiction in terms, marking the learner as inauthentic. Heritage language learners and what are now often called "new speakers" in settings around the world have been reported to experience this contradiction.[2] For example, O'Rourke and Ramallo quote a new speaker in the autonomous community of Galicia in northwestern Spain, who regrets that his Galician is "inauthentic" because he learned it at school, unlike people who have "their own variety" (O'Rourke and Ramallo 2013, 294). Similarly, Alexandra Jaffe (1993) writes that heritage Corsican learners fear making inauthenticating errors, and that having to learn one's "own" language in school was in itself "viewed by people as a contaminating, deauthenticating act." In fact, just as having to learn Corsican could be individually deauthenti-cating, the requirement to teach it in order to insure its survival "could be seen as collectively deauthenticating" for the linguistic community (Jaffe 2001, 286–287). As we will see in the next section, anonymous languages suppos-edly can be learned by anyone, but authentic languages can be learned by no one; speakers are supposed to come by them "naturally" rather than working to acquire them.

Moreover, the quality of authenticity has a tendency to become not just characteristic of but even the special preserve of minority speakers themselves. African-American, Quebecois, Corsican, Breton, London Creole speak-ers and their varieties have all been described as sharing the aura of authentic-ity and its familiar traits: rough, gritty, physical, sexual, earthy; in short, "real." Their mainstream counterparts—White, Anglo, Standard French, or Received Pronunciation English speaker—are cast in contrast as effete, stilted, artificial, strained, desexualized; in sum, inauthentic.

---

2. For the "new speaker" concept as it has been developed in recent research on minority lan-guages in a number of different settings, see O'Rourke, Pujolar i Cos, and Ramallo 2015.

Anonymity

In contrast to minoritized languages, hegemonic languages in modern society often rest their authority on a conception of anonymity.[3] Anonymity is an ideological foundation of the political authority of the public sphere of rational communicative exchange as classically described by the social theorist Jürgen Habermas (1989). By anonymity, I mean that the modern "public" itself, as a social space that generates a common public discourse, supposedly includes everyone, but it abstracts away from each person's private and interested individual characteristics to distill that common voice. If the ideological complex of anonymity acknowledges the social roots of a given public speaking position at all, it represents them as transcended. But more often such social origins are simply erased ideologically (Irvine and Gal 2000). That is, the disembodied, disinterested public is supposedly freed from the constraints of a socially specific perspective through rational discourse, allowing it to achieve what is taken to be a superior, aperspectival form of objectivity that might be called "a view from nowhere," borrowing the philosopher Thomas Nagel's term (1986). Thus deracinated, the views that dominate the modern public sphere appear not to belong to any identifiable "special interests," in the pejorative US political phrase, but rather seem to be socially neutral, universally available, natural and objective truths. In a sense then, they are anonymous.

Such anonymity is attributed not just to publics but also to the languages that articulate such publics. Ideally, the citizen participating in public discourse speaks in what we could call a "voice from nowhere." Although a minority language such as Corsican gets no authority from sounding like it is from "nowhere," dominant languages thrive on it. As Webb Keane has asserted about Indonesia, modernist national identity often seeks expression "in a variety of language that the speaker can stand outside of," a language that aspires to a universal "cosmopolitan transparency" (Keane 2003, 523).

In the modern and modernist public, the citizen-speaker is not only assumed to be an Everyman, he (or with more difficulty, she) is supposed to *sound* like an Everyman, using a common, unmarked public language. Public languages are supposed to be able to represent and be used equally by everyone precisely because they belong to no-one-in-particular. They are positioned as universally open and available to all in a society, if only, as Michael Silverstein (1996) reminds us, we are good enough and smart enough to avail ourselves of them. In contrast to the

---

3. I am indebted to Susan Gal for the conceptual framework of linguistic anonymity laid out here. It was developed largely through her contributions to the article we coauthored (Gal and Woolard 2001).

social indexicality that is the key function of minoritized languages, the referential function is ideologically all-important for the anonymous language of the public sphere. The ideology of anonymity holds that it is what is said that matters, not who says it.

Sociolinguistic case studies have shown how an ideology of anonymity allows institutionally or demographically dominant languages to consolidate their position into one of hegemony. By hegemony, I mean that they achieve what the cultural theorist Raymond Williams called the saturation of consciousness, which allows their superordinate position to be naturalized, taken for granted, and placed beyond question (Williams 1973).

English has been diagnosed with this anonymous quality in many of its incarnations. Joshua Fishman, among others, argued that the traditional assimilative power of English in the United States, at least through the mid 20th century, owed to the fact that it was ideologized as "nonethnic" in character. "It did not obviously clash with or demand the betrayal of immigrant ethnic values," he wrote (Fishman 1965, 149), and elsewhere he elaborated: "Just as there is hardly any ethnic foundation to American nationalism, so there is no special language awareness in the use of English" (Fishman 1966, 30). This is a description of what Michael Billig has called "banal nationalism": the invisible ideological habits, the daily flagging of nation in citizens' lives that is so familiar, so continual, that it isn't usually consciously registered as reminding them of anything at all (Billig 1995). Banal nationalism and its corresponding linguistic anonymity and transparency have been tools of Hispanicist discourses in the language debate in Spain and have also been goals of some segments of the Catalan political spectrum, an idea we will return to in Chapter 3.

Framed this way, English came to be seen—or rather, made invisible—by participants and in some cases social analysts as a transparent window on a disinterested rational mind and thus on truth itself (Silverstein 1996, Woolard 1989b). This was illustrated in arguments made by the English-Only/Official English movement in the 1980s against official uses of languages other than English in the United States. The English-Only supporters depicted languages such as Spanish and Chinese as obfuscating devices used by manipulative ethnic activists to cloak the truth of political discourses, while it was taken for granted that English would give unbiased access to objective facts (Woolard 1989b).

From the same period, the controversial memoir by the Mexican-American writer Richard Rodriguez, *Hunger of Memory* (1981), provides many illustrations of the banal anonymity of English in the United States, in contrast to the private, particularistic nature he attributed to Spanish. Son of Spanish-speaking immigrants, Rodriguez wrote that when he finally spoke out loud in English in school "the calming assurance that I belonged in public, had at last taken hold. . . . At last, seven years old, I came to believe what had been technically true since my birth: I was an American citizen" (22). "It would have pleased me to hear my teachers address me in Spanish ... I would have trusted them and responded with ease," Rodriguez writes, "but ... I would have evaded ... learning the great lesson of school, that I had a public identity" (19). Rodriguez illustrates just the point I wish to make about the anonymity of the public sphere and dominant languages when he writes that in public, "full individuality is achieved, paradoxically, by those who are able to consider themselves members of the crowd." "It is true that my public society today is often impersonal," he continues, characterized by "the anonymity of the crowd" (27).

Arguably, the ideological neutrality of American English was abandoned in the late 20th century, with unanticipated adverse consequences for the linguistic assimilation of later immigrants. In a study comparing American immigrant autobiographies published in the early and late 20th century, Aneta Pavlenko found that the earlier authors depicted an easy transition to the English-speaking world (Pavlenko 2004). They made little overt reference to language learning, and where they did, it was described as fast and unproblematic, a matter of a few months in school. Like Fishman, Pavlenko attributes this in part to a relatively tolerant linguistic atmosphere in 19th century and pre–World War I America, in an industrial economy in which job success required only minimal English. In optimistic tales of upward mobility in an open society, immigrant narratives appropriated the master trope of the self-made American. They successfully cast the immigrant as the "truest American," because s/he epitomized this self-made quality, and there was no need to repudiate roots or origins.

By the late 20th century, however, immigrants' autobiographies came to foreground linguistic identity and depict the acquisition of English as a slow, painful, personally anguishing process. Rodriguez's memoir actually belongs to this later narrative set, and he engages in a double discursive strategy. He both invokes his personal experience of such anguish and also repudiates it as founded on a mistaken belief about the power of ethnic languages to create intimacy. Pavlenko attributes the difference in the narrative strategies of the two periods in part to a change in dominant American ideologies of language. With World War I, a new xenophobic vision of Americanness became bound to monolingualism in English, and intolerance of English varieties marked as nonnative developed. In response, the acquisition of English came to be viewed by immigrants as a threat to identity, a difficult and painful process, and a cause for great ambivalence. As the master trope of the national text of Americanness changed to one of authenticity rather than open, anonymous universal access, so did the immigrant text, with predictable backlash. We might ask whether the linguistic circumstances of immigrant assimilation were really so different in one period than another, but it is still significant that the tales that are told publicly differ systematically. The confrontation of these two narratives of immigration was found in the recurring criticism of multilingual and multicultural policies in the late 20th century by immigrant-descent Americans who stereotypically asserted that "my grandfather came here from (Italy, Poland, Lithuania . . .) and learned English without any special help."

The ideology of linguistic anonymity continues to play an important role in debates over the analysis of English as the language of globalization in the current late modern period. "English belongs to everyone or to no one, or it at least is quite often regarded as having this property," Ronald Wardhaugh (1987, 15) wrote. Ulrich Ammon elaborated on this point: the national connotations of a language like English wear off through frequent nonnative use around the globe, and the language acquires the "touch of neutrality" (Ammon 2013, 117). Janina Brutt-Griffler recounts similar—if controversial—academic views that World English is an international language that is "deracialized" and "denationalized . . . not the property of its mother tongue speakers . . . playing a purely functional role" (Brutt-Griffler 2002, 5, 178).[4] She characterizes World English, in contradistinction to English as a national language, as a "domain in which national distinctions dissolve" (Brutt-Griffler 2002, 181). As a French anthropologist phrased it to me only half-jokingly, English is not a language, it's a metalanguage. However, the view of English as anonymous has been strongly criticized as self-interested anglophone mystification and late-colonial domination by Robert Phillipson, among others (Phillipson 1992, 2003a, 2003b).

In some cases of language standardization, such as Basque (*euskara batua*), Indonesian (*bahasa Indonesia*), or the Neo-Melanesian of Papua New Guinea, language planners have deliberately chosen leveled forms, koines, or auxiliary languages as the basis for standardization, in an attempt to construct a linguistic form literally not identifiable with any localized group of speakers. For example, Errington (1998) has argued that Indonesian has been remarkably successful as such a language not belonging to anyone. However, the project of creating linguistic anonymity often involves ideological more than actual linguistic engineering. This was true for the development of Hungarian-speaking unity from a linguistically heterogeneous polity in 19th century Hungary, as described by Susan Gal (2001). Many of the linguists and activists involved in creating modern Hungarian were not themselves native speakers of the language. They forged a standard language that they claimed was linked to no particular group or social class. Instead, they asserted that it derived only from the language's inherent laws, a striking example of a professional linguistic ideology in operation. This

4. "Functional" in this sense means the referential function.

Hungarian was a language that would be "everyone's" because it purported to be "no one's-in-particular," Gal writes (Gal 2001, 43).

In the French sociologist Pierre Bourdieu's well-known critique of the ideological project of universality that undergirds the hegemony of French, the popular understanding of linguistic authority as what I am calling anonymous is called "misrecognition" (*méconnaissance*) (Bourdieu 1982, 1991). In misrecognition, listeners recognize the authority of a dominant language, but fail to recognize the historical developments and the material power difference between social groups that underpin that authority. This ideological erasure of historical roots is what allows dominance to become hegemony in Raymond Williams's sense.

For Bourdieu, such misrecognition is the result of the deracination of language carried out primarily in institutions such as schools. They purge a language such as French of its origins in the speech of particular social groups and purvey it as a natural attribute of authority. We might think of this process as a kind of language laundering analogous to money laundering. As in money laundering, the actual source of capital (linguistic capital in this case) is obscured by transferring it through legitimate institutions. Under the persuasive power of schools and media, people come to endorse a language's power as genuinely inhering in the language itself. Having lost its social roots, it becomes a language "from nowhere."

In Bourdieu's account, accent can be just as important to the production of the anonymous standard language as it is within the framework of authenticity. Bourdieu suggests that a nonstandard accent (whether class-based, regional, or foreign) in one's French might be perceived as a particularistic trait that disqualifies the speaker in public deliberations. Despite the ideological appearance of open access, accent can trouble the citizen's identity in the most universalistic as well as the most locally oriented of contexts (Silverstein 1996).

The concept of misrecognition holds that the standard isn't really everybody's language, and that in most cases it really does belong to specific "someones" more than to others. Those who have the view from the margins, rather than the center, are most likely to see it this way. For example, many young black Americans shun the supposedly unmarked, anonymous, universally accessible Standard English of the school, rejecting it as "too white." If anything, the laundering of the standard language through the school achieves a kind of ethnic cleansing and realignment of linguistic differences that only serves to confirm the tie of Standard English to white America for them. The privileged, exclusive nature of access to the public sphere itself is all too apparent from the perspective of marginal social positions.

Catalan speakers as a group hold a position of relative socioeconomic privilege and social prestige that does not allow comparison to the situation of

African-American vernacular speakers.[5] Nonetheless, the peripheralization of the Catalan language in Spain does allow a recognition of the social and historical specificity of Castilian/Spanish, despite its advocates' claims to universality and ideological anonymity. These dynamics will be explored in detail in the next chapters.

Sociolinguistic Naturalism

On the surface, the two ideological complexes of authenticity and anonymity offer contrasting images of the relationship between language and social life. However, they do not always oppose each other as bases for authority, but may intertwine in a complex relationship. For example in US politics, Jane Hill proposed that a leaky boundary between the public and the private may be exploited linguistically, and a Bill Clinton or a George W. Bush can gain political authority from the folksy, regional voice of authenticity that bleeds into the national public sphere (Hill 2001). Even in the formation of national languages, these have sometimes been seen to be mutually reinforcing rhetorics, as in Gal's analysis of the 19th century standardization of Hungarian discussed earlier.

Moreover, the two ideological complexes share fundamental assumptions. Both anonymity and authenticity place high value on the relation of linguistic form to a vision of truth. However, in the framework of anonymity, "truth" is held to lie in the referential fit of language to the world. In contrast, in the ideology of authenticity, "truth" lies in the pragmatic fit of linguistic form to the speaker who authors it or the community that authorizes it. Sincerity, understood as speaking from the heart in one's own true language, is the best guarantee of access to the truth from the perspective of authenticity. This is the ethic of Protestantism as much as it is of hip-hop and Romantic nationalism (Hutton 2008).

Further, I want to suggest that anonymity and authenticity share a common taproot that goes much deeper in western thought than either Romanticism or the Enlightenment, in what I will call *sociolinguistic naturalism*, a subcategory of the linguistic naturalism thoroughly and insightfully analyzed by John Joseph (2000). Each of these two ideological frameworks takes a linguistic form to be rightfully authoritative because it is the natural, unmediated expression of a state of social life in the world, rather than the outcome of human will, effort, intervention, and artifice. Such naturalism is opposed to recognition of the agency

---

5. For this reason, there was derisive commentary when in a speech on the Catalan national holiday in 2013, the Catalan president Artur Mas invoked Martin Luther King's "dream speech" in relation to the demand for a referendum on Catalan independence. However, we will see that King's words formed a trope invoked in 2006 by more than one opponent of Catalanism.

of speaking subjects, and to a historicized image of language as constructed by human action.

The authentic, the anonymous, and the natural have all intertwined in the *questione della lingua* since it was addressed by Dante Alighieri in his *De Vulgari Eloquentia* in the early 14th century (first published in the 15th century). As is well known, Dante distinguished two forms of language, the *locutio vulgaris* or vernacular—"that which we acquire without any rule, by imitating our nurse"[6]— and *gramatica* (by which he meant Latin), which we acquire only with study. Dante wrote that "of these two the nobler is the vernacular . . . because it was the first used by the human race . . . and because it is natural to us, whereas the other is artificial" (Joseph 2000, 144).

Dante went on to attempt to identify the most illustrious form of the noble vernacular, that which was suited for literary use, tracking it like a panther "through all the highlands and pastures of Italy."[7] He could not find "this beast whose scent is everywhere yet which appears nowhere." Dante ultimately located this most noble form of the vernacular in the anonymous voice-from-nowhere: "Of those actions which are Italian, the noblest are those specific to none of the towns of Italy, but common to all. Among these we can now identify that vernacular we were seeking earlier, whose odour wafts through every city but which makes its bed in none" (Joseph 2000, 146). John Joseph has neatly paraphrased this originary moment in a very apt way for my purposes: "We want something common to all the people but specific to none of the towns: what all of them do, yet what none of them does" (147). In short, Dante sought the nobility of the natural and authentic in an anonymous, dislocated language.

This is a form of ideological naturalization in the sense that the French literary theorist Roland Barthes described, a process in which History is transformed into Nature through the loss of the memory that things were once made. In myth and ideology, Barthes observed, the world becomes a harmonious display of essences, emptied of history and filled instead with nature (Barthes 1972, 141–142). As Joseph points out, Dante's *volgare illustre* is "anti-historical . . . deeply mythical, creating a pan-national unity under the pretence of rediscovering and restoring it." "Whereas *gramatica* is artificial because it is the product of human history, the *volgare illustre* is not because it is the product of anti-history," created by taking away deformations added by history to each local dialect (Joseph 2000, 147).

---

6. N.B., Dante refers to the wetnurse. So much for the mother tongue!

7. My translation here is based on but slightly alters Joseph's.

In relation to linguistic authenticity, we can highlight an even more concrete, pragmatic kind of sociolinguistic naturalism in the legacy of Dante's vision of the vernacular as opposed to *gramatica*. This sociolinguistic naturalism pits the ease of a seemingly artless natural language that is a speaker's first medium, and thus not understood as a medium at all but rather as direct and unmediated reality, against the labored artifice of a secondarily learned language. To quote John Joseph once again: "The 'artificial'—the product of human will, the historical element of language—is marginalized in favour of a 'natural' language that is reckoned to be above the human will and therefore more 'real' than we, its speakers, are" (Joseph 2000, 144). Well beyond the struggle between authenticity and anonymity, this doxic sociolinguistic naturalism constrains minority language movements as well as professional linguistics and sociolinguistics.

Rethinking Authenticity's Relation to Naturalism

Linguistic anthropologists and sociolinguists have been challenging the traditional linguistic and specifically sociolinguistic naturalism of our disciplines for some time now. These fields have proposed models that emphasize speakers' agency in the making of language, rather than representing them simply as heirs to language and identity. In the last two decades, sociolinguistics has generated an important critique of its own implicit dependence on an ideology of authenticity and a central, invidious concept of the Authentic Speaker (Bucholtz 2003, Eckert 2003). Nikolas Coupland has done much to deconstruct professional notions of authenticity, even as he cautioned that we should not "give up too soon" on the concept, since it may still have some analytic utility (Coupland 2003, 417). Here I extend his efforts in order to call into question a persistent analytic conflation of the authentic with the natural, and the attendant assumption that the "natural" always has the (positive) valence of the "authentic," and vice versa.[8]

In the naturalist formulation of authenticity (the modernist form of authenticity that I have been discussing thus far) a temporal criterion is key: origins and beginnings define essence. This is a primordialist understanding that was born in the early modern period along with vernacular national languages and the territorialization of political authority and power (for an example, see Woolard 2002). The form of language acquired first and produced apparently artlessly is taken to be the most direct, unmediated expression of the true self, and this is viewed as a good thing. The natural is valued, while the artificial and the "mechanical," as one of Jaffe's Corsican informants called school learning, is spurious and suspect

---

8. Coupland himself has elaborated a closely related argument in work that appeared recently (Coupland 2014).

(Jaffe 2001, 289). This linked valorization of the primary, the natural, and the locally rooted still carries enormous clout around the world, and in my own field-work I indeed see speakers continue to struggle with it.

However, conceptualizations of authenticity are not always or necessarily founded in naturalism. As Coupland argued, speakers themselves can still value a sense of authenticity even when it is not one that comes naturally to them. Rather than being based on origins and "where you're coming from," it can be a self-aware, reflexive stance that is not an index of but rather a comment on this sense of "where you're coming from," as Coupland's media research shows. Authenticity can also be framed as "where you're going." It can be a goal, invested in the cultivation of a coherent self.

A linguistic variety habitually used in a given setting will almost certainly feel more "natural" to speakers, in that it becomes inscribed in the bodily habi-tus of which Bourdieu wrote (Bourdieu 1991). But this kind of naturalness does not automatically confer value on the variety; rather, it is a particular ideological complex of linguistic authenticity that does this. Although nat-uralness and authenticity have been entangled and generally equated in the western ideological tradition, the ethnographic and historical records sug-gest that artifice is not everywhere and always construed as antithetical to authenticity. Alternative formulations may value will, effort, or artifice rather than primordial and natural essence, including in matters of language. The literary historian Stephen Greenblatt has shown that such valued forms of "self-fashioning" through artifice were a significant development in early modern Europe (Greenblatt 2005). Alternate views have also been described in anthropological studies of various societies, particularly in Southeast Asia and Oceania. (See Tapp 2010 for a review of some relevant anthropological work.) New alternative understandings of a post-natural authenticity are now arguably coming to the fore in late modern western and western-influenced societies. In the next section I sketch a summary of several analyses from the research literature that give us, at least for the sake of this argument, illustra-tions of the possibilities.

One such alternative view is James Siegel's account of Javanese language ide-ology (Siegel 1986). Javanese is renowned for its hierarchical organization and multiple "levels" of politeness, which Siegel describes as based fundamentally in two linguistic varieties: Low Javanese (*Ngoko*) and High Javanese (*Kromo*). No one has High Javanese as a first language, according to Siegel, yet people are not considered "fully adult, *fully Javanese* . . . until they also use High Javanese." "To speak Javanese, indeed to *be* Javanese," Siegel writes, "one must translate" (3; ital-ics added). Not surprisingly, this linguistic distancing from the self troubled 19th century European colonial scholars. For example, one Dutch philologist wrote that *Kromo* was a mannered, deformed, and morbid outgrowth on "healthy" *Ngoko*, produced by "pedantic schoolmasterishness" (3).

Siegel's discussion of the Dutch philologist's distress captures the western vision of linguistic authenticity as based in the fit of the word to the speaker's interior being, and the understanding that that interior being shows forth in the speaker's first language. He says that for the Dutch philologist, "One's true intentions are formed in the first language; a second language masks those intentions" (3). And the true fit of language to the speaker's intentions is the source of value in the western and Romantic ideology of authenticity. This view aligns authentic language with the original, the first, the natural, the spontaneous, the interior, and the voice. Inauthentic language is in contrast identified with the secondarily acquired, the artificial, the schoolteachers, and the written, all of which oblige people to "suppress their 'natural' inclinations to speak spontaneously" (4).

However, according to Siegel, the Javanese themselves did not share this Romantic European view. Instead, his informants took keen pleasure in their ability to speak High Javanese as an acquired language (7). This value is not based in identification between "the self" and a single form of speech (17). Rather, Siegel claims that it is the movement *between* Javanese languages, from the natural to the nonnatural, that is valued as essentially Javanese. Granted, the Javanese do believe that Low Javanese is "natural." But rather than making it the truly Javanese language, that naturalness makes Low Javanese basically not quite language. Low Javanese is seen as pre-social and thus pre-human, according to Siegel. Thus, a speaker is not seen as betraying what s/he is "really" like or "really" thinking if s/he slips from High into Low Javanese; rather, it is as though s/he is simply not there as a socially recognizable being. The Low Javanese speaker disappears from view, to self and to others (25).[9] Since anyone (supposedly) can speak Low Javanese, it doesn't reflect the structure of the social world, and it gives its speaker no place in that world. The essence of being Javanese is refinement (*alus*), and speaking *Kromo* is the most essential ingredient of this (16). Javanese take pleasure in the accomplishment of speaking *Kromo* and thus in *not* speaking their "natural" language (28). To be sure, Siegel surmises that High Javanese developed in response to the pressure of Dutch colonialism; that is, he does not propose that this alternative view of linguistic authenticity is somehow intrinsically and eternally Javanese (22).

In Siegel's representation, then, the Javanese might well be said to embrace the position of Oscar Wilde as quoted by Coupland: "The first duty in life is to be as artificial as possible" (Coupland 2003, 417). The point that remains to be made is that the Javanese had no trouble reconciling such artifice with Javanese authenticity;

---

9. See Errington 1998 for a different analysis of the strategic interactional effects of this kind of Javanese style-shifting as a form of what Errington dubs speech modeling.

it is just such artifice that makes one truly Javanese, if Siegel's analysis is correct. I must note that Joseph Errington's analysis of Javanese language ideologies offers an apparent challenge to this view. Errington argues that the elegant, "exemplary" language of High Javanese is so closely associated with closed elite circles that it is taken as a "quasi-natural attribute of elitehood"; not as "evidence of training in linguistic technique but a perceptible index of imperceptible, intrinsically refined nature" (Errington 2001, 108). That is, there is ideological re-naturalization. It is not easy to fully reconcile these two analyses, but they both support a point that I am trying to make with this illustration: the first language variety acquired is not necessarily identified directly with a speaker's authentic, essential, and "natural" being; such an essential self can be held to be revealed in and through what is cultivated and secondarily acquired. Moreover, a true self is not necessarily monologic.

A second example of an ideology of linguistic authenticity that differs from the naturalist tradition can be drawn from the case of Hawaiian as described by Alicia Snyder-Frey (Snyder-Frey 2013). She analyzes the experience of language learners in the Hawaiian language revival movement in terms of a model of identity and social relations that has been proposed to be indigenous to Polynesia and has been characterized as performative (Salhlins cited in Snyder-Frey 2013, 8). This model resembles current models in sociolinguistics and linguistic anthropology, in that it holds that identity necessarily involves action and effort; identity must be performed to be granted (see Coupland 2003 on this point). Others who have written on Oceania have dubbed this a Lamarckian model of identity (Linnekin and Poyer 1990 cited in Snyder-Frey 2013, 8), although it is only loosely Lamarckian in the sense that it is teleological, oriented to ends rather than beginnings, not that it is then passed on biologically to descendants. A central element for Hawaiian revivalists is *kuleana*, a sense of "responsibility" that is both a duty and a privilege to carry out. *Kuleana* makes efforts to acquire one's mother tongue, so to speak, laudable rather than oxymoronic or shameful as in Corsica. Snyder-Frey argues that this allows Hawaiian language learners to avoid some of the anxieties and conflicts that heritage language learners experience in the Corsican and Galician cases mentioned earlier. Because they are enacting their *kuleana*, Hawaiian classroom learners do not have to fear inauthenticity.[10] Jonathan Friedman has argued that the Hawaiian strategy of self-production needs to be understood as a response

---

10. Hawaiian language learners are not immune to the influence of the traditional western ideology, and examples Snyder-Frey gives show that that there are tensions between the two models in the contemporary revival movement. Moreover, it is important to recognize that identity is still naturalized in this Hawaiian model, although the link of identity to language is not grounded in sociolinguistic naturalism.

to the material condition of Hawaiians in the global transformation of the local society (Friedman 1990), but he sees it nonetheless as expressive of a distinctive habitus that has been stable across a *longue durée* (Friedman, personal communication). This Hawaiian habitus allows an alternative valorization of an authentic relation to language as a project rather than as naturally given to a speaker.

An alternative form of authenticity that eschews sociolinguistic naturalism has also been described as a more recent development in late modern societies. Irony, the hallmark trope of postmodernity, distances speakers from claims to naturalness and brings to language an embrace of self-conscious artifice and agency. Much recent sociolinguistic research shows such a break with naturalism in playful language practices, especially among young people. As one example, Coupland has described the deliberate linguistic stylizations of a radio personality who plays with exaggerated stereotypes of his "own" heritage language. Coupland sees this not as inauthentic language but rather as authenticity as a second-order phenomenon (Coupland 2003, 427).

Another example of ironizing linguistic ownership is the well-known sociolinguistic phenomenon of language mixing identified by Ben Rampton as "crossing." In crossing, a kind of transgressive youth identity that we could think of as post-naturalist authenticity is enacted when speakers draw on linguistic resources that are patently not "naturally" their own (Rampton 1995). Similarly, studies of global hip-hop repeatedly explore mixed linguistic forms that have been dubbed expressions of "anti-essentialist authenticity" (Sharma 2010) and "xenoglossic becoming" (Pennycook 2007, 112). Kiessling and Mous (2004) characterize mixed-language urban youth vernaculars as part of the late modern construction of identity analyzed as "project identity" by Manuel Castells (2004). Castells defines project identity as aimed toward a collective goal expressing a cultural community of shared experience (Castells et al. 2004, 242).

On one hand, these moves away from naturalism could be understood as an abandonment of authenticity itself. But on the other hand, as Castells' concept suggests, the late modern "Do It Yourself" aesthetic might be seen as less a rejection of authenticity per se than a challenge to authenticity understood as naturally given, one that shifts the definition of self and community from origins to goals. Such post-naturalistic approaches to cultivating and projecting an authentic identity in a fragmented world can also be seen as versions of the narrative project for creating a coherent self posited by Anthony Giddens, whose work has so influenced recent sociolinguistics (Giddens 1991).

John Maher made a similar argument when he coined the term "metroethnicity" to describe the stance of contemporary youth from the minoritized Ainu group in Japan.[11] These young Ainu dabble in multiple languages (and a mélange of other cultural practices) as a challenge to ethnicity understood as a natural value, a value that, ironically indeed, Friedman tells us their elders worked hard beginning in the 1970s to establish in the face of a refusal of recognition by the Japanese official ideology of a mono-ethnic state (Friedman 1990). The "metro-ethnic" younger generation replaces the naturalistic authenticity of the Ainu movement with a kind of self-reconstruction by artful "design" (Maher 2005, 89). "Metroethnicity involves . . . focusing on what we can achieve as persons" writes Maher; it is a process in which "what we might become takes precedence over who we are" (Peter McLaren quoted in Maher 2005, 84). For the participants themselves, not just those who analyze their practices, (metro)ethnic identity becomes not causal—a root or origin—but rather a project and an effect.

As all these examples suggest, sociolinguists and linguistic anthropologists are not the only ones to take seriously the proposition "that through social action, people participate in semiotic processes that produce their identities, beliefs, and their particular senses of agentive subjectivity," as Michael Silverstein has written (Silverstein 1998, 402). At various times and places, speaking subjects and communities of speakers themselves have also recognized this principle, construing linguistic authenticity in ways that do not depend on sociolinguistic naturalism. It is not assumed everywhere that one comes by one's true linguistic self naturally through a first language and informal socialization. Artifice, in the sense of making something through deliberate human action and intervention, may be recognized and valorized in community practice as allowing the truest, most authentic realization of a social self. When conceived on other foundations than nature and origins—desire, potential, becoming, art, cultivation, will and pluck—an ideology of authenticity will have different consequences for language, its users, and its analysts.

Conclusion and Forecast

This chapter has sketched in outline the dominant modern western linguistic ideologies of anonymity, authenticity, and sociolinguistic naturalism, and relations among them. In the last section I have also posited the possibility of a less familiar, nonnaturalist understanding of authenticity, and I will argue in coming chapters that such a phenomenon has become significant in contemporary Catalonia. An emergent post-natural authenticity in Catalonia is loosely related to Castells' idea of project identity mentioned earlier. With a nod in that direction—and for

---

11. This concept has since been extended to "metrolingualism" by Otsuji and Pennycook (2010).

want of a more felicitous term—in the rest of this book I will sometimes refer to this development as "project authenticity."[12]

The next chapter will give an overview of the tensions and interplay among these ideological complexes as they have been evolving in contemporary Catalonia. Subsequent chapters will then examine their working in detail in specific public events and different domains of social life. Throughout, we will see an ongoing trend away from naturalist authenticity and toward anonymity as well as post-naturalism as bases for the authority of the Catalan language, both in the public sphere and in individual consciousness.

---

12. In work in progress I have variously used the terms teleological authenticity and nonnatural authenticity, and I have also considered achieved, artifactual, and crafted authenticity as rubrics for this concept, but all carry some unsatisfactory connotations.

3 REFRAMING LINGUISTIC AUTHORITY IN SPAIN AND CATALONIA

Not all demographically or politically dominant languages become anonymous and hegemonic in the way that I suggested in Chapter 2 that English and French did historically. When for structural or conjunctural reasons its roots in the cultural capital of one group in a society remain apparent, it is more difficult even for an institutionally dominant language to become ideologically and sociolinguistically naturalized and taken for granted as fitting, superior, and open to all. The visibility of a language's historical and social origins sustains other groups' awareness of alternative linguistic possibilities and hampers the naturalization of such dominance.

The Castilian language did not fully consolidate political dominance into hegemonic linguistic consciousness in 20th century Catalonia. Far from being an anonymous voice from nowhere, the language of the Spanish state was heard by many as being very much from somewhere specific (a place that continued to be suggested in the very name "Castilian" itself). The Spanish philosopher Ortega y Gasset wrote in the first part of the century that "Spain is a thing made by Castile"[1] (Ortega y Gasset 1921). The linguistic reflex of this was what the Spanish historian and philologist Américo Castro characterized in 1930 as "the painful fact . . . that the most important language of the nation has not been able to convert itself, like French, into the common denominator, loved and respected by all the cultures of Spain"[2] (cited in Boix-Fuster 2008, 276). This was all the more true in mid-century under the belligerently Hispanicist Franco regime and its legacy.

---

1. "España es una cosa hecha por Castilla."

2. "del dolor . . . de que la lengua más importante de la nación no haya podido convertirse, como el francés, en el común denominador, amado y respetado de todas las culturas españolas."

In response to the form of Spanish cultural and linguistic nationalism established under Franco, almost every political party in Catalonia supported reinstatement of the Catalan language as part of a program for justice in the transition to democracy at the end of the dictatorship in the mid-1970s. There was a sweeping social and political consensus for the institutional recovery of Catalan expressed in the public sphere, and voices raised against it were restricted to the political margins.

Catalanist activism during the political transition and early autonomy drew strongly—although certainly not exclusively—on an ideology of authenticity, in that it championed a territorially rooted linguistic identity framed as authentic and natural to Catalonia. Activists saw this identity as repressed but not undone by an artificial imposition of Castilian linguistic dominance by the Spanish state. The legal as well as the moral charter for Catalan language policy was grounded importantly in the frameworks of authenticity and naturalism.[3] Although this was a successful mobilizing discourse at the time of the transition, it increasingly became a constraint on the effort to extend the language to new speakers, because Catalan itself was not heard as an anonymous public vehicle of aperspectival objectivity. Rather, for many people Catalan continued to resonate as a local and private voice belonging to a particular kind of person, and not necessarily an attractive person from the perspective of young Castilian speakers (Frekko 2009a, Pujolar 2001).

In the decades since the transition to democracy and Catalan political autonomy, and particularly in the new millennium, there has been a noteworthy shift in both Hispanicist and Catalanist discourses, away from such overt framing in linguistic authenticity. When I assert there was a discursive shift, I do not mean that the discourses that became dominant toward the turn of this millennium were entirely new. As is usually the case when we periodize ideology and culture in history, it is a matter of changing priority among previously competing discourses (cf. Gal 2001, Woolard 2002).[4] Orientations toward universalism, cosmopolitanism, and a constructivist understanding of linguistic identity had been present in Catalan nationalism throughout the 20th century, but they have taken on renewed significance and prominence at the end of this period.[5] This trend was a response both to the new political logic of the post-Franco

---

3. Susan DiGiacomo has described the foundation of early 20th century Catalanism in naturalism and its evolution toward skepticism about language in its natural state (DiGiacomo 2001).

4. Xavier Vila has developed a more detailed periodization than I am able to do here of changing ideological frameworks in the struggle over Catalan language policy and identity. See, e.g. Vila i Moreno 2004a, 2004b.

5. There are many accounts of earlier phases of Catalanism as innovative and pluralistic; Joan-Lluís Marfany (1996, 137-139) gives a skeptical summary of early 20th century versions of such claims. Other analyses, including those written from a Socialist perspective, criticize the Catalan nationalist coalition party Convergència i Unió and its leader Jordi Pujol for an

Spain of autonomous communities, and to international developments of economic globalization and Europeanization, especially after Spain entered the European Union in 1986. Thus the shift is both specific to the historical conditions of Catalonia and also part of more general global trends toward new discourses in this period (Vila i Moreno 2004b, Duchêne and Heller 2012).

The goal of this chapter is to give a general overview of these competing discourses and the newer relations between them in Catalonia, drawing brief illustrations from across the decades and from a number of different domains and sources. This establishes the frame for more focused and systematic analyses of specific public controversies in Section II and of individual experiences of change in Section III of the book.

In the next sections of this chapter, I will first summarize the two concepts of *llengua pròpia* and normalization that were key to Catalan language policy, emphasizing their grounding in values of the authentic and the natural. I will then turn to examples of Hispanicist discourses that gathered strength in the 1990s under the banner of liberalism and Spanish linguistic anonymity to criticize Catalan policies. In the final sections of the chapter, we will look at examples of corresponding moves away from authenticity and naturalism in Catalanist discourses in several arenas: discourses of individual experience, official language campaigns, and electoral politics.

The *Llengua Pròpia* and Normalization

Catalan was recognized as an official language within Catalonia alongside Castilian by both the Spanish Constitution of 1978 and the Catalan Statute of Autonomy of 1979.[6] Neither text ever uses the term "co-official" for the languages, which tells of unsettled questions of priority. The Constitution established Castilian as "the official Spanish language of the State," and a second clause designated that "the other Spanish languages will also be official in their respective Autonomous Communities according to their Statutes."[7] The Catalan Statute of Autonomy reciprocated with a subtle reordering of the priorities, stating first

---

increasingly essentialist, traditionalist, and exclusionary nationalism over the decades it ruled the autonomous community. See Buxó 2001, Crameri 2008, Mascarell 1999.

6. These documents can be found online (Constitución 1978, Estatut 1979).

7. Article 3 of the Constitution states: 1. El castellano es la lengua española oficial del Estado. Todos los españoles tienen el deber de conocerla y el derecho a usarla. 2.Las demás lenguas españolas serán también oficiales en las respectivas Comunidades Autónomas de acuerdo con sus Estatutos. 3. La riqueza de las distintas modalidades lingüísticas de España es un patrimonio cultural que será objeto de especial respeto y protección.

that Catalan is "the official language of Catalonia," and then adding "as is also Castilian, official in the entire Spanish State."[8]

Of particular interest for the themes of this book is the fact that the Statute of Autonomy also declared Catalan to be Catalonia's *llengua pròpia*, its "proper language" in the sense we use in English of "proper name." This concept translates awkwardly into English and has sometimes been glossed as "autochthonous language" (Cabellos Espiérrez 2008, Segura Girard 2011). *Llengua pròpia* is probably best translated as "own language," as is usually done in English versions given on the Catalan government's official website.[9] Because of the difficulty in capturing its nuances in English, I will generally use the Catalan term (or its Castilian equivalent, *lengua propia*, when citing Castilian-medium texts or Castilianist discourses) throughout the rest of this book.

The adjective *pròpia* (f.; m. *propi*) did not have a well-established juridical or language policy meaning at the time of this designation, although some earlier such uses have been traced (Vila i Moreno 2011).[10] The term was taken up widely and has since come to be applied to all the minoritized languages of Spain. The then-president of Catalonia himself resorted to the dictionary to explain the significance of the term, emphasizing that something *propi* is "genuine" as opposed to "derived" (Süselbeck 2008, 168).[11] Among the meanings of *propi/pròpia* given by the *Dictionary of the Institute of Catalan Studies 2* are:

> of one person or thing to the exclusion of all others; belonging to oneself and not to another; not borrowed, not artificial; especially fitting to the nature, quality, etc. of someone.[12] (http://dlc.iec.cat)

The meaning and entailments of this concept became a main focus of legal challenges to the constitutionality of the revised Catalan Statute of Autonomy of

---

8. "L'idioma català és l'oficial de Catalunya, així com també ho és el castellà, oficial a tot l'Estat espanyol."

9. For example, in the translation of the revised Statute of Autonomy of 2006; http://web.gencat.cat/en/generalitat/estatut/estatut2006/titol_preliminar/. Accessed October 13, 2014.

10. The term appeared in a 1933 statute approved by the Catalan Parliament relating to the administration of Catalan autonomy under the Second Republic. For discussion of various interpretations of the term in relation to language across the years, see Branchadell 1997, Corretja i Torrens 1991, Solé i Durany 1996, Süselbeck 2008, Wurl 2011.

11. "genuí"/"derivat."

12. "Que és d'una persona o d'una cosa amb exclusió de tota altra . . . D'un mateix i no d'altri . . . No manllevat, no postís . . . Que convé d'una manera especial a la naturalesa, la qualitat, etc., d'algú."

2006 and of the Constitutional Court's reasoning in its 2010 decision on this question (see Segura Girard 2011, Tribunal Constitucional 2010).

At the time it was mobilized, the term *llengua pròpia* was a plausible alternative to more internationally familiar language policy designations that were denied to Catalan by dominant Spanish conventions, most specifically "national language." Although this latter term itself notoriously has no unambiguous meaning in language policy, it would have captured the significance of the Catalan language for a community whose rallying cry in the period was "We are a nation!"[13] (Argemí 1981). But that term was taboo for any language other than Castilian within the Spanish state, whose Constitution asserts "the indissoluble unity of the Spanish nation, common and indivisible homeland of all Spaniards."[14] Within this legal and juridical regime, only Castilian was to be considered a national language, just as only Spain was, and still is, to be considered a "nation." This exclusive status had been insisted on by the influential philosopher Miguel de Unamuno at the turn of the 20th century and still holds official sway in Spain after the turn of the 21st century (Resina 2002, 112).

Although lacking an established juridical meaning, the designation *pròpia* provided, or at least was taken by Catalan policymakers to provide, a charter to give Catalan priority in public institutions in Catalonia. The public role of Catalan was developed in two language laws in 1983 and 1998, in educational legislation and policy over the years, and in a number of public campaigns to increase use of Catalan.[15] By the 1990s, the evolution of language policy had made Catalan the usual working language of the Catalan government and the public face of most municipal administrations in Catalonia. It also established Catalan-medium instruction, generally referred to since the early 1990s as "immersion education," as the norm at all levels of compulsory education, with special emphasis on primary education. This is a significant development, given that less than half of the school-age population of Catalonia is of Catalan-speaking origins, and the majority is from Castilian-speaking families of Spanish immigrant origin, an issue that will be explored in Part III of this book.

The privilege that the Statute of Autonomy was taken to authorize for Catalan through the designation of *llengua pròpia* was trumped by a competing privilege bestowed on Castilian by the Spanish Constitution: "All Spaniards have

---

13. "Som una nació!"

14. "la indisoluble unidad de la Nación española, patria común e indivisible de todos los españoles." Preliminary Title, Section 2.

15. For the language laws, see Generalitat de Catalunya 1983 and Generalitat de Catalunya 1998. For overviews of educational policies see among others Ferrer 2000, Siguan 1988, Strubell i Trueta 1996, Vila i Moreno 2011.

an obligation to know Castilian, as well as a right to use it."[16] No parallel obligation was authorized for Catalan even within Catalonia, and in later controversies opponents mobilized public and legal challenges against the establishment of any such obligation (see, e.g. Vargas Llosa et al. 2008). After years of litigation, a clause in the revised Statute of Autonomy of 2006 that established an obligation (*deure*) to know Catalan, and another clause that derived an institutional preference for Catalan from its status as *pròpia*, were both ultimately rejected as unconstitutional by the Spanish Constitutional Court in 2010, to the continuing dismay of Catalan policymakers (Tribunal Constitucional 2010, Segura Girard 2011).

Outside of their respective autonomous communities, the Spanish Constitution recognizes the "other Spanish languages" only in this way: "The richness of the different linguistic modalities of Spain is a cultural patrimony that will be the object of special respect and protection."[17] There was no legal charter for use of Catalan by institutions or individuals at any other level within the Spanish state. Within the Spanish framework, then, Catalan is at best treated as an object, a heritage to be treasured, rather than a medium of communication actually to be used in contemporary life. Despite that special respect and protection, only ten Spanish universities outside of Catalan-speaking territories teach Catalan, in reported comparison to 21 in Britain, 26 in Germany, 23 in France, and 22 in the United States (Generalitat de Catalunya 2013, 48). This limited number suggests an active rejection or suppression rather than just a somehow natural lack of linguistic interest. It is in itself indicative of the Spanish linguistic ideology that insistently works at bounding Catalan as merely a local language of no public relevance or utility, despite paradoxical simultaneous complaints from the same quarters that monolinguals from other parts of Spain cannot get jobs in Catalonia because of its language requirements. The Spanish ideological investment in monolingualism has not gone entirely unnoticed by the international press. A column on the Catalan sovereignty movement in *The Economist* (July 20, 2014), straightforwardly entitled "How to make a country for everybody," put it in the classic pithy, commonsensical style of that neoliberal periodical:

> The cheapest solution is merely an attitudinal one: all Spaniards should treat Galician, Basque and Catalan not as regional languages. They are languages of Spain, full stop. Treating them as such, and not as a bother, would go a long way.

---

16. Article 3: El castellano es la lengua española oficial del Estado. Todos los españoles tienen el deber de conocerla y el derecho a usarla.

17. "Las demás lenguas españolas"; "La riqueza de las distintas modalidades lingüísticas de España es un patrimonio cultural que será objeto de especial respeto y protección."

The concept of *llengua pròpia*, or *lengua propia* in Castilian, grounds the value of languages so designated in the originary, the particular, and the local. Indeed, at least one publication by Catalan legal scholars translated *llengua pròpia* into English as "local language" (Vernet and Pons 2011, 70). This ideological foundation of linguistic legitimacy is further illustrated in the Catalan language law of 1998 (Generalitat de Catalunya 1998). Its preamble described Catalan as "a fundamental element of the formation and national personality of Catalonia."[18] Article 2 states that as Catalonia's own language, Catalan "singularizes" Catalonia "as a people."[19] The preamble frames this point by asserting that the linguistic community formed by Catalonia in conjunction with other Catalan-speaking territories has "throughout the centuries, with original voice, brought a valuable contribution to universal culture."[20]

This artful phrasing allows at least two interpretations of "original," in Catalan as in English. On the one hand, it can mean that the Catalan community brings to universal culture a unique voice that is unlike any other. On the other hand, it can signify that the community speaks in its originary, primordial voice when it makes its cultural contributions. The General Director of Catalan Linguistic Policy at the time the 1998 law was promulgated, Lluís Jou, used the definite article to paraphrase the preamble as saying that Catalan is "*the* original voice" (italics added), thus making clear the reading he gave it.[21] Jou wrote that in the law's phrasing, "Catalan is recognized as originary language, traditionally and historically rooted in the country"[22] (Jou 1998, 9).

The concept of *llengua pròpia* and the framework of authenticity from which it draws meaning clearly were important for legitimating and enabling the considerable successes in implanting Catalan in public institutions, public use, and most crucially, in education. Leaders and activists used this rationale to increase use of Catalan throughout the society in what is construed as a restoration of the language to its rightful status as the originary and essential language of Catalonia. Yet it very quickly also became a point of vulnerability, especially given the demographic realities of 20th century Catalonia.

---

18. "element fonamental de la formació i la personalitat nacional de Catalunya."

19. "El català és la llengua pròpia de Catalunya i la singularitza com a poble."

20. "una comunitat lingüística que ha portat al llarg dels segles, amb veu original, una valuosa contribució a la cultura universal."

21. "la veu original."

22. "el català és reconegut com a llengua originària, tradicionalment i històricament arrelada al país." The syntactic possibilities of Catalan do not force a choice between a definite or indefinite article ('an originary language' vs. 'the originary language').

An unintended consequence of this approach was the reinforcement of the complex of associations of authenticity discussed in Chapter 2, in which the localization of a language entails restriction of its communicative possibilities as well as of new speakers' access to it. The concept of *llengua pròpia* thus inadvertently contributed to limiting the language even while protecting it. Indeed, the only reading of *pròpia* that the Constitutional Court in its 2010 decision on the Statute admitted as acceptable grounds for policy hinged on its local and restricted nature as "privative" or exclusive to the community, in contrast to the common language shared across all (Spanish) communities.[23]

Thus, *pròpia* is understood as authentic, authentic is understood as territorially rooted, and territorially rooted as exclusively local; in a chain of signification, the strength of linguistic authenticity becomes the weakness of local restriction. Many examples can be drawn from across all domains of Spanish and Catalan public life that illustrate disdain for Catalan as "too local" for public communicative purposes. We have seen the dismissive contrast drawn by a Spanish sociologist between "local" versus "communicative" languages reported in Chapter 2. In popular culture, a radio sports journalist was reported to complain when the Catalan president of the Barcelona football club (long a symbol of Catalanism, "more than a club" in a popular refrain) used Catalan in a press conference. "This is a waste of time . . . [T]hat they speak Catalan at home doesn't worry me so much, but that they do it in public . . . ."; the journalist's conclusion was left hanging in the news report[24] (*e-notícies* 2007).[25]

In an example from the intersection of academia and government, a grant proposal for a symposium on Catalan theater was reported to have been rejected in 2006 by the Spanish Ministry of Science and Education because it was too local in scope (Díez 2007). I know nothing of the merits of the proposal, but I note the equation of Catalan with local in the sense of restricted in reviewers' reported condescending judgment that the applicants' publications were of a "markedly local character, which in a certain sense is very logical and reasonable

23. The Dictionary of the Royal Spanish Academy, DRAE, defines *privativo/a* thus: "1. Que causa privación o la significa. 2. Propio y peculiar singularmente de alguien o algo, y no de otros" http://www.rae.es/recursos/diccionarios/drae. Presumably it is the second meaning, basically synonymous with *propia*, that is intended by the Court, but it is interesting to consider the connotation of (de)privation that the first meaning lends.

24. "es una pérdida de tiempo . . . que hablen en catalán en su casa no me preocupa tanto, pero que lo hagan en público . . . "

25. This is not an entirely singular occurrence. Spanish journalists similarly objected to a Catalan football coach's Catalan response to questions posed in that same language during a mixed-language news conference in 2011, in an area of Aragon where Catalan is spoken. That generated media attention because the coach then walked out of the press conference. See, e.g., Garcia and Padilla 2011.

given their area of expertise, Catalan philology"[26] (Serra 2006b). As a "local" language, Catalan apparently could not fairly be expected to be treated in publications with wider audiences.

Over time a generally accepted contrast grew up in Spain between what are called in Castilian the *lenguas propias*—(principally Catalan under its several regional names, Basque, and Galician), which were seen as essentially local, and Castilian (increasingly referred to as Spanish), which came to appear not to be *propia* to any particular place or community at all. Rather, Castilian/Spanish came to be framed in a dominant discourse as the "common" language that enjoyed the enhancing value of anonymity as a territorially and socially limitless vehicle of communication.[27] If Catalan, Basque, and Galician are "*proper* languages," belonging to the territorialized few, the status of Spanish in contrast was cemented as a "proper *language*," that is, a medium of communication par excellence belonging to no one in particular. In contrast to the territorialized Catalan, Spanish was deterritorialized and equipped to be the "common language" of all, a term that took on increasing importance in the Spanish state-wide language conflict.

As the concept of *llengua pròpia* was used in Catalan language policy to give a degree of priority to Catalan in domains such as education, public administration, and cultural subvention, Castilianist critics objected vociferously. The concept itself has been rejected repeatedly as illiberal in that it violates the principle of the supremacy of individual over group rights (Royo Arpón 2000, Santamaría 1999). "Catalan is not a public language," one author wrote sarcastically; "it has legal owners"[28] (Royo cited in Santamaría 1999, 184–185). A principal slogan of this opposition is that "territories don't speak, people do"[29] (*Avui* 2006a). Such a position does not question monolingualism or the idea of single ownership of a single language. Such defining ownership is only relocated to the individual, in a thoroughly (neo)liberal mold. At the same time, the link of the Castilian language to all the territory of Spain goes unquestioned by such critics. Catalan

---

26. "Sus publicaciones son de marcado carácter local, lo cual es en cierto modo muy lógico y razonable dada su área de conocimiento, Filología Catalana."

27. Less often, the label of *lengua propia* has been claimed for Spanish/Castilian as well. For example, Irene Lozano, author of a book entitled *Languages at War* (*Lenguas en guerra*), asserted that "Spanish is also the *lengua propia* of Catalonia and the Basque Country" ("el español también es la lengua propia de Cataluña y el País Vasco") at the same time as she claimed the status of "common language" ("lengua común") only for Spanish (Torquemada 2006). In praising Lozano's book, the sociologist Amando de Miguel declared that the idea that territories where only Castilian is spoken don't have a *lengua propia* is "stupidity" ("una estupidez") (Aguilar 2005).

28. "el catalán no es una lengua pública: tiene unos propietarios legales."

29. "els territoris no parlen, ho fan les persones."

defenders point out to little avail the "enormous inconsistency" of claiming that territories don't have linguistic rights while defending that Castilian is the language of all of Spain. "Is it not a territory?"[30] asked one critic (Terricabras 2008a).

The attacks on Catalan policy grew while the proportion of first-language speakers of Catalan in the population dwindled in relation to new transnational immigration as well as the growing population of Castilian-speaking descendants of earlier Spanish immigrants.[31] Thus the fit of the authenticity framework to contemporary Catalonia and the conceptualization of Catalan as *llengua pròpia* became more and more awkward, setting the stage for discursive change.[32]

Normalization

Despite its deliberate intervention in language use, Catalan language policy has been grounded significantly in sociolinguistic naturalism, as seen not only in the naturalizing concept of *llengua pròpia* but also in its second guiding concept, that of "linguistic normalization." The 1983 law that elaborated the official language policy for Catalanizing the public sphere of Catalonia was called the Law of Linguistic Normalization, and the process it chartered is widely known by the same term.

The concept of normalization was introduced in 1965 by the Valencian sociologist of language Lluís V. Aracil, to analyze the Catalan situation in a cybernetic model of the interaction of language and society within language conflicts (Aracil 1982). Aracil's groundbreaking analysis sought to unmask ideological justifications of language shift as based in naturalized metaphysical entities and linguistic laws of nature. Yet later uses of the term that he had coined came to naturalize an ideal "normal" language in its "normal" state. As elaborated by another Valencian sociolinguist, Rafael Ninyoles, normalization meant the return to "social monolingualism" in a minoritized language as the only alternative to the replacive bilingualism that would result from diglossia, or

---

30. "Es una incoherencia enorme decir que los territorios no tienen derechos lingüísticos y defender que en España—¿no es un territorio?—el castellano sea el único idioma impuesto."

31. David Atkinson has written on the shared firm conviction that there is a minoritized language in Catalonia, and the simultaneous disagreement over which one it is (Atkinson 2000).

32. Albert Branchadell gives an excellent analysis of the constraints of the concept of *llengua pròpia* and of attempts within the Catalan nationalist political parties ERC and UDC as early as 1989 to break with such essentializing discourse. Branchadell recounts that one of the earliest alternate visions was inspired by a political activist's experience of the "supraethnic" patriotism he saw in a visit to the United States (Branchadell 1999). Branchadell himself has been an early proponent of a "third way" for Catalanism, akin to emergent visions described throughout this book, and especially one that makes room for Castilian speakers.

hierarchically organized bilingualism, which Ninyoles saw as the only actually occurring kind of societal bilingualism (Ninyoles 1971, 19–21). That is, normal societies are monolingual, and normalization strives to approximate that state. Like *llengua pròpia*, normalization has since become a term of language planning art adopted in other territories as well. As Boix-Fuster and Vila (1998, 316) point out, the diffusion of the term has created considerable variation in its meaning, and the emphasis on the need for social monolingualism has been softened (see also Woolard 1986, Süselbeck 2008, Sinner and Wieland 2008 for discussion of the variable meanings).

In most Catalan uses of the term, especially the early ones, the presupposition of normalization is that there is a normal, natural state for language in society, and in that normal state a single language fulfills all linguistic functions in its own territorial space naturally, without need of deliberate intervention, unless that natural role is stunted or distorted by artificial interference from external forces. As in cybernetic models, sociolinguistic systems are self-correcting or self-normalizing, except when pathological historical intervention from outside the system distorts this natural, normal position of a language. Such external distortion makes further willful historical intervention, i.e., normalization, necessary, for the "recuperation" of a normal (implicitly earlier) state. Like Dante's most illustrious form of the vernacular as discussed in Chapter 2, linguistic normalization aims to remove the distorting effects of history and restore a language to its true natural state.

Despite changes that will be discussed below, the foundation of Catalan language activism in sociolinguistic naturalism was still in evidence at times in 21st century Catalonia. In a homely example, a hand-made protest flyer handed to me outside the Catalan Parliament in 2006 by a self-described retired mechanic read: "Catalan is the natural language of Catalonia. Only invaded nations have to negotiate their language with the Castilian and French empires."[33]

The Anonymity of the Castilian Language

Early in the period of Catalan autonomy, elite Castilianist resistance to Catalan language policy also drew on a discourse based in the ideology of linguistic authenticity. An important example was a manifesto released in 1981 protesting against emerging Catalanist policies, signed by 2300 self-described "intellectuals

---

33. "El català és l'idioma natural de Catalunya. Sols les nacions envaïdes han de negociar el seu idioma amb els imperis castellà i francès."

and professionals who live and work in Catalonia"[34] (de Miguel et al. 1981). This self-identification was a recognizable reference to the well-known slogan of civic nationalism coined by the Catalan nationalist president Jordi Pujol, "All those who live and work here are Catalan," but in this case it was put to purposes that ran counter to Pujol's. The manifesto drew prolonged attention in the media and triggered significant organized responses from Catalanist defenders. The manifesto's opening objections were cast in terms of "liberty, tolerance, and respect among all the citizens of Catalonia"[35] and accused the Catalan government of "antidemocratic" policies. This was an early invocation of the liberal discourse that came to play an increasing role at the end of the 20th century and beginning of the 21st. Most of the manifesto, however, was developed in familiar terms that drew an essential link between language and identity. These included a defense based in the concepts of mother tongue and of *lengua propia* itself, understood in this case not as a territory's but rather as an individual's own language.

The 1981 manifesto asserted that the loss of Castilian from public life would mean "discrimination against the half of the population of Catalonia that has Castilian as its *lengua propia*."[36] The authors acknowledged that no one is born with a language or a culture, but they invoked a Herderian nexus of language, culture, heritage, and worldview as the foundation of a universal right:

> all are born with an inalienable right to inherit and enlarge the language and culture of their parents. No one is born with a language, but all have a right of access to knowledge of that intellectual and affective medium that unites a child with its parents and that, moreover, carries with it a complete vision of the world.[37]

This manifesto further asserted that students must have the right to "receive education in their own mother tongue," not only in early childhood or primary or even secondary education, but "at all levels."[38] Drawing on a psycholinguistic

---

34. "intelectuales y profesionales que viven y trabajan en Cataluña." The manifesto was published in more than one newspaper, and versions now available online differ some from the print text from the period that I have used.

35. "libertad, tolerancia y respeto entre todos los ciudadanos de Cataluña."

36. "discriminación para la mitad de la población de Cataluña que tiene como lengua propia el castellano."

37. "todos nacen con el inalienable derecho a heredar y acrecentar la lengua y cultura de sus padres. Nadie nace con una lengua, pero todos tienen derecho a acceder al conocimiento de ese vehículo intelectual y afectivo que une al niño con sus padres y que, además, comporta toda una visión del mundo."

38. "recibir la enseñanza en la propia lengua materna en todos los niveles."

rationale for mother-tongue instruction, it argued that Catalan-medium instruction discriminates against Castilian speakers and creates a " 'trauma' whose most immediate consequence is the loss of verbal fluency and a lowered capacity for abstraction and comprehension."[39] The manifesto held that to deny that two languages can coexist in the same territory would be to legitimate "the cultural genocide of close to three million people"[40] (presumably this referred to the first-language Castilian speakers of Catalonia). In these several discursive formulae, the manifesto wove language, identity, culture, and cognition together intimately to define and depict a distinctive collectivity, a people, under imminent threat. That collectivity was not Catalonia or Catalans, but rather Castilian speakers in Catalonia.

Thus in the early period of autonomy, the linguistic conflict and the policy rationales advanced by both the Catalanist and Castilianist positions drew on an ideology of linguistic authenticity and a rhetoric of essential and inalienable identities and rights defined by an originary language, whether of a territory or of a speaker. They depicted competition and struggle between two groups that were intimately defined by their "own" *lenguas propias.*

By the 1990s, a new discourse about Castilian had emerged to displace at least partially such ethnolinguistic essentialism, in response to a confluence of forces. On the one hand, new discursive strategies were needed to defend Castilianist positions in peninsular debates where the peripheral autonomous communities had claimed the high ground for their *lenguas propias* within the authenticity frame as well as on the basis of the restoration of justice after the dictatorship. At the same time, entry into the European Union and economic forces of globalization led Spain to focus on enhancing the international value of what was more often called Spanish as it competed with English, in a process of linguistic commodification that has also been seen in other language settings.[41] This effort was supported by the founding of the Instituto Cervantes in 1991 to foment what is called the "international projection"[42] of the language (*El Periódico* 2007c).

The rhetorical positions developed in the context of economic globalization served double duty and were frequently put to work in the peninsular linguistic conflicts. For example, the number of Spanish speakers worldwide is an often-repeated

---

39. " 'trauma' cuya consecuencia más inmediata es la pérdida de la fluidez verbal y una menor capacidad de abstracción y comprensión."

40. "el genocidio cultural de cerca de tres millones de personas."

41. For discussion of this globalizing linguistic campaign, see del Valle 2005, del Valle and Gabriel-Stheeman 2004, Mar-Molinero 2013. For related phenomena in other settings, see Heller 2003, 2010, Duchêne and Heller 2012.

42. "proyección internacional."

trope of the superior utility of the language. Politicians and Hispanicist public intellectuals eschewed nationalist tones and framed Castilian (increasingly referred to in these public commentaries as Spanish) as a post-national language, not the *lengua propia* of a specific ethnolinguistic group, but the "common language"[43] (Vargas Llosa et al. 2008), a "common linguistic space"[44] (Lodares 2005) of everyone in Spain and indeed beyond, belonging to no particular social group. The Socialist Spanish president Zapatero, for example, was reported to laud the Instituto Cervantes for working to insure that "nobody feels like a foreigner in the great territory of the Spanish language" (*El Periódico* 2007c).[45] Some commentary aimed at the peninsular conflict blends the frames of the *lengua propia* and the common language, as in this example from an op-ed piece by a member of the Royal Academy, rebutting criticism from the sociolinguists Llorenç Comajoan and José del Valle:

> Castilian or Spanish is not only the language of one group and the official language of Spain: it is the common language, general, of all Spain, belonging to (*propia de*) all. [The critics] don't want to hear this from me. There used to be freedom, now the aggression of the fanatics grows.[46] (Rodríguez Adrados 2006)

To be sure, expressions of Castilian linguistic essentialism and the older Spanish cultural and linguistic nationalism did not vanish and have even made a strong comeback in various political moments. For example, the youth wing of the Partido Popular launched a flag-waving (literally) "We are Spain" (*Somos España*) campaign on October 12, 2007, the "*Día de la Hispanidad*" "Day of Hispanicism" (formerly known as the *Día de la Raza* "Day of the Race"). In this campaign, PP quite literally wrapped itself in the Spanish flag, promising to carry it "where it is needed most,"[47] where others "insult the Crown,"[48] and especially to Catalonia and the Basque Country (Agencias 2007). Since 2012, there have

---

43. "lengua común."

44. "el espacio lingüístico común."

45. "Zapatero destacó que en el Instituto Cervantes se trabaja para que nadie se sienta extranjero en el gran territorio de la lengua española."

46. "el castellano o español no es sólo la lengua de un grupo y la lengua oficial de España: es la lengua común, general, de toda España, propia de todos. Esto no quieren oírmelo. Había libertad, ahora crece la agresión de los fanáticos."

47. "donde haga más falta."

48. "ultrajan la corona." This referred to specific instances of deliberate symbolic insults to the Crown by demonstrators.

been an increasing number of similarly explicit Spanish nationalist responses to the surge for Catalan sovereignty.

Nonetheless, the discourse of linguistic anonymity and accompanying claims to the openness, cosmopolitanism, and universalism of Spanish, as well as its superior communicative and economic power, became dominant in Hispanicist public discourses by the end of the last millennium and continue to carry such weight. In this chapter I give only some brief excerpts to illustrate, emphasizing the views of academic and public intellectuals. Many more examples in a similar vein are reported in recent work by Juan Carlos Moreno Cabrera (2008, 2010, 2014).

A poetic example of the image of Spanish linguistic cosmopolitanism came from Antonio Muñoz Molina, novelist, member of the Royal Spanish Academy, and then recent director of the Instituto Cervantes in New York:

> The Spanish language is a country that allows one to travel though an unlimited variety of landscapes without being detained at any border, a fluid and flexible identity that allows us to be from many places and from only one. (Muñoz Molina 2007)[49]

Ironically enough, Muñoz was here celebrating the charm and vigor of the many different varieties of Spanish representing multiple communities of origin that he heard regularly in the United States, indeed indicating that Spanish was not detained at that border. But this vigor, and the market for Spanish-medium commodities that it supports, are themselves sustained by the authenticity value of the Spanish language in those communities (del Valle and Gabriel-Stheeman 2004, Woolard 2007b).

The most notoriously controversial example of a discourse that claims social, historical, and political neutrality and free (market) choice for Spanish came from King Juan Carlos in 2001. In the course of awarding a literary prize to a Spanish author, he asserted:

> Ours was never a language of imposition, but rather of encounter. Nobody was ever obliged to speak in Castilian: the most diverse peoples made the language of Cervantes their own, in the freest of choices. (Marcos and Company 2001)[50]

---

49. "El español es un país que le permite circular a uno por una variedad ilimitada de paisajes sin que lo detengan en ninguna frontera, una identidad fluida y flexible que nos permite ser de muchos lugares y de uno solo."

50. "Nunca fue la nuestra lengua de imposición, sino de encuentro; a nadie se obligó nunca a hablar en castellano: fueron los pueblos más diversos quienes hicieron suyos, por voluntad libérrima, el idioma de Cervantes."

This speech was understood to have originated with the minister of culture of the conservative Spanish government under the Partido Popular. Although spokespersons for the King and state insisted that the comment was only meant to characterize the colonial history of the Americas, it was taken by many to be aimed at the language debates in Spain. Its obvious inaccuracy about the linguistic history of Latin America as well as of the Spanish state during the Franco period, if not earlier, provoked vociferous objections.

The promotion of a post-national Spanish language claiming its rightful economic and cultural place as a rival to English in a globalized world often implicitly supported criticism of minority languages and nationalisms within Spain. As José del Valle has observed, "Spanish is presented . . . as a tool in service to a post-nation . . . that reduces Catalan, Galician, and Basque to atavistic and reactionary particularism"[51] (del Valle 2005, 411).

In some cases the post-national Castilianist discourse of the language as socially neutral went further, to naturalize Spanish as a vehicle of aperspectival objectivity with a privileged purchase on the kinds of truths essential to modernity and democracy.[52] An early and particularly inspired argument for the ideological anonymity of Spanish was proposed by the philologist Ángel López García in a prize-winning book on the historical origins of the language, tellingly entitled *The Rumor of the Rootless* (*El rumor de los desarraigados*) (López García 1985). Because this popularizing work of scholarship on linguistic history so vividly and explicitly illustrates the ideological complex of linguistic anonymity, it is worth a more detailed consideration here.[53]

López García argued that Spanish was originally a Basque-Romance koine whose essential nature had never been that of a *lengua propia* (58–59).[54] Rather, "Spanish was born as the language of the others" (54).[55] In an echo of Dante's illustrious vernacular and Nagel's view from nowhere,

---

51. "se presenta el español como . . . instrumento al servicio de una post-nación . . . que deja reducidas al atavismo y al particularismo reaccionario al catalán, gallego y euskera."

52. This position can be found in myriad instances, many of them inventoried by the Spanish linguist Juan Carlos Moreno Cabrera in several works (Moreno Cabrera 2008, 2010, 2014). Moreno Cabrera is singular among Castilian-medium Spanish intellectuals for his outspoken critical stance toward Spanish linguistic nationalism.

53. I thank Professor López García for his gracious stance toward earlier versions of this critique.

54. On the accuracy of this historical account, see the exchange between Trask and Wright (1988) and López García (1988).

55. "el español nació como la lengua de los otros."

López García wrote that this koine "has its origins everywhere and nowhere" (72).[56] López García wrote that it made no sense to speak of its "native speaker"[57] (54). There were not any users who owned this Spanish language more than others.

Quite explicitly, then, López García proposed that Spanish was in its origins and therefore its essence a voice from nowhere, an anonymous and universal resource. In this account, the Spanish language and the public sphere that it articulated were indeed everyone's because no one's in particular. López García proposed that once the linguistic variety was established by the 10th century, the koine spread easily because, being no one's language, it was not threatening to anyone. As he put it quite poetically, "*como lengua de relación, la koiné no representa un ser, significa un estar*" (120) ("as a language of social relations, the koine represents not an essential being, but a temporal state"). Drawing here on the aspectual difference between the two Spanish verbs that correspond to the single English copula "to be," López García signaled the difference between an essential, timeless being (*ser*) and an active, if temporary, becoming (*estar*).

López García further cast these origins as endowing the language with an inherent ability to express an aperspectival political view. This was the language of "the disinherited who knew no other nation than that which they themselves could build without regard to race, sex, social class or birthplace,"[58] he wrote (54). With such origins, "the koiné implicitly carries, rather than an exclusionary communitarian sentiment an ideology, exactly the antiparticularistic and antihegemonic ideology of what is [held in] common" (*lo común*) (143).[59]

This inspiring vision of linguistic origins functions as what in anthropology is called a charter myth, a representation of historical origins that provides a foundation for a particular vision of contemporary society. In this case it provides a historical charter for a certain version of modern multilingual Spain, with which López García is sympathetic, one where distinct linguistic communities have their recognized, respected if limited place and are united through a socially rootless language of wider communication, precisely "*el rumor de los desarraigados*" ("the rumor of the rootless"), as the title of the book put it. (See López García 2009 for elaboration of his position on contemporary language politics.)

---

56. "tiene su origen en todas partes y en ninguna."

57. "hablante nativo."

58. "los desheredados que no conocían otra nación que la que ellos mismos . . . pudiesen edificar sin restricciones de raza, sexo, clase social o lugar de nacimiento."

59. "La koiné lleva implícita antes una ideología que un sentimiento comunitario exclusivo, justamente la ideología antiparticularista y antihegemónica de lo común."

López García went on to recognize that the authority of the Spanish language was transformed during the Renaissance from its original basis in what I am calling anonymity to one of territorially based authenticity. At that point, he explained, it was taken over by Castile and "*disfrazado*" (disguised) as *castellano* (Castilian), distorting its essential nature (López García 1985, 58–59). Once Spanish was localized as Castilian, he recounts, prescriptivism gained power, and perfect control of the linguistic form became crucial. López García depicted the ideological grounding of the linguistic authority of Castilian changing to authenticity this way, beautifully illustrating the idea that the indexical function of the language for signaling the speaker's identity triumphs over the referential function:

> As a koine, it did not matter much that centropeninsular Spanish was the mother tongue of some and only a second language for others; to trade, to converse, to undertake projects together, it was enough that the some and the others could understand each other. But woe to the others when Spanish became Castilian! Whoever did not have perfect mastery of it, whether as an urbane mother tongue or because a careful—and naturally, selective—upbringing had prepared him for it, was automatically excluded from or relegated to inferior conditions in public life.[60] (López García 1985, 108)

Thus López García made very clear that the basis of the authority of Spanish in the modern period has been particularistic and selective, not anonymous and universalistic. But at the same time his historical account provided a vision of the originary state to be recaptured in a post-Franco return to respectful multilingual recognition within overarching linguistic unity in an anonymous common, democratic language.

Other spokespersons for a post-national vision of Spanish have further advanced the claim that the contemporary language is especially suited to modern universality and democracy. Speaking about her book *Languages at War*,[61] Irene Lozano asserted that apart from the Franco period, Spanish had been freely

---

60. "Como koiné no importaba demasiado que el español centropeninsular fuese la lengua materna de unos y sólo la segunda lengua de otros; para comerciar, para dialogar, para emprender proyectos en común, bastaba con que unos y otros se pudiesen entender. Mas ¡ay de los otros! cuando el español se convirtió en castellano: quien no lo dominara a la perfección, por tratarse de su lengua materna urbana o porque una educación esmerada—y, naturalmente, selectiva—le había preparado para ello, quedaba automáticamente excluido o en inferioridad de condiciones para la vida pública."

61. "*Lenguas en guerra*."

chosen as "the common language"[62] because of its "character as a ductile language, without fears about 'contamination' "[63] (Torquemada 2006). The acme was probably reached by Gregorio Salvador, linguist, vice director of the Royal Academy of the Spanish language, and general scourge of minority languages in Spain, as quoted by José del Valle:

> Spanish is not a sign of identity nor an emblem nor a flag . . . it is now not vernacular anywhere . . . it has become pure linguistic essence, that is, an invaluable instrument of communication between peoples and nations, a plurinational and multiethnic language.[64] (cited in del Valle 2005, 407)

Commenting on other instances of the same refrain, a Catalan journalist lamented it as the "old and eternal excuses"[65]: " 'my' language is more universal than 'yours', so even in your territory, mine is more useful . . . When will we be the beneficiaries of this 'everyone' that excludes us?"[66] (Simó 2007).

The rhetorical turn to claims for the democratic anonymity of the Castilian language is particularly evident if we compare a second manifesto to defend it against Catalan and Basque language policies with the 1981 manifesto discussed earlier. The "Manifesto for a Common Language" appeared in June 2008.[67] Its title in itself gives an instructive contrast to the essentialist rhetoric of mother tongue and cultural genocide of the Manifesto of 2300 that had appeared over twenty-five years earlier.

This new manifesto in 2008 argued for the significance of Castilian not as someone's *lengua propia* or mother tongue, but as "common to all Spanish citizens."[68] Passages in the text refer to Castilian/Spanish not by name but simply as

---

62. "lengua común."

63. "por su carácter de lengua dúctil, sin temores a la 'contaminación.' "

64. el español no es seña de identidad ni emblema ni bandera . . . la vieja lengua de mil años y miles de caminos no es vernácula ya en ninguna parte . . . [ha] devenido en pura esencia lingüística, es decir, en un valiosísimo instrumento de comunicación entre pueblos y gentes, en un idioma plurinacional y multiétnico."

65. "les excuses són antigues i eternes."

66. "la 'meva' llengua és més universal que la 'teva', així doncs, i fins i tot en el teu territori, és més útil la meva . . . ¿Quan ens toca a nosaltres ser els beneficiaris d'aquest 'todos' que ens exclou?"

67. When published in *El País*, the manifesto was titled "For *a* common language," but most sources refer to it as the manifesto for "*the* common language." The change from indefinite to definite article is significant. The former treats this status as a desideratum; the latter presupposes that such a common language, which in this context can only be Spanish, already exists.

68. "común de todos los ciudadanos españoles."

"the common language of the country,"[69] presupposing its unquestionable status as this language. This manifesto arrogated to Spanish the role of "principal language of democratic communication in this country,"[70] asserting that its historical and global status somehow made it an especially rich democratic resource:

> a common political language is an enormous richness for democracy, and even more so if it is a language so rooted historically in all of the country and with such validation through the whole world as Castilian.[71] (Vargas Llosa et al. 2008)

This text challenged the institutional goals and gains made by Catalan and other minoritized languages of Spain, which were referred to as "the co-official languages,"[72] excluding Castilian from this group as if it were not itself also a "co-official language" in the relevant territories. The manifesto demanded that the Spanish Parliament "unequivocally establish that . . . Castilian is the common and official language in the entire national territory"[73] and the only language that Spanish citizens can be required to understand. This demand called for a performative enactment of an official state of affairs, but the use of the indicative mood rather than the subjunctive form of the verb "is" simultaneously presupposed that such a state was already factually true. This is an excellent example of what Terry Eagleton described as the performative nature of ideology in its constative or referential guise, drawing on J.L. Austin's theory of speech acts (Eagleton 1991).[74]

The manifesto demanded a fully bilingual civil service in the peripheral autonomous communities (but not in the central state apparatus or autonomous communities where only Castilian is official), to be achieved without requiring bilingualism of individual civil servants. Although the Spanish courts had repeatedly validated the Catalan policy goal of ensuring individual bilingual competency by the end of compulsory schooling, the manifesto opposed it because

---

69. "la [lengua] común del país."

70. "lengua principal de comunicación democrática en este país."

71. "una lengua política común es una enorme riqueza para la democracia, aún más si se trata de una lengua de tanto arraigo histórico en todo el país y de tanta vigencia en el mundo entero como el castellano."

72. "lenguas cooficiales."

73. "fijar inequívocamente [que] . . . la lengua castellana es común y oficial a todo el territorio nacional."

74. The logic of the manifesto is similar to that of the Official English movement in the United States, as seen in ballot initiatives in California in the 1980s. These essentially proposed that "because English is the language of civic life and the public sphere, it must be made the language of civic life in the public sphere" (Woolard 1989b).

some people might "logically" want to live their lives only in Castilian (but not, apparently, only in Catalan or Euskara). The phrasing of this logic echoes the supreme linguistic condescension that Bourdieu identified as the privilege of those associated with a dominant language:

> It is logical to suppose that there will always be many citizens who prefer to develop their daily and professional life in Castilian, knowing only enough of the autonomous community language to co-exist courteously with others and to enjoy as far as possible cultural manifestations in it.[75]

The 2008 manifesto shares with its 1981 antecedent an expressed concern for the educational and civil rights of those who have Castilian as their first language. However, the 1981 manifesto attended only to mother-tongue Castilian speakers and reinforced its demand with particularistic and essentialist arguments about individual psychological development, family ties, and cultural genocide, as we have seen. In contrast, the 2008 version mitigates any apparent particularism in the demand for Castilian-medium education by encompassing "the educational and civic rights of all those who have [Castilian] as a mother tongue or who with all rights choose this language as the preferred medium of expression, understanding and communication."[76] Driving this home as a universal rather than particular claim, the manifesto demanded official recognition that "All citizens who so desire have the right to be educated in the Castilian language, *whatever their mother tongue*" (italics added).[77] In this 2008 text, discourses of citizenship and commonality have come to dominate over identity, authenticity, *lengua propia*, and mother tongue as the terms of linguistic and moral authority.

Despite the strong claims advanced by partisans like Gregorio Salvador for the utter anonymity of the Spanish language, and the careful discourse of citizenship marshaled in this second manifesto, the frames of anonymity and authenticity are often mixed in the defense of the language. For example, an opinion piece by a teacher of Spanish language in a conservative, market-oriented newspaper bemoaned the "ferocious and constant harassment"[78] of Castilian by the Catalan government, as

---

75. "Es lógico suponer que siempre habrá muchos ciudadanos que prefieran desarrollar su vida cotidiana y profesional en castellano, conociendo sólo de la lengua autonómica lo suficiente para convivir cortésmente con los demás y disfrutar en lo posible de las manifestaciones culturales en ella."

76. "derechos educativos y cívicos de quienes la tienen como lengua materna o la eligen con todo derecho como vehículo preferente de expresión, comprensión y comunicación."

77. "Todos los ciudadanos que lo deseen tienen derecho a ser educados en lengua castellana, sea cual fuere su lengua materna."

78. "el acoso es feroz y constante."

seen in the controversy over language representation at the Frankfurt Book Fair of 2007 that we will examine in detail in Chapter 6. Such perceived harassment of Spanish (the author alternates between the two names for the language) was described as especially incomprehensible when the "vituperation" targeted

> a language that makes siblings of a multitude of human beings: three hundred million, according to some, four hundred, according to others.... All languages have identical value for those who have gotten them at birth, but not in human commerce .... Nonetheless, Spanish is attacked in so many places on the Peninsula, as an invader language. And this [attack] is hard to understand, unless deliberately manipulative and artificial mechanisms intervene in this neglect of Castilian, but with decisive influence on the citizenry.... because, as Herder said, "we think in a language, and to think is to speak. Each nation thinks, then, as it speaks and speaks as it thinks ... " More than ever it is necessary to subscribe to the constitutional assertion of national unity, and thus, the necessity of a common language, the Spanish language, without which the concept of the nation itself would be extinguished.[79] (Lázaro 2006)

This rightwing periodical had a limited readership, but the example illustrates motifs that were in play at more august levels. It moves from the brother- and sisterhood of hundreds of millions around the globe through the unequal economic value of languages to the essential, Romantic link of the "common" Spanish language to worldview and nationhood.

The late Juan Ramon Lodares, an academic Spanish philologist as well as public intellectual, was a tireless proponent of the claim that Spanish is the liberating common language of all, while the minority languages owe their existence to reactionary and manipulative rootbound particularism that strangles modern democracy. Criticizing the defense of the peripheral languages, Lodares explicitly and repeatedly wove the themes of modernity and democracy into specious arguments against them. He masterfully attached to contemporary minority language

---

79. "una lengua que hermana a una multitud de seres humanos: a trescientos millones, según unos, o a cuatrocientos, según otros ... Todos los idiomas poseen valor idéntico para quien los han recibido al nacer, pero no en el comercio humano ... El español, sin embargo zaherido en tantos lugares de la Península, como un idioma invasor. Y no se entiende bien. Al menos que en esa postergación del castellano no intervengan mecanismos decididamente manipuladores y artificiales, pero de decisiva influencia en la ciudadanía ... Porque, como decía Herder 'pensamos en una lengua; y pensar es hablar. Cada nación piensa, pues, como habla y habla como piensa' .... Pero más que nunca es necesario suscribir la aserción constitucional de la unidad nacional y, por tanto, la necesidad de una lengua común, la lengua española, sin la cual el concepto mismo de nación se extingue."

activism the most conservative Spanish traditionalism of the 19th and early 20th centuries, associating the preservation of linguistic differences with isolation, backwardness, and illiteracy across Spain:

> Representatives of all parties have appeared who consider it of the highest importance that children should learn even local linguistic forms, forms whose only value, why deny it, lies in the fact that they have been preserved practically intact in their villages and counties down through time, which in a country like Spain, traditionally full of illiterates, was hardly a good thing. (Lodares 2000, 18)

> in the history of Spain the preservation of particular languages is linked to the preservation of general illiteracy throughout the national domain.[80] (ibid., 21)

The familiar pejorative interpretation of "local" aside, this is a difficult bit of ideological sleight of hand, given Catalonia's leading role within Spain in modern industrialization and the urban mobilization that predictably accompanies this. In the 1970s, poor Castilian-speaking immigrants to Catalonia from regions of southern Spain impoverished under a Castilian agrarian oligarchy were more likely to be illiterate than were Catalonia-born citizens. Yet Lodares persisted in associating the minority languages such as Catalan with provincial isolation, illiteracy, undemocratic backwardness, and local feudal privileges, in implicit contrast to the appropriateness of the Spanish language for modern democracy:

> The linguistic Spain that is presented to us now as the height of modernity, with its five official languages . . . is, in essence, a very old Spain . . . A Spain whose minority languages are maintained not by a secular, democratic, collective will . . . but rather because there was no significant organization that could break the traditional local privileges of the kingdoms . . . People who were not mobile remained pure.[81] (Lodares 2000, 29)

---

80. "han aparecido diputados de todo signo que consideran asunto de sumo interés que los niños aprendan incluso usos lingüísticos locales, usos cuyo único valor, para qué vamos a negarlo, estriba en que se han conservado casi intactos en su pueblo o su comarca a lo largo del tiempo, lo que en un país como España, tradicionalmente lleno de analfabetos, tampoco es tanto mérito."... "en la historia de España la conservación de lenguas particulares está ligada a la conservación de analfabetos generales en todo el dominio nacional." *Particular* in Spanish has the sense not only of specific but also of private and peculiar to or particularistically distinctive of an entity.

81. "la España lingüística que se nos presenta ahora como el colmo de la modernidad, con sus cinco lenguas oficiales . . . es, en esencia, una España antiquísima . . . Una España cuyas lenguas minoritarias se conservan no por una voluntad colectiva, secular, democrática . . . sino más bien porque . . . no hubo ninguna organización de peso que rompiera la tradicional foralidad de los reinos . . . .La gente que no circulaba se conservaba pura."

Lodares drove home the point about linguistic modernity:

thirty years after the linguistic renaissance, I believe that it is clear that nationalist aims in relation to languages clash repeatedly with the necessities, rights, and typical customs of a modern society.[82] (Lodares 2000, 251) [83]

By "nationalist aims," in this quotation, Lodares meant minority nationalisms, not the Spanish program. This is a looking-glass world for Catalan activists, who would agree entirely with Lodares's judgment if "nationalist aims" was understood to refer to Spanish nationalism. Should there be any doubt about the virulence of the particularism with which Lodares associated the minority linguistic nationalisms, in a later work he asserted that

no radical differences can be found between the theories that Hitler expressed in *Mein Kampf*, with the aim of avoiding mixing between superior and inferior races, and those that are expressed in certain circles of Catalan or Basque nationalism.[84] (Lodares 2002, 184)

Lodares was far from the only one to use such inflammatory rhetoric. The liberal Spanish political party Union, Progress, and Democracy (UPyD) founded in 2007 expressly to combat Basque and Catalan nationalism rejected Catalan immersion education as "an attack on freedom and equality"[85] and "a Catalanist version of the *kulturkampf* cultural combat of Nazism"[86] (*El Periódico* 2008b). The booming Catalan sovereignty movement has elicited many such condemnations and assertions of Nazism. In one of the milder examples, the conservative former president of Spain, José María Aznar, said in 2013 that the Catalan sovereignty movement "opposes the European civic culture characteristic of our

---

82. "treinta años después del renacimiento lingüístico, creo que queda claro que los propósitos del nacionalismo en cuestión de lenguas chocan reiteradamente con las necesidades, derechos y usos típicos de una sociedad moderna."

83. The latest recurrence of this theme at the time of this writing was the assertion by a representative of the Ciutadans party in Valencia that while Catalan is "endearing" (*entranyable*), it is not very useful for finding a job. She asserted that those places where linguistic immersion was triumphing are returning to "the hamlet" (*aldea*), an assertion that was received with as much hilarity as indignation (VilaWeb 2015).

84. "no hallarse diferencias radicales entre las teorías que Hitler expresaba en *Mi lucha,* con el fin de evitar las mezclas entre las razas superiores e inferiores, y aquellas que se expresan en ciertos círculos del nacionalismo catalán o vasco."

85. "un atentado contra la libertad y contra la igualdad."

86. "una version catalanista de la *kulturkampf* combate cultural del nazismo."

Constitution to the most reactionary and destructive nationalism"[87] (Europa Press/San Sebastián 2013).

The banal invisibility of the Spanish nationalist perspective from which such critics speak is recognized with deep frustration by many Catalan commentators. One journalist observed sardonically that in Spain, "Whenever we say nationalism it seems that it has to be automatically understood that the only nationalisms that exist are Catalan and Basque; the first is suspect and the second is reprehensible"[88] (Huertas Claveria 2005). A Valencian novelist characterized the banality of "Spanish ultranationalism"[89] more wryly: "You know, the one that's not nationalist"[90] (Usó 2007). The sociolinguist Joan Argenter has written that "for Spanish nationalists, to be a 'Spanish nationalist' is not a way of being nationalist, but rather just a way of being" (Argenter 2007, 142).[91] The philosopher and Catalanist politician Josep-Maria Terricabras observed soberly:

> in many cases, those who attack the oppression of the population by Catalan do so absolutely convinced of the truth of what they say. Many, many Spaniards in their heart, head and gut believe that the Catalan language oppresses and Castilian liberates; that Catalan nationalism is tribal, retrograde and unfortunate, and that in Spain there is no nationalism of any kind.[92] (Terricabras 2008b)

Spanish Sociolinguistic Naturalism

Along with the many claims to the anonymity of the Spanish language, sociolinguistic naturalism more generally has also served as a tool of what Jacqueline Urla has aptly called "the possessive investment in Spanish monolingualism" (Urla 2012a,

---

87. "opone a la cultura cívica europea propia de nuestra Constitución el nacionalismo más reaccionario y destructivo."

88. "Quan diem nacionalisme sembla que automàticament s'ha d'entendre que només existeixen el nacionalisme català i el basc, el primer sospitós i l'altre condemnable."

89. "ultranacionalisme espanyol."

90. "aquell que, ja saben vostès, no és nacionalista."

91. "per als nacionalistes espanyols ser 'nacionalista espanyol' no és una manera de ser nacionalista, sinó tan sols una manera de ser."

92. "en muchos casos, los que atacan a la opresión del catalán sobre la población lo hacen absolutamente convencidos de la verdad de lo que dicen. Muchos y muchos españoles de corazón, de cabeza, de víscera, creen que la lengua catalana oprime y la castellana libera; que el nacionalismo catalán es tribal, atrasado y desgraciado, y que en España no hay nacionalismo de ningún tipo."

224). Naturalism is used as a weapon by critics of language planning in the peripheral communities such as Catalonia. As seen in the indictment of "manipulative and artificial mechanisms" in the extended complaint from Lázaro quoted above, Catalan policy is depicted as unnatural, and therefore undesirable, because it involves deliberate interventions. At the same time, these critiques naturalize and make invisible the institutional efforts that reinforce the status of the Spanish language.

For example, Lodares (2005) specifically deployed sociolinguistic naturalism in a neo-liberal defense of the merits of Spanish as "the common language" over the deleterious social engineering carried out by peripheral autonomies:

> In *the technical terms of language planning*, they are *working to foment* transitional bilingualism in Spain . . . in favor of the increasing replacement of the common language. Nothing will be able to stop the march toward institutional monolingualism in Catalan, Basque . . . if the local governments should make such a decision once the majority of their citizens master these languages . . . [A] different matter is whether such plans can become full reality in the face of *the spontaneous force of Spanish*.[93] (Lodares 2005, 13) [italics added]

In this passage, Lodares depicted the march of Catalan as relying on the technical artifices of language planning and government interventions, but in contrast the expansion of Spanish was represented as a spontaneous force of nature, with no recognition given to its own institutionalized governmental support. We might also notice that Lodares gives the non-Catalan-speaking citizens of Catalonia a pivotal role to play in stopping this unnatural process. They must refuse to learn Catalan, refuse bilingualism, if the artificial and anti-natural march of Catalonia toward Catalan monolingualism is to be stopped.

Another version of this discourse appeared in an extended piece labeled as a news report in *El País* in 2008. Opening with the observation that Catalonia, Euskadi, Valencia, and the Balearics have for years had "their own laws to protect their traditional languages,"[94] the reporter then observed, "The concept of 'language policy' is unheard of in the rest of Spain, where there is only one official

---

93. "en términos técnicos de planificación lingüística, se trabaja en España para fomentar un bilingüismo transitorio, . . . en pro de la sustitución progresiva de la lengua común. Nada podrá impedir la marcha hacia el monolingüismo institucional en catalán, eusquera . . . si los gobiernos locales tomaran esa decisión una vez que una mayoría de ciudadanos dominase tales lenguas—asunto distinto es que planes así puedan hacerse realidad plena ante la fuerza espontánea del español."

94. "tienen hace años leyes propias para proteger sus idiomas tradicionales."

language"[95] (Ximénez de Sandoval 2008). Official status for Castilian is so taken for granted that it is not recognized as a language policy; whether the journalist was slyly pointing out the unawareness of Spaniards in general or simply revealing his own is not clear. The sociolinguist Xavier Vila has also identified the banal nationalism found in a strikingly similar view expressed by Xavier Pericay, a longtime Catalan adversary of Catalan language policy who will be heard from in the controversies analyzed in later chapters. Vila quotes a 2007 opinion piece by Pericay in the arch-conservative newspaper *ABC*: "Spain does not have a language policy . . . the State, trusting and generous, delegates its constitutional mandate to the Autonomous Communities"[96] (Vila i Moreno 2011, 119). The hyperbolic adjectives used here suggest that Pericay's is not the naïve and genuine conviction that Terricabras granted to some opponents of Catalanism.

In the second of several books on this general subject, Ángel López García (2004) also drew on sociolinguistic naturalism, when he characterized the minority languages of Spain as "obscene" in a putatively etymological sense of "excessively obvious."[97] That is, in a now-familiar indictment from the standpoint of anonymity, such languages do not have the invisibility of "just talk," the referential transparency that is supposed to be the function of a public language. López García estimated that it is now "almost impossible"[98] to carry out all the activities of everyday life in a language like Catalan "naturally"[99] (López García 2004, 40–41). For second-language speakers of Catalan, López García found the reason obvious: a stutter or an error causes Catalan interlocutors to switch languages immediately. But how, he asked, could they not make mistakes, "if it's a learned language!"[100] Nonetheless, if second-language speakers don't make mistakes, "They will speak like a book and that will be even worse"[101] (López García 2004, 41). In this view, Catalan has the defective unnaturalness that the grammar had for Dante. It is not clear how López García imagined that Catalan speakers come by their second language, Castilian, or how that would not entail the same problems of unnaturalness.

---

95. "El concepto de 'política lingüística' es inaudito en el resto de España, donde sólo hay una lengua oficial."

96. "España no tiene política lingüística . . . el Estado, confiado y generoso, delega el mandato constitucional en las Comunidades Autónomas."

97. My Latin consultant advises that this etymology may not be correct.

98. "casi imposible."

99. "con naturalidad."

100. "si es una lengua aprendida!"

101. "hablarán como un libro y todavía será peor."

If it is true that as a minority language Catalan remains "excessively obvious" in some spheres of public activity, it is in large part because it is still relatively absent in others. The social origins of Catalan's institutional power have not been obscured by the invisible hand of the market, that most naturalized and naturalizing of modern institutions. And if minority languages are excessively obvious, then hegemonic languages are in turn excessively invisible. In counterpoint to the efforts to universalize Castilian and provincialize Catalan that I have just sketched, some Catalan activists have attempted to denaturalize the anonymity and the unmarked status of the Castilian language in the Spanish state. For example, a small group called the Organization for Multilingualism founded in 1999 mounted systematic challenges to monolingualism in official documents issued by the Spanish state such as national identity cards, postage stamps, the national lottery, and even the names of the offspring of the royal family. The group circulated designs for identity cards and stamps that placed the other languages of Spain on equal footing alongside Castilian. These seemed to some observers to be trivial and quixotic campaigns. But I believe their point was not simply to change the specific linguistic practices targeted so much as to disrupt invisibility, anonymity, and misrecognition of the hegemony of Spanish. They insistently highlighted and questioned the underpinnings of the still taken-for-granted linguistic authority of the state language in what is now sometimes imagined to be the structurally multilingual society of modern Spain. These campaigns attempted to move Castilian from its transparent position and make its invisibility "obscene" by placing it on par in official text and images with the other languages of Spain.

Catalan and the Limits of Authenticity

Given how widespread the ideology of sociolinguistic naturalism is, López García was correct in his diagnosis of the unnaturalness of Catalan for many potential speakers not exposed to the language from an early age. Despite the status of Catalan as the principal medium of communication in government institutions and education, as well as its broad everyday and even very natural use by many speakers, other people still do not hear it as an anonymous public vehicle of aperspectival objectivity. Since Catalan is vastly overshadowed by Spanish in commerce, mass media, and popular culture, the social roots of Catalan's institutional power are still evident. Quite the opposite of the situation that Fishman diagnosed as contributing to the hegemony of English in the United States (see Chapter 2), there is often considerable special language awareness in the use of Catalan. It was traditionally ideologized as ethnic in character rather than supra-ethnic as was English in the United States.[102] For better and worse, as a *llengua pròpia* Catalan was obviously someone's own language, a marked and private voice indexing a particular kind of person, perhaps with a particular political agenda, rather than focused on communicating a referential message. Catalan's status as a signifier of a valued Catalan identity made it difficult for nonnative speakers to assume as their own; this will be explored further below and in Part III.

Joan Pujolar described a further constraint on acquisition of Catalan created by the logic of sociolinguistic authenticity. In his ethnographic work in the 1990s he found an ideology of what he calls "monologic truth" and "simplified masculinity" among some young Castilian-speaking working-class men in Barcelona. The essence of the desirable masculine self was a rough, unadorned directness, and this was conceptualized as expressed directly and naturally in a stylized Andalusian Spanish. For these men the desired self could never be expressed in a Catalan perceived as artificially and secondarily imposed (Pujolar 1997, 2001; cf. Frekko 2009a).

To be sure, one really can become authentically socially Catalan by mastering and using the Catalan language. It is worth noting that Spanish citizenship and identity is based on *ius sanguinis*, blood or parentage, rather than *ius solis*; birth in Spanish territory does not automatically grant citizenship. In contrast, Boix-Fuster and Sanz characterize Catalan identity (there is at this point no juridically distinct Catalan citizenship) as based on *ius linguae*, linguistic practice (Boix-Fuster and Sanz 2008). Someone who speaks Catalan habitually in daily life is for most purposes taken to be Catalan. This linguistic criterion for Catalan identity has worked for many speakers, including a number of the informants in my research over the years. Víctor and Rafael, for example, were a pair of bilingual L1 Castilian boys in my 1987 classroom study who made a pact to speak only Catalan when they started high school, in order to cement their Catalan identities. They so thoroughly transformed themselves that they were classified as Catalans by their peers at their new school, and Rafael in particular was assumed by many to be an L1 Catalan speaker (Woolard 1997a, 2003). Twenty years later, Rafael was still strongly Catalan-identified and a confirmed Catalanist and committed supporter of independence, as well as a progressive backer of social justice movements. Víctor, whose Catalan identity was not as passionate, looked back at his high school linguistic transformation and commented on its motivation:

---

102. I use the term "ethnic" in its anthropological sense as a social rather than biological category (Barth 1969).

V: Era també una manera doncs de-de volíem ser d'aquí. Volíem tenir un lloc on dir que érem i que:: que:. Formàvem part i:: no sé, com que vols estimar algu- jo de fet la gent més radical que-que hi havia llavors lluitant per la: pels per-per la independència de Catalunya o pels drets dels catalans, la majoria no eren d'aquí.

KW: Ah, sí?

V: No eren-no eren nascuts aquí. Eren gents, això, d'inmigrants, eren molt més radicals. Io crec que era una mica perxò, no? Perquè:: com que: els-els nostres pares no tenien:: havien perdut lo seu, d'alguna manera, no?

KW: Sí, sí.

V: I nosaltres volíem tenir algo. Volíem ser d'algun lloc.

V: It was also a way, then, of- of, we wanted to be from here. We wanted to have a place to say we were and tha::t, tha::t, we were a part of a::nd I don't know, it's like you want to love somethi- I, in fact the most radical people, that that were then fighting for the: for for for the independence of Catalonia or for the rights of Catalans, the majority weren't from here.

KW: Ah, yes?

V: They weren't, weren't born here. They were people, like, immigrants, they were much more radical. I think it was a little for this reason, no? Becau:se, si::nce our parents didn't ha::ve, had lost their own [place], in a way, no?

KW: Yes, yes.

V: And we wanted to have something. We wanted to be from somewhere.

Despite experiences of acceptance for Catalan converts like Víctor and Rafael, the indexical value of the language for identifying "authentic Catalans"—"Catalan Catalans" as they were called—hampered as many would-be second-language speakers as it encouraged during the early years of autonomy. This can be seen in the following example from my earlier work.

In the late 1980s, I sat in on a discussion of diglossia in a Catalan class with Castilian-dominant, working-class students in their final year of high school in Barcelona. The teacher asserted that bilingualism was abnormal and that the decision to speak Catalan reflected whether one feels oneself to be Catalan or Spanish. The students rejected this construction of language choice as an expression of the self, asserting that such a view created problems for them. They did not want to be forced to choose one identity or the other, or to have their own language use construed as such a choice of identities. For these students, speaking Catalan should not be considered to be about *who* you claimed to be, but rather *where* you moved in society. "We don't speak Catalan because we are socially marginalized" (*marginats*), they asserted matter-of-factly (Woolard 2003). They believed that if and when they made it to the university, a Catalan-speaking public domain, they would naturally assume that language. (We will explore the accuracy of such a prediction in Part III.) Their teacher herself was a second-language speaker of Catalan, but she never spoke of this fact, and she passed as Catalan among her students. The teacher and her students evidenced two different language ideologies. While the teacher embraced the equation of language with the authentic self, the students were moving away from seeing Catalan within the logic of authenticity and beginning to place it instead within a schema of anonymity. They associated open access to the language not with an enduring commitment to a personal identity but with open access to mainstream social institutions (rather like a less dolorous version of Richard Rodriguez's view of English in the United States, discussed in Chapter 2).

Examples of more recent reports of the constraints of the ideology of authenticity can be found in internet communication. For example, in 2008 one blogger complained:

> We adoptive Catalan speakers are followed day and night by the question [in Catalan]: "And you, why do you speak Catalan?" And worse yet [in Castilian], "If you aren't Catalan, why do you speak Catalan?"... It's a problem that in a supposedly free society like ours, there are people who can't understand that individuals who weren't born Catalan speakers can speak Catalan. The problem is in the head of people who can't accept the full normality of Catalan. Would anyone find it strange that a Moroccan who lives in England speaks English?[103] (Veu Pròpia Bages 2008)

This perception is not just hypersensitivity on the part of new speakers. Traces of a nonnative accent in Catalan, particularly one that shows Castilian influence, could trigger a switch to Castilian on the part of Catalan speakers—as López García also asserted—and sometimes continues to do so even now (Alexandre 2014). This has long been part of a generally unconscious, double-edged linguistic etiquette that accommodates an interlocutor at the same time as it reinforces boundaries. In the earlier periods of my research, I sometimes experienced this exclusionary switch myself. Indeed, more recently even the most Catalanist student in the high school class that will be described in Chapter 7 discouraged me from speaking Catalan to new international immigrants in the class. "He's Brazilian, he doesn't

---

103. "sovint els catalanoparlants d'adopció ens veiem perseguits dia i nit per aquesta pregunta: 'I tu per què parles català?' . . . 'y si tú no eres catalán por qué hablas en catalán?' . . . el problema és que en una societat suposadament tan lliure com la nostra, hi hagi gent [que] no pugui entendre que hi ha persones nascudes no catalanoparlants que parlin en català . . . El problema està al cap de la gent que no pot assumir la plena normalitat del català, algú s'extranyaria que un marroquí que resideix a Anglaterra parlés anglès?"

understand Catalan," and "he's Romanian, he doesn't speak Catalan," I was told by more than one student, directing me to speak only Castilian to these Romance-speaking classmates. Even otherwise nearly monolingual Catalan speakers took it for granted that Castilian would somehow be more transparent for these immigrants than was Catalan, despite the linguistic relationship Catalan shared with these languages. This is a particularly striking symptom of what Aracil called the "interposition" to which minority languages are routinely subjected ideologically, in which all their relations to a larger world are assumed to be mediated necessarily by the dominant language (cited in Pujolar 2010).

In the naturalistic authenticity complex, accent matters, and as discussed in Chapter 2, those with a nonnative accent are not viewed as authentic. An example of the tenacity of this essentialist view of Catalan appeared in a media commentary on the Catalan spoken by Alberto Fernández Díaz, the Barcelona mayoral candidate in 2011 (and again in 2015) from the conservative Partido Popular, which has an anti-Catalanist, pro-Castilian platform. Although born and raised in Barcelona, the candidate is a first-language speaker of Castilian, and (at least at that time) he preferentially used the Castilian version of his given name, "Alberto," rather than the Catalan "Albert." Both of his surnames are among the most common ones in Catalonia, but they are classically Castilian, ending in the Castilian patronymic "-ez." Albert Pla Nualart, a regular commentator on Catalan sociolinguistic matters, played on the candidate's name when he wrote:

> The Catalan of Alberto Fernández Díaz, like his name, has Castilian DNA. The soul of the language, what unites us to it viscerally, is phonetics. And the phonetics of the PP candidate tells us that, even if he's made a significant effort to speak Catalan well, he hasn't given himself over to it. He hasn't let the language penetrate his intimate self, or maybe he tried to do it late, when he was already too complete.[104] (Pla Nualart 2011a)

"DNA" is a fashionable metaphor in contemporary Catalan and Spanish discourse, applied in a light key and often to entirely inorganic matters. Pla Nualart no doubt intended a playful, nonbiological mobilization of it and referred to the candidate's given name (*nom*, over which one exercises choice), not his surnames (*cognoms*). But in this context the metaphor bordered into a racialized view of language and identity, and comments posted online objected to it. Although the biological image was not

---

104. "El català d'Alberto Fernández Díaz té, com el nom, un ADN castellà. L'ànima de la llengua, el que ens hi uneix visceralment, és fonètica. I la fonètica del candidat del PP ens diu que, si bé ha fet un notable esforç per parlar bé el català, no s'hi ha entregat. No ha deixat que la llengua penetrés en el seu jo íntim o, potser, ho ha intentat tard, quan ja estava massa fet."

intended literally, the identification of pronunciation with the true, intimate self was deliberate. Pla Nualart in fact went on to praise the lexical and syntactic correctness of Fernández Díaz's speech as better than that of "many lifelong Catalans" (*catalans de tota la vida*). (Fernández Díaz was born in Barcelona and technically he too is a lifelong Catalan, although the phrase is rarely used in that technical way, and Pla Nualart's comment reveals the implicit linguistic criterion of Catalan identity, the *ius linguae* mentioned earlier.) The correctness of Fernández's speech, wrote Pla Nualart, is

> a symptom of just how much Catalan is the language of prestige in Catalonia today. That the *espanyolista* rightwing in a city as Castilianized as Barcelona speaks the Catalan that he speaks is reason for optimism in a usually discouraging context. We believed, until not long ago, that whoever spoke Catalan had become one of our own. And now we know that it's not like that.[105] (Pla Nualart 2011a)

And now, indeed, it is arguably "not like that" anymore. Contained within Pla Nualart's sense of the contradictions in the language-identity equation is an indication of the ongoing ideological shifts in relation to Catalan.[106] Those turns away from traditionalist linguistic authenticity move sometimes toward the assumptions of anonymity, sometimes toward a more post-naturalist construction of authenticity and identity. The following chapters will examine this ongoing process in systematic detail. In the next section of this chapter I will just give an overview of the change as visible in samples from several different domains.

The Turn from Naturalistic Authenticity in Catalonia

> Everyone has the right to construct freely their own linguistic biography. We're free; no one is linguistically predetermined by their mother tongue (an anachronistic concept, what's more). (Tudela 2013)[107]

This assertion by the Catalan sociolinguistic observer Joan Tudela, first published in 2006, summarizes an important premise of the emergent post-naturalist discourse.

---

105. "un símptoma de fins a quin punt avui el català és una llengua de prestigi a Catalunya. Que la dreta espanyolista parli en una ciutat tan castellanitzada com Barcelona el català que parla ell és un motiu d'optimisme en un context sovint desolador. Havíem cregut, fins no fa tant, que qui parlava català es feia dels nostres. Ara sabem que no és així."

106. Joan Pujolar has given a carefully nuanced critical view of such contradictions within some of the manifestations of the conscious effort at change (Pujolar 2007b).

107. "Cada persona té dret a construir, lliurement, la seva pròpia biografia lingüística. Som lliures: ningú no està predeterminat idiomàticament per la llengua materna (concepte, a més a més, anacrònic)."

That premise was shared by the new speaker of Catalan whose blogpost I quoted earlier in this chapter, but not by the interlocutors who he reported questioned his use of Catalan.[108] That post appeared on the website of a small organization of "new Catalan speakers who have adopted Catalan as a *llengua pròpia*"[109] called Veu Pròpia "Our Own Voice." This group spoke out against political elites like those behind the Castilianist manifestos discussed above, who claimed to speak for Castilian speakers and protect them against an alleged linguistic dictatorship of Catalan. In its very name, this organization (in which some leaders were both new speakers of Catalan and professional academic analysts of language) adopted the trope of the *pròpia* in a playfully ironic way. Veu Pròpia takes an anti-naturalistic, historicizing perspective on linguistic appropriation, with a strong focus on the free choice so emphasized by their opposition, as will be discussed below.

The blogger, a first-language speaker of Castilian, complained about twenty years of questioning of his choice of Catalan and responded with "14 reasons why I, a newcomer, have chosen to speak in Catalan as well."[110] Among these reasons were:

> 1. Because I'm not a Castilian speaker . . . in this country, the mistaken habit has formed of dividing the society between Castilian speakers and Catalan speakers according to people's origin . . . And that is false, language is not something genetic, you aren't born speaking any language. A person is a speaker of the language or languages that s/he feels like speaking. The fact that a person is born a Castilian speaker doesn't mean s/he has to be that for the rest of his/her life. Isn't it true that nobody finds it strange that those who are born Catalan speakers speak Spanish? So why do people find the reverse so strange?[111]
>
> . . .

---

108. A comment posted on Pla Nualart's blog about Fernández-Díaz's Catalan by "benyu Barcelona" reported a nearly identical sense of frustration about responses to his L2 Catalan as that of the blogger discussed here.

109. "nous catalanoparlants . . . que no vàrem tenir el català com a llengua inicial però que l'hem adoptat com a llengua pròpia . . . "

110. "14 motius pels quals jo, un nouvingut, he triat parlar també en català." "Newcomer" is a euphemism for "immigrant" in this usage, and it may connote higher social class than the latter label does. That one can be a self-designated "newcomer" for twenty years reveals tensions related to authenticity and identity that appear in some of the excerpted text.

111. "Perquè no sóc castellanoparlant: . . . en aquest país s'ha agafat el costum erroni de dividir la societat entre castellanoparlants i catalanoparlants segons l'origen de les persones . . . I això és fals, la llengua no és una cosa genètica, no es neix parlant cap llengua, una persona és parlant de la llengua o les llengües que li dóna la gana, que una persona neixi castellanoparlant no vol dir

5. To stop being an immigrant: .... where there is a minoritized language as is the case of Catalonia ... once you adopt the language they think of you as one of them.[112]

...

8. Because I have the right to. Because Catalan isn't the sole property of Catalans, languages aren't the property of anyone, not even of their speakers. I live here and I have the same right as anyone else to speak Catalan.[113]

9. Because it's fun. Speaking Catalan is fun, learning new words, new sounds, speaking Catalan is another reason to laugh and enjoy. It's fun to ... learn that a *berenjena* [eggplant] is an *albergínia*, it's very amusing to learn how to say "*xiuxiuejar*" [whisper].[114]

10. Because it belongs to me. I worked hard to speak Catalan ... It took a lot to speak Catalan and now that I've managed to do it I won't let anyone step on my language/tongue, now it's my language and it belongs to me, too ...[115]

...

12. Because I'm as Catalan as anyone else[116] ... "*Català no s'hi neix, se n'exerceix*" ('One isn't born as a Catalan, one acts as a Catalan').

...

14. Because I feel like it .... Isn't that reason enough? ... "and you, why do you speak Catalan?" Geez, I've never seen a more stupid question.[117]
(Veu Pròpia Bages 2008)

---

que ho hagi de ser tota la vida. Oi que ningú troba estrany que els que neixen catalanoparlants parlin castellà? Doncs per què la gent troba tan estrany el contrari?"

112. "per deixar de ser immigrant ... on hi ha una llengua minoritzada, com és el cas de Catalunya ... un cop adopta[da] la llengua et consideren un més."

113. "Perquè hi tinc dret. Perquè el català no és propietat dels catalans, les llengües no són propietat de ningú, ni tan sols dels seus parlants, jo visc aquí i tinc el mateix dret que qualsevol altre de parlar català."

114. "perquè és divertit. Parlar català és divertit, aprendre nous mots, nous sons, parlar català és un motiu més per a riure i gaudir. És divertit ... descobrir que una berenjena és una albergínia, és molt divertit aprendre a dir xiuxiuejar."

115. "Perquè em pertany. M'he esforçat molt per parlar català ... M'ha costat molt parlar català i ara que ja ho he aconseguit no deixaré que ningú em trepitgi la llengua, ara ja és la meva llengua i també em pertany a mi ... "

116. "perquè sóc tan català com qualsevol altre."

117. "perquè em dóna la gana .... no és prou motiu aquest? ... i tu per què parles català? Ostres, mai he vist pregunta més estúpida."

In this mix of motives, we see not a loss of the importance of linguistic authenticity, but a redefinition of it, along the lines of what in Chapter 2 I discussed as post-natural, project authenticity. The blogger describes this in conscious contradistinction to a naturalist conception of authenticity as defined by origins. His emphasis is on play, free individual choice, and performative construction and achievement of identity. This is not to say that there is no ideological naturalization at work. "Do what you feel like," doesn't ask who you are or why you feel like it. But what is naturalized is not origins and originary language.

Who is it that questions this new speaker's use of Catalan? Is it Castilian speakers or L1 Catalan speakers? Is this a struggle over the potential attrition of Castilian-speaking identity in Catalonia, or over ownership of the Catalan language? The blogger does not make this clear, and the patterns discussed above allow for skepticism coming from any direction. Readers familiar with other situations may assume that first-language speakers of Catalan jealously guard their linguistic capital, but that is not necessarily the case. I will discuss empirical evidence on this question at the individual level in Part III of this book.

At the public level, similar shifts away from traditional naturalist discourses of linguistic authenticity can be seen in various language campaigns by Catalan civic organizations that promote Catalan, as well as in the official normalization campaigns sponsored by the government (Boix-Fuster, Melià, and Montoya 2011). In response to the criticisms from the high ground of enlightened Spanish linguistic anonymity that denigrate Catalan as a local language and a tool of retrograde nationalism on the one hand, and to the appreciable counterproductivity of essentialist discourses for recruiting new speakers on the other, the public defense of Catalan also began moving away from the ideological framework of authenticity. Just as among Castilianists, newer approaches among Catalanist activists and policymakers draw on modernity, universalism, and anonymity in the struggle to reposition the Catalan language. Most notably, since the turn of the millennium, fewer defenses of Catalan have celebrated it as the *llengua pròpia*, despite decades of linguistic advocacy based on exactly that status.

In place of *llengua pròpia*, the trope of the "common language" is used by Catalanists in what appears to be a surprising appropriation of the Castilianist rhetorical strategy, but may have been borrowed from Quebec (Riera Gil 2013). In a head-on challenge to the Castilianist discourse discussed above, the civic group Plataforma per la Llengua "Platform for the Language" had begun using "Catalan, the common language"[118] as a slogan of its campaigns at least by 2005

---

118. "el català, llengua comuna." In some of its materials, Plataforma itself translates "comuna" as "shared" (see Fig. 5.1), but I have used the cognate form elsewhere in this book and retain it here.

(Biosca 2009, Sànchez 2005). Plataforma also published a bilingual Castilian-Catalan "guide for new and future speakers of Catalan"[119] entitled *Catalan Is Also Mine* (Plataforma per la Llengua 2010). In a dialogic format, the book reassures potential speakers that they do not have to renounce anything, change their identity, or become nationalist to speak Catalan. It also reminds them of the invisible Spanish nationalism behind the official Castilian policy. Along with these elements of a critical discourse of anonymity, Plataforma also employs playful and transgressive motifs in its visual materials. Punning on the double meaning of "*llengua*" as tongue and language, one of its slogans urges "*Utilitza la llengua*" "Use your tongue/language." In one publicity campaign, this slogan appeared over a drawing of an androgynous pair kissing (Fig. 3.1); in another, over photographs of young people sticking their tongues out at the viewer.

Similar if tamer rhetorical strategies appeared in official government language campaigns, particularly after the political leadership of Catalonia changed in 2003 from the center-right nationalists who had held the Generalitat throughout the autonomous period to left-leaning, Socialist-led coalition governments. One campaign designed to encourage "social use" of Catalan, introduced by the Secretary of Linguistic Policy in January 2005 and renewed in March 2006, had the theme "Wind up Catalan" (*Dóna corda al català*) (Generalitat de Catalunya 2005a).[120] It featured a windup toy as its mascot. The campaign was aimed at getting younger generations to use in various domains of their daily lives the Catalan that they had already acquired to some degree, whether at home as a first language or through schooling.

The absurd mascot of this campaign is la Queta (short for la Boqueta "the little mouth"), a windup set of chattering plastic teeth. Thousands of such plastic toys were distributed in the campaign. In videos on mass and digital media, la Queta sings the theme song—"Speak without shame, speak with freedom, and for a start, speak Catalan"[121] in a notably nonnative, or at least nontraditional, accent (Fig. 3.2). La Queta cheerfully asserts that if she makes a mistake, she just starts over again. One of the first speech acts that la Queta comically modeled on the campaign's website was how to insult people in Catalan.

The goal of the campaign was described as making the language seem appealing (*engrescadora*), especially to those who are not fully fluent by reassuring them

---

119. "guia per a nous i futurs parlants de català."

120. The slogan doesn't translate well into English, in which the literal equivalent is ambiguous in an unfortunate way. The idea is to give something energy by winding it up, like a windup toy, not to bring something to a close.

121. "parla sense vergonya, parla amb llibertat, i per començar, parla en català."

FIGURE 3.1 "Use your tongue/language." Plataforma per la Llengua civic campaign for use of Catalan.

Reproduced by permission of Plataforma per la Llengua.

that it doesn't matter (*no passa res*) if they make mistakes. The secretary of linguistic policy when the campaign was introduced, Miquel Pueyo, is a sociolinguist who has no doubt read the same classic studies of language and youth that I have, and the campaign showed that it was informed by such sources. The explicit goal was to give Catalan "a modern image," to represent it to young people as "not imposed" but rather as a "transgressive language" that "makes things happen and erases labels" (Generalitat de Catalunya 2005b).[122] These themes resonate with well-known sociolinguistic ideas such as Rampton's analysis of linguistic crossing as a form of youth transgression that challenges rigid ethnic categorization (see Chapter 2 for discussion).

An image on the reverse of the foldout triptych for the campaign described the Catalan language as "integrative, useful, modern, necessary, friendly, a language

---

122. "una imatge moderna"; "una llengua trangressora"; "potenciar els valors del català com a llengua que facilita les coses, que esborra etiquetes."

FIGURE 3.2 La Queta, mascot of the "Dóna corda al català" ("Wind up Catalan!") language use campaign, 2005. La Queta says "Speak without shame. Speak with freedom. To start, speak in Catalan." "Dóna corda al català"

FIGURE 3.3 Reverse of the la Queta flyer in Figure 3.2. "Catalan, language of opportunities, the future, social relations; shared, integrative, modern, useful, necessary, friendly." "Dóna corda al català"

© *Generalitat de Catalunya. Reproduced by permission of the Generalitat de Catalunya.*

of relationships, opportunities, the future"[123]—a good summary of much of the new discourse (Generalitat de Catalunya 2005a) (Fig. 3.3). No trace of *llengua pròpia* was to be seen in this publicity. Authenticity, essentialism, purity, tradition, and victimization were all repudiated quite manifestly in this campaign as well as in its choice of mascots. What could be less authentic or serious and more ironizing and playful than toy plastic dentures?

The campaign was renewed the following year with a new theme song recorded by first- and second-language speakers in various international music styles: reggae, disco, hip-hop, and rumba (a version of which has Catalan roots). Video ads showed la Queta dj-ing and comically suggested her having sex in a rocking car parked at Barcelona's best-known locale for such activities (Alós 2006). La Queta's new accent was indeed transgressive, enough so to be criticized by a Mallorcan Catalan linguist as a "repugnant Hispanicized pronunciation" associated not just with nonnative but also with youthful first-language Catalan speakers in Barcelona, "formed by imitation of all the articulatory habits of Spanish"[124] (Bibiloni 2006). Thus both the social

---

123. "integradora, útil, moderna, necessària, amiga, [una llengua] de relació, d'oportunitats, de futur."

124. "aquesta repugnant pronúncia espanyolitzada"; "formada per la imitació de tots els hàbits articulatoris de l'espanyol."

and linguistic typifications indexed by la Queta were a notable change from "la Norma," the linguistic martinet and mascot of the first public campaign for "normalization" in 1983. Norma was a rather priggish, know-it-all little girl who in widely distributed cartoons admonished people about their linguistic habits and whose very name oriented speakers to linguistic normativity (Woolard 1986).

Another official campaign for the "social use" of Catalan was introduced in 2009 and was entitled, loosely translated, "Spread Catalan around."[125] This one was explicitly designed to encourage Catalan speakers not to switch to Castilian (the language of interposition between Catalan and the world) when speaking in "multilingual contexts" to interlocutors who might understand but who on the basis of physical appearance are assumed to be foreigners.[126] A Bollywood-style musical video for this campaign featured Indian dancers and a protagonist whose appearance suggested foreign origin, among various other actors representing the increased number of transnational immigrants who altered the face of Catalonia in the last decade. Again there was no endorsement of traditional authenticity concerns, but instead an overt rejection of them: "You speak Catalan to him?!"[127] sings one surprised character. "Of course! . . . that way I can practice!"[128] responds the young protagonist. The campaign used globalized popular culture and multicultural images, as well as the artifice and playful irony seen in the la Queta campaign, to represent Catalan as an open, cosmopolitanism language (that should be) available to all.

Like the Castilianist discourse of the common language seen above, the Catalanist version also sometimes mixed the frames of anonymity and authenticity and moved easily from the language of universalism and democracy to the assumption of the natural and essential. An opinion piece in 2007 by the spokesperson for CAL, the coordinating association of civic organizations supporting the Catalan language, was entitled "The Common Language."[129] The article began by debunking the "supposed defense of the individual rights of persons"[130] and the appeals to universal rights made by Castilianists. It pointed out that the rights of members of the 300 other linguistic communities living in the Catalan

---

125. "encomana el català."

126. http://llengua.gencat.cat/ca/serveis/informacio_i_difusio/campanyes/encomana/participa-hi_encomana/.

127. "Li parles en català?"

128. "és clar, així el puc practicar!"

129. "la llengua comuna."

130. "suposada defensa dels drets individuals de les persones."

Countries are not defended by these same forces, nor the rights of non-Castilian speakers living in Madrid. The author argued that this reveals that it is not actually persons, but rather the legal framework of the Spanish state and the interests of Castilian speakers, that are defended. In response, he advocated that it is Catalan that should become

> the common language of the Catalan Countries, that is to say, the cohesive element of a society that expresses itself in a great diversity of languages, but that has *la pròpia* as its backbone and as an instrument of welcome and integration."[131] (Vila i Ros 2007)

Here we see the specialized usage that has come to reserve the concept of *llengua pròpia* strictly for the territorial language, and not for diverse speakers' "own" diverse languages.

Anonymity in Catalan Electoral Politics

The final domain that I will sketch in this chapter is electoral politics. That the discursive ground was shifting away from a battle between competing Spanish and Catalan authenticities to one of competing anonymities (oxymoronic as that phrase may seem) was further illustrated in the campaign for the Catalan Parliament in fall 2006. This election and its outcome were the backdrop to the public debates over language use that will be examined in close detail in the three chapters of Part II.[132] Here I give a brief overview of new campaign rhetoric from two opposing political parties that illustrates the emerging change to the ideological framework of anonymity over authenticity in electoral strategies. These two parties have since come to take the lead in framing the ideological positions for and against sovereignty in the movement that blossomed into international news in 2012, and that ideological positioning was foreshadowed in the campaign of 2006.

Ciutadans: The Citizens' Party

The ideology of language as a universalistic, anonymous tool of democracy was embraced by a new political force in the 2006 elections, a party with the bilingual

---

131. "la llengua comuna als Països Catalans, és a dir, l'element que cohesioni una societat que s'expressarà en una gran diversitat de llengües, però que tindrà la pròpia com a eix vertebrador i com a instrument d'acollida i d'integració."

132. Skeptics in fact diagnosed electioneering as the root cause of the two controversies examined in Chapters 5 and 6.

name Ciutadans–Partido de la Ciudadanía "Citizens–Party of the Citizenry" that formed officially only months before the electoral campaign period opened.[133] The principal name of the party, Ciutadans, was chosen to echo the words of the president of Catalonia in exile and in the post-Franco transition, Josep Tarradellas, a member of the historic Republican Left Party of Catalonia (Esquerra Republicana de Catalunya, ERC). When Tarradellas returned to Barcelona from exile in 1977 as acting president of the provisionally reinstated Catalan government, he famously chose to greet the populace in Catalan not as "Catalans," but rather as "Citizens (m. pl.) of Catalonia." The new Ciutadans party was running in direct opposition to ERC's Catalanist platform, and the reference was deliberate. The party was generally known at the time as Ciutadans although it has since become known by the shorthand "C's" and most recently by the Castilian version Ciudadanos as it has expanded its campaigns into other parts of Spain.

In 2006 Ciutadans was successful beyond most expectations and won the votes required to gain recognition in the Catalan Parliament, resulting in three seats. Most but not all of the leadership of the Ciutadans party was drawn from earlier civic groups that had mobilized repeatedly against the Generalitat's language policies and in defense of Castilian over the years. Ciutadans labeled itself as non-nationalist and anti-nationalist, but it was perceived as specifically anti-Catalanist and pro-Spanish nationalist not just by convinced Catalan nationalists but by diverse observers. For example, Elena, a bilingual informant of Castilian-speaking background who will be introduced in Chapter 8, was an avowed "anti-nationalist" herself. Yet she did not hesitate to label the Ciutadans party as Spanish nationalist and "*facha*," a common slang term for fascist, referring to far-right positions redolent of Francoism. After the elections, the party scrambled to recover from the revelation that its leader, Albert Rivera, had been a member of the youth group of the conservative Partido Popular until just months before being elected president of the new party (Andreu 2006). The photogenic young politician successfully rode out the news and has gone on to lead the challenge to Catalanism within Catalonia in response to the gathering sovereignty movement. He expanded his party's presence to other areas of Spain in the anti-traditionalist political atmosphere of elections in 2015, bringing the change of the party's name to its Spanish form, Ciudadanos.

The Ciutadans party positioned itself as eschewing identity politics. It staked a claim to representing an anonymous Everyman, free of all linguistic and cultural constraints. This was depicted boldly and nakedly in the party's sensationalistic campaign images, featuring the candidate Albert Rivera posing unclothed

---

133. The first and commonly used name, before the hyphen, is in Catalan; the noun phrase after the hyphen is in Castilian.

FIGURE 3.4 Bilingual campaign flyer of the Ciutadans party, Catalan parliamentary elections 2006, featuring lead candidate Albert Rivera. "Your party has been born. We only care about people. We don't care where you were born. We don't care what language you speak. We don't care what clothes you wear. We care about you."

(Fig. 3.4). In parallel monolingual texts in Catalan and Castilian, the campaign flyer read

> We only care about people (persons). We don't care where you were born. We don't care what language you speak. We don't care what clothes you wear. We care about you.[134] (Ciutadans-Partido de la Ciudadanía 2006)

_____

134. "Sólo nos importan las personas. No nos importa dónde naciste. No nos importa la lengua que hablas. No nos importa qué ropa vistes. Nos importas tú./Només ens importen les

In the text and the image, "the person" was celebrated as a culturally uncon-strained individual exerciser of free will, just as unfettered by language as by fash-ion. Rivera was "selling us anonymous citizenship,"[135] wrote a critical journalist and political figure, Pilar Rahola (2006b).

To challenge the Catalan nationalist agenda and Catalanizing linguistic poli-cies in particular, the Ciutadans party explicitly emphasized universalism and cosmopolitanism. Campaign posters and T-shirts bore a design made up of a number of phrases, some in Catalan (*italics* below), some in Castilian (roman type below), some in English (<u>underlined</u> below.) (Fig. 3.5). No phrase was inter-nally mixed (although *bilingüe* is bivalent, both Catalan and Castilian):

> I'm a citizen of the world; *I'm bilingual*; I'm rational; *I'm european*; I'm cos-mopolitan; *I'm solidary, I'm open to dialogue, I speak castilian, I'm spanish*; I'm bilingual; <u>I am european</u>; *I'm a citizen of catalonia*; I'm universal, I speak catalan, I'm a citizen of catalonia; <u>I am spanish</u>; I'm solidary.[136]

Nowhere did the design say "I'm Catalan" in any language. Its absence perhaps implied that unlike Spanish and European identity, Catalan identity was not to be viewed as compatible with the modern, cosmopolitan, solidary, universal, and rational.

The Ciutadans party criticized Catalan linguistic normalization policies as particularist nationalistic attacks on individual freedom. "Freedom" (*liber-tad*) was a key term in their campaign. They adopted as their own the slogan "Territories don't speak, people do"[137] mentioned above (*Avui* 2006a). Printed campaign literature and platforms as well as most of the rhetoric in public events emphasized bilingualism as the Ciutadans' goal. As will be discussed and evi-denced in more detail in Chapter 5, "bilingualism" is a loaded term in Catalonia, rejected by Catalanists as anti-Catalan and as designed principally to facilitate individuals' monolingualism in Castilian.

---

persones. No ens importa on vas néixer. No ens importa la llengua que parles. No ens importa la roba que vesteixes. Ens importes tú (*sic*)." The reader was addressed with informal second person singular form. The pronoun *tu* was rendered in its Castilian form in the Catalan por-tion, presumably an overlooked error.

135. "nos vende ciudadanía anónima."

136. "Soy ciudadano del mundo, *sóc bilingüe*, soy racional, *sóc europeu*, soy cosmopolita, *sóc solidari, sóc dialogant, parlo castellà, sóc espanyol*, soy bilingüe, <u>I am european</u>, *sóc ciutadà de catalunya*, soy universal, hablo catalán, soy ciudadano de cataluña, <u>I am spanish</u>, soy solidario." Regular typeface represents phrases that appeared in Castilian, italics represent Catalan, and English in the original is underlined here.

137. "els territoris no parlen, ho fan les persones."

FIGURE 3.5 Trilingual campaign poster for the Ciutadans party, October 2006. "I'm a citizen of the world, I'm bilingual, I'm rational, I am european, I'm cosmopolitan, I'm solidary, I am spanish, I'm bilingual, I'm universal, I'm a citizen of catalonia. . ."
Photograph by K. Woolard.

The lead candidate Rivera frequently spoke publicly in fluent Catalan as well as Castilian during the campaign, and generally codeswitched between the two in a pattern not traditionally used in the speech community. Celebrating his party's surprising success on election night, Rivera echoed Martin Luther King and also switched languages mid-sentence, a form of codeswitching rarely heard in public events. On this occasion Rivera corrected himself to monolingual Castilian. His self-repair created the appearance that the mixing of Catalan (*italicized* here) and Castilian was an unconcious habit of bilingualism that had just slipped out:

Fa molt de temps que tenemos un sueño-
((Audience cheers))
Hace mucho tiempo que tenemos un sueño
For a long time we have had a dream
((Audience cheers))
For a long time we have had a dream
that we can live where it doesn't matter what language you speak
((Cries of "Freedom!" from audience))[138]

Bilingual political and public rhetoric was so unusual and so specific to Rivera that he was caricatured on a popular television show of political humor (discussed in the next chapter) by an unclothed actor repeating everything he said in both languages. This linguistic joke was turned back on the show's producers when they themselves spoke in both Catalan and Castilian to an audience at a media awards ceremony "in the purest style of Albert Rivera,"[139] as a newspaper reported. "Have you joined the Ciutadans party, or what?"[140] asked a Catalan actor (Jordan 2006).

Less personal bilingualism was modeled by other leading Ciutadans candidates, and the designated Catalan speakers at some events forgot to speak in Catalan. In a campaign rally I attended in the working-class, Castilian-dominant city of Bellvitge in the industrial belt of Barcelona, the candidate José Domingo did speak Catalan briefly, as seen in the next extract (Catalan in *italics*). However, it was used only in its authenticating function to claim Catalan identity, rather than as an unmarked medium of referential value. After a sarcastic inventory of his Catalan credentials, Domingo returned to Castilian and drew on a stylized Andalusian accent to narrate his account of the reason he took up political activism:

Jo parlo català, tinc el nivell C, sóc un bon català. He nascut a Barcelona, tinc el 'pedigree', sé cantar el Virolai . . . digamos que cumplo los requisitos del buen catalán tal como nos lo han imbuido desde los medios públicos . . .	*I speak Catalan, I have the Level C [linguistic credential], I'm a good Catalan. I was born in Barcelona, I have the 'pedigree', I know how to sing the Virolai* [Catalan patriotic hymn]. Let's say that I fulfill all the requirements of the good Catalan as they have been imbued in us through public media. . . .

138. TV3 election news Nov. 1, 2006, 10:25 pm; see also Mars 2006. I transcribed the first two lines verbatim as the news report aired. My fieldnotes give only a close approximation of the Castilian for the rest of the quote, so I do not represent in Castilian the part that I did not fully capture in the original.

139. "al més pur estil Albert Rivera."

140. " 'us heu afiliat a Ciutadans o què?' "

Mi madre que es de Graná((da)),. . .
vive en el Verdún, . . . y en su mundo
nunca ha tenido necesidad de hablar
catalán. . . . En ese entorno en el que el
catalán ha sido un elemento anecdótico
porque . . . ((donde)) se vivía no era
presente, . . . el catalán no ha sido un
elemento social porque no era necesario. . . . Acontece que este familiar tan
directo tiene una grave enfermedad,
yo vivía entonces fuera de Cataluña. El
informe médico de cuatro páginas detal-
lado en el que se estaba anunciando una
importante enfermedad fue redactado
exclusivamente en catalán. Entregado
en un sobre y cerrado esperando a que
el hijo viniera de Mallorca, . . . para que
cuando llegara me dijera 'niño, ¿qué
eh lo que pone aquí? Porque yo no lo
entiendo.'

My mother is from Graná((da)) . . .
she lives in Verdún ((a working-class
Barcelona neighborhood)), . . . and
in her world she has never had the
need to speak Catalan . . . .In this
environment, Catalan has been an
anecdotal element because where she
lived it wasn't present . . . Catalan
hasn't been a social element because
it wasn't necessary . . . It happens that
this relative, so close ((to me)), had a
serious illness, and I lived outside of
Catalonia then. The detailed four-
page medical report that announced
an important illness was written
exclusively in Catalan. Delivered in an
envelope, it was sealed and waiting for
her son to come from Mallorca . . .
so that when I arrived she said 'Son,
what does it say here? Because I don't
understand it.'

Además del lenguaje médico tan
complicado tan costoso de entender,
se había introducido un elemento
irracional, conociendo la persona a la
que iba destinado el informe . . . .
Y eso es lo que queremos introducir,
cambiar, desde Ciutadans, queremos
que las administraciones atiendan con
normalidad en las dos lenguas y en
función del usuario. . .es decir, ¿usted
cómo quiere ser atendido? En catalán,
pues en catalán. En castellano, en
castellano.

In addition to the complicated medical
language that is so hard to understand,
they had introduced an irrational
element, knowing the person to whom
the report would go . . . . And this is
what we want to introduce, change,
from Ciutadans, we want the administrations to address ((clients)) normally
in two languages and according to the
client . . . that is, "How do you want to
be addressed?" In Catalan, well then in
Catalan. In Castilian, in Castilian. [141]

141. Field recording, Bellvitge, October 27, 2006. In this transcript, Catalan is represented in
italics in both the original and translation, and Castilian is in plain Roman type.

The Ciutadans platform position was that social issues such as health and safety are more important than nationalist linguistic ones, and that the latter merely distract from the former: "More social welfare, less nation"[142] was among the slogans in its campaign flyers and newspaper ads. Yet it was only the linguistic issue, not health care delivery, that was the focus of this account from the candidate. The diagnosis of "irrationality" was introduced in the narrative only in relation to a Catalan document sent to a Castilian speaker. The purpose of the institutional bilingualism that Ciutadans advocated was to accommodate individual monolingualism. Domingo's point was that the system should be prepared to communicate in Castilian for those who prefer Castilian, and apparently even without the specification of preference in the case of his mother. The rationality of informing any patient of a serious illness in a mailed four-page written report in "complicated medical language" in any linguistic medium, without expert mediation, was not raised. Nor was there any concern for what would happen in such a situation for speakers of Tamazight, Chinese, or Romanian, or for the many Spanish immigrants from Domingo's mother's generation who were illiterate. The commonsense position from which Domingo's criticism was formulated rested on doxic assumptions about the place of Castilian in Catalonia and brought only that one language into focus. Arguably, this distracted attention from the underlying social welfare issue of healthcare delivery.[143]

The Ciutadans party asserted that identitarian questions should be set aside so that action on social issues could be the focus of political concern, but more than one Catalan observer noted that it was the Ciutadans who in fact consistently raised issues of language and identity in the 2006 campaign and promised to do so throughout their incumbency. One critic complained,

> The worst part is that after three very long years of talking every day about essentialist questions, sick to death of the debate about the new statute [of autonomy], about rhetorical questions of being or not being Catalan, and with the open wounds of society in housing, insecurity, immigration, etc., that nobody resolved, now these bores come along and open up the identitarian debate again. They're going to be the most ultranationalists in the parliamentary chamber; they are such antinationalist Catalans that they're going to contaminate politics again with sterile debates. Just

---

142. "Más benestar social, menos nación" / "Més benestar social, menys nació."

143. The circularity of the argument that Catalan should not be necessary in Catalonia because it has not been necessary in Catalonia is another issue that Catalan activists continually confront, despite the gradualness with which Catalan was introduced through the schools in an effort to avoid such difficulties. Complaints about medical communication like the one

what we needed, three delegates obsessed with identitarian questions![144] (Rahola 2006b)

ERC: The Quest for Banal Catalanism

A parallel, countervailing attempt to frame Catalan as an anonymous public language emerged in the campaign of the Catalanist, left-of-center Catalan Republican Left party (Esquerra Republicana de Catalunya), known as ERC. ERC was historically the party of progressive Catalanism during the Second Spanish Republic and in exile during the Franco period. Its often controversial leader in 2006 and candidate for president, Josep-Lluís Carod-Rovira, was himself a Catalan philologist. In his campaigning, Carod asserted that it was necessary to "depoliticize the language"[145] and relieve it of its ideological charge (Sans 2006). He argued that Catalan would have to stop being the language of Catalanism so it can be the language of everyone, of all Catalans (González 2007). These statements drew considerable critical comment from diverse perspectives (Branchadell 2007a, La CAL 2007). Former president Pujol, of the formerly hegemonic Catalan nationalist coalition party Convergència i Unió (CiU), was described as dumbfounded by Carod's remarks[146] (*Avui* 2006d). They also drew more than a little fire from within Carod's own party, which was riven by internecine struggles that Carod eventually lost (see, e.g., Carretero i Grau 2007a, 2007b).

Carod claimed that the Catalanism of his government if elected would be a new kind, not "weekend Catalanism"[147] but "*la pluja fina*," the "fine rain" that soaks you through without your noticing, a "quotidian Catalanism of daily construction"[148] (X. Bosch 2006, Carbó 2006). Some segments of the party and other Catalanists were outraged by what they saw in such gnomic remarks as an

---

Domingo recounts have been reported across the years, and another was reported in the press during the period of this study.

144. "lo peor es que después de tres años larguísimos hablando cada día de cuestiones esenciales, hartos hasta la hartura del debate estatutario, de cuestiones retóricas, del ser o no ser catalán, y con las heridas de la sociedad abiertas en canal en las llagas de la vivienda, la inseguridad, la inmigración, etcétera, sin que nadie las resuelva, llegarán ahora estos pesados y volverán a abrir el debate identitario. Es decir, van a ser los más ultranacionalistas de la Cámara ... Son tan antinacionalistas catalanes que van a ser los culpables de contaminar nuevamente la política con debates estériles. Sólo nos faltaban tres obsesos de las cuestiones identitarias!"

145. "despolititzar la llengua."

146. "estupefacte."

147. "catalanisme de cap de setmana."

148. "un catalanisme de la quotidianitat i de construcció diària."

embrace of post-nationalism, "mental colonization"[149] (Carretero i Grau 2007a), and an abandonment of the defense of the Catalan language and of Catalan nationalism (Vallory 2007).[150] But I believe that what Carod was advocating was better understood not as post-nationalism but rather as *banal nationalism*, the invisible nationalism of hegemonic nations and their ubiquitous cultural and linguistic resources (Billig 1995).[151] (Whether it is possible to advocate for invisibility is another matter.) Banality was in fact ERC's campaign motif in the 2006 elections; we are "just like you"[152] was a key slogan addressed to voters. Images showed candidates doing everyday activities: preparing iconic but everyday Catalan food, petting a dog, using power tools (all fodder for humorists).

After the elections, Carod became vice president in a governing coalition of three center-left to left parties.[153] In a speech just a few months later, Carod elaborated on the campaign slogans that some Catalan traditionalists had found so baffling and offputting, and he explicitly cited Billig and the concept of banal nationalism as he did so. He further pointed out the invisibility of banal Spanish nationalism:

> The Spanish national idea is very essentialist. And nationalist, regardless of the fact that the majority of Spanish nationals live it with such naturalness that they don't even notice it . . . [154]

---

149. "colonització mental."

150. For explicit advocacy of a "post-national" 21st century Catalanism in contrast to the nationalist Catalanism of the 20th century, and a discussion of the relation of both of these forms to cultural vs. political identity, see Bilbeny 2001.

151. Kathryn Crameri (2000) has argued that a form of banal Catalan nationalism had already been introduced earlier, perhaps counterproductively, by the center-right nationalist coalition party, Convergència i Unió, which under Jordi Pujol ruled autonomous Catalonia for the first twenty-three years. I take Crameri's point that Catalan policy made Catalan language and identity "normal" in some realms, particularly among younger generations, as we will see in Part III of this book. This view is also to some extent corroborated by the analysis of Manuel Castells (Castells et al. 2004). However, such acceptance may be different from Billig's banal nationalism. As Albert Branchadell has pointed out, it is practically impossible to have two invisible, banal nationalisms in the same territory (Branchadell 2012). The many critics of Pujolism quoted in this chapter as well as Chapters 5 and 6 show that the banality of Catalan nationhood and its linguistic and cultural signs was not well established in all domains and social strata in the period.

152. "com tu."

153. The Catalan Socialist Party (Partit Socialista de Catalunya), ERC (Esquerra Republicana de Catalunya), and EU-ICV (Iniciativa per Catalunya Verds-Esquerra Unida i Alternativa).

154. "La idea nacional espanyola és molt essencialista. I nacionalista, per més que la majoria de nacionals espanyols ho visquin amb tanta naturalitat que no se n'adonin."

Curiously, it is the most identitarian and essentialist who most frequently use anti-essentialist expressions . . . From the most unmistakable identitarian essentialism, but never recognized, with the protective cover of the structural shelter of the state, they are accustomed to being anti-identity . . . of the others, of those of us who don't have a state.[155] (Carod-Rovira 2007, 7, 9)

In response to such Spanish claims to anonymity and allegations of Catalan essentialism, Carod asserted that

it is indispensable to overcome definitively the essentialism that holds that there is an essence, a seed or specific gene that is the distinctive sign of being Catalan. That whoever is a little distanced from it or doesn't have it doesn't figure in the ranks of the "authentic" Catalans.[156] (Carod-Rovira 2007, 8)

Urging that Catalans abandon essentialism, Carod went on to argue in a very recognizable but unacknowledged echo of Manuel Castells,

identity then will not be understood in a static, rigid, eternal, immutable manner, but in a historical, evolving, changing form . . . .For the majority of Catalans in our time, being Catalan is not family inheritance, but rather a choice, a decision, a will. . . . The Catalan nation is not a past-identity, but rather a project-identity.[157] (Carod-Rovira 2007, 9)

Carod's appointee as minister (*conseller*) of culture and communications media, Joan Manuel Tresserras, articulated the same stance.[158] In response to a journalist's assertion of public fears that ERC would institute an "identitarian" cultural policy, Tresserras insisted that ERC—and indeed, the dominant

---

155. "Curiosament, els més identitaris i essencialistes són els que més freqüentment utilitzen expressions antiessencialistes . . . Des de l'essencialisme identitari més inequívoc, però mai no reconegut, amb la cobertura protectora de tot l'aixopluc estructural de l'estat, s'acostuma a ser antiidentitat . . . dels altres, dels que no tenim estat."

156. "és imprescindible superar definitivament l'essencialisme, segons el qual hi ha una mena d'essència, de pinyol, de gen específic que és el senyal distintiu de ser català. Qui se n'allunya una mica o bé no el posseeix, ja no figura en els rengles dels catalans 'autèntics.'"

157. "la identitat ja no s'entendrà d'una manera estàtica, rígida, eterna, immutable, sinó de forma històrica, evolutiva, canviant . . . per a la majoria de catalans dels nostres dies, ser català no ha estat una herència familiar, sinó una elecció, una decisió, una voluntat. La nació catalana no és una identitat-passat, sinó una identitat-projecte."

158. I translate *conseller* as minister because it is the most recognizable English equivalent, but I note that news media in Catalonia conventionally retain the form *conseller* in Castilian-medium reports. This allows a shorthand distinction between the administration of the Catalan government and that of the Spanish government, which has *ministros* 'ministers.'

discourse of contemporary Catalan politics in general—rejected the "essentialist discourse of 25 years ago."[159] This was replaced in ERC, he said, with a vision of Catalan culture as "broad, inclusive, and open"[160] at a historical moment that "offers us the possibility of reinventing almost everything, of redefining collective subjects"[161] (Moix and Massot 2006).

On the question of language specifically, Carod urged collaborative effort to "free the language from the heavy political and ideological load that . . . prevents it from advancing with naturalness and optimism."[162] "Catalan has to stop being only, preferentially, above all, the language of Catalanists in order to become the language of Catalans (m. & f. forms)."[163] He specified, "The 'political' dimension of the language is a brake for many Catalan speakers . . . and it can be that for newcomers"[164] (Carod-Rovira 2007, 11). And again he exhorted, "We have to separate [the language] . . . from any type of conflict . . . Catalan has to pass from being a political language to a national language, the common meeting place for everyone, regardless of their private language" (Carod-Rovira 2007, 12).[165]

In these quotes from ERC leadership, the ideological foundation of authenticity was repudiated and replaced with a discourse of anonymity inspired by Billig's analysis, and in some passages with a post-natural project identity apparently inspired by Castells.[166] Carod wanted "to construct a national community from pluralism"[167] (Carod-Rovira 2007, 14), one "implicated in multilingualism"[168] (Carod-Rovira 2007, 16). Albert Branchadell has pointed out the

---

159. "discurso esencialista"; "de hace 25 años."

160. "amplia, inclusiva y abierta."

161. "nos ofrece la posibilidad de reinventarlo casi todo; de redefinir los sujetos colectivos."

162. "alliber[ar] la llengua de la feixuga càrrega política i ideològica que . . . li impedeix avançar amb naturalitat i amb optimisme."

163. "el català ha de deixar de ser – només, preferentment, sobretot – la llengua dels catalanistes, per ser la llengua dels catalans i catalanes."

164. "aquesta dimensió 'política' de la llengua fa de fre a molts catalanoparlants . . . i pot fer-ho per als nouvinguts."

165. "L'hem de separar . . . de tota mena de relació de qualsevol tipus de conflicte . . . El català ha de passar de llengua política a ser llengua nacional, l'espai comú de trobada per a tothom, al marge de la llengua privada d'ús personal que cadascú tingui."

166. Among a number of other noteworthy statements of anti-essentialist projects in support of Catalonia in the period is the cleverly titled book *Els altres andalusos* (Cabrera et al. 2005), a play on the classic description of Andalusian immigrants to Catalonia, *Els altres catalans* (Candel 1964).

167. "Volem construir una comunitat nacional des del pluralisme."

168. "implicar-nos en el terreny del multilingüisme."

limits of this plurilingual vision, since in other parts of Carod's representation the nation is still only achieved through public monolingualism, for example in his expressed desire to convert all Catalans into Catalan speakers, and these into "people who use the language in all domains of use without exception" (cited in Branchadell 2012, 6).[169] De-naturalizing Catalan's authenticity, Carod's project in Branchadell's analysis was mostly aimed at re-naturalizing the language as the anonymous, common, universal language of all citizens of Catalonia, not at achieving a new plurilingual form of society.

Carod's often poetic and inspiring rhetoric was also sometimes muddled, and it nonplussed even his own constituency during the 2006 campaign and the years of his vice presidency. He lost the internal power struggle in his own ERC party. Nonetheless, in its turn away from the essentializing ideology of authenticity toward the power of the anonymous public and of a post-naturalist national project, much of Carod's and ERC's campaign rhetoric has since come to appear prescient. In fact, a book Carod published in 2008 entitled *2014* predicted that Catalonia would express its will about sovereignty in that year (Andreu 2008).[170]

Conclusion and Forecast: Catalonia, Anonymous Society

By the end of the 20th century, construals of and conflicts over language in many spheres of public discourse in and about Catalonia rested less and less on the traditional ideology of authenticity that had sustained earlier periods. Spanish nationalist and Castilianist discourses on the one hand increasingly based the authority they attributed to, and demanded for, that language on claims to its anonymous universality and its global clout. On the other hand, by the turn of the 21st century, Catalanists were also increasingly pushing back against the constraints of the local and the authentic to move Catalan out of the frame of traditional authenticity and into the frame of anonymity, advocating that it be understood not as a marker of ethnolinguistic identity but as a common public

---

169. Branchadell is without doubt better able to interpret the nuances of Catalan phrasing than I am, but I read Carod's "without exception" as modifying "domains" rather than use of the language. That is, I do not take it that Carod was urging monolingualism, but rather the presence of Catalan across all domains, including those where it currently has little, such as judicial processes.

170. The date was not plucked out of thin air. September 11, 2014 brought the 300th anniversary of the fall of Barcelona to Bourbon forces, an event that is traditionally observed as the defining moment when Catalonia lost its independent political character and autonomy from the Spanish state. Moreover, Carod was far from a passive oberver predicting an inexorable natural event; he was an active agent in the evolution of the demand for sovereignty.

language available to all. There were also inchoate movements of language activists and political strategists to counter sociolinguistic naturalism and to reconstrue linguistic authenticity itself as an anti-essentialist, goal-oriented project of active construction through flexible and even playful artifice.

Two diametrically opposed political parties, the "anti-nationalist" Ciutadans and the Catalanist Esquerra Republicana, exemplified some of the newly ascendant discourses about language and identity in their campaigns for the Catalan Parliament in 2006, and each had an impact on the outcome of the elections. Ciutadans made a startling mark by winning seats in its first electoral run. ERC gained the votes it needed to be the decisive player in the formation of a left-leaning coalition government and in setting ensuing cultural and linguistic policy. The discourses that these parties newly foregrounded in the 2006 elections have since come to articulate the movements for and against Catalan sovereignty. Civic groups occupy the foreground of the sovereignty movement, and Artur Mas, the head of the center-right Convergència party who became president of Catalonia, stepped belatedly but then resolutely into a leading role. Nonetheless, under different leadership ERC has both contended and collaborated with Mas in the movement and has formulated much of the ideological program for sovereignty, striking many of the same notes as Carod did in 2006.[171] In the opposition to the sovereignty movement, Albert Rivera continues at the head of the Ciutadans party, which has displaced the Partido Popular within Catalonia as the opposition to Catalan sovereignty and has also springboarded to Spanish statewide politics as a leading contender for votes of disgruntlement against corruption, economic disaster, and politics as usual. Thus, there continue to be important resonances and repercussions of the discursive turns that I have surveyed in this chapter.

The most immediately significant outcome of the 2006 election for my sociolinguistic theme, however, was the emergence of an unprecedented president, a Castilian speaker of immigrant origin. Although Artur Mas and his center-right Catalan nationalist party won more votes, the Catalan Socialist party was able to broker leadership of a governing coalition. This brought to the presidency José Montilla, who was both an immigrant-origin Castilian speaker and an uncharismatic and managerially oriented Socialist party stalwart. Montilla, who is the focus of the next chapter, pledged to reduce the political drama that had plagued the earlier coalition government of his charismatic Catalan Socialist predecessor, Pasqual Maragall. He also sought to tamp down the nationalist agenda in favor of what Socialists called the social agenda focused on policies to address social

---

171. The current ERC leader, Oriol Junqueras, has espoused official status for Castilian as well as Catalan in the hypothetical independent Catalonia.

inequality and welfare. And to many, he appeared to represent personally the linguistic future of Catalonia, for good or ill.

Soon after the election the journalist and media figure Toni Soler described the direction in which the new governing coalition could be expected to lead Catalonia, using terms that aptly summarize the theme of this book. Soler punned on the Spanish phrase for "Incorporated," *Sociedad Anónima*, which is abbreviated *S.A.* ("Inc.") and translates literally as "Anonymous Society":

> the Government . . . opts for management alone, and it has decided . . .
> to convert us all into members of the board of directors of Catalonia S.A.
> ("A" for anonymous, because anonymity is the ideal of those who are
> against identities.)[172] (Soler 2006)

We will return to the theme of the corporate enterprise model for the new Catalonia in Chapter 6. In the next chapter, we will take a close look at the linguistic leadership of this newly anonymous Catalan society, as personified by its president José Montilla and parodied in a hit television show directed by Toni Soler himself.

---

172. "el Govern . . . apuesta por la gestión a secas, y ha decidido . . . convertirnos a todos en miembros del consejo de administración de Catalunya S.A. ('A' de anónima, porque el anonimato es el ideal de los que están en contra de las identidades)."

SHIFTING DISCOURSES OF LANGUAGE IN CATALAN POLITICS AND MEDIA

4 "DEEDS NOT WORDS"

AN IMMIGRANT PRESIDENT AND THE POLITICS OF LINGUISTIC PARODY

Out of the scrum of coalition politics after the 2006 Catalan parliamentary elections, the Socialist party leader José Montilla emerged as president of the Generalitat, the government of the autonomous community of Catalonia. He held that position until 2010. Montilla is a Castilian speaker who immigrated to Catalonia from the province of Cordoba in Andalusia, arriving at age sixteen with his father. His story began as that of a typical immigrant, but his rise to the Catalan presidency, as an immigrant, was unprecedented.[1] Montilla liked to characterize himself as an Andalusian by birth and a Catalan by choice.

During thirty years in politics, Montilla had ascended through the ranks of the Catalan and Spanish Socialist parties (PSC and PSOE).[2] From long service as mayor of the working-class and immigrant-based city of Cornellà de Llobregat in the Barcelona industrial belt, he moved on to head the administrative council (*Diputació*) of the province of Barcelona, then to a cabinet position in the Spanish central government of José Luis Rodríguez Zapatero, and from there to the presidency of Catalonia. Montilla had not been elected president through the popular vote, in which he actually fared relatively badly, but rather through agreements among parties that collaborated to form a parliamentary majority.

---

1. Montilla was the first president of the restored Generalitat born outside of Catalonia, although he was also only the third president in that same period. Two Andalusians reportedly had served as president of a Generalitat in a quite different form in the 17th century (*Avui* 2006c). For comment on the common application of the term "immigrant" to those who move within the Spanish state but across historic national boundaries, see note 4 in Chapter 1.

2. The two parties are at least nominally distinct. There have been tensions between them in many periods including Montilla's presidency and the preceding one, as well as during the current sovereignty movement.

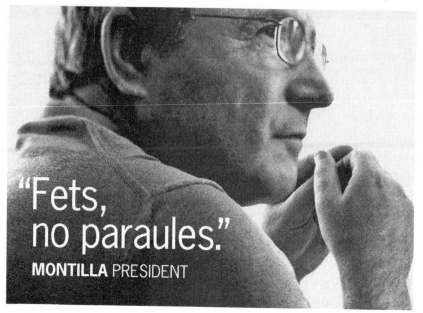

FIGURE 4.1 "Deeds not words." 2006 campaign slogan and image of Catalan Socialist Party (PSC) candidate for president of the Catalan government (Generalitat), José Montilla.

Source: La Rosa de Barcelona 47, October 2006.

By his own admission Montilla was an infrequent and poor speaker of Catalan, despite his many decades in Catalonia and in Catalan electoral politics. He was also known as wooden, colorless, and inarticulate even in his native Castilian language, the antithesis of the Andalusian stereotype. One journalist reported that Montilla was known as "el Mudito" ("the Little Mute"), adding that "when he speaks Catalan, he looks like someone is winding him up"[3] (de Sagarra 2006c). Another commented that he read his speeches in a weary tone devoid of any trace of emotion, whether enthusiastic or sad (Fonalleras 2007). For both of these reasons it was not surprising that Montilla's campaign slogan was *Fets no paraules* "Deeds not words" (Fig. 4.1). The slogan gave a wry sidelong acknowledgment of his lack of Catalan skills and his lack of rhetorical ability. (In the accompanying campaign photo the "deeds" were represented by piles of bureaucratic papers, the top ones printed in Castilian, Fig. 4.2.)

When Montilla emerged as the likely presidential choice, the information media and internet filled with commentary on the idea of an immigrant-origin president who was relatively unassimilated linguistically. Montilla was perceived

---

3. "cuando habla en catalán parece que le estén dando cuerda."

FIGURE 4.2 Lower section of PSC campaign material in Fig. 4.1, showing Montilla at work (on documents in Castilian).
Source: La Rosa de Barcelona 47, October 2006.

as a party plodder and administrator, not a charismatic leader, and his elevation was the uninspired outcome of Spanish Socialist party pressure and Catalan political horsetrading celebrated by few. This presidency had none of the brilliance or historic weight of the Obama election in the United States that followed soon after. Nonetheless, just as the question was raised whether the Obama era is "post-racial," Montilla's presidency provoked discussion of whether Catalonia was now "post-national," and whether that would be a good or bad thing (Villatoro 2006). One tongue-in-cheek commentary characterized Montilla as a "post-Catalan" (Alzamora 2006). For an immigrant and a non-fluent speaker of Catalan to become president of Catalonia seemed like a watershed moment to most observers. But just what social and linguistic significance should be attached to the event; which way was the linguistic water flowing?

Particularly during his first year in office but continuing throughout his tenure, there was a wealth of explicit commentary on Montilla's origins and his linguistic competence, and many comic skewerings of his speech style. These overt representations allow us an especially good view of the competing and changing as well as some unchanged discourses about language in Catalonia. Ambivalence about Montilla's poor control of Catalan was frequently handled with irony and parody. This chapter analyzes views of Montilla and his language expressed by public figures and in news and digital media, as well as by some of my informants in interviews. It then explores in detail several examples of humor about Montilla's Catalan in the mass and digital media and considers the complex politics of parody.

The Reception of President Montilla and His Catalan

The ethnolinguistic meaning of Montilla's presidency was ambiguous because the positioning of Castilian and Castilian speakers is ambiguous in Catalonia. First-language speakers of Castilian number among both the lowest and highest social classes in Catalonia. Castilian is at once a language of working-class immigration and a language of centralist Spanish political domination. Fitting the personal and political ambiguity of Montilla's biography, the reception of both his presidency and his poor linguistic skills in Catalan was mixed. The problem illustrates the question of scale that has become the focus of recent work in linguistic anthropology (Blommaert 2010). As president, should Montilla's voice not be understood to be speaking for and representing the interests and legitimacy of Catalonia, a public responsibility? Or were Montilla's speech patterns to be evaluated on a personal scale, as part of the life history of an immigrant worker who had toiled to build a successful career? Public discussion of the president's language shifted between these scales of interpretation, sometimes collapsing and sometimes distinguishing them.

From one perspective, Montilla's origins as a working-class immigrant from Andalusia placed him as a relative underdog compared to native Catalans and Catalan speakers. "I know what it is to work from age sixteen; I began as an apprentice working twelve hours a day,"[4] said Montilla when asked by an interviewer to defend his credentials as the only presidential candidate without a university degree (Sala i Martín 2006). (To be sure, Montilla had not risen directly from the factory floor. He began two different courses of university study, but left both to work in municipal politics.)

In the 1960s and 1970s, some 1.5 million workers had migrated to Catalonia, most from relatively impoverished areas of the south of Spain. Although they were able to find jobs as skilled or unskilled laborers, the majority lived in relatively poor housing in the industrial belt of Barcelona with scant infrastructure and public services during the Franco era. The population of the city of Cornellà de Llobregat, where Montilla came to be long-term mayor, had swelled almost tenfold between 1950 and 1980 to 100,000, with almost all of the growth coming from Castilian-speaking working-class immigration.[5] Clustered in de facto ghettos under the

---

4. "Sé lo que es trabajar desde los 16 años; empecé de aprendiz doce horas al día."

5. Website of the city of Cornellà del Llobregat, http://www.cornella.cat/ca/Historia.asp#.

demographic pressure of such massive immigration, most immigrants had little access to cultural or linguistic integration into existing Catalan social structures. They became known as "Other Catalans" at best, and more often as *xarnegos*, a slur of not entirely certain origins (Candel 1964, Vilarós 2003).[6]

This immigrant-origin working class formed the popular base of the Catalan Socialist party, and the hope had been to mobilize that base to vote in the Catalan election with Montilla as a candidate perceived as one of their own. (The hope was not fulfilled.) A video for Montilla's campaign featured fellow residents of Cornellà speaking in Castilian-accented Catalan much like his own. Private talk among politicians that Catalonia was not yet ready for a "*xarnego* President" leaked out (de Sagarra 2006b).

Some journalists cast the immigrant Montilla's Catalan political arrival as the story of a "self made man" (Puigverd 2006a) or the script of a Capra film (Ellakuría 2006). Others interpreted it in terms unflattering to traditional Catalan politics. For example, one asserted that Montilla's selection "completed the recognition of Catalans who came from outside as first class citizens, to the disappointment of the exclusionary nationalists"[7] and that it was the sign of the ascent of the immigrant-origin politicians from their longstanding subaltern position within the Catalan Socialist party (Hernàndez 2007). Others put a more positive spin on this for Catalanism as a sign of the inclusive character of Catalonia. Having a "*xarnego*" president is a way of opening things up, wrote one commentator (de Sagarra 2006b). For others, Montilla's presidency confirmed the demise of the very concept of the *xarnego* as well as the term. "The end of the '*xarnego*'" signifies a "new collective reality made of up the existing pluralism,"[8] declared a well-known Catalan author (Porcel 2007). A letter to the editor of the leading center-right Barcelona newspaper *La Vanguardia* declared Montilla's selection as president a happy day for all Catalans, one that made the letter writer (whose own first and surnames were of Castilian origin) "proud of this land" and "more convinced today that Catalonia is a nation"[9] (Rodríguez Pérez 2006).

The vice president of Montilla's uneasy coalition government was Josep-Lluís Carod-Rovira, the hopeful architect of Catalan banal nationalism whom we met

---

6. The term *xarnego* has passed out of use and is now mobilized primarily self-consciously by authors and activists who reclaim and rehabilitate the pejorated identity. Most of my teenaged informants in 2006 had never even heard the word *xarnego*, while their counterparts from twenty years before still remembered it as a stinging insult.

7. "completa el reconocimiento de los catalanes llegados de fuera como ciudadanos de primera, para disgusto de los nacionalistas excluyentes."

8. "una nueva realidad colectiva compuesta por la pluralidad existente."

9. "me siento orgulloso de esta tierra . . . hoy estoy más convencido de que Catalunya es una nación."

in Chapter 3 and will hear more from in Chapter 6. Carod was a leader of the Catalan independentist party Esquerra Republicana de Catalunya (Republican Left of Catalonia). In exchange for joining the coalition government headed by Montilla, Carod's party took charge of the Department of Culture, and language policy was brought directly under the purview of the vice president. Carod characterized strengthening Catalan cultural and linguistic policy as a main task facing the new government (Barbeta and Bracero 2006). Commenting on the significance of his support of Montilla's presidency, Carod asserted:

> [the fact] that an independentist political formation such as Esquerra votes for a gentleman named José who was born in Andalusia to be president of the Generalitat is the best demonstration that our national project is neither essentialist nor ethnic nor para-religious, but rather that it is democratic, inclusive and absolutely integrative."[10] (Barbeta and Bracero 2006)

That the president continued to use the Castilian form of his given name was seen as significant by more than one commentator; "the history of Catalunya changed the day that a José presided over the Generalitat"[11] wrote another (Hernàndez 2008). (We will see a less sanguine view shortly.) Montilla's surname was as much a trope as his first name for commentators on the significance of his presidency. The Catalanist newspaper *Avui* editorialized on it:

> Surnames are never informative about the political preferences of any citizen, and even less about the degree of their sentimental attachment to a given territory or human collectivity, but they leave on record that some societies, like the Catalan one, are a set of sediments that have been deposited successively over the demographic base of the country. Catalonia is, surely, the most open society in all of the [Spanish] state; the place where it is easiest to juxtapose identities.[12] (*Avui* 2006e)

---

10. "que una formación independentista como Esquerra vote como presidente de la Generalitat a un señor que se llama José y que nació en Andalucía. Es la mejor demostración de que nuestro proyecto nacional no es esencialista ni étnico ni pararreligioso, sino que es democrático, inclusivo y absolutamente integrador."

11. "la historia de Catalunya cambió el día en que un José presidió la Generalitat."

12. "Els cognoms no informen mai sobre quines són les preferències partidàries de qualsevol ciutadà, i encara menys sobre quins són els graus de pertinença sentimental a un determinat territori o a un col·lectiu humà, però deixen constància que algunes societats, com la catalana, són un conjunt de sediments que s'han anat dipositant de forma successiva sobre la base demogràfica del país. Catalunya és, segurament, la societat més oberta de tot l'Estat; el lloc on és més fàcil juxtaposar identitats."

In these constructions, Montilla's name, his biography, and even his lack of linguistic skills allowed the display of the superior moral, social, and political character of the Catalan community as inclusive and open. Even some of the strongest supporters of Catalan independence among my informants shared this positive view. One high school student welcomed Montilla's selection even while she categorized him as "not Catalan":

Ex. 4.1 Montilla's presidency

S: em sembla molt bé, que hagi sortit aquest senyor.

KW: El=

S: =Sé que no és català=

KW: =Sí

S: I em sembla encara millor, perquè=

KW: =Sí?

S: també és hora de que surti un que no sigui català. *¡No pasa nada!. . .*

KW: Per què? Explica'm una miqueta això.

S: Perquè normalment els-, se'ns veu que els catalans som molt tancats que, si és de fora, ja no el volem.

KW: Sí

S: Tampoc és això, i que surti un que no és català, *pues,* està molt bé . . .

S: I think it's very good that this gentleman has won.

KW: The=

S: =I know that he's not Catalan=

KW: =Yes

S: And I think that's even better, because=

KW: =Yes?

S: it's also time that someone win who isn't Catalan. *It's okay!. . .*

KW: Why? Tell me a little about this.

S: Because normally, they see us Catalans as very closed, that, if someone is from outside, we don't want him.

KW: Yes

S: But it's not like that, and that someone has won who is not Catalan, *well,* that's very good . . .

Other informants specifically welcomed Montilla's markedly second-language Catalan. For them an audibly nonnative president made believable the longstanding nationalist slogan, "all those who live and work here are Catalan" and signaled the arrival of Catalonia as a normal nation, a much-sought status. Rafael, a 34-year-old independentist and cosmopolitan, elaborated on this in an interview in 2006:

Ex. 4.2 Rafael on Montilla's Catalan

R: em sembla genial que tenim un president que és andalús.

KW: Sí. Volia preguntar-te això.

R: Fantàstic. Parla un català fatal.

((KW laughs))

R: I think it's great that we have a president who is Andalusian.

KW: Yes. I wanted to ask you that.

R: Fantastic. He speaks terrible Catalan.

((KW laughs))

R: Terrorífic. El seu català és patètic. Em sembla una gran idea. I que sigui president gràcies al als independentistes, em sembla fantàstic!

KW: Sí?

R: Ens treuen l'etiqueta de identitat i (això). No ens importa. Em sembla que Esquerra Republicana ho està fent genial això. I em sembla que és una gran notícia de futur. Crec que, crec que tindrem Esquerra Republicana al poder d'aquí vint anys.

R: Horrific. His Catalan is pathetic. I think it's a great idea. And that he's president thanks to the the independentists, I think that's fantastic!

KW: Yes?

R: It takes the identity label off us and (that). It doesn't matter to us. I think that Esquerra Republicana is doing a great job, and I think it's great news for the future. I think, I think that we'll have Esquerra Republicana in power in twenty years.

Even after his presidency ended, the limitations of Montilla's Catalan continued to get similar positive commentary in the media, e.g.: "The labored Catalan of President Montilla . . . thanks precisely to its limitations, is the best example of the commitment to Catalan as a common language"[13] (Cirici 2011).

From a different perspective, by the time he was elected to the Catalan Parliament, Montilla was a well-off career politician. He sent his children to one of the most expensive private schools in Barcelona, a German-medium school, which was perceived as indicative of his dismissive attitude toward the Catalan language. As a cabinet member in the Spanish Socialist government, Montilla was widely understood to have been picked by the Spanish Socialist president Zapatero to muscle out the more charismatic and Catalanist incumbent Catalan Socialist president of the Generalitat, Pasqual Maragall, whose chaotic presidency had given too much trouble over matters such as the revised Statute of Autonomy. Montilla was thus part of a political strain within that party that is viewed by many Catalans (and not exclusively ardent nationalists) as subsidiary to the Spanish statewide party, jacobin at best, and systematically uncomprehending of Catalonia and of Catalan linguistic concerns in particular.

Montilla looks in this frame not like an underdog at all, but instead like another member of the centralist Spanish political elite, one who presumed to

---

13. "el català esforçat del president Montilla com el de l'entranyable Alberto Fernández Díaz són, precisament gràcies a les seves limitacions, els millors exemples de l'aposta pel català com a llengua comuna."

take the reins of the Catalan government without bothering to acquire the linguistic competency required by law for the clerical workers in his own government offices. Moreover, Montilla's campaign had attempted to use the language issue as a wedge by proposing that the presidential candidates debate in Castilian on Spanish statewide television. This was a violation of a consensus that had long held among the main political parties not to exploit linguistic differences in electioneering, as well as an oddly inappropriate proposal to bring a regional election to a Spanish statewide forum. The bid was dismissed as a nonstarter, but it strongly suggested cynicism on Montilla and the Socialists' part about the language question (Culla i Clarà 2006).[14]

Some of Montilla's political opponents professed to be scandalized that such a poor representative of Catalan should lead the nation, and treated it as a sign of the weak position of the Catalan language and the paltry political will to defend it. The wife of Jordi Pujol, the former longtime Catalan president and leading figure in the nationalist opposition party Convergència i Unió (CiU), criticized Montilla not only for speaking Catalan poorly but because he "has his name in Castilian."[15] She referred here to Montilla's use of the Castilian form of his first name, "José," rather than the Catalan form, "Josep." Whereas Carod took the president's Castilian first name as a positive sign, Marta Ferrusola cast it as negative (Mauri 2008).[16] Former president Pujol, who had coined the slogan "All those who live and work here are Catalan," distanced himself from his

---

14. See Boix-Fuster and Sanz (2008) for discussion of the divisive tactics employed in Montilla's campaign. Notably, the assumption was always that the debates must be monolingual, in one language or the other, evidence of the conceptualization of bilingualism as parallel monolingualisms of which Monica Heller has written (Heller 1999). One journalist commented on Montilla's demand for a presidential debate in Castilian on Spanish statewide television by saying that if one is "ready to ask the impossible, he could have asked for a debate on Eurovision in French or English. Or, better yet, proposed that in the debate in Catalonia, each one should choose his own idiom, the way that they chose arms in 19th century duels." (*puesto a pedir imposibles, hubiera podido solicitar un debate por Eurovisión en francés o inglés. O, mejor aún, plantear que en el debate en Catalunya cada uno eligiera idioma, como en los duelos del XIX se escogía armas.*) (Carol 2006). In this perspective languages are like weapons, and a bilingual public interaction is—or at least then was—simply unthinkable.

15. "tiene el nombre en castellano."

16. We have seen in Chapter 3 that the linguistic form of a name was also treated as a significant social diagnostic in the case of the PP candidate Alberto Fernández Díaz. Carod himself later became involved in a statewide flap when he insisted on Spanish television, in Castilian, that a questioner from the audience address him as "Josep Lluís," the Catalan version of his name, rather than "José Luis," the Castilian version: "that's my name here and in China, and you [formal] have no right to modify my name." (*Yo me llamo así aquí y en la China, y usted no tiene derecho a modificar mi nombre.*) (Mauri 2007). This view of the linguistic medium as an integral part of one's personal (proper/own) name is relatively new but significant in Catalonia

wife's criticism, saying that Montilla's presidency proved the integrative spirit of Catalonia.

Another leader of CiU later declared that one of the worst aspects of a parliamentary session was hearing Montilla "destroy" the Catalan language. "Not even when reading is he capable of a minimum level of correct diction and pronunciation in our language,"[17] Felip Puig complained (*El Periódico* 2008a). Puig's criticism, apparently intended as humorous, failed to acknowledge that the written text itself could hamper linguistic performance by adding a layer of decoding to speech production. Montilla no doubt habitually decodes orthographic symbols according to Castilian patterns. It could be expected that his pronunciation would be worse, not better, when reading than in spontaneous oral production.

Puig's indictment of Montilla's pronunciation was not just linguistic but moral and political: it implied that Montilla had not taken his adopted country seriously enough to work on acquiring the language. Just as Montilla's speech was interpreted on the positive side by Carod not simply as a linguistic phenomenon or index of personal character, but rather as an index of the political community, so Puig also explicitly cast his criticism as a comment not just on Montilla, but also on Catalonia. Puig asserted that "nowhere else in the world is there a president who does not know how to speak the *llengua pròpia* of his country properly"[18] (*El Periódico* 2008a).[19] Perhaps Puig had never heard of George Bush, either *père* or *fils*. (Consider the joke headline: "Bush suspends agreement between noun and verb" (Laura Graham, personal communication.)) The Bushes' inarticulate misrenderings of English are known internationally and have been the subject of myriad jokes as well as linguistic anthropological analysis (Silverstein 2003), but there are reasons that I'll discuss below why such a parallel would not be recognized.

---

and Spain. Under the Franco regime, only Spanish given names were allowed in official identity papers. For many Catalans it was very meaningful to have those papers and names changed after the transition. But the culture of translation persists in Spain, and other Catalans still use the two versions of their personal names with more indifference.

17. "destroza"; "ni siquiera leyendo es capaz de tener una mínima dicción y pronunciación correcta de nuestra lengua."

18. "en ningún lugar del mundo ocurre que el presidente de un país no sepa hablar con propiedad la lengua propia."

19. This theme appears more than once in commentaries on Montilla's Catalan. For example, a blogger complained, "many will call me a linguistic essentialist, but frankly, what normal country would allow its president to speak its own language badly?" (*molts em qualificaran d'integrista de la llengua, però, francament, a quin país normal permetrien que el seu president parlés malament la llengua pròpia?*) (Riera 2006).

In response to Puig's attack, Carod-Rovira, who was trained as a Catalan philologist, rose in Parliament to defend Montilla's phonetics. He applauded Montilla, as someone not born in Catalonia and arriving as an adolescent, for achieving the presidency of the country and for studying to improve his Catalan (Noguer 2008). Carod rebuked attacks on a second-language speaker's pronunciation as discouraging others from learning it, a problem that we saw in Chapter 3 stemmed from the authenticity framework, in which Catalan was traditionally placed. Further criticisms from a CiU party member brought cries of "Xenophobe!" from other legislators (Noguer 2008). In his regular newspaper column, the popular journalist and media figure Toni Soler concurred that thousands of immigrants who speak Catalan the way Montilla does, or worse, would feel themselves targeted by Puig's remark. Soler asserted that it was acceptable to criticize Montilla's own Catalan, because as president he should set a better example. However, he concluded that Puig's criticism of Montilla's Catalan was out of place, because "Montilla is an Andalusian by birth who has chosen to be Catalan and who, although a little late, has adopted the language of the country; this—unfortunately—doesn't happen every day, and it's what really matters"[20] (Soler 2008). This was a particularly noteworthy defense of Montilla's Catalan because Soler is the director of the hit television show that developed the most well-known linguistic parody of Montilla, which will be discussed later in this chapter.

Montilla disarmed some of his linguistic critics immediately after taking on the presidency by freely admitting his deficiencies in Catalan (Santos 2006) and announcing that he would take language classes (Hinojosa 2006), which he did with noticeable improvements and to good reviews a year later (Rico 2007). He collaborated in some of the ribbing, for example appearing on a radio show that announced that Montilla would speak "clear and Catalan,"[21] a joking use of a Catalan idiom for straight talk. (Montilla apparently appreciated the joke, because his own 2013 memoir bears the same title, *Clar i català*.) In an appearance on an audience-participation Catalan television show, Montilla responded to a woman who apologized for not speaking Catalan well by saying that he did not speak it well, either. "But you've improved a lot," the woman replied. "And you can, too," countered Montilla[22] (Foix in Montilla and Jorba 2013, 14). During the 2010 election campaign, a commentator wrote that Montilla had

20. "Montilla es un andaluz de nacimiento que ha elegido ser catalán y que, aunque un poco tarde, ha adoptado la lengua del país; eso, que—por desgracia—no pasa cada día, es lo que realmente importa."

21. "Clar i català."

22. "Però vostè l'ha millorat molt"; "També ho pot fer vostè."

provided an authentic lesson that *"xarnegos"* can integrate perfectly if they want to (Pitarch 2010).

Thus Montilla turned his linguistic faults into a virtue as an exemplar of a late language learner. As president he always used Catalan when speaking in public, providing a model that some observers felt could encourage other immigrants to overcome their fear of speaking it, unless the model was overshadowed by the jokes (Puigverd 2006b). Moreover, Montilla added to those virtues by explicitly pointing to his own deficient skills as evidence of the need for legal protections for Catalan, whenever such policies were challenged as unjust by Ciutadans or other political representatives (Santos 2006).[23] The semiotic process by which Montilla bolstered his own image is nicely captured by Michael Silverstein's concept of orders of indexicality (Silverstein 1995). At a first order of social indexicality, Montilla's poor Catalan proficiency pointed to Montilla's own shortcomings and weakness. But Montilla strategically repositioned his linguistic failing from this first order to a second order of social indexicality, where the poorly speaking president could himself be read as a sign of the precariousness of the Catalan language. In this order, Montilla's linguistic limitations said something about the state of the Catalan language, not about Montilla. Exploiting the weakness of his Catalan by escalating the social indexicality of the linguistic form to yet a third level of meaning, Montilla claimed an image as a Catalanist through the act of pointing to himself as such a sign of the need to protect Catalan.[24]

What Was Montilla's Catalan Actually Like?

The most journalistically objective report on Montilla's actual linguistic patterns appeared not in the newspapers of record but rather in a free newspaper of the kind found in subway stations (*Què!* 2006). The article highlighted five lexical errors identified in a single radio interview with Montilla, and additionally commented on his phonetic difficulties.

Montilla's lexical errors were generated by morphophonemic formulae for transforming cognate words from Castilian to Catalan, and these formulae can sometimes work. Their over-application is widespread among L1 as well as L2 speakers of Catalan. This news article reported examples from Montilla's interview including *enfermetat* (from CS *enfermedad*) for Catalan *malaltia* "illness",

---

23. The columnist Iu Forn (2006a) pointed out that Montilla's presidency was the perfect way to foil the complaints of the new Ciutadans party about discrimination against Castilian and Castilian speakers.

24. This semiotic strategy is reminiscent of the joking definition of the Yiddish word *chutz-pah*: a man kills his parents and then asks for the mercy of the court because he is an orphan.

and *reflexa*, which was a stab at a morphophonemic transformation from the Castilian *refleja* that missed the CT target *reflecteix* "reflects."[25]

A sidebar in this article reported on pronunciation issues and observed that voicing of the Catalan orthographic "s" is one of the greatest challenges for "an Andalusian such as Montilla." Catalan has a phonemic contrast between the voiceless alveolar fricative /s/ and the voiced /z/, but Castilian does not. Between vowels, the orthographic single "s" represents the voiced /z/ in Catalan. This creates pronunciation differences between standard Catalan and Castilian in many common words that are spelled alike in the two languages, such as *casa* "house", which has the voiced alveolar fricative in Catalan and the voiceless one in Castilian. The intervocalic voiceless sibilant is represented in Catalan writing as "ss" or "ç," as will be discussed in examples below.[26] The voiced alveolar fricative, like other voiced obstruent consonants, doesn't occur in word final position in Catalan, but obligatory word liaison calls for voicing of that segment in connected speech, which Montilla also did not do.

The free newspaper used the occasion of Montilla's presidency to report on adults studying Catalan, as the headline indicated: "Montilla will study Catalan as 75,000 people already do."[27] The story commented on professional soccer players from the famed Barcelona team who already took such language lessons, and reported advice from language professionals on good ways to proceed ("Let yourself be corrected by those who speak Catalan").[28] "Montilla motivated me to study Catalan again," a subhead announced.[29]

In contrast to the neutral to positive tone of this news report and its normalization of second-language acquisition of Catalan, signed columns and features in mainstream newspapers evaluated Montilla's Catalan humorously and/ or negatively, poking fun particularly at his ninety-minute speech at the presidential investiture ceremony. Montilla's way of speaking was depicted as if it were a

---

25. The form belongs to a set of Catalan verbs called inchoative, which doesn't have an immediate morphological parallel in Castilian. One of Montilla's opponents, the eloquent native-speaking Catalan Josep Piqué of Partido Popular was caught hypercorrecting Catalan *"perceben"* to *"percebeixen"* ('they perceive') in his reply to Montilla's speech (Serra 2006a).

26. Catalan also has a phonemic contrast of voicing in the palato-alveolar fricatives and affricates. The voicing distinction of fricatives as well as affricates is often lost in Castilian-influenced speech.

27. "Montilla estudiarà català com ja fan 75.000 persones."

28. "Deixar-se corregir pels qui parlen català."

29. "Montilla m'ha animat a tornar a estudiar català." One or two of my informants reported that their immigrant parents who had never been heard to speak Catalan before were now beginning to do so.

distinctive dialect of Catalan and dubbed with various invented names: *montillés, montillès, montillà,* "Level S Catalan," and "post-Catalan."

A number of Castilian-influenced features could be heard in Montilla's Catalan, but just a few became iconic in a stereotype that circulated across the media. A newspaper columnist diagnosed "post-Catalan" *montillès* as an "allergy to voiced s's and neutral vowels, a frankly bad relationship with double l's, and mass extermination of the weak pronouns (taking advantage of the fact that, as their name indicates, they can't defend themselves)"[30] (Alzamora 2006). Days later a blogger described *montillés* as "without voiced s's, without weak pronouns, and without the neutral vowel" (Babunski 2006), strongly suggesting intertextual borrowing of the stereotype.[31]

Iconic Catalan Linguistic Features: A Brief Explanation

Before discussing humorous representations of Montilla's speech in detail, a very brief explanation of these iconic linguistic features is in order for those not familiar with Catalan. Castilian and Catalan are closely related Romance languages, and there is, therefore, much lexical and syntactic common ground. Morphophonemics and phonology are key areas that distinguish the two languages.

The lack of voiced "s" has already been discussed. The neutral vowel refers to schwa [ə] (similar to the "uh" sound in unstressed syllables in American English, as represented by the "a" in "alone" and "cola"). In the standard central variety of Catalan spoken in the Barcelona area, /a/, /e/, and /ɛ/ in unstressed syllables are all reduced to [ə]. Castilian influence (among other factors) leads speakers to use full forms and to replace unstressed [ə] with a full-value [a] or [e].[32]

The standard variety of Catalan spoken in the Barcelona area also reduces all unstressed /o/ and /ɔ/ to [u]. This is a pattern that Castilian speakers can acquire relatively easily, since they have the [u] sound in their repertoire, so it is not

---

30. "al·lèrgia a les esses sonores i a les vocals neutres, una relació francament dolenta amb les dobles eles i exterminis en massa de pronoms febles (aprofitant que, com el seu nom indica, no saben defensar-se)."

31. "el dialecte montillés: sense esses sonores, sense pronoms febles i sense vocal neutra." The change from grave to acute accent mark in the joking name of the dialect is interesting but it is unclear what the intention was, e.g., to represent Castilian influence in orthography or Montilla's inability to distinguish between tense ("closed") and lax ("open") vowels. The blogger was from Lleida, where vowels pattern differently than in central Catalan, making the criticism of Montilla's lack of vowel neutralization especially curious and likely to have been taken from elsewhere.

32. Some varieties of Catalan do not have this vowel reduction, but it is standard in the provinces of Barcelona and Girona.

mentioned in these commentaries on Montilla's speech, even though Montilla often does not reduce the vowel when reading a prepared text. Reducing orthographic unstressed "o" in word-final position to [u] is in fact one of the strategies often used by both L1 and L2 speakers to create Catalan words out of Castilian ones. For example, *buenu* from Castilian *bueno* "good" is a widespread discourse marker in vernacular Catalan censured by purists. The pattern of overusing [u] in unstressed syllables to make Catalan out of Castilian is a feature of many parodies of Montilla's speech.

The assertion of a "bad relationship with double l's" refers to the palatal lateral consonant represented in writing by "ll" and part of the phonemic inventory of standard Castilian as well as Catalan. It is systematically more frequent in word-initial position in Catalan than in Castilian (e.g., CS *libro*, CT *llibre* "book"; CS *libre*, CT *lliure* "free"; CS *lengua*, CT *llengua* "tongue/language"). The palatal lateral does not occur at the end of words in Castilian, but it does in Catalan, causing particular trouble for Castilian speakers, who generally substitute either a palatal offglide [y] or occasionally an alveolar lateral [l]. Moreover, the variety of Castilian spoken by most Castilian speakers in Catalonia is well advanced in the change of the palatal lateral to the glide [y] in any position in words, a pattern that is known as *yeísmo*. Catalan has not experienced this change very widely, and *yeísmo/ieisme* in Catalan is usually attributed to Castilian influence.

The weak pronouns (*pronoms febles*) play an important role in every discussion of the distinctive character of the Catalan language. They are an extensive set of cliticizing unstressed direct and indirect object pronouns and adverbial pronouns, which linguists have described as the "most intricately exacting aspect of Catalan grammar" (Wheeler, Yates, and Dols 1999).[33] In prescriptive standard Catalan, there are multiple forms of each pronoun, depending on their combination and their position in relation to the verb. A complex grid of up to 169 cells (13 x 13 units) appears in many teaching grammars, even basic ones, to show the proper forms for combining two weak pronouns, varying according to position in the clause. This prescriptive system was derived from alleged logical principles rather than oral forms when modern Catalan was standardized by the engineer and grammarian Pompeu Fabra early in the 20th century. (One Catalan speaker described the prescriptive weak pronouns to me as "pure science fiction.") The consequence of such abstract prescriptivism even among native Catalan speakers has been "rejection by speakers and difficulties in learning, and thus in application, for the written as well as spoken language" (Segarra 1985, 186). Despite—or more likely because of—this widespread difficulty with the weak pronouns

---

33. Clitics are words that cannot stand alone when unstressed and instead attach to a stressed word.

as prescribed, they are treated by many as the emblematic icons of the Catalan language, par excellence. The Catalan weak pronouns are the frequent focus of sociolinguistic stereotyping, prescriptive commentary, and linguistic complaint writing, as well as of parodies and humor in the media.

If they are difficult for native speakers, the weak pronouns are often viewed as impossible for Castilian learners of Catalan. Obligatory adverbial weak pronouns have no counterpart in Castilian (although they do in French), some object pronouns have inexact cognates in the two languages, and all of them are subject to the phonological rules such as vowel reduction and liaison that distinguish Catalan from Castilian. My informant Josep, to whom we will return in Chapter 8, put it this way:

Ex. 4.3 Josep on the weak pronouns

The Catalan turns of phrase, the- the weak pronouns. . . . A Castilian is never in his life going to master those. The- the weak pronouns, this is mother-freaking complicated. Because on top of it, Catalan has- it's archaic, it's very archaic, and it has some phrasings that are very complicated, it has complicated sounds for a Castilian speaker.[34]

In addition to these features and the lexical calquing discussed earlier, we will see several more patterns of Castilian influence on Catalan singled out for criticism in the examples analyzed below. However, the devoicing of the voiced /s/ and the weak pronouns were the prototypical recurrent emblems of Catalan as a mediatized object that brought critical commentary on Montilla's speech. For example, reporting that Montilla planned to study Catalan, one newspaper suggested he might be heard "pronouncing voiced s's and using weak pronouns in a matter of months"[35] (Hinojosa 2006).

Two cartoons published in the newspaper of a small Catalan city further demonstrate the salience of these linguistic features. One entitled "Urban legends of today" showed one schoolboy telling another "If Montilla wins, they say everyone will be given a passing grade in language class to celebrate." Behind him, Montilla can be seen on a television stringing together gratuitous weak pronouns (and calquing Castilian verbal syntax, as well): "I'm going to go say something about there to at him" (Fontdevila 2006b) (Fig. 4.3).

---

34. "los-los giros del catalán, el-los *pronoms febles* . . . Un castellano no te lo va a dominar nunca en la vida. Los-*els pronoms febles*, eso es complicao como la madre que los parió. Porque encima, el catalán, tiene-es arcaico, es muy arcaico, tiene unos giros en el lenguaje muy complicados, tiene- una sonoridad complicada para un castellanoparlante."

35. "Escuchar a José Montilla pronunciando las eses sonoras e introduciendo *pronoms febles* en su dicurso puede ser cuestión de meses."

FIGURE 4.3 "Urban legends of today." One student to another: "If Montilla wins, they say everyone will get a 'Pass' in language studies to celebrate!" Montilla on TV in background: "I'm going to go say something about there to at him." Cartoon by Manel Fontdevila.

Reproduced by permission of the artist.

A second cartoon by the same artist depicts the difficulty of voicing two inter-vocalic segments in the single word *desitjo* [dəziʤu] ("I wish" in "I wish you happy holidays") as "The Challenges of the Montilla Government" (Fontdevila 2006a) (Fig. 4.4). In the cartoon, multiple letters represent Montilla trying to pronounce the voiced fricative "s" [z] and the voiced affricate "tj" [dʒ] in the holiday greeting.

Mediatized Representations and Parodies

Humorous criticisms and parodies of Montilla's Catalan emanated from many different sources. In the next sections, we will look closely at four examples of such humor, to see what they say about perceptions of Catalan as well as about perceptions of the president himself. Before turning to the Catalan examples, let us briefly consider analytic approaches to the politics of such representational work.

Public representations that purport to capture the speech style of nonnative, nonstandard, and minority language speakers are generally diagnosed by sociolinguists and linguistic anthropologists as forms of ethnic derogation and discrimination. A particularly relevant example is Laura Graham's analysis of linguistic imagery in the Brazilian print press (Graham 2011). Graham demonstrates how an indigenous Brazilian activist, Mario Juruna, was politically undermined when newspapers reproduced his limited syntactic and lexical control of Portuguese

FIGURE 4.4 "The challenges of the Montilla government: 'I wish you happy holidays.'" President Montilla tries without success to voice the "s" [z] and "tj" [dʒ] in the holiday greeting. Cartoon by Manel Fontdevila.
Reproduced by permission of the artist.

in verbatim quotations. Graham finds such putatively objective representations to have been in effect pejorative and to have helped end Juruna's political career:

> As linguistic prejudice swelled against Juruna, other media also sanctioned forms of linguistic discrimination. In his popular weekly television show, the comedian Jô Soares roasted the Xavante politician by parodying his semiconversant Portuguese. His jokes objectified Juruna's manner of speaking in ways that many people today would consider extremely offensive and politically incorrect. Soares's imitations . . . provoked audiences to laugh "at" Juruna and his way of speaking and promoted ridicule of the formerly celebrated Xavante leader (Graham 2011, 176).

Even more than such broad parodies, it was the verbatim representations within straight news reports that Graham sees as particularly damaging to Juruna's authority. The literary theorist Mikhail Bakhtin told us that even the most exact quote is always an ideological revoicing that can be heard as mockery (Bakhtin 1981). In the memorable phrasing of *Saturday Night Live*'s Tina Fey impersonating Sarah Palin, "I hope the lame stream media won't twist my words by repeating them verbatim."[36] A biting satire of the conservative American politician Newt

---

36. From a skit that aired on NBC television's *Saturday Night Live* in May 2011.

Gingrich was a 2007 video clip of Gingrich himself reading in heavily English-accented Spanish. In exquisite irony, the performance was an apology for having dismissed Spanish as a "ghetto language" just days before. The clip was reproduced by a team of video commentators called the "Young Turks" who simply shouted over it with derisive laughter at features of Gingrich's incompetent pronunciation.[37] Gingrich's arrogance in appropriating a language he obviously didn't know and had treated dismissively revealed more directly than usual the complex that Jane Hill has argued is a form of racism underlying Anglo Spanish (Hill 2008).

These examples show how verbatim reproduction, particularly of imperfect linguistic control, can be a powerfully negative comment, as Graham argues. If this is true of oral performances, when produced through nonstandard orthography the effect can be even more devastating. The textual practices that Graham describes were likely to be especially powerful because, as Janina Fenigsen has observed, it is one thing to hear nonstandard speech, but quite another to see it written, or worse yet printed (Fenigsen 1999). Standard language ideology is much stronger in relation to written than to spoken language. Fenigsen observes, "In . . . cultures of writing and print that are characterized by the hegemony of standard spelling . . . any divergence from the standard invites censure and is saturated with social and moral contrasts" (Fenigsen 1999, 64). Sometimes nonstandard spellings are used to reflect pronunciations that actually are nonstandard. Other times they are used as what has been called "eye dialect," that is, deviant spellings to represent oral forms that are not deviant at all, but rather phonologically correct standard pronunciations (e.g., "wimin" for "women" in English). Eye dialect insistently frames forms as deviant, making them appear "sloppy" or "wrong" even when they are not, because they are spelled incorrectly. Both kinds of ad hoc spelling can communicate negative valorizations of a speaker (Fenigsen 1999, 74), but gratuitous eye dialect is less ambiguously a strategy of derogation.

Standard language is standard precisely because, as a component of ideological anonymity, it is supposed to be devoid of particularistic inflections. Nonstandard orthography violates this expectation and communicates just such a particularistic, locatable identity. The transgression is especially egregious because it introduces traces of an embodied voice into printed text, where ideology holds that none should be heard. Voice is bodily, and the bodily traces contaminate the purity of the standard, like someone spitting on the language. Thus, standard language ideology endows transgressions in the print medium with particularly violent symbolic force in comparison to aural modalities. This distinction will be relevant to the analysis of different forms of commentary on Montilla's speech.

---

37. The original segment had been taken down from Gingrich's own website but the Young Turks' version was found at http://www.youtube.com/watch?v=Og0HqSZVKqA.

An initial approach to parodies of Montilla's poor Catalan might reasonably assume the representations of the nonnative Catalan president to be analogous to those of the indigenous Brazilian activist. However, mimesis is by definition ambivalent and all parodies are not equal. Are representations of Montilla's second-language speech most appropriately compared to those of the indigenous Brazilian activist Juruna that Graham studied, or to mockery of Newt Gingrich's Spanish? Does Montilla's Catalan index the linguistic struggle of an up-by-the-bootstraps immigrant or arrogant condescension from the privileged position of a dominant state language? Some of the examples we will see in this chapter are derogatory by any standard. To be sure, the audience's political stance will always affect the reading of linguistic representations of public figures, regardless of the nuances of the signi-fiers used. We can be appalled by parodies of disadvantaged minority speakers and still guffaw at Gingrich's Spanish. Nonetheless, different metalinguistic commen-taries and humor have different semiotic dynamics, and thus potentially different social effects, that can be dissected with some of the analytic tools we have.

I hope to demonstrate in the next sections that the social semiotics of linguis-tic mimesis are affected by the nature and status of both the linguistic medium and the technological medium involved. When the target linguistic variety is a minoritized language rather than an anonymous, hegemonic language, the social meaning of such linguistic parodies of public figures is significantly affected. Hyperbolic stylizations and humorous parodies of hybridity can have especially complex layered meanings in such situations, as seen in Nikolas Coupland's inter-pretation of the stylized accent of a Welsh radio personality (Coupland 2001), or the parody of the hybrid Irish of a media figure analyzed by Kelly-Holmes and Atkinson (2007). Moreover, the sociopolitical effects of parody—always to some extent ambiguous—depend on whether the mimicked variety is unambiguously linked to a social persona or position. When it is not, the social semiotics of par-ody will in turn be even more ambiguous than is usually the case. Finally, I hope to show that there are significantly different possibilities afforded by different parodic genres and the different technological media through which they appear.

With these arguments in mind, in the next sections we will look at four dif-ferent examples of humor about Montilla's Catalan. The examples are taken from different media sources (one from a mainstream newspaper, two that circulated in digital media, and one from television) in order to see the different semiotic strategies that were used and the concomitant potential differences in the social meaning of linguistic parodies.

Print Criticism of Montilla: *"Pressident del Gover (d'Enteça)"*

The day after Montilla gave his formal presidential investiture speech, a humor-ous feature article about it appeared in the leading Castilian-medium Barcelona newspaper, *La Vanguardia*, a center-right paper that did not support Montilla or the Socialists.[38] In the article Màrius Serra, a Catalan author and frequent commentator on language, dissected Montilla's Catalan. Despite the humorous tone, there was sting in the strategies of textual representation used (Serra 2006c).

Since Montilla read a prepared text, he was surely not the sole author of his parliamentary speech. As one humorous columnist put it, "Montilla read everything, including the watermark of the paper the speech was written on"[39] (Forn 2006b). Given that expert Catalan writers had vetted the text, his errors in this instance were mostly confined to pronunciation. Montilla's address came across as perfect Catalan in textual quotations that observed the regular journalistic practice of standard orthography. Serra's piece, however, represented Montilla's faulty Catalan pronunciation visually through the extraordinary measure of nonstandard orthography. This technique played with what Briggs and Bauman call an intertextual gap, a distance between a representation and its target, where in normal journalistic conventions none would have been seen (Briggs and Bauman 1992). On the one hand, the unconventional spellings could be taken as narrowing the (phonetic) gap between the printed text and the oral production that it represented, making it more truly verbatim. But in narrowing the phonetic gap between original speech and print reproduction, the newspaper article visibly widened the gap between Montilla's speech and its target, standard Catalan. The symbolic violence of deviant spelling heightens the pejorative force of the critical linguistic commentary, over those that were made by others in more conventional graphic terms.

The headline of the article alone, *"Pressident del Gover (d'Enteça)"* (standard Catalan orthography: *President del Govern (d'Entesa)*; "President of the Government (of the Accord)"), used three nonstandard spellings to represent phonological traits of Montilla's speech. Montilla's replacement of the voiced intervocalic fricative [z] in *President* and *Entesa* with a voiceless [s] was represented by two different Catalan graphemes for the voiceless intervocalic fricative—"ss" in the first case and "ç" in the second –in place of the orthographically correct single "s." The third nonstandard spelling in the header depicted the inappropriate deletion of the final [n] from *Govern*, an error that Montilla continued to make after years at the helm of the government. Like the devoicing of "s," it most likely derives from transfer of Castilian phonological

---

38. *La Vanguardia* now also publishes a Catalan-medium edition prepared through automatic translation from the Castilian.

39. "Montilla va llegir fins i tot la marca dels fulls on duia escrit el discurs."

constraints.[40] Using invented spelling to represent the new president's pronunciation of his own official title and the name of the government itself is a particularly glaring tactic.[41]

Serra's article focused on "the absolute extermination of the voiced s." He asserted that Montilla did not produce a single one in his speech in Parliament; "he devoiced them all without pity."[42] We have already seen a similar use of "extermination" in a commentary on Montilla's speech above, in that case the extermination of the defenseless weak pronouns. These critics played humorously on the allegation of "linguistic genocide" that some Catalanists level seriously against the Spanish state and Castilianists.[43] Although their humor distances both of these critical commentaries on Montilla from such earnest complaints, their use of the term nonetheless conjures an image of a willful speaker actively victimizing the Catalan language, rather than a second-language speaker struggling with a difficult linguistic obstacle.

Making this feature emblematic, Serra dubbed Montilla's style as "Level S Catalan," in a mocking play on "Level C Catalan," the bureaucratic classification of linguistic proficiency required of civil servants (Frekko 2013).[44] However waggishly, Serra was criticizing not just Montilla's speech but what he characterized as a linguistic variety; whether this should be considered an "enregisterment" of the variety in the sense Asif Agha (2007a) has proposed is a question I will address shortly. Other features Serra attributed to this variety were: the yodization of

---

40. As a learner of Catalan myself, my intuition was that the deletion of the final "-n" was the overgeneralization of final segment deletion calquing strategies and of Catalan phonological simplification of homorganic final consonant clusters (see Wheeler 2005, 220-227 for the latter). Speakers often try to transform Castilian lexemes into Catalan by deleting any final segment, but in particular /n/, following the models of CS *pan* = CT *pa*, CS *ningún* = CT *ningú*, CS *catalán* = CT *català*, etc. Ivan Tubau, a Catalan critic of Catalan purism, complained that some Catalan speakers are so wary of final [an] in Catalan for fear of sounding Castilian that they pronounce his name as "Ivà" (Tubau 1990, 17). However, more knowledgeable linguists of Catalan advise me that direct transfer of the Castilian prohibition of final consonant clusters is the more likely source of this deletion in Montilla's case.

41. Another columnist warned of political backlash if "anthropological catalanism" (*catalanismo antropológico*) recriminated Montilla for not voicing intervocalic orthographic "s," a concern that he characterized as "more ethnic than philological (*más étnica que filológica*)" (Juliana 2006). I note that this understanding of the "anthropological" is not the one from which this book is written.

42. "el exterminio absoluto de la s sonora . . . el futuro president no pronunció ni una s sonora. Las ensordeció todas sin piedad."

43. The trope of "linguistic genocide against the weak pronouns" was broadly satirized in a later Catalan television series; see Ribot Bencomo 2013; Woolard, Ribot Bencomo, and Soler Carbonell 2014.

44. The Level C requirement is not particular to Catalonia. It is based on the Common European Framework of Reference for Languages, which designates the "Effective Operational Proficiency" or "Advanced level" required to work or study in the countries of the European Union.

almost all "j" sounds, that is, substituting palatal glides for voiced alveo-palatal fricatives, such as *proiectes* for *projectes, aiuts* for *ajuts*; the loss of phonological liaison between articles and nouns; and the direct transfer of function words from Castilian, such as *como* (CT *com*) and *por* (CT *per*). The description of this deficient variety concluded "about the weak pronouns, don't even ask."[45]

No instance was cited of either of these last two problems in Montilla's actual inaugural address, and a mistake with the weak pronouns was unlikely because of the text's preparation. In the sleight of hand that is the forte of linguistic enregisterment, Serra altered the target from Montilla's individual speech to what he presented as a widespread variety of bad Catalan. However, it is important to observe that the criticism remained linguistic, and could not easily be given the "characterological" indexicality that is part of Agha's conceptualization of speech register. Level S Catalan cannot be unambiguously located socially or tied to a social persona, as registers can (and must be) in Agha's formulation. Although most of the distinctive traits of Level S Catalan are transferred from Castilian, very different social types are associated with them. Certainly Andalusian immigrants like Montilla, most of them working class at least in origin, would be likely to have such features in Catalan. However, the linguistic enregisterment of the Andalusian immigrant is not usually produced through any form of Catalan at all. Rather, a form of Castilian marked by stylized Andalusian features is enregistered as indexing this working-class social type (formerly the *xarnego*), and it is iconized in aspiration of the voiceless sibilant /s/ (e.g., *loh ehpañoleh* for *los españoles*) (Pujolar 2001).

Equally important to the social meaning of so-called Level S Catalan, the urban Catalan bourgeoisie of Barcelona who grew up speaking Castilian as a primary language also often shows the devoicing of the voiced fricative, and the trait is found among a number of Montilla's bourgeois native Catalan political contemporaries. To the extent that transfers from Castilian might be taken to typify Montilla as an immigrant or second-language speaker, Serra neutralized these associations by asserting that Level S Catalan is "nothing new: neither among adopted Catalans nor among fellow citizens with the purest [Catalan] roots."[46] Indeed, Castilian-influenced varieties of the language especially as spoken by Barcelona Catalans had provided fodder for comedians for decades.[47]

Serra's critique of Montilla's Catalan echoed specific criticisms of native-born Catalan-speaking politicians that another commentator had made three years earlier, precisely after the investiture debate of the previous Catalan government in 2003 (Moliner 2003). Then too, the devoiced "s" was the key feature singled

---

45. "De los *pronoms febles*, ni se sabe."

46. "Nada nuevo . . . ni entre catalanes de adopción ni entre conciudadanos de pura cepa."

47. For analyses of earlier forms of linguistic humor, see Woolard 1987, 1995.

out in the speech of several politicians from parties right to left, but those were all natives of Catalonia, one of them a member of an influential Catalan family from the region generally held to speak the purest Catalan.[48] That critic characterized the devoiced intervocalic fricatives as emblematic of *xava*, a variety of Catalan generally thought to be phonetically Castilianized and strongly associated with urban Barcelona.[49] Again in 2011, the same criticisms of devoiced fricatives were leveled at a native Catalan politician, this time at the newly elected mayor of Barcelona, Xavier Trias, who was described as a "gentleman of Barcelona":

> His Catalan has as much a genetic base as a social history of the city. It carries the imprint of families with a *de* in the middle of their surnames [i.e., haute bourgeoisie], that on the tragic stage of the twentieth century, lost their voiced consonants in the measure that they moved up [in the city] and tried to speak with more refinement . . . This social class . . . is returning to wave the flag of their grandparents' language after fratricidal confrontations . . . (Pla Nualart 2011b)[50]

Coming from such a Catalan bourgeois family, the critic continued, Trias was not exposed much to Catalan until he was already an adult, "with an unrecyclable identity. Too late to ever have a clear grasp of the boundary between Catalan and Castilian" (Pla Nualart 2011b).[51] We see the indelible mark of the ideology of linguistic authenticity in this description of Trias's "unrecyclable identity."[52]

Thus, while the linguistic enregisterment of this phonologically and phonetically Castilianized Catalan is clear, with the same features recognized repeatedly, its

---

48. Joaquim Nadal, from Girona. It is rumored that he was advised to speak in this way to appeal to a popular vote. Joan Saura was the other politician whose *xava* style was the subject of frequent comment.

49. *Xava* has spread upward socially in recent decades, rather like Estuary English in the London area. Although the devoiced fricative may be characteristic, its most salient feature is usually seen to be the full [a] in place of [ə] in unstressed syllables (Ballart 2002, 2013).

50. "El seu català té tant de base genètica com d'història social de la ciutat. Porta l'empremta de famílies amb un *de* al mig del cognom que, en el tràgic escenari del segle XX, van anar perdent les consonants sonores a mesura que pujaven Eixample amunt i intentaven parlar més fi . . . "; "La classe social . . . aquí està tornant a fer bandera de la llengua dels seus avis després que enfrontaments fratricides . . . "

51. "quan ja era . . . d'identitat irreciclable. Prou tard per no tenir mai clara la frontera català-castellà."

52. "Recycle" is a reference to the program of linguistic normalization called "linguistic recycling" that required teachers and bureaucrats to take courses in Catalan within a certain period of time in order to keep their posts and/or advance in the system.

social enregisterment is not at all straightforward. The stigmatized linguistic forms do not come from one particular social location, and are as characteristic of a native-born Catalan bourgeoisie as of an immigrant working class, if not more. They are not enregistered to a single social type. This ambiguous, bidirectional indexicality itself epitomizes the paradoxical social situation of Catalan in relation to Castilian.

A second factor also mitigated the potential symbolic violence of Serra's linguistic critique of Montilla. The nonstandard representation of his pronunciation was based in Catalan orthography, mobilizing graphemes not used in modern Castilian (ç, ss). To decode those graphemes presumes a Catalan frame of interpretation and contains it within the boundaries of the Catalan language, even making it look more Catalan, given that the critical discussion was itself written in the medium of Castilian. Standard ideology applies differently not only to print versus oral media, but to dominant versus subordinate languages. Because of institutional limitations, the latter are simply not quite as ideologically standard as the former, despite sometimes very rigid beliefs. Catalan is subject to a strong ideology of standardization, as Susan Frekko has shown in her analysis of complaints about "Catalan that hurts the eyes," but standard Catalan orthography still does not have the hegemony among a broad reading public that Castilian has (Frekko 2009a, 2006, 2009b). Because they were educated in Castilian, many Catalan speakers of middle age and above (i.e., the main audience of *La Vanguardia*, in which Serra's critique appeared) have little eye for correctness in Catalan writing. Around the time of Montilla's election, only about 25% of readers in the population over age 14 reported reading books in Catalan, while 72% read in Castilian (FUNDACC 2012). Serra in fact commented within his critique that he had debated which orthographic device to use to represent devoicing, since he doubted that many readers would even recognize the "sonoricide" if he used "ss." Given this, violations of standard orthography in Catalan would not be likely to carry all the negative characterological indexicality of illiteracy discussed by Fenigsen and others. They are less noticeable, and when noticed they may be taken less as a matter of low intelligence and lack of cultivation than of the limited proficiency in written Catalan that many readers share.

Email Parodies

As might be expected, anonymously authored parodies of Montilla's Catalan circulated in email, and I will discuss two of them here. Both involved hyperbolic exaggerations and targeted not only phonetics and phonology, but also lexical, morphological, and syntactic features of Castilian-influenced Catalan. In contrast to Serra's article, these apparently grass-roots lampoons explicitly drew on social stereotypes to associate Montilla's speech with the working-class urban periphery and with Andalusian immigrants. What Serra had enregistered as a socially neutral, bureaucratic Level S Catalan was located in the immigrant urban periphery by these jokes. They are reminiscent of the Ebonics parodies that circulated in the United States in response to the Oakland school board controversy in the 1990s (Ronkin and Karn 1999).

The linguistic features ridiculed in these texts were not remotely factual representations of Montilla's actual speech, but rather were bold caricatures of a macaronic Catalan derived from linguistic strategies to transform Castilian to Catalan. Underlying these parodies is the not entirely misplaced notion that some Castilian speakers don't exactly learn Catalan, but rather they make it up on the fly when it becomes necessary to speak it. What is mocked is not so much a dialect or register, as a set of translinguistic strategies that figure into what Boix-Fuster and Sanz (2008, 103) have called Catalan Interlanguage.

Email Quiz

The first, and milder, example of the email parodies takes the form of a quiz (Fig. 4.5). The task is to "Translate the following words from Catalan to Montillan."[53] An example is given that features yodization: *Ajuntament = Aiuntament* ("town hall"). Here the Catalan voiced palato-alveolar fricative [ʒ] is replaced by a palatal glide [y], making it more similar to the Castilian form of the word, *ayuntamiento*.

The putatively correct answers given in the quiz (Fig. 4.5) are incorrect forms of Catalan. Some of these are simply actual Catalan words pronounced with a feature transferred from Castilian. For example, we see yodization in the pronunciation of the first segment of *Generalitat* as a glide, [y]: *Yeneralitat* (the proper name of the Catalan government). *Yeísmo* is the only unusual feature in the pronunciation of Catalan *ull* "eye" as Montillan *ui*, with no resemblance to Castilian *ojo* [oxo].

The incorrect weak pronoun is another feature of the parodic linguistic profile. *Lu* (from Castilian *lo* with correct Catalan vowel reduction to [u]) replaces the correct Catalan *ho* "it" in five different examples. The *lo* form, pronounced [lu] as it is phonetically spelled in this parody, is actually widespread in colloquial Catalan among L1 as well as L2 speakers.

Other forms parodied result from over-application of the most common rule of thumb to transform a Castilian word into a Catalan one: delete the last segment of a Castilian word. In this parody the strategy was applied to very common words. They resulted in forms even most semi-speakers would recognize as absurd, especially since several of the Montillan forms retain distinctively Castilian

---

53. "Tradueix de català a montillà les paraules següents."

Vols apendre el nou idioma que neix a Catalunya?
T'oferim la possibilitat de fer una primera prova de "Montillà".
Només cal que superis aquest breu test.

Tradueix de català a montillà les paraules següents.
P. ex. Ajuntament = Aiuntament

Ull		
Generalitat		
Pruna		
Figa		
Oli		
Pa amb tomàquet		
Pernil		
Tu ho veus		
T'ho he dit		
Què puc menjar?		
T'ho porto		
Ho has vist?		
T'ho he portat		
Total		o

Si vols veure les respotes correctes només
cal que premis la pestanya de SOLUCIONS.

SOLUCIONS

CATALÀ	MONTILLÀ
Ull	Ui
Generalitat	Yeneralitat
Pruna	Ciruel
Figa	Ic
Oli	Aceit
Pa amb tomàquet	Pam tumaca
Pernil	Jamó
Tu ho veus	Tu lu veus
T'ho he dit	Te lu e dit
Què puc menjar?	Que puc cumè?
T'ho porto	Te lu portu
Ho has vist?	Lu as vis?
T'ho he portat	Te lu e purtat

Perdoneu les molèsties i gràcies per la vostra atenció.

Si sacas de un **0** a un **3** el teu Montillà es desastrós. Que as fet tu tuts lus ains a Catalunya? Tens que cambiar els teus habitus i sulament fe vida a alguna zona de Sabadel.

Si sacas de un **4** a un **6** el teu Montillà es de nivel baix Tens que passar els caps de setmana sulsament a una sona d'oci comercial. Per saber la fluydessa del llenguatge.

Si sacas de un **7** a un **10** el teu Montillà és de nivel mitx- alt. Per se un bon seguidor del Montillà, tindries que cambiar lu nom de la teva pareia. P.ex. Si la teva novia es diu Gisela dili Yennifé io si el teu compañ es diu Joan digali Yónatan.

Si sacas de un **11** a un **12** el teu Montillà és de nivel altissim. Sacat las opos per fer de profesó de Montillá.

No et perdiss el ssegüent fasscicle t'enssenyarem a parlar el Ssaurà.
Al tercer fascicle el català de Xavier Trias.
I al quart, el Cadot-Duvidà

FIGURE 4.5 Quiz circulated anonymously by email, 2007. "Do you want to learn the new language that's been born in Catalonia? Here's a chance to test your 'Montillan.' You just have to pass this short quiz. Translate the following words from Catalan to Montillan. For example, Ajuntament = Aiuntament." Answers to the quiz show hyperbolic phonological and morphological strategies for creating Montillan from Catalan.

diphthongs that do not correspond to Catalan, e.g., *ciruel* from Castilian *ciruela* for Catalan *pruna* "prune", and *aceit* from Castilian *aceite* for Catalan *oli* "oil". Other parodic deletions include *jamó* from Castilian *jamón* "ham" (CT *pernil*), *cumé* from Castilian *comer* "eat" (CT *menjar*), and *ic* from Castilian *higo* "fig" (CT *figa*).

Where Serra used nonstandard orthography only to represent actual phonological interference from Castilian in Catalan, the email quiz also uses gratuitous nonstandard forms, or eye dialect. This is seen in the misspellings that replace orthographic "o" with orthographic "u" to represent what would be perfectly correct reductions of the unstressed vowel /o/ to [u], seen in *tumaca, lu, portu, purtat*.

The quiz's interpretations of the scores, given on its first page, all written throughout in this mock variety, tie them to social spaces and character types.[54] The lowest score for Montillan places the variety in the industrial urban periphery, telling low scorers that to master Montillan they must "go live in a zone of Sabadel."[55] This is a nonstandard rendering of the name of a peripheral city associated with heavy working-class Andalusian immigration to its textile mills in the 1960s and 70s.[56] By spelling Sabadell as "Sabadel," the form itself represents an emblematic bit of Castilian linguistic influence, the "frankly bad relationship with double l's" mentioned earlier, which results in this case in substitution of an alveolar lateral for the palatal lateral sound.

The interpretation of scores of 7–10 points links the variety to the typified character of lower-class Castilian speakers through their given names: "If your girlfriend is named Gisela call her Yennifé and if your boyfriend is named Joan call him Yónatan." The instruction is to replace clearly Catalan names that begin with the challenging voiced fricative with ones that index young lower-class Castilian speakers from the industrial periphery. The spelling represents the yodization of "j," and the name Yennifé is emblematically associated in the media with the stereotype of young women from this social sector.[57] For example, in a self-mocking Catalan hit song of

---

54. An English gloss of the interpretation of scores given in Fig. 4.5, with no attempt to reproduce the mostly nonstandard form: "If you get 0–3 your Montillan is disastrous. What have you been doing all these years in Catalonia? You have to change your habits and only spend your life in some part of Sabadell. If you get 4–6 your Montillan is at a low level. You have to spend weekends only in a commercial leisure area. To learn the fluency of the language. If you get 7–10 your Montillan is mid-high level. To be a good follower of Montillan, you'll have to change your partner's name. E.g., if your girlfriend's name is Gisela call her Yennifé and if your boyfriend's name is Joan call him Yónatan. If you get 11–12 your Montillan is the highest level. Take the qualifying exam to become a teacher of Montillan."

55. "Tens que cambiar els teus habitus i sulament fe vida a alguna zona de Sabadel."

56. It may be that this quiz was authored in Sabadell; I received or heard of it from more than one informant who lived in the city.

57. These names themselves represent the influence of American popular culture on this demographic group.

summer 2011 entitled "Jenifer," a Catalanist male confesses to falling in love with a *choni*—a term for this Castilian-speaking, working-class peripheral female style (also known as *quilla*, which will be discussed in Chapter 7)—named Jenifer. Little more than the name was needed to recognize the social gulf that he had crossed, but the lyrics wryly detail a list of stereotypical cultural specifics of this Romeo and Juliet's "forbidden love."[58] Even former president Jordi Pujol weighed in on the social significance of "Jenifers." In another example, the television political parody *Polònia* (to be discussed in a later section of this chapter) similarly used the name "Yennifé" to index this social type. A skit represented Montilla's wife screaming over flamenco music to "Yennifé" to come to dinner, in a ruse to convince people that they behave like stereotypical (*xarnego*) immigrant Castilian speakers at home.[59]

The emailed joke quiz, then, exemplifies the processes of biographical identification and social characterization that are phases of the ideological institutionalization of a linguistic variety that Asif Agha terms enregisterment. With its spatial and characterological anchors, the quiz resolves the ambiguity of Montilla's social location. This is the pejorative representation of a working-class immigrant, Montilla as *xarnego*. This contrasts with Serra's critique, moving further into the terrain of symbolic violence against nonnative Catalan speakers. Nonetheless, in a sort of postscript the quiz also plays on the social ambiguity of the nonstandard linguistic forms by promising that the next lessons will teach how to speak the languages of three other politicians who do not have Montilla's immigrant origins. These were Joan Saura ("el Ssaurà,", with the double "s" satirizing the icon of his *xava* style); Xavier Trias, whose bourgeois Catalan and devoiced consonants were targeted in critical comments reported above; and Carod-Rovira, whose idiosyncratic difficulties pronouncing "r" were mocked ("Cadot-Duvidà").

An Email Letter from the "Pacident de la Cheneralitat de Catalunia"

A second parodic text that circulated in email depends on many of these same boldly hyperbolic phonological, morphological, and eye-dialect strategies. Its stigmatizing effects are even stronger because it is framed as an official letter from the president, rather than as a list. This textual genre heightens the expectation of standard orthography and the negative effects of its absence. Moreover, both the content and linguistic form of the mock letter go even further to tie Montilla and his speech to working-class Andalusian immigrants. The letter is addressed "*Dere*

---

58. "amor prohibit." Els Catarres, https://www.youtube.com/watch?v=O2gFkpx-vew.

59. Episode 34, broadcast December 22, 2006, viewable at https://www.youtube.com/watch?v=3t0Sn9huwmU.

immigran,"[60] and "Montilla" assures immigrants—"like me"—that they don't really have to learn Catalan. The substance of the text, reproduced here with boldface to highlight the deliberate errors, not only identifies Montilla as an immigrant but also depicts him as politically, culturally, and linguistically anti-Catalan:

> **Querid** immigrán
>
> com a presidén de Cataluña t'adresu aquestas líneas per dunar-ta la benvinguda. Has **llegat** a un país milenariu, amb una cultura y una llengüa própias. Pero no t'**asustis** parqué aixó **mu** pensu carragá **yó** en cuatra dies. Da fet, el país milenariu no **mi**mporta parqué **sá** da mirá endaván. De la cultura, milló ni pa**l·l**á. **Y** la llengüa, ¿**cá té** da **dí**? Da todas formas, com he d'aparentá una mica par guardá las formas, t'ascric aixó par anima**r**ta a **ca** t'integris. Esperu que demostris que no tods **los imigráns** són tan inadaptads com **yó**. **Yá** veus, 40 añs viv**ín** aquí da la pulítica i mira com parlo. És que a mí aixó del catal**áng** sempre me **la traid** fluixa, pr**ó** no'm prucupa. Aquesta regió está plena d'idiotas que van di**én** pels **puestus** que **mi** partid **es** catalanista. **Y** no sé si la **llén su** creu, pr**ó** ells sag**ú** que sí. O no. M**é**sigual. **Y**o cuan sigui presid**én** pudr**é** f**é lu** que vulgui y no estaré lligat de **pens** i **maus** per **nad** ni nadi. Da mum**én**. **Y**ó dirillir**é** la pulítica lingüística. **Y** par que no s'anfadi **mi** sosi Carod **y se** pensi que fach alguna cosa per la llengua **tanviu** un kit **ca mé** truvat pal daspach dal prugrama "**Dale cuerd** al catal**áng**". També **me** ofereixo a fer-te de v**u**luntari lingüístic, a v**é**ure si **c**unsegu**exu cargar**-me l'idioma. **I** ya saps, si alguns **te** diuan **cal** catal**áng** és nesess**á**ri per prusper**á** a Cataluña, ni cas.
>
> José Montilla
> **P**acident de la **C**heneralitat de Catalunia[61]

Some of the nonstandard orthography used in this example represents stigmatized Andalusian vernacular phonology transferred most improbably to Catalan, e.g. substitution of [l] for [r] in *pal·la* for CT *parlar* (to speak). The velarization of final /n/ represented in *cataláng* had already been mediatized to typify Castilian speakers from the working-class periphery of Barcelona, in the television character of a car-pimping, techno-pumping young idiot called El Neng de Castefa "The Kid

---

60. Here I gloss the nonstandard forms with approximations in English.

61. Here I give an English gloss for the entire text, with no effort to reproduce nonstandard equivalents to the nonstandard forms in boldface:

> Dear immigrant, as president of Cataluña ((Spanish form)) I write these lines to welcome you. You've arrived at a millenarian country, with its own language and culture. But don't be afraid, because I plan to get rid of that in no time. Actually, the millenarian country doesn't matter to me because you have to look ahead. About culture, better not to even speak. And the language, what can I say? Anyway, since I have to pretend to maintain the form a little, I'm writing this to you to urge you to integrate. I hope that

from Castefa" who is the male counterpart of the Yennifé/Jenifer type.[62] The real Montilla used neither of these stigmatized linguistic features.

Again in contrast to Serra's critique, which used Catalan orthographic conventions to represent Montilla's Castilian-influenced pronunciation, many of the representational strategies in both of these email texts are based on Castilian orthographic norms. In this one, they include *Cataluña* for *Catalunya*.[63] *Cheneralitat* for *Generalitat* glaringly emphasizes the Castilianizing transfer of affrication and devoicing of the initial consonant by using the Castilian form "Ch" instead of the equivalent Catalan "Tx." *Querid* "dear" strikes the eye as a deformation of Castilian *querido*, not of the Catalan equivalent *estimat*. Eye dialect is used in this text as in the other emailed parody to encode phonologically correct Catalan vowel reductions and consonant cluster simplifications. Here again, this gratuitous nonstandard spelling filters the speech through Castilian orthographic conventions, not Catalan; e.g., "u" to reflect correct Catalan pronunciation where standard written Catalan would show "o"; correct non-pronunciation of final /t/ in *immigran(t) and presidén(t)*.[64] That is, this email parody is represented not through a Catalan orthographic lens, but through a Castilian one.

Presumably this was intended to represent the Castilianizing way that Montilla would write Catalan.[65] But a potentially consequential result is that although it is supposedly bad Catalan that is lampooned, it appears visually as

---

you'll show that not all immigrants are as unadapted as I am. You see me, forty years living from politics here and look how I speak. It's just that for me, this thing of Catalan, I've always been weak, but I don't worry. This region is full of idiots who go around saying that my party is Catalanist. And I don't know if people believe that, but they [themselves] surely do. Or not. I don't care. Me, when I'm president I'll be able to do whatever I want and I won't be tied hand and foot by anything or anybody. For the moment. I'll be in charge of linguistic policy. And so that my associate Carod doesn't get mad and so that he thinks I'm doing something for the language, I'm sending you a kit that I found at the office from the program "Wind up Catalan." And I also offer to be a volunteer linguistic partner for you, to see if I can bring down the language. And as you know, if someone tells you that Catalan is necessary to prosper in Cataluña, don't even pay any attention.

62. "Castefa" itself is a stylized Castilian version of the Catalan toponym of Castelldefels, a town where such working-class youths go to discotheques. The slang name elides a challenging "double l" and is itself a marker of this social type.

63. The Catalan form of toponyms has been established as official in Catalan law. The Castilian spelling is now a marked form in Catalonia even in the Castilian media, and here it helps construct Montilla as anti-Catalanist.

64. Many of the grammatical forms in this fictive letter are markedly correct Catalan, such as regular and irregular subjunctives (*demostris, sigui*) and inchoative verb infixes that differ significantly from Castilian and that media evidence showed the real Montilla had not mastered (*ofereixo, consegueixo*).

65. Some of it may also be unintended. Even Catalans tend to subscribe to the widespread belief that Spanish orthography has a superior one-to-one correspondence of symbol to sound that makes it a true representation of linguistic form, of the way a language really is.

much like bad Castilian. And I have argued earlier that standard written Castilian still saturates public consciousness more than standard Catalan does. When eye dialect frames a Catalan parody with Castilian orthography and sets the implicit visual reference point as Castilian, its force may be all the more violent to many readers' eyes, because it violates both Catalan and Castilian.

Moreover, diacritics are inappropriately strewn or omitted throughout the text (*llengüa, llén, Yó, lingüística, véure, nesessári*), unmotivated lexical errors are made (*pens i maus* for *peus i mans* "hands and feet"), and the spelling of key words is inexplicably unstable (*presidén/pacident, Cataluña/Catalunia*). All in all, the extreme orthographic deviancy of this text depicts Montilla not just as having a poor command of Catalan (and as anti-Catalan), but also as illiterate, with all the conventional ideological implications that brings.[66] This text unquestionably mobilizes linguistic parody to make a derogatory caricature of Montilla, as derogatory as representations of Mario Juruna were. In this case there is none of the characterological ambiguity of Serra's newspaper critique of Level S Catalan; the persona derogated is explicitly an immigrant.

The Television Parody: *Polònia*

On the surface, audiovisual media might be expected to have even stronger, more cutting parodic effects than written forms because of the greater semiotic affordances of the multiple channels involved. However, I discussed the claim earlier that standard language ideology is more vigorously applied to written than oral forms. That in turn means that ideological filters on embodied oral forms may be more forgiving than those on the ideologically depersonalized print medium. In contrast to the derogatory effect of textual parodies, characterizations embodied in human form have the possibility of adding personal dimensions that soften a parody and perhaps even its target (Moritz Schwarcz 2013). I propose this is the case for the best-known parody of Montilla in Catalonia, a televised caricature of the notoriously wooden politician.

This faux Montilla character appeared every week for four years, and continued to appear sporadically after Montilla's presidency, on *Polònia*, an extremely popular program of political satire launched in 2006 on the Catalan public broadcasting television channel, TV3.[67] (The director of the program, Toni Soler, is also a columnist and political commentator whose articles I quote in several chapters.) The show's

---

66. Some readers may have been aware that Montilla does not have a university degree and was for that reason the target of some criticism about his lack of learning and cultivation.

67. The primary television channels in Spain, as in most of Europe, were traditionally state-owned, so TV3 was not exceptional, except for being affiliated with an autonomous community's government rather than the central state.

title is a reference to a traditional denigration aimed at Catalans by other Spaniards during their military service in other parts of Spain. It was said that they sounded like *polacos* "Poles," which provides the motif for many of the show's conceits and graphic design.[68] The program's political sketch humor is of the sort found elsewhere, e.g., on the British "Spitting Image," but it features actors in generally elaborate makeup rather than puppet heads. Among US shows, *Polònia* most resembles a hybrid of the *Daily Show* and *Saturday Night Live*, but the Catalan program's title indicates how ethnolinguistic issues are foregrounded. *Polònia* is often discussed by politicians and the press as having significant and possibly worrisome political impact, paralleling concerns in the United States about the *Daily Show* and the *Colbert Report* (Ferré-Pavia and Gayà-Morlà 2011, Sintes i Olivella 2010).[69]

Unlike the caricatures of other politicians in the show, the physical representation of Montilla was based primarily on the resemblance of the actor who plays him, Sergi Mas, to the politician (Fig 4.6). Where the elaborate makeup for most characters took an hour or more, makeup for Sergi Mas as Montilla reportedly took only fifteen minutes (Ventura and Escribano 2007).

The Montilla character appeared as an utterly nondescript, normal man, unlike all the other characters for whom some distinctive features or physical mannerisms were exaggerated. His colorless normality was in fact the real Montilla's distinctive feature as a politician; during the electoral campaign, Montilla described himself as "a normal person," in contrast to most political leaders (Albiñana 2006). Next to other characters, *Polònia*'s Montilla came across as entirely realistic. The only thing that was exaggerated was his nonnative Catalan. An unrealistically macaronic linguistic caricature combined uncannily with the naturalistic physical portrayal by the actor.

The result, I propose, was that the caricature gave Montilla's linguistic frailty a warmer, more human image than the original himself had. The sympathy generated by this portrayal was not restricted to the imitation, but transferred to the original. Marçal Sintes, a Catalan media observer, noted that viewers themselves say that after having watched *Polònia*, when they see real political figures such as Montilla on the news, they "cannot help but see and hear the corresponding figures from *Polònia* . . . . In the mind of many people, 'Polonized' politics seems to hold more authenticity

---

68. There is no intrinsic reason that a comparison to Poles should be considered derogatory, but it is offered and taken as such in this well-documented usage.

69. *Polònia* debuted in spring 2006 to great success. The character of Montilla first appeared in the third episode (March 2006), at that time as a cabinet minister in the central Spanish government, with little development and a low profile. When Montilla emerged as the head of the Socialist list for the November 2006 Catalan parliamentary elections, the character became a protagonist and began to develop. The first gags focused on his woodenness and lack of charisma, mocking his difficulties in smiling for campaign materials. The linguistic profile became the focus in the run-up to the elections. Although fully developed by the time of his selection as President, it continued to evolve over the years until the Socialists decisively lost the elections of November 2010 and Montilla stepped down.

FIGURE 4.6 José Montilla (right) with the actor who represents him, Sergi Mas (left), on the set of *Polònia*, 2006.
Reproduced by permission of Televisió de Catalunya.

and more intensity than the politics that are seen through conventional information media"[70] (Sintes i Olivella 2010, 51–53). Sintes quoted *Polònia*'s director Toni
Soler as saying "at times parody is so strong that it can eclipse the real person," adding that it was not really desirable for the audience "to think that the president of
Catalonia is Sergi Mas"[71] (ibid., 53), thus suggesting that at some level they do think
just this. This is a concern that Montilla himself echoed recently (Montilla and Jorba
2013, 84). Another television show based a feature story on the premise that the
two figures, president and actor, had merged in the public mind.[72] Reporters showed
photos of the faux Montilla to people in the street to see if they would take him for
the real Montilla. This rarely happened, but there was considerable hesitation and
comment by interviewees on the possibility of mixing up the two. The premise of the
segment itself showed how much there was a public sense that the two figures were

---

70. "no poden evitar *veure* i *sentir* els personatges corresponents del Polònia"; "En l'imaginari
de moltes persones, la política polonitzada sembla que agafa més autenticitat i més intensitat
que no la política que es manifesta a través dels espais informatius convencionals."

71. "'A vegades la paròdia realment és tan forta que pot eclipsar el personatge real'"; "'no és
desitjable' que l'audiència 'es pensi que el president de Catalunya és Sergi Mas.'"

72. TVist, March 3, 2008.

merged in the audience's mind. And indeed, in at least one reported case a media outlet mistakenly reproduced the photo of a *Polònia* actor in place of the political figure he parodied (Ferré-Pavia and Gayà-Morlà 2011, 48).

The particular effects communicated from an imitation to the original depend on the particular representational techniques used. *Polònia*'s linguistic parody of Montilla was based in some—but significantly, not all—of the same hyperbolic techniques as the email texts discussed above. Like those texts, it relied heavily on absurd overextension of morphophonemic formulae for transforming cognate words from Castilian to Catalan. Hyper-application of the rule of thumb that deletes final segments of Castilian to produce Catalan generated absurd forms repeatedly used by the Montilla character, such as *bona notx* (from CS *buenas noches* "good evening") in place of Catalan *bona nit*; *de acuerd* (for CT *d'acord*, from CS *de acuerdo* "ok") and *des de lueg* (from CS *desde luego* "obviously"; there is no Catalan cognate). The first form was particularly ludicrous because it butchered a salutation heard everywhere literally every day, even by and from nonspeakers of Catalan. The last two were ridiculous because, as in the email text examined earlier, they preserved a salient diphthong from Castilian that does not occur in Catalan, even while Catalanizing other parts of the lexical items.[73] Another example of this deletion strategy, *xist* from CS *chiste* "joke", for which Catalan has no cognate, became one of the faux Montilla's best-known taglines, *era un xist* "It was a joke", as we will see below. In a related strategy, the faux Montilla Catalanized words by simply inserting [u] where unstressed [o] is found in Castilian or adding it to the end of words, which the real Montilla infamously did when he substituted *"repitu"* for Catalan *repeteixo* "I repeat" (Serra 2006). Examples of this strategy of mock Montillan abound, but particularly ridiculous and memorable ones on *Polònia* were *catalanus* for *catalans* and Montilla's song, *Els meus amigus* "My Friends" (CT *Els meus amics*).[74]

Apart from these iconic morphophonemic translation strategies shared between print and television media, in *Polònia* there was little other reliance on phonemic or phonetic transfer to sketch the character. Two key function words were regularly pronounced with the full vowels of the Castilianized form instead of the reduced vowels of Catalan (*de, que*), and the Montilla character was generally *yeista* and often devoiced [z], but there is evidence in other broadcast material that these were the actor's own linguistic traits (as he himself suggested) and not a deliberate caricature of Montilla. Several of the salient Castilianized traits of Montilla's actual speech that were singled out for criticism by Màrius Serra and in the textual parodies were underplayed or even rehabilitated in the television persona. These included yodization of [j] (*aiuts* for *ajuts*), failure to reduce unstressed vowels, and failure to make liaisons between articles and nouns; even the devoicing of [z] was never hyperbolic.

---

73. I must acknowledge that the borrowed discourse marker *buenu* does exactly this, and it occurs frequently in L1 as well as L2 colloquial speech.

74. Viewable at https://www.youtube.com/watch?v=4Ky0RbqNM0M.

For example, in a mock inaugural greeting to citizens (a parallel to the email letter to immigrants), *Polònia*'s Montilla, unlike the real Montilla, pronounced the [n] in *govern* and the "g" (as [dʒ]) of *nogensmenys*. He neutralized a number of the unstressed vowels in positions that the real Montilla does not, and he even appropriately voice a word-final /s/ in liaison with the following segment. That is, the television satire observed the rules of linguistic fair play advocated in Parliament by the philologist and vice president Carod-Rovira, in contrast to other critiques and parodies we have seen that happily targeted the second-language speaker's phonetic abilities. In his classic work on black and white talk among British youth, Roger Hewitt warned that pronunciation is the most socially dangerous and the most likely form of imitation to be perceived as unacceptably derogatory (Hewitt 1986). We might say that because it is the most bodily of the linguistic subsystems, phonetics strikes closest at the speaker's self. As a Catalan sociolinguistic commentator quoted earlier observed, phonetics unites us most viscerally to a language (Pla Nualart 2011b). *Polònia* and Sergi Mas's choice to downplay phonetic mimicry, whether deliberately made or not, mitigated the derogatory effect of the parody of Montilla.

The *Polònia* parody played with the intertextual gap between standard Catalan and Montilla's Catalan, sometimes widening it, as with lexicon, morphology, and morphophonemics, and sometimes narrowing it, as with phonetics and aspects of phonology. This play with form made the parody richer and complicated and decentered its social meaning.

The richness of this play in contrast to the blunt heavy-handedness of the emailed digital parodies is in keeping with a lamination of narrative frames that is one of the program *Polònia*'s trademarks. The director Toni Soler regularly punctuates skits featuring the faux politicians by stepping into the scene and declaring, "*Talleu, és bona!*" "Cut! It's a wrap!,"[75] at which point the characters—still in character—step off the "set" (onto a larger set) and pursue the director with complaints about their roles and lines, further layering the levels of representation. In these liminal moments, the director and other characters often gave the faux Montilla critiques of his Catalan. And in these interstices, the real politicians who are being mocked, including Montilla himself, also sometimes make appearances. Thus there is a complex self-reflexive interplay of the representers, represented, and representations in this televised parody that is not found in the print and digital media.[76]

Instead of the phonetic features that were the focus of the newspaper critique and that figured strongly in the email texts, morphosyntactic and lexical elements were key to the *Polònia* parody of Montilla's Catalan. In what follows I will focus on two specific strategies.

---

75. Literally, "Cut, it's good!"

76. Such self-reflexive Catalan metacommentary will be seen again in another venue in Chapter 6, in the speech of the author Quim Monzó at the Frankfurt Book Fair in 2007.

The first recurring hyperbolic strategy of interest is the televised Montilla's inability to correctly produce the weak pronouns. As I discussed earlier, these are often treated in serious as well as humorous commentary as the essence of the Catalan language. Week after week, *Polònia*'s Montilla was continually shown struggling to produce the pronouns, in long nonsensical strings. My informant Josep's view of weak pronouns as impossible for a nonnative speaker to acquire, quoted earlier in this chapter, is not so far from the perspective offered in one *Polònia* skit, in which Montilla gave a rather literal rendering of the idea that language is inscribed in the bodily habitus (Bourdieu 1991). In this episode, while speaking to his vice president Carod, the Montilla character compared the weak pronouns to circumcision:

Ex. 4.4 Montilla speaks Catalan in private[77]

CAROD: Well, Pepe, remember what we said, eh? You have to work harder on your Catalan.
MONTILLA: Carod, buddy, I do work hard. It's just that I have a problem with the weak pronouns, you know? It's like circumcision. If it's not done to you when you're a child, then when you're older -' ((grimaces, shakes head)).

In another sketch entirely structured around this linguistic emblem, the faux Montilla appeared before the Parliament to present a proposal to abolish the weak pronouns (reminiscent, perhaps, of the joke about Bush cancelling the agreement between subject and verb). He argued that it was necessary in order to make Catalan a more efficient language suited to getting work done (recall the director Soler's print commentary, quoted at the end of Chapter 3, on the corporate managerial emphasis of the new government). Montilla's complaint about the inefficiency of the weak pronouns was illustrated in several wildly exaggerated strings of nonsense syllables and non-linguistic sounds, punctuated by a hyperactive laugh track that insured that the audience would find these sequences hilarious.

Ex. 4.5 Montilla abolishes the weak pronouns[78]

Bones <u>tards.</u>	Good <u>aftnu.</u>
((laugh track))	((laugh track))
La m<u>o</u>ció que presentaré avui al	The motion I'll present today to the
<u>pl</u>enu és una me<u>s</u>ura qu<u>e</u> Catalunya	<u>Congressu</u> is a measure that Catalonia
necessita com <u>l'aigua de maig.</u>	needs like <u>the spring rain.</u>

---

77. *Polònia*, Episode 34, December 22, 2006. Skit can be found at https://www.youtube.com/watch?v=3t0Sn9huwmU.

CAROD: Bé, Pepe, recorda't del que hem parlat, eh? T'has d'esforçar més amb el català.
MONTILLA: *Amigo*, Carod, si <u>yo</u> m'esforço. Però <u>yo</u> tinc el problema dels pronoms febles, eh? Que és això com la *circumcisión*. Si no te la fan de petit, de gran <u>ya</u> ((grimaces, shakes head)).

78. *Polònia*, Episode 35, January 11, 2007; DVD 9.3. Since linguistic form is the point of this extended example, I attempt in the transcription and gloss to indicate nonstandard

Es tracta de la derogació ad eternum dels pronoms febles.
((laugh track))
De manera que un President de la Generalitat
Que li digui a la seva secretària que el dia de ahir
Va demanar un informe

It is about the derogation ad eternum of the weak pronouns.
((laugh track))
So that a President of the Generalitat
Who tells his secretary that yesterday he asked for a report

No es vegi obligat a fer-se la pixa un lio
Amb elocucions del tipu: "Vaig demanar-li-lo-la?"
((laugh track))
O per exemple: "Vaig demanar-li-s'ho-lo-ho? Hi?"
((loud laugh track))

Doesn't find himself obligated to tie his prick in a knot
with locutions like "Did I ask him that it?"
((laugh track))
Or for example: "Did I ask him his that it that? There?"
((loud laugh track))

Comença la votació. Vots a favor?
((camera switch to stock footage of stone-faced members of real Parliament, none voting in favor. Laugh track.))
Bé, ja veig que no els s'hi-ho-um-als-la-s-f-th-rur-tehk-l'he-ho convençut.

Voting begins. Votes in favor?
((camera switch to stock footage of stone-faced members of real Parliament, none voting in favor. Laugh track.))
Ok, I see that I haven't you-them-it-that-um-them-her-s-f-th-rur-tchk-it-I-it convinced. ((laugh track overlaps)).

Bé, era el meu deure intentar-lo-sh'ho-lo-qu-ho-l'hi-li.
((loud laugh track))

Well, it was my duty to try that sh-there-that-it-what-it-there-him.
((loud laugh track))

Veuen com s'han de: abolir?
Moltes gràcies! ((laugh track throughout))

See how they have to: be abolished?
Thank you very much! ((laugh track throughout))

---

and nonsensical forms in the Catalan. Underlining in the original indicates notable phonological, lexical, and idiomatic transfers from Castilian, as well as hyperbolic syntactic errors in the faux Montilla's Catalan. Underlining and solecisms in the English gloss approximate the most glaring solecisms in the Catalan. Double parentheses (()) enclose contextualizing comments I have added. Skit may be viewed at https://www.youtube.com/watch?v=VnGgjife1N8.

It is entirely obvious that this skit made fun of Montilla, but I believe that it was also a joke about the most infamous complexity of standard Catalan, lampooning it as an overly fussy, absurdly difficult language that gets in the way of modern management.[79] Despite the faux Montilla's conviction that the weak pronouns are less painful if acquired early, L1 Catalan speakers as well as L2 learners feel hectored about them by teachers and purists, and discrepancies between colloquial habits and formal conventions are widespread (Wheeler et al. 1999, 167). The different linguistic constituencies in Catalonia get the weak pronouns wrong in different ways, but most ordinary speakers do get them wrong, one way or another, at one time or another. This sketch fits a media tradition of Catalans laughing at Catalan, in which the weak pronouns are a recurring trope for an arcane preciosity and hyperformality of the language and its more punctilious speakers. For example, Susan Frekko has aptly analyzed a particularly hilarious parody of *CSI* in which a mysterious series of deaths has occurred among Catalan teachers. Careful detection reveals that attempts to use the weak pronouns correctly caused all the victims' heads to explode (Frekko 2009a). Such jokes bring a laugh not just from or about struggling L2 speakers, but from almost anyone who has attended school in Catalonia since autonomy and the restoration of Catalan teaching. (Further examples of such jokes are explored in Woolard, Ribot Bencomo, and Soler Carbonell 2014.)

A second recurring motif of *Polònia*'s parodic Montilla was the inappropriate use of lexical items that seem to a Castilian ear uniquely Catalan, and particularly of formal, quaint, and archaic terms. In the faux Montilla's inaugural greeting at the beginning of his presidency, accompanied by another insistent laugh track, he assured the citizenry:

Ex. 4.6 Montilla's inaugural greeting

Volem un govern que actuï	We want a government that acts
nogensmenys, ple de àdhuc,	nonetheless, full of even, with firm
amb fermes cabòries i (..) andròmines!	preoccupations and (..) useless furniture![80]

Politicians are often lampooned for meaningless rhetoric, but there is play with the non-referential use of language at more than one level here.[81] "Montilla" nonsensically uses especially salient forms of a linguistic medium that we have seen Spanish elites characterize as having no referential value. This is in part a

---

79. Cf. Kelly-Homes and Atkinson's comment on representations of Irish's lack of utility in the modern world (Kelly-Holmes and Atkinson 2007).

80. *Polònia* season 1, DVD 7 Chapter 4.

81. See Dana Carvey's classic *Saturday Night Live* sendup of the handwaving presidential candidate George H.W. Bush in debate: "Stay the course . . . on track . . . a thousand points of light . . . stay the course."

satirical enactment of the idea we have seen in Part I, that Catalan is useful only to signal an identity, not to "communicate."

The brief skit is full of odd linguistic forms and usages. *Nogensmenys* "nonetheless" and *àdhuc* "even" are archaic lexemes that few first-language Catalan speakers use even in writing today. Adult learners are sometimes taught them and then (if they're lucky) warned not to use them, to avoid sounding "letter-wounded" (*lletraferit*) or "letter-burned" (*lletracremat*) (that is, speaking like a book, in just the way that Angel López García bemoaned in Chapter 3). "It's not an accident" that *Polònia's* ridiculous caricature of Montilla used expressions like *nogensmenys*, wrote one Catalan language teacher, warning that with their high formality, these words are hard to handle and need special care (Serra i Casals 2010). *Cabòries* "preoccupations, worries" has variably quaint resonance and regionalized formality in Catalan ears.[82] *Andròmines* "useless furniture" is in more general Catalan use but, in addition to being entirely silly in this context, shares with the other words the trait of having no cognate Castilian equivalent.[83] They seem to sound "very Catalan," as well as nonsensical.

Cabòries and *àdhuc* mispronounced with stress shifted to the second syllable as *adhúc* were both used inappropriately as exclamations, and these became taglines of the Montilla character on *Polònia*. This repurposing as exclamations further commented playfully on the stereotyped idea that Catalan isn't really used for its referential value.[84] I know of no source in the real Montilla's actual speech for any of these misused lexical forms; they were simply projected onto the persona. One part of the joke, mentioned explicitly in a book based on the program, was that *Polònia's* Montilla brandishes letter-burnt vocabulary in response to accusations of being uncultured and uneducated, and to unflattering comparisons to the family literary heritage of his immediate predecessor (to be discussed in Chapter 6) (Ventura and Escribano 2007). The archaic and misused vocabulary suggested that Montilla learned Catalan from a dictionary rather than from actual use—"communication"—with interlocutors in everyday life. The running joke displayed ambivalence toward studied learning in contrast to natural acquisition of Catalan, again as López García warned. Emphasizing the inauthenticity of efforts to sound

---

82. Josep Soler-Carbonell gathered impressions from a small set of contacts. Evaluations ranged from "not archaic but I would never say it" and "not in my village" to "only in the village, and formal" and "totally antiquated, nobody would use it if it weren't for *Polònia*!" My thanks to Pep and those who contributed comments.

83. For anecdotal evidence that the word may sound antiquated to Spanish speakers, see the "adopt an endangered word" entry on the Word Reservation website http://www.reservade-palabras.org/apadrina-listar.php?palabra=andr%F3mina.

84. Possibly the faux Montilla is meant to imagine that *cabòries* is a Catalan version of a Castilian exclamation such as *caramba* or *caray*. It was such a popular tagline that it was used as the title for a book of *Polònia's* sketches in 2008.

authentically Catalan, it played with the discomfort we have seen in Chapter 3 about secondarily acquired Catalan.[85]

As with the weak pronouns, I suggest that in *Polònia*'s play with vocabulary it was not only the speaker but also the Catalan language itself that became the object of scrutiny and evaluation. In these jokes about the grammar and the lexicon, questions about the persnicketiness and the referential value of Catalan were held up for consideration as well as ridicule. The humorous connotations of the archaic, quaint, and nonsensical accrue to the language as well as to Montilla, "sticking" to Catalan even if it is not the direct target of *Polònia*'s gags (Chun 2004, Jaffe 2000). The famed stiffness of the politician Montilla is played off the increasingly mythic stiff formality of Catalan, about which we will hear from young people in Part III of this book. Catalan itself is more than faintly ridiculous here.

The difficulty and hyper-Catalanism of the learned words that *Polònia*'s Montilla used contrasted to the repeated complaints that the real Montilla couldn't be bothered to learn Catalan in his thirty years in local politics. The strained vocabulary of the parody depicted a Montilla who was in certain respects "really trying," and this came to be a more general trait of the caricature as it developed over the years of Montilla's presidency. As Michael Silverstein wrote of the real-life malapropisms of George W. Bush, the embodied message that a leader is "really trying" can be more important to a late modern public than the punctilious language-focused criticisms of "conceptualizing elites" (Silverstein 2003, 71).

In contrast to the printed criticisms and digital text parodies, the televised caricature displayed nuance and ambivalence about the Catalan language as well as about the misrendering of it. The Montilla character grew across the seasons, and in the end the linguistic foibles created an affable image. (We do well to recall here, as media commentators have, that the television channel on which the program appears is under the aegis of the Catalan government.) Montilla as a candidate was initially lampooned as entirely wooden; for example, in one skit, his jaw cracked when he tried to smile. Then as president, he was first represented as rather childlike, in large part through his linguistic confusions. But the character quickly developed and the linguistic errors became less nonsensical, with many of the jokes highlighting the real Montilla's reputation as hardworking and self-effacing.[86] Again as Silverstein (2003, 70) wrote of the real Dubya, the "whole bodily posture

---

85. On hearing an earlier version of this analysis I gave at a conference, a specialist in the teaching of Catalan as a second language confirmed that jokes are often made about students in adult Catalan classes, representing them not only as trying to use "*àdhuc*," but also mispronouncing it by shifting the stress to the second syllable, as *Polònia*'s Montilla does.

86. This contrasted notably with the characterization of his chief opponent (and successor as President of the Generalitat) Artur Mas as insincere, vain, and narcissistic. However, anecdotal reports suggest that since Mas became president, the caricature of him has also become more positive.

of earnestness has got to make our hearts go out to the guy," and earnestness was a key feature of *Polònia's* Montilla, despite his absurdly terrible Catalan.

Overall the humorous effect was relatively affectionate and humanizing for the president who in real life was described as having a "cold and distant image"[87] (Lasalas 2006), as a "cold and hard strategist"[88] (Ellakuría 2006), and as "not amusing, witty, or even likeable"[89] (Bueno 2006). To celebrate the program's fifth anniversary in 2011, the newspaper *El País* asked those caricatured to comment on the show. Several observed that the program's humor worked to "humanize"[90] politicians. Even more to my point, two respondents singled out the caricature of Montilla as a favorite, "a kind portrait"[91] that "provokes tenderness"[92] (*El País* 2011). A survey and focus group study of general viewers found agreement that the humor of the show humanized politicians, and nearly unanimous opinion that *Polònia* presented Montilla in particular more favorably than others (Ferré-Pavia and Gayà-Morlà 2011, 54). The physical affordances of embodied, multimodal communication as opposed to the print medium, as well as the specific parodic strategies exploited, allowed this television send-up to warm and humanize the extremely contained personality of the real politician Montilla.

Two skits in particular support my claim that the overall tone and effect of the *Polònia* linguistic parody was positive and affectionate toward Montilla. In each, there was deliberate play with laminations of the Montilla persona and the actor who portrayed him—in one case Sergi Mas, but in the other, the real Montilla.

In the first, during his ultimately unsuccessful campaign for re-election in November 2010, Montilla himself turned up, and not just as a bystander between skits. With remarkable gusto, he played Montilla the character within an extended skit. The real Montilla delivered with a gleeful wink one of the exaggerated forms of Castilian transfer mentioned above, which had become a tagline for the parodic character: "*era un xist*" "it was a joke" based on the Castilian word *chiste*, for which there is no Catalan cognate. This triple lamination, of the real Montilla as the TV Montilla parodying the real Montilla, earned the president positive reviews for his performance; "An artist is born"[93] said one (*El Periódico* 2010).[94]

---

87. "imatge més aviat freda i distant."

88. "un duro y frío estratega."

89. "no es gracioso, ni ocurrente, ni siquiera simpático."

90. "humaniza."

91. "retrato amable."

92. "provoca ternura."

93. "ha nascut un artista."

94. Nonetheless, Montilla's party went down in one of its worst defeats. Good humor, comedic warmth, and the power of the mass media only go so far, as American politicians who have gamely appeared on shows such as *Saturday Night Live* have also found.

The second skit that supports the positive, warm effect that I am claiming for the Montilla parody is the farewell speech that the actor Sergi Mas gave to the president—and thus to the character he played—when his term ended in late 2010. The skit began with Sergi Mas in character as Montilla, but playing on the fact that Mas was also the surname of the incoming president Artur Mas, the actor continued to speak while delaminating character and self, stripping off his jacket, rolling up his sleeves, and lowering his voice. Once the transition was complete and he was in character as "himself," the actor addressed President Montilla directly (using the formal second person form) and asserted that Montilla's way of speaking was in part his own. Like Montilla, Sergi Mas's first language was Castilian, although he spoke fluent, nearly native Catalan where Montilla did not. Mas's avowal of linguistic and personal identification with Montilla in this sketch revealed the political intimacy that laughter and parody can express (Klumbyte 2011). The sympathy resonates throughout the monologue, as can be seen here:

Ex. 4.7 Farewell to Montilla[95]

De fet, avui ja no hauria de fer jo el monòleg.	Actually, I shouldn't be doing the monologue today.
L'hauria de fer en Mas.	Mas should do it.
Per tant, que ho faci el Mas.	So let Mas do it.
Em refereixo, evidentment, al Sergi Mas.	I mean, of course, Sergi Mas.
I aquest sóc jo, President, sóc jo.	And that's me, President, that's me.
Ja ho veu, que jo estic igual que vostè.	As you see, I'm in the same situation as you.
Bueno, igual, igual.	Well, not exactly the same. Governing is
Governar no és fàcil, suposo que no és fàcil.	not easy, I guess it's not easy.
Imitar-lo a vostè tampoc.	Nor is it easy to imitate you.
Per tant, per tant, es podria dir que aquests quatre anys ens ha tocat patir als dos junts.	So, so one could say that for the past four years, the two of us have had to suffer together.
A mi, a mi no em toca dir si vostè ha estat un bon president o no, no sóc ningú.	It's not my job to say whether you have been a good president or not, I'm no one.
Però sí que puc constatar que durant aquests quatre anys, en aquest programa	But what I can state is that in the last four years, in this show

---

95. *Polònia*, December 17, 2010. Video viewable at https://www.youtube.com/watch?v=BCJ3iY6Pjw4.

l'hem parodiat, l'hem ridiculitzat
ens hem rigut de la seva forma
de parlar
-que és una mica la meva-
hem estat <u>punyeteros</u>. I ho hem fet
des de la televisió pública i amb
total llibertat.
En fi, molta sort i gràcies pel seu
<u>fair play</u>.
Ara ens arriba el moment de
deixar-ho.
Vostè què farà?
Perquè jo, jo jo no sé, jo encara no
sé què faré, li dic *en serio.*
Si s'*entera* d'*algo*, avisi'm, *vale*?
O igual ens anem veient per
aquí,sobretot si vostè la lia
una mica.
Que no té molta pinta de liar-la,
també sigui dit.
I també crec que no té perquè
abandonar vostè la política, no sé.
Igual Zapatero li dóna un càrrec.

Amb la bona relació que tenen.

<u>Xist</u>, era un <u>xist</u>, d'aquell és <u>xist</u>!
Bé, Catalans, catalanes
President Montilla
Visca Catalunya! Visc, a
Catalunya!
I fins aviat!

We have parodied you, we have
ridiculed you
we've made fun of your way of talking
-which is a little bit mine-
we've been <u>sons of bitches</u>. And we've
done that on public television and with
complete freedom.
So, best of luck and thanks for your
<u>fair play</u>.
Now the moment has come to end this.
What will you do?
 Because me, I I don't know, I don't
know what I'll do yet. I'm *serious.*

If you *hear* of *anything*, let me know, *OK*?
Or maybe we'll see each other around
here, especially if you screw up a bit.

But let me say, you don't look like you're
going to screw anything up.
And I also think that you don't have any
reason to abandon politics, I don't know.
Maybe Zapatero will offer you a
position.
Given the good relationship that you
two have.
<u>Joke</u>, that was a <u>joke</u>, like, "that's a <u>joke</u>"!
So, Catalans (m.), Catalans (f.),
President Montilla,
Long live Catalonia! I live in Catalonia!

And see you soon!

The actor's apparent emotion (whether for himself, the character, the politician, or all three) was communicated not only in his words but also in the catch in his voice and the gleam of tears in his eyes as he said goodbye to the president at the very end of this segment. Comments on the website where this clip was posted show that some of the audience shared this fond sentiment and attached it to the merged character of José Montilla, "José Montilla," and Sergi Mas.

Conclusion

This chapter has examined the linguistic dimensions of the presidency of an immigrant, nonnative speaker of Catalan. José Montilla's ambiguous status as a member of the Spanish political elite and also an immigrant to Catalonia of working-class Andalusian origins gave rise to considerable ambivalence about his nonnative Catalan and its significance for the viability of Catalan as an expanding public language available to all.

In analyzing examples of the several kinds of media commentary and mediatized humor that expressed censure, ambivalence, and some grudging affection for Montilla's Catalan, I have argued that not all political and linguistic parodies are equal as forms of symbolic violence against speakers. When it comes to interpreting the specific social and political nuances of linguistic parody, the technological medium and the status of the linguistic medium, as well as the specific details of the strategies and targets of representation, are all relevant.

Standard language ideologies surrounding print text can allow it to be an even more brutal parodic weapon than multimodal technologies precisely because of, rather than in spite of, the constrained and regimented form that print takes. In turn, embodied performances can add human dimensions that cut against the grain of a linguistic parody. Moreover, parodies of public figures arguably have different force when the targeted linguistic medium is not an anonymous dominant language but rather a language that is marked in the public sphere because of a history of minoritization. A hegemonic, anonymous language, even when a vehicle of parody, is itself transparent, taken as a direct window on thought. Linguistic quirks in such a context are understood to display qualities of mind, not the peculiarities of the language itself.[96] In contrast, even the most institutionally well-established minority language, which Catalan is, does not easily become referentially transparent, as we have seen in Chapter 3.

In such circumstances, a historically subordinated language easily becomes what Bakhtin called an objectified word: not a tool of direct referential communication, but rather its own opaque representational object and a target of scrutiny and evaluation (Fenigsen 1999, 79, Johnson and Ensslin 2007, Jaffe 2007a). The medium is the message. This is another way to phrase what Ángel López García meant when he called minoritized languages such as Catalan "obscene," or too obvious (see Chapter 3). Because of this objectification of the medium, mockery of incompetent speakers of such a language can easily meld with mockery of the language itself. There is always already a fundamental doubleness in the parodic

---

96. For example, Americans never let Vice President Dan Quayle live down the evidence that he didn't know elementary-school spelling, but rarely paused to ask why *is* it "potato" but "potatoes"?

and critical commentary carried out through play with such a language. It has the potential to be at once a comment on the character and on the language itself.

The very existence of a President José Montilla placed the questions of Catalan linguistic authority and authenticity, as well as of broader access to the Catalan-speaking public and political sphere, in a new light—some said dimmer, some said brighter, as we have seen in this chapter. Criticisms and parodies of Montilla's Castilian-soaked Catalan revealed continuing struggles over the status of Catalan relative to Castilian as well as the continuing power of the ideology of authenticity in establishing ownership rights in the language. Nonetheless, there *was* a President Montilla, a nonnative, non-fluent Catalan speaker with full exercise of powers in the Catalan political sphere (or as full as the leader of such a complex coalition could hope). Differing views on Montilla's control of phonetics and even his choice of the linguistic form of his personal name revealed different interpretations of the social significance of language and linguistic hybridity. They also showed ongoing conflicts over the weakening ideological grounding of linguistic authority in authenticity and its extension to new speakers in 21st century Catalonia.

5 LINGUISTIC COSMOPOLITANISM IN THE CELEBRATION OF LOCALITY

In September 2006, just as I returned to Barcelona for fieldwork, a public dispute broke out over language choice. It concerned the city's festival of la Mercè, the annual municipal celebration or *festa major* to be held later that month. [1] Controversy surrounded the speaker who had been invited by the mayor to give the keynote address opening the festival, and it focused on the language she would use, Castilian.

All towns and cities in Catalonia as elsewhere in Spain have a traditional public celebration on their annual patron saint's day (*festa major/fiesta mayor*). These have grown markedly in the post-Franco period, and Barcelona's has expanded vertiginously since it was essentially reinvented in the late 1970s (Richards 2007). Already dismissed by some of my informants in 1979 as "bread and circuses" offered by the city government to distract citizens from public problems, la Mercè has taken on an increasingly spectacular character (in both senses) across the decades. In addition to traditional popular cultural forms, it features commercial popular musical performances for spectators, with growing appeal to tourists as well as local residents (Abril 2006). In 2006, the festivities for la Mercè included 800 events and performances spread over nine days, many of them sponsored by major commercial enterprises and featuring Spanish and international musical acts (Colás 2006). Whether by the turn of the millennium the festival of la Mercè was to be viewed as a local and participatory popular event or a more tourist-oriented commercial spectacle is a subject of debate. It is a recognized condition of late modernity in Barcelona as elsewhere that the local and the global intertwine in the "glocal" (Bastardas i Boada 2007). At least one study has shown that many of those who attend events around la Mercè in Barcelona see the two orientations as coexisting in the celebration (Richards 2004). But the

---

1. Catalan distinguishes between *festa*, a traditional celebration, and *festival*, a modern commercial event. I use the English term "festival" for both.

controversy around la Mercè in 2006 set the local at loggerheads with the global. The ideologies of linguistic authenticity and anonymity underpinned this conflict, with the former weakening in the face of challenges from the latter, in the guise of the cosmopolitan.

The celebration of la Mercè always officially opens with a keynote speech known as the *pregó*, given by an invited speaker—*pregoner/-a*—who usually has some renown in the arts or sciences and some recognizable connection to Barcelona. In early September 2006, it was announced that the speaker that year would be Elvira Lindo, an author based in Madrid and best known for a popular children's book series in Castilian, *Manolito gafotas*. It was not incidental to the invitation (and perhaps not to the uproar that followed either, though this remained unacknowledged) that Lindo's husband was Antonio Muñoz Molina, the recent director of the New York branch of the Instituto Cervantes, the institute created in 1991 by the Spanish government to promote the Castilian/Spanish language globally. (Muñoz's own praise of the borderless anonymity of Spanish was discussed in Chapter 3.) The outgoing Socialist mayor of Barcelona, Joan Clos, had invited Lindo to speak at the Mercè festival, reportedly after finding himself charmed by her at a New York event connected with the Instituto Cervantes (Navarro 2006). Thus, the global and cosmopolitan character of the Castilian language was presupposed by the occasion of the invitation itself. The mayor failed to discuss his choice with his partners from more Catalanist parties in the city's fragile coalition government before it was announced, leading to a public contretemps.[2]

Lindo had no recognized public connection to Barcelona and no ability or inclination to speak in Catalan. Moreover, she had published opinion pieces in the Spanish newspaper of record, *El País* (known for its own liberal jacobinism), that were critical of nationalism, which she implicitly attributed only to the peripheral communities of Spain (Lindo 2005). "We would like to be able to live in a world where the Andalusians are a little less Andalusian, the Basques less Basque, and the Catalans less Catalan,"[3] Lindo had written just a few months earlier (Lindo 2006a). Critics observed that she had not said that in such a world, Spaniards should also be a little less Spanish (Izquierdo 2006, Portabella 2006). Lindo's opinion pieces were symptomatic of the anonymity of Spanish

---

2. Barcelona's government was formed by the same tense coalition of left-of-center parties that governed Catalonia in this period, as discussed in Chapters 3 and 4: The Socialist Party of Catalonia (PSC) in the lead, supported by the left Catalanist party Esquerra Republicana de Catalunya (ERC) and the left-green coalition, Iniciativa per Catalunya Verds-Esquerra Unida i Alternativa (ICV-EUiA).

3. "nos gustaría poder vivir en un mundo en el que los andaluces fueran un poquito menos andaluces, los vascos menos vascos, los catalanes menos catalanes."

nationalism, its banality in Billig's sense as discussed in Chapter 2. It appears that it was so much a part of the environment that it was invisible, or at least literally unremarkable, to Lindo herself.

Protests were raised against Lindo's selection and specifically against her giving the *pregó* in Castilian, which the mayor's office acknowledged she could be expected to do. A call went out online for a demonstration of mourning in protest against Lindo's speech as "an act of genocide against the Catalan language and its people"[4] (madafaka 2006). A more circumspect formal petition supported by some ninety organizations, small and large, also objected to the selection and demanded that the *pregó* be given in Catalan (Cia 2006).

In response, the mayor's office defended Lindo's designation not on grounds of her relationship or relevance to the city—that is, her authenticity—but rather as a way to showcase the city's "cosmopolitanism." This claim was characterized by critics as an "absurd" arrogation of cosmopolitanism to Madrid and Castilian and a gratuitous insult to Barcelona and Catalan (Ros 2006). "Obviously there is at least an equal percentage of Catalan-speaking cosmopolitans as Castilian-speaking cosmopolitans,"[5] said Jordi Portabella, a deputy mayor from Esquerra Republicana de Catalunya (ERC), the independence-oriented Catalanist party in the city's coalition government (Portabella 2006). The claim that Lindo's selection represented cosmopolitanism was nonetheless repeated by the new Catalan Socialist mayor Jordi Hereu in the face of increasing criticism, which he dismissed as unseemly and "alien" to a city like Barcelona that is "open to the world and to the rest of the [Spanish] State"[6] (Castán 2006). Portabella in return announced that he would boycott the event (Ferro 2006).

Elvira Lindo had been put in a difficult situation by an invitation that she did not seek and the controversy it triggered. Those who objected to the invitation were also in a difficult position of either accepting a fait accompli that they found high-handed and insulting or engaging in a game of "get the guest." Despite the uproar, Lindo carried through. She gave her entire speech in Castilian, with the telling exception of the final phrase, which will be discussed below. Hundreds of Catalanist protestors gathered in the Plaça Sant Jaume in front of the City Hall where Lindo spoke, and a number of them opened black umbrellas in mourning as called for on the internet. A column in a mainstream newspaper branded such protestors the "linguistic Taliban"[7] (Gimeno 2006). Organized by the Ciutadans

---

4. "acte de genocidi a la llengua catalana i al seu poble."

5. "és evident que existeix un percentatge, com a mínim igual, de cosmopolites catalanoparlants que de cosmopolites castellanoparlants."

6. "oberta al món i a la resta de l'Estat."

7. "talibanes lingüísticos."

party, Lindo's defenders turned out in the same location in smaller numbers. They carried a banner declaring, "We are all Elvira Lindo," mobilizing the framing slogan that is used internationally to express solidarity with victims of tragedy, terrorism, and major injustices (Sala and Espanyol 2006).[8] Deputy Mayor Portabella boycotted Lindo's speech as promised and was branded "inquisitorial" in a conservative periodical (Marhuenda 2006). A fellow deputy mayor from a progressive party in the uneasy city government coalition bemoaned that the protests made it appear that in Barcelona and Catalonia there is "intolerance toward Castilian and toward other cultures"[9] (Redacción 2006). Those who protested Lindo's speech represented a "closed and intransigent Catalonia,"[10] editorialized the leading center-right newspaper of Barcelona, *La Vanguardia*. In contrast, the editorial praised the festive nature of the week's celebrations as "the best demonstration that the city is open, plural and integrative"[11] (*La Vanguardia* 2006). Online, Castilianist bloggers posted comments denouncing those Catalanists who protested against Lindo as "Khomeini-esque," "xenophobic," "racist" "linguistic police" who hid their "pure fascism" behind the "protection" of the Catalan language[12] (*e-notícies* 2006). Lindo's husband Antonio Muñoz Molina was quoted as saying "What I saw that day in the Plaça Sant Jaume shouting against Elvira Lindo was the black Spain. The intolerant, brutal Spain" (*Avui* 2006b).[13] Masterfully, Muñoz Molina not only identified Catalanists as Spanish (an identity many of them would reject), but also tarred them with the most demonized vision of Spain, legacy of the well-known anti-Spanish "black legend" that long circulated in Europe.

These invocations of genocide, racism, global injustices, fanaticism, fascism, and the black legend of Spanish inquisitorial cruelty may seem hyperbolic even in this age of mediatized moral panics about language that have become familiar internationally, but they have proved to be only a foretaste of the Spanish response to the sovereignty campaign. Although the most vitriolic language (in print as well as online) came from Castilianist defenders of Lindo, meta-commentators

---

8. A photo accompanying the Castilian-medium news report showed a banner with the slogan in Catalan: "Tots som Elvira Lindo."

9. "intolerancia hacia el castellano y hacia otras culturas."

10. "una Catalunya cerrada e intransigente."

11. "la mejor demostración de que la ciudad es abierta, plural e integradora."

12. "jomeiniana," "xenòfoba," "racista," "policia lingüista [sic]," "fascismo puro y duro," "feixisme q s'amaga darrera d l 'protecció' d'l llengua (catalana)."

13. "El que jo vaig veure aquell dia a la plaça de Sant Jaume cridant contra Elvira Lindo era l'Espanya negra. L'Espanya intolerant, brutal." In 2012, both Muñoz Molina and Lindo would sign a petition against Catalan independence.

who positioned themselves as the voice of reason primarily blamed Lindo's Catalan critics for starting the trouble by overreacting to a minor aggravation. The protest by Catalanists was dismissed by well-known public commentators, even some usually known to defend Catalan, as "sad, hackneyed, and trivial"[14] (Serra 2006b), "puerile, tiresome, provincial"[15] (Rahola 2006a), "ridiculous"[16] (de Sagarra 2006a), and "laughable"[17] (Arasa 2006). These critics of the Catalanist critics lamented that the protest against Lindo in itself showed a lack of cosmopolitan savoir faire and "gave ammunition to those who feel cosmopolitan when they brand us as provincials"[18] (Izquierdo 2006). As one online commentator put it in criticizing the Catalanists who objected to Lindo:

> What an example of provincialism. Would these people . . . say the same thing if an American or a Russian or a German writer came to give the opening speech? Is this the cosmopolitan Barcelona? What an embarrassment and what a way to hand arguments to the anti-Catalans.[19] (Manel 2006)

Underpinning the inflamed rhetoric and the rejections of it is a clash not only between partisan politicians gearing up for an election season, but also between the familiar ideologies of linguistic authenticity and anonymity. The next sections will examine the premises and unfolding logic of the debate as it was prosecuted in the print and digital media. This analysis is based on approximately sixty articles about the controversy and many more with some bearing on it.[20] The brief excerpts I quote are taken from across the spectrum of these sources to

---

14. "triste, trillado y, sobre todo, trivial."

15. "pueril, cansina, provinciana."

16. "ridícul."

17. "risible."

18. "da munición a quienes se sienten cosmopolitas tachándonos de provincianos."

19. "quin exemple de provincianisme. Aquests del CAL i el CIEMEN dirien el mateix si vinbgúes [sic] a fer el pregó un escriptor americà, rus, alemany . . .? Aquesta es [sic] la Barcelona cosmopolita? Quina vergonya i quina manera de donar aruments [sic] als anticatalans."

20. The print items were collected during fieldwork in 2006 and augmented by searches in fall 2013 of the nearly exhaustive database of print journalism maintained by the Centre de Documentació of the Generalitat de Catalunya. Search terms used were Elvira Lindo, la Mercè, pregó, and Hereu. This search yielded articles from rightwing Spanish sources and smaller, less frequent Catalan periodicals that I would not otherwise have accessed. To complement these print sources, I did an online search on these same key terms in fall 2013, which netted blog posts and aggregated news sources still available; these included extended threads of comments that are incorporated in this analysis.

illustrate overall trends in this data set. They show a turn away from authenticity as a legitimating frame for linguistic authority, and a struggle to claim other ground for the defense of Catalan.

Authenticity vs. Cosmopolitanism in la Mercè

When Lindo's selection as *pregonera* was announced, the first objections were raised on grounds of authenticity. What was this speaker's relation to Barcelona? How did she or the Castilian language she could be expected to use represent this particular place? These first criticisms presupposed that the status of Catalan as the *llengua pròpia* of Catalonia, its "own language," as discussed in Chapter 3, could be automatically transferred to Barcelona. For example an online comment called for use of "the *llengua pròpia* of the city, the way they do in London, Madrid, Amsterdam, Rome"[21] (ReiDelMam 2006b). As we have seen earlier, Catalan is juridically defined as the *llengua pròpia* of Catalonia by the Catalan Statute of Autonomy. But is it therefore, a fortiori, the *llengua pròpia* of Barcelona, as the de facto capital of Catalonia? Although this comment treated it as unproblematic to transpose this link to the urban entity, public figures were generally more cautious and used careful circumlocutions.

The online accusation quoted above that the selection of a Castilian speaker from Madrid was an act of "genocide against the Catalan language and people" is an extreme example of the essentializing ideology of linguistic authenticity that lay behind the first mobilization against the choice of Lindo as *pregonera*. However, this frame did not sustain the extended debate that ensued. Lindo's proponents in the mayor's office simply did not engage the question of authenticity and did not argue the merits of Catalan vs. Castilian as appropriate to Barcelona. Instead, they quickly raised a defense of "cosmopolitanism." Once raised, it rapidly displaced authenticity as the reference point and set the terms of discussion. Through the month of September and beyond, the controversy of la Mercè whirled around cosmopolitanism.

Where Lindo's defenders simply did not enter the framework of authenticity, Catalanist critics of Lindo's selection did in contrast directly engage the challenge to their cosmopolitanism, and stepped into that framework to construct their arguments within it. For example, the Catalanist comments below were posted on an online article that briefly reported on the proposed speaker and language of the *pregó*. They developed a thread on cosmopolitanism (possibly an organized effort) and turned the complaint back against Castilian and Madrid:

---

21. "la llengua pròpia de la ciutat? Ho fan així a Londres, a Madrid, a Amsterdam, a Roma."

What's this about cosmopolitan? . . . It's cosmopolitan never to give the *pregó* in the language of the city? Is that how they do it in London, Madrid, Amsterdam, Rome, New York, Paris, Stockholm?[22] (ReiDelMam 2006b)

Cosmopolitan means you can speak in any language as long as it's not Catalan? . . . Cosmopolitan=Castilian? Closed=Catalan?[23] (ReiDelMam 2006a)

So, you go preach Catalan cosmopolitanism in Madrid. And then apply the response here.[24] (MSerrallonga 2006)

In Madrid a lot of languages are spoken, why is it that none of these "cosmopolitans" and "citizens of the world" take a single step toward having a *pregó* in any other language?[25] (Sabadellenc 2006)

Catalanist political and public leaders adopted the same focus. Deputy Mayor Jordi Portabella, as well as the ninety organizations that joined together to lodge a formal objection, insisted that their protests arose not in response to Lindo herself nor even to Castilian as the medium of the *pregó*, pointing out that there had been others given in Castilian in recent years without such mobilization.[26] Rather, they asserted that their objection was specifically to the claim that these would enhance the cosmopolitanism of Barcelona (Ros 2006, Castán 2006, Portabella 2006).

Those who criticized the choice of Lindo not only repeatedly raised the questions of what constitutes cosmopolitanism and who can claim it on what basis, but they also offered definitions, redefinitions, and counterarguments about its meaning, as I will illustrate below. Their arguments resonated with larger debates in international academic circles over the nature of cosmopolitanism and proposals for new versions of it. Before examining the controversy over cosmopolitanism in la Mercè in further detail, then, let us briefly consider the wider significance of this fraught concept, and particularly its relations to authenticity and anonymity.

---

22. "però i de cosmopolita? . . . És ser cosmopolita no fer mai el pregó en la llengua pròpia de la ciutat? Ho fan així a Londres, a Madrid, a Amsterdam, a Roma, a Nova York, a París, a Estocolm?"

23. "cosmopolita vol dir que es pot fer en qualsevol llengua sempre que no sigui en català? . . . .cosmopolita = castellà? Tancat = català?"

24. "doncs ves [*sic*] tu a predicar el cosmopolitanisme català a Madrid. I després aplica la resposta aquí."

25. "A Madrid es parlen moltes llengues [*sic*], com és que cap d'aquests 'cosmopòlites' [*sic*] i 'ciutadans del món' fa un pas a favor que el pregó es faci en qualsevol altre llengua?"

26. But see Emili Boix-Fuster's commentary on another such flap in 2002 (Boix-Fuster 2015).

Cosmopolitanism: Theoretical Debates

At the time that this controversy broke out in Barcelona, cosmopolitanism was also a significant subject of politically and morally charged debate among social and cultural theorists internationally. Who and what is cosmopolitan? The European tradition that derived from Greco-Roman Stoicism and developed in the Enlightenment and in the philosophy of Kant provides the deceptively simple first answer that a cosmopolitan is a "citizen of the world" who recognizes bonds to all humanity rather than just a local community. But given the structural changes in economy, social relations, communication, and security wrought by globalization, who is a citizen of the world in the late modern period—and who is not?

The challenges of globalization brought renewed theoretical and policy interest in cosmopolitanism from more than one corner. On the one hand, cosmopolitanism was proposed as a response to seemingly relentless homogenizing forces of globalization and the neoliberal market, a response that would restore weight to "Others" and to difference and variation. On the other hand, a quite different vision of cosmopolitanism was proposed to address the perceived dangers of identitarian and multiculturalist programs that had developed in part in response to transnational migrations. Cosmopolitanism also opposed resurgent nationalisms perceived to be "xenophobic, ethnically exclusionary, anti-democratic, and prone to violence" (Kymlicka 2001, 209).[27]

In the different tellings, cosmopolitanism is placed in contradistinction to communitarianism/nationalism/particularism on the one hand, or to imperialism/universalism/global homogeneity on the other (Beck and Grande 2007, 71). These two poles exert so much force that different accounts of cosmopolitanism pull tendentiously to one side or the other. In the theoretical debates that arose, cosmopolitanism thus came to be variously and confusingly aligned by different proponents or critics with or against Enlightenment universalism, with or against the celebration of cultural difference, with or against cultural hybridity, with or against tolerance, with or against the forces of imperialism and globalization. Such different perspectives led to proposals of more refined categories in order to remedy the perceived deficiencies of cosmopolitanism as an unmarked term. "Rooted cosmopolitanism" (Ackerman 1994, Appiah 1997, 2005), "vernacular cosmopolitanism" (Bhabha 2001, Werbner 2006), and cosmopolitanism

---

27. In addition to the references on late modern cosmopolitanism cited in this very brief summary, a number of other sources are useful and provocative. For a fuller discussion see inter alia Appiah 2007, Benhabib 2006, Breckenridge et al. 2002, Featherstone 1990, Fine 2007, García Canclini 2005, Knowles 2007, Nussbaum and Cohen 1996, Rumford 2007, Urry 2003, Vertovec and Cohen 2002a, Werbner 2008. For discussion of the nature of cosmopolitanism in another peripheralized linguistic setting, see McLaughlin 2013.

"from below" (Beck and Grande 2007) are some of the modifications that have been influential. The unmodified or linguistically unmarked term came more and more to be understood and treated skeptically as universalistic Enlightenment cosmopolitanism.

Some of the theoretical differences involved in these debates stemmed from a variable focus on political philosophy, morality, or cultural practice. Other differences developed when some theorists distinguished the cosmopolitan as a biographical person, modern condition, or banal lived experience from cosmopolitanism as a philosophy, program, or privileged reflexive outlook on such lived experience (Beck and Grande 2007, Hannerz 1990). A third source of theoretical differences, the one that is most important for our discussion of this Catalan case, is the stance taken toward cultural and linguistic difference in practice. Does cosmopolitanism entail rising above cultural difference, or does it mean reveling in such difference and taking on board multiple cultural forms? Do we master human difference by shrugging off cultural variability as unimportant? Or by dabbling in it, collecting and mixing bits and pieces? Or by becoming adept and more fully engaged in multiple cultural and linguistic forms? Beck and Grande argue that the cosmopolitan must be a very specific way of "dealing with otherness in society," in which differences are neither arranged hierarchically nor replaced by common norms, but rather "accepted as such" (Beck and Grande 2007, 71). But it has been hard even for those who might agree on such a dictate to agree what it means to "accept differences as such" in actual cultural and linguistic practice. This dimension of disagreement among avowed advocates of cosmopolitanism became particularly relevant to the dispute over la Mercè, as we will see.

Traditional Enlightenment cosmopolitanism's fundamental stance toward cultural difference has been subjected to two main criticisms in the literature, both focused on its hidden foundations in the easily assumed privilege of dominant societies and elites. First, (Enlightenment) cosmopolitanism is criticized as a mask for the universalizing cultural project of imperialism. Like the allied ideology of anonymity that imagines some cultural practices to be from "nowhere" and therefore universally available, the cosmopolitans who comfortably see themselves as "from everywhere" have been accused of simply hiding and denying their own privileged social and cultural rootedness. Posing as the rational foundation of modernity in opposition to irrational cultural vernaculars, such cosmopolitanism is an extension of the universalizing project (Briggs 2005, 77). In this critique, cosmopolitanism is "simply one more imperialistic particularism dressed up in seductive universal garb" (Gilroy 2004, 4), at best "an invitation to those who are different . . . to become like us" (Lloyd Rudolph quoted in Pollock 2000, 602).

In the second and related criticism of its attitude toward cultural difference, late modern cosmopolitanism has been derided as the self-indulgent and self-congratulatory aesthetic project of elites who can be caricatured as "frequent travelers," a "globetrotting bourgeoisie," and "champagne liberals" (Calhoun 2002, Friedman 2002, Vertovec and Cohen 2002b). In such a jaundiced view, cosmopolitanism reduces to the superficial consumption practices of "liberals on safari" (Appiah 2005, 214) who can rely on privileged economic means to move easily around the globe, "consuming the world" (Friedman 2002, 33) and collecting culture as artifacts to adorn their metropolitan apartments. The cachet endowed by such discretionary mobility is denied to those who travel the world as labor migrants and refugees, or who encounter cultural diversity through incursions of the globalized economy and popular culture into their dominated home territory.

Given such criticisms of unmarked cosmopolitanism as imperialistic and elite consumerism, cosmopolitan defenders of cultural variation proposed the various modified new brands of cosmopolitanism mentioned earlier, the rooted and vernacular cosmopolitanisms from below. For Appiah, a rooted cosmopolitan is "attached to a home of one's own, with its own cultural particularities, but taking pleasure from the presence of other, different places that are home to other, different people" (Appiah 1997, 618). All of these revisions of cosmopolitanism seem intended, as Sheldon Pollock wrote, to refuse the dichotomy imposed between modernizing cosmopolitanism and vernacular traditionalism (Pollock 2000, 624). They propose a "both/and" view of local (or national) and cosmopolitan identity as compatible, in place of the older either/or spirit of Enlightenment cosmopolitanism (Beck and Grande 2007, 70).

In Pollock's words again, the goal of such new conceptualizations of cosmopolitanism is to create an alternative to the "desperate choice . . . between on the one hand, a national vernacularity dressed in the frayed period costume of violent revanchism and bent on preserving difference at all costs and, on the other, a clear-cutting, strip-mining multinational cosmopolitanism that is bent, at all costs, on eliminating it" (Pollock 2000, 593). This is the struggle to find an alternative to the rock of authenticity and the hard place of anonymity, a struggle with which we see Catalanism engaged in debates such as that over the *pregó* of la Mercè. With this in mind, we will now return to Barcelona.

The Cosmopolitanism of Catalonia and Barcelona

There is some irony in references to cosmopolitanism to criticize Catalanism. From its late 19th century renaissance through the early post-Franco period, Catalonia had carried the flag of cosmopolitanism and modernity in contrast to an allegedly provincial Spain. With its economic and social base in industrialization, Catalanism long presented itself as modern and outward looking, and European rather than (pen)insular, in contrast to a hidebound, anti-modernist Spain dominated by a landed oligarchy. As a city, Barcelona was an icon of cosmopolitanism in contrast to Madrid. Yet soon after the transition to democracy and political autonomy, external and internal political struggles combined to recast Catalonia and Catalanism as backward-looking, narrow-minded, and provincial, as we saw in Chapter 3 (see also Pujolar 2007a). As Socialist municipal governments of Barcelona (and of the Spanish state in periods, as well) emphasized their modernity, progressivism, and cosmopolitanism, the nationalism of the center-right party that governed the autonomous region of Catalonia for nearly twenty-five years, Convergència i Unió (CiU), appeared more and more culturally conservative and provincial (Crameri 2008, Mascarell 2007). "The citizen [i.e., city-dweller] is cosmopolitan and therefore socialist, while nationalism makes for rustics," a leading journalist affiliated with CiU commented sardonically about this mythic division in the brands of Barcelona versus Catalonia (Villatoro 2007).[28]

The cosmopolitan image of Barcelona (under Socialists) was nonetheless entangled in the alleged provincialism of Catalan nationalism (under CiU) during the preparations for the 1992 Olympics in Barcelona, when tensions rose over the role of the Catalan language in the games.[29] Susan DiGiacomo (1999) has shown how in the name of cosmopolitanism, accusations of provincialism were leveled at putative attempts to "impose" use of Catalan on the event. For example, the Peruvian writer Mario Vargas Llosa, later a lead signatory of one of the manifestos against Catalanism discussed in Chapter 3, lamented that Barcelona, "a great cosmopolitan center in Spain" was now "defending Catalan peculiarity" and thus closing itself off from outside influences, in "a tragedy for a city with a great tradition of universalism" (translated quote given in DiGiacomo 1999, 119). Vargas Llosa thus explicitly equated cosmopolitanism with universalism, and he set both against local language and culture depicted as tragically closed and particularistic. Just as would happen again in 2006, Catalan commentators in 1992 tried to unmask the implicit arrogation of universality to Spanish in criticisms such as Vargas Llosa's. "Behind this pretension to universality lies a badly disguised chauvinism," a Hispanic pride that casts Catalan as second-class and

---

28. "El ciutadà és cosmopolita i per tant socialista, mentre que el nacionalisme fa pagès."

29. Pasqual Maragall, the Catalan Socialist mayor who had led Barcelona in the Olympics, became president of Catalonia in a coalition government 2003–2006. Elections to replace this coalition formed the backdrop to the controversy over la Mercè.

merely "local," wrote one Catalan columnist who was also an ERC political representative (translated quote given in DiGiacomo 1999, 120).

When Pasqual Maragall, the Catalan Socialist mayor who had led Barcelona to the Olympics, became president of Catalonia in the first and most unstable of the coalition governments (2003–2006), his administration attempted to rebrand Catalonia and encompass it within the trademark modernity of Barcelona. That mercurial political period was the immediate backdrop to this dispute over la Mercè, in which the same criticisms that DiGiacomo analyzed were mobilized again some fifteen years later. Although the debate was Sisyphean rather than new, three aspects make this instance of the discourse of cosmopolitanism worth a closer look. First, in la Mercè, cosmopolitanism was made the relevant criterion not in an explicitly global event, as in the Olympics, but in a traditionally local one, a municipal festival. Secondly, even though the 2006 controversy concerned an explicitly local event, the question of cosmopolitanism drove out other grounds for argument and framed the public debate. And third, when cosmopolitanism became the frame for debate, defenders of Catalan elaborated alternative visions of cosmopolitanism that illustrate the larger theoretical issues reviewed briefly above. All three of these circumstances indicate the degree to which since the return to political autonomy the ideological ground had shifted away from authenticity as a legitimate and legitimating foundation of linguistic authority, making this controversy particularly interesting for the thesis of this book.

The Cosmopolitanism of Elvira Lindo

Elvira Lindo herself attempted to defuse the controversy and did not claim to represent or bring cosmopolitanism to Barcelona. "I don't have any desire to be or to appear cosmopolitan,"[30] she said in response to a reporter's query on the topic (Navarro 2006). Yet supporters made her the flagbearer of that cause. After the event, there were reports on the graciousness and cosmopolitan openness of the speech that Lindo delivered. Lindo had given her detractors "a lesson in 'cosmopolitanism,'"[31] according to the approving headline in one conservative newspaper (Sala and Espanyol 2006). In contrast, perhaps to downplay the appearance of small-minded personal attacks on an invited guest, her critics refrained from commenting publicly on Lindo's performance at all, much less challenging her demonstration of cosmopolitanism (but see Tree 2007, Gabancho 2007). Nonetheless, a number of passages in Lindo's speech as well as assertions attributed to her in news reports are worth reviewing to see the kind of cosmopolitan

---

30. "No tinc l'afany de ser o de semblar cosmopolita."

31. "una lección de 'cosmopolitanismo.'"

stance that Lindo took and that she was depicted to represent by the media. These reveal facets of the elite cosmopolitanism discussed critically above.

In interviews before the event, Lindo asserted that she would participate, and participate in the language of her choice, because Barcelona "doesn't belong to anybody" (EFE 2006b).[32] She also said that she preferred to stay out of the linguistic controversy. This was understandable given the difficult position she was placed in, but it showed no recognition that in speaking in any language she would inevitably take part in the controversy. The Lindo of these reports treated the use of Castilian as neutral and transparent, not itself positioned. This is in keeping with the assumption of the anonymity of Castilian among many leading language professionals that we saw in Chapter 3.

The actual *pregó* gives a fairer representation of Lindo's own voice. In it, she claimed not to recognize herself in the descriptor "a writer from Madrid."[33] Instead, she asserted that she is at home everywhere she goes, in the many places that are "my cities,"[34] such that

> I am *gaditana* [f. Cádiz-ian], tomorrow *madrileña* [f. Madrid-ian]; a few days from now a New Yorker, and in the fall I'll feel that I am from Buenos Aires . . . and here I always want to be *barcelonina* [f. Barcelonan].[35] (Lindo 2006b)

In this baldly proprietary phrasing, Lindo represented herself as a global citizen from everywhere and nowhere, quite in the way others quoted in Chapter 3, among them Lindo's husband, represented the language she used as a global language from everywhere and nowhere. In the speech, Lindo characterized herself as having "innate chameleon-like abilities" that allow her "never to feel out of place." She had learned early, she announced, that wherever one goes, "if they sing, sing; if they dance, dance."[36] But apparently not "if they speak Catalan, speak Catalan." For Lindo a language such as Catalan appeared to be of a different order, not assumable by even the most innately chameleon-like Castilian-speaking Spaniard.

---

32. "no pertenece a nadie."

33. "escriptora madrilenya."

34. "les meves ciutats."

35. "Sóc gaditana, demà madrilenya, d'aquí a uns dies novaiorquesa i a la tardor em sentiré de Buenos Aires . . . i aquí desitjo sempre ser barcelonina." Although all but one sentence of Lindo's speech was given in Castilian, source quotations given throughout this discussion are in Catalan because that is the only language in which the text of the speech can now be retrieved from the official website for la Mercè.

36. "habilitats camaleòniques innates per no sentir-me fora de joc"; "si canten, canta; si ballen, balla."

Lindo closed her speech by comparing the Catalan question to black-white race relations. In doing so she simultaneously discounted the contemporary significance of both, in a rhetorical move that I admit I find breathtakingly naïve. Lindo did this by recounting an anecdote about a beloved Catalan jazz pianist, Tete Montoliu (who was white and blind). When asked by an expert why he played like a black man, Lindo reported, Montoliu had replied with a smile, "Because I am black."[37] Lindo explained that Montoliu's retort meant that "in this day and age we cannot talk about race anymore."[38] She went on to say: "It is the same idea as Martin Luther King's: 'we are fighting for a racially blind society.'"[39] Lindo concluded that if she had to justify her presence in Barcelona's la Mercè festival, she would use the phrasing of Tete Montoliu and say, in Catalan: "Because I am Barcelonan."[40]

In advancing this identity claim, Lindo produced the only Catalan phrase of her entire speech (Suñé 2006a). She used Catalan not for referential substance, but only indexically, to authorize a claim on Catalan identity, in an enactment of a key tenet of the ideology of linguistic authenticity discussed in Chapter 2. Lindo thus reinforced the image we have seen of Catalan as a "local" language, one that is useful primarily to index who one is, not to "communicate" semantically what one has to say about the world.

Lindo's claim to global citizenship and Barcelonan identity and her references to Montoliu and Martin Luther King sketch a striking profile of her as the jet-setting liberal cosmopolite seen in the theorists' caricatures I discussed earlier. Setting aside Lindo's apparent naiveté about race and the supposed post-racialness of the period, in asserting that her own experience paralleled Montoliu's, she failed to recognize that Montoliu's putative blackness was not self-styled. In her own telling, Montoliu had been credited by a connoisseur for his actual ability in an art form rooted in black America. Montoliu walked the walk, if you will. In advancing her supposedly parallel claim to a Catalan identity, Lindo did not even talk the talk.

Lindo's appropriation of a Barcelonan identity was presumably intended as a Kennedy-esque offer of solidarity: "Ich bin ein Berliner," or perhaps better, "We are all Tete Montoliu." But it was boldly problematic under the controversial circumstances. It was, however, completely in keeping with the certainty Lindo expressed in her speech that "a person can construct her own personal geography

---

37. "És que jo sóc negre."

38. "a aquestes altures ja no es pot parlar de races."

39. "és el mateix pensament de Luther King—'lluitem per una societat racialment cega.'"

40. "és que jo sóc barcelonina."

to suit her own heart."[41] Resonant with the do-it-yourself ethos of the neoliberal self and of project identity, in this case such a sense of happy entitlement allowed the construction not just of a self but also of the world around that self, and it was facilitated by the privilege of using one's own first language while moving about that world.[42] Lindo's Catalan critics did not feel that they could assume this same privilege of constructing the character of their own personal geography, even "at home."

Rooted Catalan Cosmopolitanism vs. Provincialism

Lindo's partisans presupposed but rarely provided any explicit warrants in their discourses for the claim on cosmopolitanism with which they legitimated the choice of speaker. They drew implicitly on the ideological complex of anonymity, which associates universal availability and aperspectival objectivity with dominant languages such as Castilian in Spain and correspondingly represents "local" languages such as Catalan as restricted perspectivally as well as spatially and socially.

One of the few explicit warrants given in the print media for the claim that it would be more cosmopolitan to have a speech in Castilian from Lindo than one in Catalan from another speaker did not address the cosmopolitanism of Castilian but rather Catalan's lack of it. The author asserted the "basic observation" that Catalan doesn't have the diffusion of English, Spanish, or French. Therefore many of those who speak at invocations, conferences, and congresses wouldn't do it in Catalan, "Fortunately. Poor us if our cultural horizon had to be limited to speakers from the Principality!"[43] (Arasa 2006). At work here is the familiar assumption of the restrictedness of "local" language (see Chapter 2). This premise makes it unthinkable that outsiders might speak in Catalan. A requirement to speak in Catalan is understood as the same as a requirement that a speaker be "from the Principality." Catalan, as a local language, is then by definition *not* cosmopolitan and not capable of mediating cosmopolitanism, because it is simply not usable by outsiders. This logic overlooks, or in Irvine and Gal's (2000) terms ideologically

---

41. "una persona pot construir la seva geografia personal a conveniència del propi cor."

42. This is a privilege that I share as an English speaker.

43. "por fortuna. ¡Pobres de nosotros si nuestro horizonte cultural tuviera que limitarse a ponentes del Principado!" The "Principado" ('Principality,' Catalan *Principat*) is a historical reference to the Catalonia of its ascendant medieval period which is the basis of the politically recognized territory of modern Catalonia. It is a particularly odd and infelicitously localizing choice of terms in this quote, because it distinguishes Catalonia from other Catalan-speaking territories in Spain, France, and Italy (Sardinia) from which a Catalan-speaking *pregoner/-a* could be invited.

erases, readily available counterexamples such as the best-selling and indubitably cosmopolitan Australian author Robert Hughes, who reportedly had given the *pregó* in Catalan just a few years earlier. It even erases the existence of the other Catalan-speaking areas of Spain, France, and Sardinia.

Catalan opponents fought against such spatial allocations of cosmopolitanism. "Cosmopolitanism has nothing to do with where a person is from," nor with the use of a given language, asserted representatives of ERC, the party in the governing coalition that led the opposition to Lindo's selection (Ros 2006). ERC's deputy mayor Portabella said:

> If cosmopolitanism were reduced to bringing people from outside who speak in other languages, then Madrid, London, Paris, Berlin or New York would not be open or cosmopolitan cities.[44] (Suñé 2006b)

From their linguistically peripheralized perspective, Catalan critics are acutely aware of the ideology of anonymity and the banal nationalism that underpin such a partisan Castilianist assumption of cosmopolitanism. A familiar accusation traded in such controversies is that of "rancid nationalism,"[45] which Spanish and Catalan opponents often used to brand each other as reactionary particularists (Huertas Claveria 2005). One commentator on the Mercè flap—Màrius Serra, the same columnist who skewered José Montilla's "Level S" Catalan (Chapter 4)—played on this formula to depict the self-ascribed progressive cosmopolitanism of Lindo's defenders as in fact retrograde, by terming it the "rancid cosmopolitanism exuded by those who style themselves non-nationalists from an inalienable Spanish national paradigm" (Serra 2006b).[46] Nonetheless, Serra dismissed the *pregó* as insignificant compared to more consequential cases of discrimination against Catalan in the name of cosmopolitanism, such as the denial of government funding to academic projects because their focus on Catalan literature was dismissed as provincial localism (see Chapter 3).

Leaders of the Catalanist opposition to Lindo's selection turned the accusation of "provincialism" back on Lindo's defenders. They asserted that provincialism is actually, as the ERC politician Jordi Portabella put it, "the lack of confidence in one's own possibilities . . . the belief that granting greater distinction to that

---

44. "Si el cosmopolitanismo se redujera a traer gente de fuera que habla en otras lenguas, Madrid, Londres, París, Berlín o Nueva York no serían ciudades abiertas ni cosmopolitas."

45. "nacionalisme ranci."

46. "El rancio cosmopolitanismo que destilan quienes dicen ser no nacionalistas desde un paradigma nacional español irrenunciable."

which comes from other territories enhances your image" [47] (Portabella 2006). Portabella suggested that the Socialist mayor's office had a linguistic inferiority complex masquerading as cosmopolitanism. Jordi Porta, head of the Catalanist cultural organization Òmnium Cultural, concurred: "in trying not to appear closed, we fall into the most complex-ridden provincialism" [48] (Díaz 2006). This same trope of a false cosmopolitanism as itself provincial also circulated the following year in the controversy that will be discussed in the next chapter. Online posts echoed the theme, associating provincialism with Castilian:

> Couldn't they bring some author who's American, or German, or Indian . . . to give us an opening speech in Catalan full of global awareness and humanism, something of a culture respectful of minorities, instead of Hispanic cheesiness? Cosmopolitan, open Barcelona is becoming provincial.[49] (Pol 2006)

Pressing the counterclaim of provincialism further, Josep-Lluís Carod-Rovira, head of ERC and a philologist by training, argued that a genuinely cosmopolitan writer in any Romance language should easily be able to read a speech in another Romance language (ElMundo.es/Agencias 2006). Online comments suggested that translation is part of genuine cosmopolitanism, and that not to consider it is provincial:

> The provincials are those who want to see the Spanish language in our institutions and events. If a German, Russian, etc. author were to come, . . . s/he'd give it in the language of the place, wouldn't s/he? If not, they would furnish an interpreter, right?[50] (Jordi 2006)

The mayor's office indeed offered to prepare a translation of Lindo's text for her to read, but she did not take up this possibility, saying that she preferred to stay out of the controversy, which she found to be too political. "I can't invent a history that I don't have, so about the language, I can't say anything and I don't

---

47. "la manca de confiança en les nostres pròpies possibilitats . . . .el fet de pensar que donar major categoria a allò que procedeix d'altres territoris t'engrandeix l'opinió."

48. "per tal de no semblar tancats caiem en el provincianisme més acomplexat."

49. "No podrien dur algun autor americà, alemanys, indi, . . . per fer-nos un pregó en català trufat de globalitat i humanisme, algú de cultura respectuosa amb les minories, comptes de cutrerisme hispànic? La cosmopolita i oberta barcelona es provincialitza."

50. "Els provincians son [sic] els que volen veure la llengua espanyola en les nostres institucions i actes. Si vingués un autor alemany, rus, etc . . . oi que ho diria en la llengua del lloc? Oi que si no posarien un interpret [sic]?"

want to see myself involved in it,"[51] Lindo was reported to have said in explanation (Díaz 2006). This again suggests that for her the use of Catalan was tied both to local politics and to the self in the complex of authenticity, in ways that other languages—and other practices like joining the locals in singing and dancing—are not. Speaking in Catalan was as out of the question for Lindo herself as it seemed to be to the *La Vanguardia* columnist Arasa quoted above, who assumed that people who came from outside of Catalonia simply could not speak the language.

In the controversy, ERC leaders attempted not only to unmask the complicity of Spanish nationalistic prejudices with pretensions to cosmopolitanism, but also to articulate an alternative vision that we might call "rooted Catalan cosmopolitanism," recognizably related to the proposals of Appiah and others discussed above. An op-ed piece by Jordi Portabella that appeared in *La Vanguardia* as well as on his website is an extended example (Portabella 2006). Portabella defined cosmopolitanism as "having an open, non-sectarian mentality acquainted with different languages and cultures that recognizes the cultural diversity of different peoples around the world and their ways of doing things as a rich heritage to be safeguarded."[52] From this perspective a genuine display of Barcelona's cosmopolitan character would mean "to show, without embarrassment, our personality and our singularity to the world, so that they can do what they want with it."[53] To bring "our difference and our diversity to an increasingly homogeneous world"[54] would be the mark of true cosmopolitanism. The question of "our personality" implicates the ideology of authenticity and attempts to reinstate its legitimacy within the framework of cosmopolitanism that had come to dominate the discourse. Rather than cosmopolitanism as rising above and leaving behind diverse particularities, cosmopolitanism was reconceptualized as true immersion in and mastery of just such diversity.

Like the postcolonial cosmopolitans that Appiah and Pollock defend, Portabella attempted to move the debate over cosmopolitanism beyond the opposition between authenticity and anonymity in which it had been cast, between cultural revanchism and cultural stripmining, to a form of "rooted cosmopolitanism." This was neither the first nor the last 21st century effort to reformulate the relationship between the Catalanist and the cosmopolitan. Calls had been made before by engaged intellectuals to resolve this same opposition with a synthesis

---

51. "no em puc inventar una història que no tinc, per tant, sobre la llengua, no puc dir res i no m'hi vull veure ficada."

52. "És tenir una mentalitat oberta no sectària que coneix cultures i llengües distintes i que reconeix la diversitat cultural i maneres de fer dels diferents pobles del món com una riquesa per defensar."

53. "És mostrar, sense complexos, la nostra personalitat i la nostra singularitat al món perquè faci amb ella el que li vingui de gust."

54. "aportar la nostra diferència i la nostra diversitat a un món cada vegada més homogeni."

in a new Catalanism, and the political scientist Montserrat Guibernau explicitly proposed a cosmopolitan Catalanism (Buxó 2001, Guibernau 2004, 2013). Moreover, in the years following the controversy over la Mercè, the Catalan nationalist party Convergència under the leadership of Artur Mas, later president of Catalonia and uneasy collaborator with ERC in the sovereignty movement, developed a platform specifically for "cosmopolitan nationalism" and a cosmopolitan Catalanism (Fundació CatDem 2013, *In Transit* 2012).[55] The phrase was largely left behind as calls for the "right to decide" and "sovereignty" garnered more positive attention than any term for nationalism could in the international media. But the various political efforts to formulate Catalanism as a both/and enterprise with cosmopolitanism continue undiminished.

Whose Roots for Cosmopolitanism?

Portabella's defense of a rooted cosmopolitanism left open a question with deeper roots than the issue of who is the most cosmopolitan, and those roots were in the ideology of linguistic authenticity. That question was, what *is* the "true personality and distinctiveness" of Barcelona (and Catalonia)? Specifically, what is the relationship of that true personality to the Castilian language? The bone of contention in the la Mercè controversy was not that the *pregó* would not be in Catalan; it was that it would be in Castilian. What is the rightful place of Castilian in Barcelona?

Online posts by Catalanists were often explicit about how they understood the role of Castilian in Barcelona. Many commentators discounted "cosmopolitanism" as merely a mask for a Hispanicist (*espanyolista*) colonial imposition of Castilian. Here are three examples from the blog thread cited earlier:

> Barcelona will be cosmopolitan, but the presence of Castilian in our institutions and institutional and public events will never be an innocent act.[56] (Jaumot 2006)

> The fact that Barcelona is cosmopolitan doesn't mean the opening speech of its city festival should be given only in Castilian.... If you want cosmopolitanism, we could read it in 54 different languages, including our own. That's what it means to be cosmopolitan; only in Castilian is colonialism.[57] (J. 2006)

---

55. For a proposal of cosmopolitan nationalism in another setting, see Brett and Moran 2011.

56. "Barcelona serà cosmopolita però la presència del castellà en les nostres institucions o actes institucionals o públics mai serà un acte innocent."

57. "El ft [*sic*] que Barcelona sigui cosmopolita no implica que el pregó de les seves Festes Majors es faci només en castellà.... Si vols cosmopolitanisme, el podríem llegir en 54 llengues diferents, inclosa la nostra. Això és ser cosmopolita: només en castellè [*sic*] és colonialisme."

I'm not an enemy of the Castilian language, but yes, of the colonization my people are subjected to. That isn't being cosmopolitan, it's applauding the one who's pissing on you.[58] (FrancescCiuta 2006)

In these views, a *pregó* in Barcelona in Castilian would not be innocent as one in English, Chinese, or German would be, because it is not just any world language, nor is it an aperspectival voice from nowhere. For these online commentators, Castilian is a language imposed by the central Spanish state, still redolent of the Franco dictatorship or even centuries of political subjugation. For them, the veneer of cosmopolitanism masked a use of a local festival to strengthen the position of Castilian in the cultural canon of Barcelona and Catalonia. From this perspective, what was really a contest over the internal, authentic linguistic identity of Barcelona was being fought falsely on the ground of cosmopolitanism, where it was assumed that Catalan, as strictly local in the view of some, would fail.

Such an interpretation of the real meaning of the debate was not necessarily the alarmist projection of Catalanists in online posts, a medium that notoriously draws hyperbolic discourse from the easily outraged. Although the mayor's office advanced no such arguments, the *pregó* was represented in the print media by some of Lindo's defenders as well as opponents to be significant precisely because of the place of Castilian in Catalonia. For example, the *La Vanguardia* editorial quoted earlier, which celebrated Lindo's speech as representing "Open Barcelona,"[59] shows that newspaper's vision of the fundamental issue: "respect for bilingualism must be demanded of all,"[60] it asserted. The editorial argued that one should "never abridge freedom of expression for ideological reasons or for the language used, whether it be Catalan or Castilian."[61] Such an attitude is "anti-democratic"[62] and not in accord with the values of the "citizens of Catalonia,"[63] it concluded (*La Vanguardia* 2006).

La Vanguardia's version of the true Barcelona, then, is one that honors not cosmopolitan multilingualism but rather bilingualism; not all languages but only Catalan and Castilian; not a global cosmopolitan society, but the *citizens* of a

---

58. "Jo no som [*sic*] enemic de sa llengua castellana, xò [*sic*] sí de sa colonització a sa que està sotmès es meu poble. Açò no és se [*sic*] cosmopolita, açò és aplaudir a aquell que et pixa damunt."

59. "Barcelona abierta."

60. "el respeto al bilingüismo debe exigirse a todos."

61. "nunca debe coartarse la libertad de expresión por razones ideológicas ni por el idioma utilizado, sea catalán o castellano."

62. "antidemocráticas."

63. "ciudadanos de Catalunya."

bounded polity. As depicted by the Socialist politicians who proposed her, Lindo was coming from outside Catalonia, from Madrid, and bringing her worldliness with her. But for *La Vanguardia*, the Castilian language that Lindo used came from inside Catalan society. Given that *La Vanguardia* had long been a monolingual Castilian-medium institution of the Barcelona public sphere, it had a vested interest in this vision of the integral place of the Castilian language in Barcelona society.[64]

In another pointed example, a columnist for a neoliberal business-oriented periodical wrote that "non-nationalist political leaders of Catalonia" (to be read as the Socialist mayor and his associates) were dodging "the question that nobody wants to ask in Catalonia today: is Catalan culture expressed in one language or two?"[65] (Leguino 2006). The columnist's own answer was clearly, if implicitly, "two." He portrayed Catalan nationalists as denying the true status of Castilian in the city. Why? The author sardonically caricatured the way that Catalanists think about Castilian, in a phrasing that echoes the online comments just discussed:

> Because Castilian, the mother tongue of the majority of inhabitants of the Barcelona metropolitan area, is an imposed language. And [imposed] by whom? By Franco. Therefore what is a writer from Madrid doing reading an opening speech in Barcelona? Imitating Franco, imposing an invader language.[66]

In this columnist's account, the local status of Castilian as a first language of citizens of the Barcelona metropolitan area was ideologically erased not only in the Catalanist attacks on Lindo's selection, but also in the rationales given for it by the mayor's office:

> What is the opinion of the non-nationalist leaders of Catalonia: is Catalan culture expressed in two languages or only in one? They don't know or they don't answer.[67] (Leguino 2006)

---

64. Several years later, *La Vanguardia* instituted a Catalan edition, created through automatic translation.

65. "la pregunta que nadie quiere hacerse en la Cataluña de hoy: ¿la cultura catalana se expresa en una o en dos lenguas?"

66. "Porque el castellano, la lengua materna de la mayoría de los habitantes . . . del área metropolitana de Barcelona, es un lengua impuesta. Y por quién? Por Franco. Por tanto, qué hace una escritora madrileña leyendo un pregón en Barcelona? Emular a Franco imponiendo una lengua invasora."

67. "Qué opinan los líderes no-nacionalistas de Cataluña: la cultura catalana, se expresa en dos lenguas o sólo en una? No saben o no contestan."

Is Catalonia Bilingual?

Is Catalan culture expressed in one language or two? The leader of the Ciutadans party, which organized the public protest against the Catalanist protesters at Lindo's *pregó*, seemingly put the answer flatly: "Catalonia is bilingual, it's not a problem,"[68] Albert Rivera was reported to declare (*El País* 2006). However, in this assertion Rivera mobilized a term that is not at all flat in Catalan language politics; "bilingual" is not simply an objective linguistic description. Whether characterizing a person, territory, or institutional policy, it is a politically fraught term that has long been rejected by Catalan linguistic activists as a myth and a mask for continued Castilian dominance leading to language shift (Aracil 1966, Ninyoles 1971), and there has very recently been a renewed declaration of that thesis (Vidal 2015). If a "normal" language fulfills all communicative functions in a society, as the normalization model proposes, then bilingualism can be seen to make linguistic normality impossible. (See Boix-Fuster and Vila i Moreno 1998 for discussion.) The concept of bilingualism itself as well as of bilingual policies is therefore rejected by many Catalanists.

Bilingualism is generally understood from this Catalanist viewpoint as a code word for Castilian speakers' freedom to remain monolingual (Vila i Moreno 2004b, 160). As an official policy, bilingualism is most often taken (and intended) to mean the provision of institutional facilities in two languages, allowing individuals to exercise what language planning calls the personality principle and choose to use only one: "those who preach bilingualism are the ones who do not practice it," Josep-Lluís Carod-Rovira wrote recently[69] (Carod-Rovira 2013). While bilingualism as an ideological position purports to achieve social and linguistic peace—"it's not a problem" is the common refrain—critics insist that such a peace only allows further language shift and replacement of a socially minoritized language within its own territory by a more powerful one (Broch 2005). It is, in Carod-Rovira's words, an "anesthetic" for language shift (Carod-Rovira 2013).

Just a month before the dispute over la Mercè, in a related controversy that will be examined in the next chapter, a blogger asserted:

> Our Hispanicist heroes . . . have proposed to demonstrate . . . that you can be bilingual and not say even "good morning" in the language of the country. Bilingualism for some . . . is actually an alibi that allows them never to write the way that [canonical Catalan novelist] Mercè Rodoreda did. (Mel 2006)[70]

---

68. "Cataluña es bilingüe . . . no es ningún problema."

69. "Els que el prediquen són els que no el practiquen."

70. "Els nostres herois hispànics . . . s'han proposat demonstrar . . . que es pot ser bilingüe i no dir ni un "bon dia" en la llengua del país. El bilingüisme per a uns . . . és en realitat una coartada que els permet no escriure mai com ho feia Mercè Rodoreda."

Most of the criticism of "bilingualism" is aimed at institutional policies that go by that name. However, as an individual descriptor, a claim to bilingual identity is also taken as a rejection of Catalan identity. For this reason, many Catalan speakers who are fluent bilinguals in Spanish avoid claiming that designation (Vila i Moreno 2003). This online commentary on the controversy over la Mercè illustrates:

> We're not bilingual simply because nobody is . . . we're monolingual and the first foreign language we have, many times unfortunately, is Castilian.[71] (Josep de la Trinxera 2006)

The manifesto of organizations protesting Lindo's selection to speak at la Mercè showed this same skeptical view of bilingualism, saying that the *pregó* in Castilian:

> does not benefit the cosmopolitanism of Barcelona, but rather it replaces Catalonia's own [*pròpia*] common language, *as always happens with institutionalized bilingualism,* and it is also in detriment to the other hundreds of languages spoken in this city.[72] (italics added, EFE 2006a)

As this statement suggests, while Catalan supporters reject bilingualism, they are more positively disposed to multilingualism or polyglossia, a condition that promises escape from the binary relations of domination and subordination between two languages. For example, Jordi Portabella, the politician at the center of the storm over la Mercè, said in another context:

> To be able to live in Catalan in a polyglot Barcelona would be the best therapy against the deformations and fabrications about bilingualism preached by political groups like Ciutadans and PP.[73] (Baulenas 2007)

Another example of the welcome extended to plurilingualism in contrast to bilingualism appeared in a later opinion piece baldly entitled "Catalunya is not bilingual." It contrasted a "Catalonia that has become a plurilingual society" with a fearful Spain that "to the anachronistic tune

---

71. "No som bilingües per la senzilla raó que ningú ho és . . . Som monolingües i la primera llengua estrangera que tenim, per desgràcia moltes vegades, és el castellà."

72. The original Catalan-medium text of the manifesto is no longer available in online databases and so is quoted here from a Castilian-medium news report. "No beneficia al cosmopolitismo de Barcelona, sino que sustituye la lengua común y propia de Cataluña, *tal y como sucede siempre con el bilingüismo institucionalizado,* y va también en detrimento de los centenares de lenguas que se hablan en la ciudad."

73. "poder viure en català en una Barcelona poliglota seria la millor teràpia contra les deformacions i invents sobre el bilingüisme que prediquen formacions com ara Ciutadans i el PP."

of bilingualism, hides its real intention: to implant Castilian, in place of Catalan, as the linguistic medium." (Ribera 2010)[74]

As terms that undercut the power of Castilian, multilingual and plurilingual are more widely welcomed than the term bilingual by Catalan political and cultural leaders. It was a point of great pride for the Catalan sovereignty movement that in an international press conference about the proposed November 2014 referendum, the president of Catalonia, Artur Mas, spoke without notes in four languages and was happy to field media questions in all of them (Catalan, Spanish, English, and French, with a nod to Italian as well). The sharp contrast to the prerecorded monolingual Castilian statements of the Spanish president Mariano Rajoy did not escape the notice of the international press (Frayer 2014).

Researchers have observed in other settings that modern states are commonly seen to have minorities, and so in a bit of faulty logic, having minorities is taken by some state actors to make polities appear modern (Handler 1988, Hankins 2014). This effect encourages policymakers to adopt multiculturalism and multilingualism in forms that create commensurable minority groups that are made manageable within the dominant social framework (Hale 2005, Povinelli 2002). The Catalan acceptance of "the hundreds of languages spoken in the city" and its celebration of the polyglot fit this pattern, but the historical specificities of the Catalan case provide even more pointed motivation for celebrating multilingualism. Recognition of Castilian can be framed within a multicultural policy that puts it on a footing with hundreds of language that are not *pròpia* to Catalonia. This framing is represented graphically in Figure 5.1, an image from a bilingual Catalan-Tamazight pamphlet entitled "Catalan, the Common [Shared] Language" published by the civic organization Plataforma per la Llengua (2008). Proponents of Castilian perceive this frame as an infuriating backhanded demotion of the official language of the state and co-official language of Catalonia.

Castilian is now, and for at least half a century has been, the first language of more than half the population of Barcelona, much of it Catalonia-born. This is primarily the legacy of mass immigration from other parts of Spain rather than of language shift on the part of the autochthonous population, although Catalan elites did participate in such a shift, complicating the social semiotics of the language, as we have seen in Chapter 4. In view of this status as a first language, some

---

74. "Catalunya s'ha convertit en una societat plurilingüe . . . sota la cantarella anacrònica del bilingüisme, oculta la intenció real: implantar el castellà, en comptes del català, com a llengua vehicular."

FIGURE 5.1 Catalan as the common language of a plurilingual society. From the bilingual Catalan-Tamazight pamphlet "El català, llengua comuna/Takatalaniyt, tutlayt ax ismann," published by Plataforma per la Llengua, 2008.

Reproduced by permission of Plataforma per la Llengua.

social scientists and sociolinguistic activists sympathetic to Catalan advocated a "new Catalanism" for the new millennium that finds a way to recognize the possibility of a stable bilingualism (e.g., Buxó 2001) and "the structural bilingualism of Catalan society" (Branchadell 2007b) without accepting the presumptions of Castilian hegemony. Others assert that, with the numbers of Castilian speakers educated since autonomy who have working knowledge of Catalan (if not necessarily high levels of use), bilingualism now has different sociolinguistic significance and is not a predictor of loss of Catalan. Rather, it is pointed at acquisition of and even shift toward Catalan, observers such as Rudolf Ortega argue (Ortega 2015), and we will see some evidence of that in Part III of this book. Nonetheless, the history of uses of the term bilingualism discussed above makes it difficult to accept new uses of it at face value.

Conclusion

In the controversy over the *pregó* of la Mercè, municipal leaders on both sides shifted the ground of explicit contention to a contest over cosmopolitan visions, rather than directly engaging a struggle over the true linguistic nature of Barcelona. The status of Castilian as a first language of many of its citizens and therefore its potential to be a structural or authentic language of Catalonia were ideologically erased in the public debate over the *pregó*, not only by traditional defenders of Catalan but also by the Socialist mayor's office that proposed and defended the Castilian keynote speaker. In a division of political labor within the Catalan Socialist party, however, the structural status of Castilian within Catalonia was at the same time asserted by its candidate for the presidency of the Catalan government, José Montilla, whose own problematic linguistic status and initial campaign strategy of stressing the Castilian language were discussed in the last chapter. Weighing in on the municipal controversy and reinforcing the longstanding ambiguity of the Catalan Socialists' linguistic ideology, the candidate Montilla did not speak of cosmopolitanism but of local linguistic conditions behind the *pregó*: "It's normal for it to be in Castilian, given that it's a language that a very important part of Catalan society speaks"[75] (Gubern 2006).

Although it was downplayed in the conflict over cosmopolitanism in the festival of la Mercè, the stubborn question remained: is Catalan culture expressed in one language or two? In fact, that question was at the very same time being debated in the same media by politicians and elite language professionals (authors, publishers, critics) in another cosmopolitan controversy. That debate concerned how Catalan culture was to be represented to the world at the Frankfurt Book Fair in 2007. The Catalan author Alfred Bosch, who has since become a significant political figure in ERC and the sovereignty movement, winked at the link between the two controversies by waggishly nominating Elvira Lindo as "spokesperson for Catalan culture at the Frankfurt Book Fair in 2007"[76] (A. Bosch 2006). We will follow his lead and turn in the next chapter to an examination of the key discursive themes of authenticity, anonymity, and cosmopolitanism as they played out in this second controversy.

---

75. "Es normal que sea en castellano, dado que es una lengua que habla una parte importantísima de la sociedad catalana."

76. "com a portaveu de la cultura catalana a la Fira de Frankfurt del 2007."

6 "SINGULAR AND UNIVERSAL"

BRANDING CATALAN CULTURE IN THE GLOBAL MARKET

Chapter 3 closed with a quote from the media commentator Toni Soler, who gave the name "*Catalunya S.A.*" or "Catalonia, Inc." to the coalition government that materialized in 2006 under the presidency of José Montilla. The quote is worth reprising here, as it sounds a theme of this chapter:

> the Government . . . opts for management alone, and has decided . . . to convert us all into members of the board of directors of Catalonia S.A. ("A" for anonymous, because anonymity is the ideal of those who are against identities.)[1] (Soler 2006)

Soler's wry label for the Montilla government highlighted both its corporate-style managerial culture and the fact that it distanced itself from themes of national identity.[2] The metaphor of the corporation suggests that even as a stateless nation, 21st century Catalonia participated in the modality of governance often described as characteristic of the contemporary era of neoliberalism and globalization, in which the state engages in the practices of corporate culture. But Soler's description of the Catalan government's corporate model as "anonymous" and "against identities," also suggests something different about the Catalan case, especially compared to other small language communities in politically peripheralized territories. "Catalonia S.A."

---

1. "el Govern . . . apuesta por la gestión a secas, y ha decidido . . . convertirnos a todos en miembros del consejo de administración de Catalunya S.A. ('A' de anónima, porque el anonimato es el ideal de los que están en contra de las identidades)."

2. The corporate management style was contrasted to the chaotic excess of charisma for which the previous administration was known, which Soler dubbed "the Age of Aquarius."

appears here to contrast with the widespread nation branding pattern known as "Ethnicity, Inc.," in which the state emphasizes identity in order to commodify and brand it (Comaroff and Comaroff 2009, Urry 2003). This chapter explores this tension between corporate practices, anonymity, and identity as it played out in a controversy around linguistic commodities in an international marketing event.

Catalonia S.A. put its wares (and itself) on display at the Frankfurter Buchmesse "Book Fair," where Catalan culture was featured as the invited guest of honor in 2007. The annual Buchmesse is the largest publishing trade fair "on the planet," as a leading Barcelona newspaper put it (*La Vanguardia* 2007b). Although publishing may seem like a quaint industry in the late modern era of digital communication, the Frankfurt Book Fair is a principal international venue where publishers and agents spot rising cultural trends and negotiate commercial relations, licensing, and translation rights in the global industry, increasingly not only for print but also for digital "content" across the "creative industries," as the fair's website stresses.[3] In March 2005, after several years of groundwork by the Catalan government, the Frankfurt Book Fair's administration designated "Catalan culture" as the guest of honor for its October 2007 event.[4]

The Frankfurt Book Fair was an opportunity to project the Catalan language, culture, and identity to a global audience of industry professionals, with the hope of reaching a broader international public through them. It was also an opportunity for competing interest groups to contend over the nature and status of Catalan language, culture, and identity, and for all sides to try to capitalize on those displays and challenges for professional and political gain. Claims for the place of the Catalan and Castilian languages in Catalan society were publicly pitted against each other throughout nearly three years of preparations for the Frankfurt Fair.

In this chapter we will examine those competing claims as they were represented in over 200 media reports across those three years (2005–2007).[5] Those reports show the controversy moving over the same bumpy ideological terrain

---

3. http://www.buchmesse.de/en/company/.

4. "Cultura catalana." The general agreement between the Frankfurt Book Fair and the Catalan government was reported to have first been made in October 2004, but the specific year in which Catalan culture would be honored was set later (A.V. and B. 2007).

5. I gathered these from the print media during my field stay 2006–2007; from the two extensive (but not exhaustive) digital dossiers on the topic assembled by the Centre de Documentació of the Generalitat de Catalunya, which cover the political spectrum of print periodical newspapers in both languages as distributed in Catalonia during the period 2005–2007; and from my own supplemental online searches of weblogs and the archives of three major newspapers, carried out in April 2014.

of linguistic authority in autonomous Catalonia that is familiar from earlier chapters. In the case of Frankfurt, Catalan language politics were strategically redirected away from the traditional logic that set linguistic authenticity against anonymity and cosmopolitanism, and refashioned within a discourse of branding in the global marketplace befitting a corporate, cosmopolitan "Catalonia S.A." summarized in its slogan as "Singular and Universal."

The Frankfurt Book Fair 2007: A Narrative Account

The Frankfurt Book Fair administration began inviting annual guests of honor as a marketing tool in the late 1980s (Weidhaas 2007). Invited status was usually bestowed on independent states (e.g., Italy, Japan, Spain, Ireland, Brazil, Switzerland, Lithuania, India), some of them officially monolingual, others notably multilingual. In two earlier years the invitee had been defined by a language that cut across juridical states (Dutch, including the Netherlands and Dutch-medium Belgium in 1993, and the Arab world in 2004), but never before had the honored guest not been identified with at least one independent state.[6] The designation of Catalan "culture" may have been chosen to avoid the political pitfalls of territorially based terms such as "Catalonia" or the "Catalan Countries"[7] which could imply an endorsement of an independent geopolitical entity (Simó 2006). Why "Catalan culture" rather than "Catalan literature" was chosen, and who was responsible for the designation, were not questions answered in public documents.[8]

If the label was chosen to avert political controversy (and it is not at all clear that it was), it failed spectacularly. From the contention discussed in the last chapter, we know that the term Catalan culture would be an invitation for polemics,

---

6. Catalan is one of three co-official languages of the principality of Andorra, but that micro-state is tied nominally to ritual rule by Spanish and French officials rather than fully independent.

7. "Països Catalans." This term is favored by irredentist Catalan nationalists to encompass territories beyond Catalonia proper, which is itself often referred to as the Principat de Catalunya 'Principality of Catalonia,' a historical reference to the medieval period. The umbrella term includes traditional Catalan-speaking areas of Spain: Valencia, the Balearic Islands, and a strip of Aragon. It also extends beyond the borders of the Spanish state to include areas in France and Sardinia that were traditionally Catalan-speaking and maintain it as a heritage language, as well as Andorra. In the Frankfurt exposition, "Catalan culture" was taken to include Catalan-medium production from these areas.

8. There were insinuations on the one hand that Catalan politicians with a weak commitment to Catalan preferred the "culture" label as more comfortably vague (Cònsul 2005), and on the other hand that the Frankfurt Fair authorities preferred it as more likely to stir up controversy and therefore publicity (Geli 2007b).

immediately raising exactly the question said to underlie the controversy over la Mercè: "Is Catalan culture expressed in one language or two?" The question in the Frankfurt case was more narrowly focused on high culture: should literature written in Castilian—or more exactly, authors who write in Castilian—be featured as part of "Catalan culture" at the Frankfurt Fair?

Barcelona is the major base of the publishing industry in Spain, comprising 55% of Spanish publishing (Cuadrado 2007d) and over 43% of publication export business (*Avui* 2007), with substantial production not only in Catalan but also in Castilian, addressed to a Latin American market as well as the Iberian peninsula. The most prestigious as well as the internationally best-selling novelists from Barcelona, such as Juan Marsé, Eduardo Mendoza, and Carlos Ruiz Zafón, all write in Castilian.[9] All these authors are known for works deeply informed by the history and culture of Barcelona. What was to be their status and that of their Castilian-medium works at the Frankfurt Book Fair? Were they "Catalan authors," and were their books part of "Catalan literature"? Were such well-known figures (not to mention their less famous co-lingual colleagues) to be presented as part of "Catalan culture"?[10]

This question of the categorization of the Castilian-medium Catalan author was far from new. For example, leading authors in Catalonia had conducted a survey of their colleagues on this very question and published it in the leftwing Catalan cultural journal *Taula de canvi* in 1977, during the early effervescence of the post-Franco transition (Carbonell et al. 1977).[11] There was fiercer contention

---

9. The debate focused almost exclusively on elite fiction writers and essayists. One editor finally complained about the exclusion of nonfiction from culture and publishing in the public debate, despite this being the mainstay of the publishing world and of industry events such as the Frankfurt Fair (Pontón 2007).

10. Catalan media figure Toni Soler asserted that when Spain was the guest of honor in 1991, no authors who wrote in Catalan were included in the delegation to Frankfurt (Soler 2007). A German newspaper reportedly characterized those languages as "relegated" (*relegados*) by "provincial Madrileños" in 1991 (Bassets 2005a). However, the Spanish minister of culture in 2007 asserted that Spain had in fact brought authors who wrote in "the co-official languages of the State" to the fair (Alsedo 2007). All other journalistic reports I have found completely ignored this basic factual question while they covered the ongoing controversy assiduously, so I have been unable to verify the facts of that earlier event.

11. Among the leaders of this survey was the author and supporter of a progressive Catalanism as well as Catalan Communism, Manuel Vázquez Montalbán, who wrote most of his very successful books in Castilian but also published often in Catalan. Vázquez Montalbán quickly regretted the idea of the survey, compared himself to Kafka in his own ironic and regretful response to it, and refused to answer his own questions. See DiGiacomo (1985, 219–223) for a discussion of the acrimony the survey raised around the question that persisted into the Frankfurt exposition. Vázquez Montalbán died suddenly in 2003, and the loss of his voice was often lamented in relation to the Frankfurt controversy.

over the issue between competing cultural elites once Catalan government subventions that supported Catalan-medium literary and cultural production came to be at stake under political autonomy (Crameri 2008, King 2005). This was largely a matter of status politics or the politics of recognition, that is, a competition for official canonization of cultural emblems as a validation of a social group itself (Gusfield 1986, Fraser 2000). But it was also a struggle between stakeholders over resources, since even limited financial support affects the survival of lesser-known artists in the rarefied high cultural markets of literature and particularly of theater (Berger 2005, Pericay 2006). Moreover, the Frankfurt invitation poked a finger in the unhealed wound of the recently concluded 2004 book fair in Guadalajara, Mexico, where Catalan literature had also been the guest of honor. A controversy had broken out there when the handful of Castilian-medium authors among the Catalan delegation became publicity stars of the event alongside world-famous Latin American writers, overshadowing Catalan-medium authors. Some of the latter were publicly indignant and determined not to let this happen again at Frankfurt (Alós 2007a).

Although the explicit terms of the agreement were not published, newspapers reported that the contract between the Catalan minister (*conseller*) of culture and the Frankfurt Fair, as well as other fair directives, specified that Catalan "writers and artists who do not express themselves in Catalan"[12] were to be included (Alós 2007a, Cuadrado 2007d, Morán 2007b).[13] The Catalan authors whom the fair's organizers enthusiastically cited when issuing the invitation all in fact wrote in Castilian. Nonetheless, soon after the agreement between the Frankfurt Fair and the Catalan government was announced, the Association of Catalan-Language Writers (AELC), still burning from the perceived slight at Guadalajara, demanded that official representation at Frankfurt be limited to writers who published in Catalan. The Socialist-led Catalan administration replied with a reminder that "Catalan culture" was the invitee, and asserted that "Catalan writers are as much those who write in Catalan as those who write in Castilian."[14] However, the first Catalan minister of culture to handle the matter, a Catalan Socialist, also announced that there would be affirmative action (*discriminació positiva*) in favor of the Catalan language (*ABC* 2005, J.B. 2005).

---

12. "escriptors i artistes que no s'expressen en català."

13. Changes in administrative personnel of the Frankfurt Fair organization as well as the Catalan government during the time the official details were hammered out make it difficult to know what might originally have been agreed. Multiple news sources in 2007 gave this same report.

14. "escritores catalanes son tanto aquellos que escriben en catalán como los que escriben en castellano."

This position, which will be explored in more detail below, was received with more howls than applause. A few weeks later, the Catalan Parliament passed a motion to give Catalan-medium literature priority at Frankfurt (Bassets 2005b). A stronger motion in July 2006 to *exclusively* invite "writers in the Catalan language"[15] failed to pass, notably because the leaders of the opposition parties that presented the motion—Convergència i Unió (CiU) and Esquerra Republicana (ERC)—were absent from the vote (Hevia 2006, *Racó Català* 2006a, 2006c). On the question of language, there were factions within factions not only in the coalition governing Catalonia at that time, but also within the opposition parties.

Indignant reports and op-ed pieces in the Castilian-medium and Spanish statewide press did not register the distinction between priority for Catalan-medium writers and exclusion of Castilian-medium ones. Objections were made to the effort to prioritize Catalan-medium works as "hyperprotectionist nationalism"[16] (Ferran and Fernández 2005) and more vehemently as a "scandalous" example of an "intolerable" "absolute provincialism"[17] (Güell 2005), that demonstrated the "exclusionary nature . . . of closed-minded provincialism"[18] of the Catalan government (*El Mundo* 2005).

Over the two and a half years between the announcement in 2005 and the actual fair in October 2007, this question of Castilian-language authors continued to be mooted repeatedly in the Catalan, Spanish, and German press, the shrillness of tone rising and falling with political vicissitudes across the period. The organization of the Frankfurt exhibition was placed under the direction of the Institut Ramon Llull (IRL), a government-sponsored consortium that had been created in 2002 to promote Catalan language and culture, on the model of the Spanish Instituto Cervantes (itself modeled on the British Institute). The labyrinthine road to Frankfurt was littered with political corpses, their demise attributed to this controversy (Alós 2007a, A.V. and J.B. 2007). The Frankfurt possibility had first been explored by the center-right Catalan government administration of CiU under Jordi Pujol (Cuadrado 2007c). Preparations then ran through three different incarnations of Socialist-led governing coalitions, under the direction of three different ministers of culture and three different heads of the IRL. Political maneuvering involved the Spanish state as well. Two successive Socialist Spanish ministers of industry—one of whom was José Montilla, the future president of Catalonia, and the other the former mayor of Barcelona who had invited Elvira

---

15. "escriptors en llengua catalana."

16. "nacionalismo hiperprotector."

17. "escandaloso"; "intolerable"; "absoluto provincianismo."

18. "el carácter excluyente . . . de la cerrazón y el provincianismo."

Lindo to speak at la Mercè—pledged a total of twelve million euros of subventions to the Catalan publishing and cultural industries in 2006–2007, largely to support participation in Frankfurt (Cuadrado 2007b, Piñol 2006). Revived at each turn in the political road, the controversy created such a sense of déjà vu that one author reported that his friends asked him well before the actual event how Frankfurt had gone (Palol 2007).

Unsurprisingly given the several changes of political regime as well as the minefield the question represented, the Catalan government gave vague and conflicting signals of its interpretation of "Catalan culture" over time. It was widely agreed that many missteps were made across the years of preparations, each seized on by one side or the other for criticism, now as too Catalanist, now as too Castilianist.

In August 2006, the Socialist minister of culture (at that time) of the Catalan government, Ferran Mascarell, announced a compromise that a reporter labeled "Solomonic" (Hevia 2006); the baby would be cut in half. The Institut Ramon Llull as the organizing body would officially invite only authors who wrote in Catalan as part of its entourage, but through a different institute the Catalan government would subsidize Catalan publishing houses to bring their Castilian-medium Catalan authors to Frankfurt. Demonstrating that this was a struggle over recognition rather than resources, this solution did nothing to mollify critics of Catalanism or to assuage Castilian-medium authors (Pericay 2006).

After continuing controversy, the third and final director of IRL to handle the Frankfurt preparations, the ERC appointee Josep Bargalló, made announcements in March 2007 that revised the Solomonic decision on the official delegation to Frankfurt. The official invitees would now include Castilian-medium authors because "a good part of the strength of our culture is fruit of this dialogue [between Catalan and Castilian literature], of this creative and creating co-existence."[19] Including "Catalan writers in the Castilian language"[20] in the program would underline this dialogue and enable them "to speak to us about their relation with the Catalan language"[21] (Bassets 2007). At the beginning of March illustrious international authors were mentioned as invitees; by the end of the month writers from Barcelona were being mentioned (Bassets 2007, Geli 2007a). These authors were to be encompassed within a tripartite structure for the program of exhibits: Catalan literature, exclusively in Catalan; the publishing industry, including authors in Castilian; and Catalan culture in an extended sense,

---

19. "Buena parte de la fuerza de nuestra cultura es fruto de este diálogo, de esta convivencia creativa y creadora."

20. "escritores catalanes en lengua castellana."

21. "nos hablen de su relación con la lengua catalana."

including gastronomy and visual and performing arts in these two languages and more (Bassets 2007). The plan fit the model, a kind of three-ring circus, that had been successfully established in 1988 by Italy, and met with the approval of the Frankfurt Fair directors. However, closure on the language debate was not to be achieved with this solution.

By June, several top Castilian-medium Catalan writers were contacted about participating at Frankfurt as invitees of the Catalan government. However, the press reported that they were to be ambassadors of Catalan-medium literature rather than of their own work (Europa Press 2007). This idea had been introduced as early as June 2005 by a publisher (Capdevila 2005) but was scorned by various observers from all sides (Branchadell 2007b, *Racó Català* 2006c, *El Mundo* 2007b). The new plan for bringing Castilian-medium authors on the one hand was criticized by the Catalan nationalist opposition party CiU as a deferential bow to the hegemony of Spanish culture (Branchadell 2007b), and on the other hand only increased the number of Castilian authors who felt personally insulted by the Catalan government (*La Vanguardia* 2007c, Fernández 2007a, Vallbona 2007). One author and steadfast critic of Catalan nationalism, Félix de Azúa, reportedly suggested that Castilian-medium authors should not accept their invitations unless President Montilla issued a public apology for the past twenty-five years of cultural policy under other administrations, which had subsidized Catalan-medium literary production (Alós 2007a). All the Castilian-medium authors who were invited declined to attend. Most claimed publicly, some with more perceptible condescension than diplomacy, that they preferred to leave the limelight to their Catalan-medium colleagues ("with or without their Catalan caps on,"[22] as one put it scornfully) (Fernández 2007b). The president of the augustly Catalanist Institute of Catalan Studies (IEC), Salvador Giner, expressed dismay that writers who live in Barcelona and write in Castilian would not be going to Frankfurt as part of the official delegation (*La Vanguardia* 2007a). A conservative legislator in the Spanish Parliament termed their absence "the greatest episode of exclusion, sectionalism, and abuse" (Alsedo 2007).[23]

In the event, some 130 Catalan-medium authors (Fernández 2007b), a troop of politicians, and figures from the visual and performing arts, gastronomy, and the Castilian- as well as Catalan-medium music industry joined the official delegation, but no Castilian-medium authors. Agents, editors, and publishers in

---

22. "con o sin barretina." The *barretina* is a red hat in the style of a Phrygian cap that typifies traditional, provincial images of Catalonia and Catalanism. (However, Salvador Dalí was often photographed wearing one.) The author who made this comment, Juan Marsé, an inspired chronicler of working-class Barcelona, would not want to be seen wearing one.

23. "el mayor episodio de exclusión, de sectarismo y de atropello."

both languages went to Frankfurt and conducted their annual business as usual, outside the limelight.

Catalan author Quim Monzó opened the exposition with an "ingenious meta-speech"[24] that played on multiple levels of knowing reflexivity about the impossibility of representing Catalan culture under the circumstances, wittily disarming the audience and defusing the controversy (Castells 2007). The central exhibit was an artistic "forest of words" with 2000 paper leaves bearing the names of Catalan authors and artists over the centuries, Castilian-medium as well as Catalan. In video recordings, authors from a variety of linguistic backgrounds—Castilian, Catalan, English—spoke of their relation to Catalan culture (Morán 2007a). Musical performances in Castilian and Catalan included a hybrid duo of flamenco and Catalan folk-pop artists. The conservative Spanish press continued to criticize what it billed as the exclusionary and retrograde nationalist character of the Catalan literary delegation, but other reports even in some conservative papers characterized the central exposition of Catalan culture at the fair as "much more open-minded and open to dialogue,"[25] conceding the representation of cultural *convivència* claimed by the Catalan administration (Morán 2007a). The mainstream press of Catalonia, both Catalan- and Castilian-medium, rallied around to declare the event a success for Catalonia and its publishing and culture industries, while still criticizing the political leadership for needless missteps along the way.

As in the case of la Mercè, the mediatized controversy around the Frankfurt Fair intertwined cultural celebrity and professional rivalries and egos with conflicting cultural nationalisms and political point scoring in election season.[26] This time the intrigues were brought to an international rather than a local forum, in a kind of miniature hybrid of the Olympics of 1992 and a "Big Brother" reality television show. It was clear in most of the complaints from both sides that it was not the publications that were to be displayed and promoted at Frankfurt that were at issue; it was the personal protagonism of literary figures (Pontón 2007). Editors complained that it was simply a mistake to put so much focus on authors at a working venue where they had little role to play (Morán 2007b).

Our interest is not in the professional rivalries as such (though they hold a certain embarrassed fascination), but in the linguistic ideological foundations

---

24. "una metaconferència enginyosa."

25. "abierto y dialogante."

26. Xavier Marcé, who participated in the organization and the debate at the time, commented several years later that behind the "monumental polemic" there was no real difference in the positions of nor real conflict among the political parties, except for Partido Popular. Rather, the language question was exploited out of partisanship, he affirmed (Marcé 2011).

and discursive construction of language in this struggle over status and recognition. The following sections take a closer analytic look at the key themes that framed the public discussion as reported in the media.

The Defense of Castilian

What were the discursive terms in which the Castilianist criticisms of the Catalan government's evolving plans were phrased? We saw that although the linguistic character of Catalonia was the issue underlying the dispute over la Mercè, critics of Catalanism in that case rejected the framework of linguistic authenticity itself rather than stepping into it in order to contest the privileged authenticity of the Catalan speaker. Instead, they presupposed the moral validity and persuasive value of anonymity and cosmopolitanism. This was largely true in the Frankfurt controversy as well.

For example, the head of the Collegial Association of Writers of Spain was quoted as saying that literature "is above nationalisms and does not have frontiers"[27] (Fernández 2005). Another critic admonished that the classic definition of Catalan identity has no linguistic limitations,[28] and that languages should not be turned into flags (Pernau 2007). "To deny someone [the right to be] part of Catalan culture for not writing in Catalan becomes an act of intellectual cruelty,"[29] wrote two Catalan Socialist politicians early in the controversy (Ferran and Fernández 2005). The canonical Barcelona novelist Eduardo Mendoza reportedly dismissed localizing authenticity concerns in general: "Local and universal aren't important today; what's troubling is the localist spirit."[30]

There was more open assertion in the Frankfurt controversy than in la Mercè that what was in question was the "real" and legitimate linguistic character of Catalonia as "bilingual" (*El Mundo* 2007a). Calls were explicitly made for the (equal) inclusion of Castilian-medium authors as part of Catalan culture, not as "foreigners, not Francoists,"[31] as the critic de Azúa put it in an authors' roundtable organized by the conservative newspaper *El Mundo* (*El Mundo* 2007a). De Azúa nonetheless spoke

---

27. "por encima de nacionalismos y no tiene fronteras." Andrés Sorel, Asociación Colegial de Escritores de España. No irony appears to have been intended or recognized in the fact of this criticism coming from an organization so named, nor in relation to an invitation based on both the explicit recognition as well as crossing of national frontiers.

28. "Una postura sense limitacions idiomàtiques, coherent amb la clàssica definició de la identitat catalana."

29. "Que se le niegue a alguien el formar parte de la cultura catalana por no escribir en catalán deviene un acto de crueldad intelectual."

30. "Local y universal hoy no es importante; lo preocupante es el espíritu localista."

31. "que no somos extranjeros, que no somos franquistas."

disdainfully of the concept of Catalonia and associated it with former president Jordi Pujol, whose politics he despised. De Azúa reported that as a university student he loved Barcelona, but that, "I didn't know anything about Catalonia until Pujol showed it to me, and I still don't understand what there is beyond the city."[32] Eliminating any doubt on his view of Catalan national identity as an authorizing framework, the urbanite de Azúa went on to compare Catalan nationalism to the Spanish fascist Falange, and to reject the concept of nation as "invented by Napoleon, a bourgeois counter-revolutionary invention"[33] (*El Mundo* 2007a).[34]

A rare example of a sensibility for Catalan authenticity from a Castilian defender came from a fellow participant in the authors' roundtable. Francisco González Ledesma (b. Barcelona 1927), the oldest of the authors, said that as the child of Spanish immigrants in Barcelona,

> I learned to read and write in Catalan, and I would have been a writer in Catalan, but Bargalló forgets Francoism and that many of us Catalan speakers were obliged to accept Castilian culture. Whose fault is it that I chose the Castilian language because that's where I find the difficult word, the magical word? . . . In my novels, I've presented Barcelona to the world. But now I find that I love my country but my country doesn't love me, and moreover, that it thinks I'm not part of it . . . This fills me with pain and perplexity. I don't give a fig about Frankfurt.[35] (*El Mundo* 2007b)

González Ledesma responded directly against his co-panelist de Azúa's condemnation of Catalan nationalism: "I'm prepared to defend that Catalonia is a nation. That's why it hurts me so much that they don't consider me Catalan"[36] (*El Mundo* 2007a). His words resounded as a rare cri de coeur of a wounded sense of Castilian-medium Catalan authenticity.

---

32. "no supe de Cataluña hasta que me la descubrió Pujol y todavía no entiendo lo que hay más allá de la ciudad."

33. "las naciones las inventó Napoleón, que son una invención de la burguesía contrarrevolucionaria."

34. See among others Patricia Gabancho's comments on the identity of well-known Castilian-medium authors as not Catalans but Barcelonans (Gabancho 2007, 75–76).

35. "aprendí a leer y escribir en catalán y hubiera sido un escritor en catalán, pero Bargalló olvida el franquismo y que mucha gente de habla catalana nos vimos obligados a aceptar la cultura castellana. ¿Quién tiene la culpa de que yo escogiera la lengua castellana porque es donde encuentro la palabra difícil, la palabra mágica?. . .En mis novelas . . . he paseado Barcelona por el mundo. Y ahora me encuentro con que yo quiero a mi país pero mi país no me quiere a mí y, además, piensa que no formo parte de él.. . . Esto me llena de perplejidad y de dolor. Me importa un pepino Fráncfort."

36. "yo estoy dispuesto a defender que Cataluña es una nación. Por eso me duele tanto que no se me considere catalán."

As with la Mercè, in most cases advocates of Castilian framed the issue less as a battle of competing authenticities than as a rejection of the ideology of authenticity entirely, in favor of intellectual, linguistic, and market freedom. Labels of provincialism, reactionary nationalism, and exclusionary politics, familiar from debates discussed in earlier chapters, were used throughout the Frankfurt controversy, regardless of the government's shifting positions on sponsoring Castilian-medium authors as part of the delegation. For example, when the Catalan Parliament refused to exclude Castilian authors but approved a vague motion to give Catalan priority in the representation, the cry of "provincialism" rose immediately from leading critics of Catalanism such as Xavier Pericay (Güell 2005).[37] A year later when a new Catalan minister of culture announced the plan to take both Catalan- and Castilian-medium authors to Frankfurt, but under different auspices and avenues of subvention, Pericay again indicted this as monolingualist, protectionist nationalism. Through such subvention policies, he wrote, it protected a monolingual institutional literature and made a second class of the "actually existing bilingual literature ruled by the law of supply and demand," whose authors are the only ones "with any real weight in the world. That is to say, outside of Catalonia"[38] (Pericay 2006). Such endorsements of the authority of the market will be discussed in detail in the next sections.

With equal consistency, *El Mundo* editorialized in 2005 and 2007, first against the parliamentary motion that gave priority to Catalan authors in the Frankfurt delegation, writing that it demonstrated the excluding character, the "closed-minded provincialism"[39] of the Generalitat (*El Mundo* 2005). Two and a half years later, after a reversal of policy and the extension of government invitations that were declined by Castilian-medium authors, *El Mundo* continued to criticize the exposition for "amputating a part of Catalan culture for the sin of expressing itself in Castilian" and excluding "autochthonous writers who write in Castilian."[40] Here *El Mundo* drew on the authenticity framework in organic metaphors of origins and the bodily integrity of culture at the same time as it indicted

---

37. In the 1980s and 1990s, Pericay had begun as one of the leaders of a group of iconoclastic young Catalan philologists who from professional positions in mass media contested traditional and institutional Catalan linguistic authorities. They championed what they saw as a modern and others saw as a Castilianized form of Catalan characterized dismissively as "Catalan light" (Woolard 1999). By the time of the Frankfurt controversy Pericay was well established as a critic of all facets of Catalan nationalism and a regular writer for the rightwing Spanish newspaper *ABC*. He also collaborated in founding the civic organization that gave rise to the Ciutadans party, introduced in Chapter 3.

38. "la literatura efectiva, verdaderamente existente, bilingüe, regida por la ley de la oferta y la demanda"; "el segundo es el único con algún peso en el mundo. Es decir, fuera de Cataluña."

39. "La cerrazón y el provincianismo."

40. "amputar una parte de la cultura catalana por el pecado de expresarse en español"; "se excluyera a los escritores autóctonos que escriben en castellano."

"the disloyalty committed by the Generalitat that has, with the [Spanish] State's money marginalized the common language of all"[41] (*El Mundo* 2007c).

Some reporters for German newspapers such as *Der Spiegel*, allergic to expressions of nationalism for their own historical reasons, adopted this same critical perspective with the same implicit reliance on the banal nationalist assumptions that legitimate only the languages associated with sovereign states. German journalist Margit Knapp unfavorably contrasted the Catalan plans with the success of the Dutch exposition in 1993, which was an "eye-opening experience for all book lovers." Knapp did not notice that "the joint exhibit by Belgium's Flanders region and the Netherlands," in classifying Dutch-medium literature from Belgium with Dutch literature from the Netherlands, sundered Belgian literature on a linguistic criterion. Such a taxonomy was an exact parallel to the definition of Catalan literature adopted for the Frankfurt Fair. Yet Knapp lauded the Dutch for "raising the profile" of Dutch authors and securing "Dutch literature a permanent place in German publishing houses and book stores," while Catalonia came in for harsh criticism for its "close-minded policy of not including the many Catalans who write in Spanish in its definition of Catalan literature." Such an "airing of old nationalist sentiments" narrowed rather than widened perspectives, Knapp wrote (Knapp 2007). The status of Dutch as a language backed by a state seems to have made invisible to the German author the old nationalist sentiments that excluded Belgians who write in French.

What Is Catalan Literature? The Market and Commodification

Despite such complaints, a relatively broad agreement emerged fairly early about what constituted "Catalan literature." "Catalan culture" proved more persistently controversial across the years of preparation, but a modal definition was finally achieved—or imposed—by the coalition government that brought the project to fruition. As one Catalan author asserted approvingly and overoptimistically, there was a general conclusion "accepted by all," that "Catalan literature is unified by virtue of its language, while all of us who operate from this reality belong to Catalan culture without distinction based on linguistic or artistic medium of expression" (Bru de Sala 2007).[42] The discourses that framed this ultimately dominant position are examined in this and the next sections. We will hear in them

---

41. "la deslealtad cometida por la Generalitat, que ha marginado con el dinero del Estado la lengua común a todos."

42. "una especie de conclusión general, un distingo por todos aceptado, según el cual la literatura catalana es una por razón de lengua, mientras que todos los que operamos desde esta realidad pertenecemos a la cultura catalana sin diferencia de medio de expresión artístico o lingüístico."

recognizable echoes of the market themes and the commodification of language that Monica Heller and other analysts have identified as displacing earlier nationalist logics of identity and rights in the late modern period.[43]

The primary criterion used to define Catalan literature by supporters of the administration's view was the linguistic medium, but claims to a Romantic linguistic authenticity and the central traditional trope of *llengua pròpia* were given little air. Instead, this was defended with a presumption of hardheaded common sense as simply the criterion used by librarians, historians of literature, and the commercial marketplace, the last of which was characterized by some as the model for rational decision-making, as will be discussed below. What were asserted to be booksellers' and librarians' standard conventions were advanced from a number of positions as settling a cut-and-dried classificatory question with an obvious answer (Fernández 2005, J.B. 2007b). "A literature is a language,"[44] a Catalan publisher wrote in one of the earliest commentaries in March 2005 (Cònsul 2005), and thus "Catalan literature" was that written in Catalan. At the opening of the fair in Frankfurt two and a half years later, the former longtime president of Catalonia (by then in the opposition) Jordi Pujol asserted that all histories of literature confirmed this same principle: "the defining element is the language"[45] (Geli 2007c). "This is a librarian's debate, about bookshelves,"[46] said a well-known journalist and media director affiliated with Pujol's party, dismissively (J.B. 2007b). "As anyone who has ever set foot in their town library knows, literatures are classified by their languages,"[47] wrote another in one of the conservative Spanish-medium dailies (Sintes 2007). Most relevant to the point I want to develop, another commentator asserted "The head of the bookstore at El Corte Inglés [Spain's leading department store chain] has it straight: Catalan literature is that which is written in Catalan, and for that there are specific display cases"[48] (Cuyàs 2007).

---

43. Heller has developed this influential thesis in a number of works. For summary statements of the thesis, see among others Heller 1999, esp. 10–20; Heller 2013, 352; Heller and Duchêne 2012, esp. 1–3. For case studies, see Duchêne and Heller 2012, and Pietikäinen and Kelly-Holmes 2013. For further discussion of the exploitation of the iconic indexicality of language in marketing, see Cavanaugh and Shankar 2014.

44. "una literatura és una llengua."

45. "el elemento de definición es la lengua."

46. Vicenç Villatoro: "és un debat bibliotecari, sobre prestatgeries."

47. "Como sabe cualquiera que haya pisado la biblioteca de su pueblo, las literaturas se clasifican por su idioma."

48. "l'encarregat de la llibreria d'El Corte Inglés ho té clar. Literatura catalana és la que es fa en català, i per això té uns expositors especialment dedicats."

Comparisons were made to conventions by which English literature is that written in the English language even when written by a Pole or a Russian.[49] German literature is that which is written in German, even by a Jew living in Prague. Kafka—Czech citizen but German author—was put forward as an exemplar immediately after the March 2005 announcement of the invitation (Cònsul 2005, Piquer 2005), in a trope reproduced repeatedly across the years of debate and again by former president Pujol in Frankfurt.[50] Following this model (which no one criticized as Kafkaesque!), Catalan literature is that and only that written in Catalan, regardless of the subject matter, birthplace, or residence of the author (Geli 2007c). It is indicative of the canonically monolingual nature of publication in Catalonia that this classificatory schema was not much confounded by linguistically hybrid forms (but see King 2006 for discussion of such hybridity). Although some authors have experimented with mixing the two languages in some of their work, and some write occasionally in the second language, no hybrid literary genre is recognized, much less marketed, in Catalonia (Crameri 2005). Publishing in Catalonia, like other domains of language use, largely fits the dominant model that Monica Heller (1999) identified of multilingualism as a set of parallel monolingual practices.

There were a few rejections not of marketing principles as such, but rather of the use of linguistic criteria to establish the market's taxonomy (Ferran and Fernández 2005). Felix de Azúa, the critic of Catalan nationalism quoted earlier, embraced a neoliberal, anti-protectionist market standard: "there are things that defend themselves . . . it's not necessary to defend Catalan literature, because it defends itself"[51] in the marketplace. Endorsing an absolute free market principle, de Azúa rejected the classification of literatures according to language as a "19th century idea." He criticized the Catalan cultural administration as belonging to

> an archaic political order . . . with ideas from the 19th century—not even the 20th even though we're already in the 21st—and it continues to consider the condition of literature according to the 19th century manuals that said that it was defined by language. . . . In the 21st century, everyone knows the difference between university manuals and reality, which says that literature

---

49. As honored guest in 2006, India had excluded English-medium literature in a similar move, with a similar accompanying controversy (Cal 2007).

50. This was not the first time that Kafka had been cited among Catalan writers. The popular Castilian-medium writer Manuel Vázquez Montalbán had alluded to Kafka in 1977 when asked—in a survey he instigated himself—to characterize his own status in Catalan culture (Carbonell et al. 1977); see brief discussion earlier in this chapter.

51. "Hay cosas que se defienden por si mismas . . . no es necesario defender la literatura catalana porque se defiende sola."

doesn't belong to a nation or a language, but to publishers, marketing and the market.... A culture ... is a market.[52] (*El Mundo* 2007b)[53]

De Azúa drove home the point again later in the roundtable: "More than nations there are markets"[54] (*El Mundo* 2007a). He did not specify on what ground, literally or figuratively, post-national literature was to be demarcated and re-marketed. Voicing the ideology of anonymity, de Azúa here formulated the market and its culture as from nowhere and everywhere, floating free from any constraints at all—territorial, linguistic, or other. (Yet he had previously been the Paris director of the Instituto Cervantes, founded by the Spanish government to promote the Spanish language internationally, and has since become a member of the Spanish Royal Academy.) In practice it was specifically the treatment of Castilian-medium authors from Barcelona that was the focus of his indignation, rather as if under cover of anonymity, the free market and government sponsorship of Castilian were the same thing.

More generally, the convention of one language, one literature was accepted when the debate could be confined to "Catalan literature" rather than "Catalan culture" (as it seldom could). Objecting to the parliamentary motions that stated the allegedly obvious in service of status politics, an editorial director of a major publishing house complained dismissively: "To say that Catalan literature is that which is written in Catalan is like saying two plus two equals four"[55] (Fernández 2005).

In this debate, then, advocates from both sides attempted to frame the definition of Catalan literature as not a matter of authenticity, origins, national identity, or sentiment. Rather they treated it explicitly, unabashedly, and common-sensically as an issue for the marketplace to settle, or even as an issue already resolved there.[56]

---

52. "un orden político arcaico . . . con ideas del siglo XIX—ni siquiera del XX aunque ya estamos en el XXI—y sigue considerando la condición de literatura según los manuales del XIX donde se decía que quedaba definida por la lengua . . . .en el XXI todo el mundo diferencia entre manuales universitarios y realidad, que dice que la literatura no pertenece ni a una nación ni a una lengua, sino que pertenece a los editores, al mercadeo y al mercado . . . ."; "[U]na cultura . . . es un mercado."

53. See King (2006, 2010) for a related critique of the linguistic definition of Catalan literature. King discusses the merits of the proposal to replace the category of "Catalan literature," with its strong monolingual tradition, with a new category of "Catalan letters" that acknowledges bilingual production (King 2010, 239–240).

54. "más que naciones hay mercados."

55. "decir que la literatura catalana es la que se escribe en catalán es como decir que dos y dos son cuatro."

56. The second director of IRL to try (briefly) to organize the Frankfurt event, Emili Manzano, was one of the few to express reservations publicly about emphasizing the market in relation

The objects this framework placed in contention were not languages as such but books, which were depicted as commodities, to be located on library and store display shelves for easy identification by potential consumers. As one publisher wrote, "all languages and all literatures have to do everything possible to widen the market for their use"[57] (Broch 2005). A columnist for a business periodical explained the quest for honored guest status itself in the same terms, tinged by sarcasm: "We've decided that the label 'Made in Spain' doesn't sell anymore, and everybody has gone into business for themselves"[58] (Echart 2007). A Catalan author put it in even more strongly cynical terms: "We have to sell ourselves the way the prostitutes in Amsterdam do: displaying ourselves. We put ourselves in the shop window and whoever wants us can buy us"[59] (Piquer 2005).

The rhetoric of markets and commodities is strong here. If we are tempted to see this case as an example of what Jacqueline Urla characterized with doubt as "the inevitable colonization of the field of language politics by neoliberal rationalities" (2012, 74), her skepticism is a useful perspective on Catalonia as well as the Basque case that she studied. Rather than the neoliberal market colonizing language politics, in the Catalan case there were accusations from the publishing industry that politicians and language politics were colonizing a well-established commercial enterprise. "This is an event for publishers, not the Olympics"[60] grumbled one (Fernández 2005).[61] As the most important book market in the world and a "global display window," the Frankfurt Fair was deemed by another publisher to be too important an event to be left in the hands of "cultural functionaries" and "the politicians of the day"[62] (Cònsul 2005). In 2007, scoffing at the government's efforts to portray the actual event as a success, a Catalan

---

to language. He asserted that although Catalan had been able to survive a "criminal" political institutional oppression, pure market criteria would be a serious threat to its survival (Amela 2006).

57. "tota llengua i tota literatura han de fer el possible per eixamplar el seu mercat d'ús."

58. "Hemos decidido que la marca *made in Spain* ya no vende y cada uno ha puesto un negocio por su cuenta."

59. "Ens hem de vendre com fan les putes a Amsterdam: mostrant-nos. Ens posem a l'aparador i qui ens vulgui, que ens compri."

60. "es una cita para editores, no unas Olimpiadas."

61. These complaints from the publishing industry did not acknowledge that long-term government efforts and negotiations were what put Catalan publishing houses in the position of being featured players in the 2007 fair, nor that it was precisely the allocation of government funding that was in dispute.

62. "funcionaris culturals"; "polítics de torn."

journalist and poet who writes in Castilian asserted again that this was a case of government meddling in market matters, rather than vice versa: "When ideology imposes itself on industry, when the matter is one about industry, it is never good news"[63] (San Agustín 2007).

Editors, publishers, and literary agents from Catalonia had in the past attended the Frankfurt Fair annually to place their products and to purchase translation and publication rights to others, and more than one was indignant about being displaced now by government authorities and authors (Morán 2007b). Publishers' efforts to protect a central role for themselves in the production of the Frankfurt event recall Benedict Anderson's (1991) thesis of the origins of nationalism and of standard languages themselves: that it was print capitalism, and specifically printers and publishers, that first made the linguistic objects that only later would be brought under political aegis as national languages. For Anderson, standard languages, and thus ultimately nations themselves, are things made by printers in order to consolidate their markets. National languages in this view were born commodified. Anderson's thesis exaggerates the role of print publications in the complex historical emergence of both standard languages and modern nationalism and plays loosely with periodization, but its emphasis on the early capitalist commodification of what became national languages provides a useful long view on their commodification in late capitalism. Susan Gal similarly provides a historical perspective on tropes of linguistic commodification associated with European nation-states over a century and a half (Gal 2012, 22, 24). Gal's overview suggests it may be less linguistic commodification itself that is distinctive in the contemporary period than the particular forms that it takes, the uses to which it is put, and the broad swath of linguistic workers and consumers that it affects.

In the Frankfurt controversy, some commercial publishers felt that their prior claim to this field of activity was threatened, and they argued that politicization was contaminating the rational—the market—with the irrational—nationalism. One wrote that publishers knew very well how to sell Catalan culture to the directors of the Frankfurt Fair, but when management was transferred to a government institution, "what was a market matter was transmuted into patriotic essences; commercial rationality was replaced by nationalist irrationality"[64] (Pontón 2007). Languages were represented as coexisting happily in the marketplace; it is only when subjected to political management that they become conflictive, charged, and exclusionary (Ferran and Fernández 2005). But as we have

---

63. "Que la ideologia s'imposi a la indústria, quan la cosa va d'indústria, no és mai una bona notícia."

64. "lo que era material de mercado se transmutó en esencias patrias. Al ser sustituida la razón comercial por la irracionalidad nacionalista."

seen in earlier chapters, the political management of language by the central state is itself invisible.

Supporters of the focus on Catalan-medium literature also endorsed the rationality of the marketplace. For example, if the manager of El Corte Inglés had been put in charge of the Frankfurt Fair, none of this controversy would have arisen, Manuel Cuyàs hypothesized in a humorous tone. Sensible decisions about books as commodities to be sold would have been made. Cuyàs acknowledged that the government is not the same as a department store, but proposed that "a government has to have ideas as clear as those of a salesman," and "the government has to take [to the fair] the books that the manager of El Corte Inglés would take"[65] (Cuyàs 2007).

From a more jaundiced perspective on the market, some, including Josep Bargalló, the director of IRL who was ultimately in charge of the event, hinted that it was precisely marketing imperatives that created an artificial linguistic controversy. The suggestion was that in choosing the annual guest of honor (as with India the year before, which generated a similar controversy about English) the Frankfurt Fair actually sought or manufactured conflictive cases to stir interest (Cal 2007, Geli 2007b, Bru de Sala 2007). In his history of the Frankfurt Fair, its former director Peter Weidhaas (2007) recounted prolonged controversies surrounding guests of honor from Italy in 1988 through India in 2006, and he indeed reported that increased media attention and marketing success were attendant on such controversies. Moreover, the fair's new director in 2007, Jürgen Boos, was described as interested in reviving the "political aspect" of the guest of honor appearance; he was particularly happy about the choice of Turkey as honored guest for the following year because "it's politically charged" (Knapp 2007). Boos told the press on opening day of the Catalan event that despite a smooth start there would be continued controversy in the following days, strengthening the suspicion that he fanned the flames of controversy to increase publicity (Alós 2007c).

Other commentators took up the talk of market rationalism but turned it to a different effect, pointing out seeming inefficiencies and artificial constraints on the free market in Spain, where translation opportunities were being lost.[66] The great irrationality, one Catalanist op-ed piece asserted, is that in the 21st century, there were still people with political, social, and cultural clout in the Spanish state who didn't want to know anything about Catalan literature (Loste

---

65. "El Corte Inglés és una cosa i un govern català n'és una altra"; "però un govern ha de tenir les idees tan clares com un venedor"; "el govern hi ha de portar els llibres que l'encarregat d'El Corte Inglés hi portaria."

66. See Crameri 2008 for corroboration of this complaint.

i Romero 2007). The implication was that such gatekeepers obstructed the free flow of Catalan literature and ideas to the wider market. A Catalan-medium author, Rafael Vallbona, similarly suggested that there was a constraint on the market at work when it was much more common for his books to be translated into Italian, which he did not see as a natural market for him, than into Spanish, which he felt logically should be his (*El Mundo* 2007b).

What Is Catalan Culture? Authenticity and Pluralism

"Culture" does not have the same bounded reification in the marketplace that could be claimed for literature. Thus, the problem of defining Catalan culture—the original problem posed by the Frankfurt invitation—could not be resolved so flatly by recourse to an allegedly established criterion. Nonetheless, a dominant position emerged that was expressed and accepted by a broad (not the entire) political spectrum. We look in this section at the competing criteria for the linguistic belonging of culture, the emergence of this dominant position, and the rhetoric in which the event was finally framed by government authorities.

Discourses of Authenticity

In sociolinguistic research generally, nationalist discourses of language are usually characterized as monolingualist and essentialist; they are seen to be based in and to reinforce the equation of one language, one culture, one nation (Blommaert and Verschueren 1998). In the transition to democracy and the post-Franco period, official Catalan nationalism took ambivalent stances on this question. On the one hand, from the earliest stages of autonomy in 1980, Catalonia was characterized by administration leaders such as the head of language policy as one community that expresses itself in two languages. On the other hand, as seen in the 1979 Statute of Autonomy and reinforced in the language laws of 1983 and 1998, Catalan language policy has revolved around the concept of Catalan as Catalonia's *llengua pròpia*, its "own language" (see Chapter 3). As the *llengua pròpia*, Catalan is deemed an authenticating characteristic of Catalonia not only juridically, but also ideologically and morally.

Both the generalized sociolinguistic view and the official Catalan policies might lead us to expect the trope of *llengua pròpia* to have had a central role in justifying priority for Catalan as representing Catalan culture at Frankfurt, and an ideology of linguistic authenticity more generally to have framed the rhetoric. Alternatively, from the ideological shifts and newer public rhetorics of language that we have seen in previous chapters, we might expect the discourse of authenticity to be muted. And indeed, this muting was generally the case. Explicit defenses of the *llengua pròpia* were heard from some voices in the political and public sphere, and these will be discussed in this section. However, for the most part the leaders of the governing coalition damped this theme and amplified other rationales in the planning for the fair, as will be shown in the next section.

An essentializing view of language as defining a culture was advanced from some Catalanist quarters in the Frankfurt controversy. For example, the center-right Catalan nationalist coalition party CiU that had ruled Catalonia for over two decades objected on this ground to the Socialist-led government's differentiation between language and culture. Positing a Whorfian foundational link between language and culture, a CiU spokesperson argued that the entire distinction between literature and culture was itself inappropriate (Europa Press 2007). This was unsurprising given both CiU's parliamentary position in the opposition and also the relatively traditionalist vision of language and culture established in its subvention policies in the decades it held the government of autonomous Catalonia (the policies for which de Azúa had demanded an apology from the new president).[67]

The ideological frame of authenticity and its attendant terms made frequent appearances early in the debate, as partisans of different views competed for position before the definition of the event solidified. In 2005, the spokesperson for the Catalanist ERC party, Marina Llansana, wrote of "*la nostra llengua i la nostra cultura*" ("our language and our culture")—that is, our one culture and one language—to advocate a Catalan-only official presence at Frankfurt.[68] She asserted that the party, and specifically its leader Josep-Lluís Carod-Rovira (from whom we will soon hear a different position), rejected the claim that Catalan culture is the sum of cultural manifestations produced in the country. That claim had been made explicitly by Catalan Socialist cultural policy leaders in earlier years (Crameri 2008, Mascarell 1999). Llansana asserted that such a claim would make Catalan culture "the only one in the world that doesn't have its own signs of identity."[69] She used the same rhetorical tactic that we saw ERC also applied in the debate over la Mercè, characterizing as "provincialism" the desire to hide *la*

---

67. See again Crameri 2008. Although it was not the case at the advent of autonomy, CiU came to own the label "nationalist" in the press; any political reference in Catalonia to "nationalists" was to that party. At the same time, it must be recognized that CiU had a longstanding official policy of anti-essentialism when it came to defining Catalan identity. It was the CiU leader Pujol who in the 1970s introduced the definition that became hegemonic "All those who live and work in Catalonia are Catalan."

68. Catalan syntactic rules, unlike Spanish, require the definite article (in this instance, f. sing. *la*) with possessive adjectives (e.g., *nostra* "our"). This construction makes more explicit a commitment on whether "our language" is one or can be more.

69. "l'única al món que no tindria senyals d'identitat propis."

pròpia identitat cultural "our own cultural identity" at exactly the moment when its "difference" is of most value (Llansana 2005).[70]

Another important example of the equation of language and culture appeared early in the debate in an op-ed piece written by Jordi Porta, the head of the non-governmental organization Òmnium Cultural, known for its defense of traditional Catalan linguistic and cultural forms (and a leading force in the current sovereignty movement). "The health of Catalan literature, and by extension Catalan culture, is a recurrent object of our public debate,"[71] the op-ed asserted. While the essay thus explicitly proposed that a literature can metonymically or synecdochically represent "a culture," it further implicitly rested on the unexpressed presupposition that only *Catalan-medium* literature represented the Catalan culture. Porta elided the very question of a place for Castilian-medium literature in Catalan culture—the original question—through a chain of equivalents that rhetorically suppressed their foundational premise.

> Literary production is often identified with the global state [of health] of a given *culture*. And in *our* case, that of a *literature* that has to compete in a market where the potential readers are also capable of reading in a *language* that is spoken by more than 300 million people . . . it always demands extra quality or an extra, complementary effort at promotion.[72] (Porta 2005; italics added)

With no textual antecedent to anchor the possessive pronoun, "our case" artfully allowed slippage from a *literature* to a *culture* first and from a *literature* to a *language* second as the "case" in question; closing the logical circuit completes the equation of a language and a culture. Through these equivalences, the author implicitly placed the Castilian language (the one "spoken by more than 300 million people") outside of Catalan culture, and Castilian-medium writers outside of the Catalan "us," without ever articulating the proposition or mentioning the *llengua pròpia* much less arguing the point.

---

70. ERC had earlier formed part of the coalition government with the Socialists and left-green party that continued to govern in this period before the fall 2006 elections discussed in Chapter 3. ERC and specifically Carod-Rovira had been ejected from the coalition after public gaffes and unsurprisingly took critical stances toward the remaining governing coalition's policies.

71. "l'estat de salut de la literatura catalana i, per extensió, de la cultura catalana, constitueix un objecte recurrent del nostre debat públic."

72. "la producció literària s'identifica sovint amb l'estat global d'una determinada cultura. I en el nostre cas, el d'una literatura que ha de competir en un mercat en què els possibles lectors són capaços de llegir també en una llengua que és parlada per més de 300 millions de persones . . . reclama sempre un plus de qualitat o rebre un plus un esforç complementari de promoció."

The Catalanist nongovernmental meta-organization for linguistic activism CAL (Coordinadora d'Associacions per la Llengua Catalana) used the concept of *llengua pròpia* to charter Catalan-only representation at Frankfurt without any circumlocution. CAL baldly asserted that the literature that the Generalitat of Catalunya must sponsor at the Frankfurt Fair was "none other than that conceived and written in the *llengua pròpia dels Països Catalans* ('The Catalan Countries' own language')."[73] "To invite Castilian-language writers who reside in the Principality of Catalonia would be deceitful," it continued, "because those authors are already represented by another culture: the Spanish one"[74] (*Racó Català* 2006b).

The concept of *llengua pròpia* made another relatively rare positive public appearance in a panel discussion in February 2007, but in a form that repudiated this equation of language and culture. Author and former director of the official Catalan television and radio corporation Vicenç Villatoro was reported to assert that all cultural manifestations in the territory "should be considered *propias*," but that there should be a special commitment to cultural production in Catalan as the "*lengua propia del país*" ("the country's own language") (Guillaumet 2007).[75] That is, multiple linguistic forms are *propia* to Catalonia as *culture*, but only one form is *propia* as *language* in Catalonia: Catalan. The distinction may be finely made, but it is a reminder of the de jure status of the language.[76] The Statute of Autonomy designates only linguistic, not cultural, propriety.

The term *pròpia* was also used by opponents, albeit negatively. A longtime critic of Catalanism, the Catalan journalist Ivan Tubau described the Frankfurt official delegation as the latest representation of the "grand fiction" found throughout the democratic period, in which advocates "pretend that Catalan is the *propia* and 'national' language of Catalonia"[77] (Tubau 2007).

---

73. "No és altra que aquella concebuda i escrita en la llengua pròpia dels Països Catalans."

74. "Convidar els autors en llengua castellana residents al Principat de Catalunya és un engany, ja que aquests autors ja hi són representats per una altra cultura: l'espanyola."

75. "Debe 'considerar como propias' todas las manifestaciones culturales del territorio, aunque reclamó un compromiso especial con la creación hecha en catalán como 'lengua propia del país.'" Although it is likely that Villatoro spoke in Catalan, the news report put the quote in Castilian, which is preserved here.

76. Another journalist, Marçal Sintes, reminded readers parenthetically of this status in an opinion piece (Sintes 2007). Òmnium Cultural also used the concept of *llengua pròpia* when it issued an official statement in September 2006, but it was notable for its caution about invoking any essentialist formulations at all, and its historicization of arguments for featuring Catalan literary production. When the statement used the term *llengua pròpia*, it was not to refer to Catalan specifically, but rather to "*territoris amb llengua pròpia*," 'territories with their own language' that are home to the diversity that is obscured by powerful dominant states.

77. "Fingir que el catalán es la lengua propia y 'nacional' de Cataluña."

Pluralist Visions of Language and Culture

Despite Tubau's assertion, in the more than 200 print and online reports I examined for this analysis, the term *llengua pròpia* itself was not reported to be used at all in relation to the Frankfurt project by administration representatives during the two-year period before Tubau wrote his criticism, and only sparingly in the following period of preparations up until the opening of the fair itself, when it made a notable reappearance that will be discussed below.[78] The successive Socialist-led coalition governments, even with the Catalanist ERC at the helm of the Culture Department and IRL, publicly defended an anti-Whorfian stance: a single culture can be multilingual. Catalan culture was to be seen as expressed not only in one language or even in two languages, but in all languages used in producing culture (whatever that might be) by those who live in Catalonia.[79]

This was entirely in keeping with the Catalan Socialist party's traditional stance toward culture and language, a tradition long criticized by others as insufficiently Catalanist. For example, the leader of the Catalan nationalist CiU party, Artur Mas, had blamed the insult that Catalan authors perceived at the Guadalajara book fair on the "socialist philosophy" that "empties Catalonia of Catalanness"[80] (Alós 2007a). It had thus been unsurprising when in discussing the Frankfurt invitation in 2006, José Montilla, who was at the time both the Spanish minister of industry and the designated Socialist candidate for president of Catalonia (see Chapter 4), described "the reality" of Catalonia as "the co-existence (*convivencia*) of two languages within a single culture"[81] (Piñol 2006). It was more surprising, however, when after the Catalan elections this same stance was taken by Montilla's vice president in charge of the Department of Culture, Josep-Lluís Carod-Rovira. As has been mentioned earlier, Carod's ERC party was the most Catalanist of the coalition government. Carod agreed to support the Socialist-led coalition only if ERC could hold the portfolio for cultural and linguistic policy. Less Catalanist forces assumed—and feared—that in this position ERC would impose strong preferences for Catalan language and culture (Moix and Massot 2006). After all, from the parliamentary opposition, ERC legislators had

---

78. Even the conservative Spanish press that was vigilant for such claims did not report any Catalan officials using the term until the Fair itself, which will be discussed later. Related terms that may be seen to draw on essentializing links, such as "our language" and "our culture" did appear in some statements from government officials.

79. Although the meaning of "culture" was vague in this formulation, it was generally equated to expressive and artistic culture; examples given included not only high culture but popular cultural forms.

80. "La filosofia socialista"; "buidar Catalunya de catalanitat."

81. "la convivencia de dos lenguas dentro de una misma cultura."

presented the motions to represent only Catalan-medium literature at Frankfurt, as discussed earlier.

Yet we have seen in Chapter 3 that during the electoral campaign of fall 2006, Carod-Rovira took an unorthodox position on Catalan nationalism as well as on the language. In keeping with this, Carod as vice president was reported to declare in January 2007 that "Castilian has become a structural element of Catalan society practically since the beginning of the 20th century and forms part of Catalan reality at the beginning of the 21st century"[82] (Branchadell 2007b). This position was supported publicly by the ERC frontline of cultural administrators appointed by Carod, right up to the opening of the Frankfurt Fair. For example, the new minister of culture, Joan Manuel Tresserras, asserted that "Catalan culture is that which is produced by anyone who lives in Catalonia,"[83] reportedly specifying that this would include a rumba sung in Castilian (Branchadell 2007b). The new IRL director Josep Bargalló, also an ERC appointee, explained that a culture is a territorial concept, and everything that happens in that territory forms part of the culture, while a literature is a concept based in a single language. (Bargalló added that they were not going to Frankfurt to explain two literatures.) (Geli 2007b).

That ERC officials should take such a position on the relationship of culture and language surprised observers (*El Mundo* 2007a). It was decidedly not the position that had been expressed by the ERC spokesperson Marina Llansana months earlier when ERC first took over the Department of Culture: "We are clear that not all culture that is produced in Catalonia in a given moment is Catalan culture"[84] (Massot 2006), and it was still not supported by all factions of the party (Branchadell 2007b). We can recognize in the newer stance, however, the outline of the cosmopolitan nationalism that had emerged as an ERC position in the la Mercè debate and in Carod's own electoral campaign rhetoric.

Rather than endorsing cultural purity or an essentialist form of authenticity, the political and cultural leaders who put the stamp on the Frankfurt event under the auspices of ERC publicly and repeatedly framed Catalan culture as pluralistic, cosmopolitanism, modern, European. Ringing the changes of neoliberalism, a report on an interview with the new minister of culture, Tresserras, represented him as advocating "the degovernmentalization of culture," and as endorsing an "open and inclusive" vision of Catalan culture that eschewed "politics of victimism" in favor of "realism, economic rationality, and modernization" (Moix and

---

82. "El castellà s'ha convertit en un element estructural de la societat catalana pràcticament des dels inicis del segle XX i forma part de la realitat catalana de principis del segle XXI."

83. "Cultura catalana és la que fa qui viu a Catalunya."

84. "tenemos claro que no toda la cultura que se hace en Catalunya en un momento determinado es cultura catalana."

Massot 2006).[85] The director of the cultural exhibit at Frankfurt, Xavier Pla, emphatically struck similar notes, stressing the "plurality of voices, generations, languages and artistic idioms of the Catalonia of today" and its "multicultural and plurireligious" character. The exposition showed Catalonia to be an "open and cosmopolitan society" and was reported to belie the prejudiced view of Catalan as a "regional and folkloric culture and a closed nationalism." Pla was quoted as asserting that "the very concept of Catalan identity has come to be declined in the plural"[86] (Alós 2007b).

Particular exhibits at the fair were reported to emphasize the contributions of immigrants from widespread origins to Catalan culture and their participation in the construction of a shared identity (Cuadrado 2007a). Center-right and center-left Catalan newspapers editorialized positively about the "open and tolerant Catalonia" that they saw displayed in the fair (Antich 2007b; see also *El Periódico* 2007a). At both the beginning and the end of the organizational process, some commentators went so far as to refer to Catalans and the Catalonia that was ultimately displayed at the fair approvingly as "mestizos" (*mestissos, mestissa*) (Alós 2007b, Huertas Claveria 2005).[87]

In sum, the ideology of traditional authenticity, even within the discourse of Catalan nationalism, was attenuated throughout the nearly three years of debate over the representation of Catalan culture at the Frankfurt Book Fair, as it was in other public discussions in the period. As was to be expected, longstanding opponents impugned linguistic authenticity and instead drew on an ideological framework of anonymity, calling on the free market and freedom of expression to legitimate the representation of Castilian authors at Frankfurt. Catalan government authorities in return eschewed overt rhetorics of authenticity. Traditional, naturalistic, and monolingual visions of cultural and linguistic authenticity were avoided or even repudiated by administration spokespersons throughout the years of preparation for Frankfurt. Reflecting the uneasily shifting grounds of linguistic legitimacy, it appeared that *llengua pròpia* in particular had become something of a politically taboo term in this controversy.

---

85. "desgubernamentalización de la cultura"; "una visión 'amplia, inclusive y abierta de la cultura catalana'"; "por acabar con la política del victimismo, en favor del realismo, la racionalidad económica y la modernización."

86. "la pluralitat de veus, generacions, llengües i llenguatges artístics de la Catalunya d'avui"; "multicultural i plurireligiosa"; "una societat oberta i cosmopolita"; "del prejudici que la catalana és una cultura folklòrica i regional"; "el concepte mateix de catalanitat o d'identitat ha passat a declinar-se en plural."

87. These applications of the term to Catalan culture are striking. Crameri (2008) comments astutely that while racial and ethnic hybridity are endorsed by Catalan nationalism as a matter of historical pride, cultural and especially linguistic hybridity have been treated as threats.

The prevailing definition that framed "Catalan culture" and the place of languages within it was the same in the beginning of the public controversy as in the end. But at the beginning it had come predictably from Socialists with whom it had long been associated, and whose Catalanist credentials were always treated as suspect. At the end it came from ERC, the explicitly Catalanist, longtime independentist party, in consonance with the new formulation of its vision that was mobilized in the electoral campaign.[88] This constituted a potentially significant shift in the discursive terrain, recognized, albeit grudgingly, even by the ardent opponent Félix de Azúa (*El Mundo* 2007a). Whether it was taken (or given) as sincere or empty political talk was another question (Sàlmon 2007).

Alternate Modes of Privileging Catalan: Market Weakness, Market Strength

If "Catalan culture" was the invited guest of honor at Frankfurt, and if Castilian-medium authors were to be treated indubitably as producers of a Catalan culture celebrated for its pluralism, on what grounds did the Catalan political leaders and organizers for the fair justify the focus on Catalan-medium authors and the late, minimal overture to Castilian-medium authors? The priority of Catalan at Frankfurt rested on two points, both hinging on the commercial market. (It is useful to recall that the market to be cultivated at the international event was not directly that of readership *in* Catalan; it was the market for Catalan works in translation, which would of course in turn help maintain the market in Catalan.) The first and more controversial rationale was Catalan-medium products' weak position in a market depicted as inefficient or irrationally constrained, a kind of market failure. The second took the opposite tack, arguing that Catalan's distinctiveness would enhance Catalonia's position in the publishing and cultural markets. I will discuss examples and the logic of each argument in turn in the next two sections.

Weak Position in the Market: Affirmative Action

The first justification given for the focus on Catalan-medium literary production was as affirmative action for commercial reasons. This rationale mixed social justice and market resource discourses (Heller 2013, Ruiz 1984). As in contemporary diversity discourses in the United States, the argument was advanced that affirmative action is good for business, not just for its direct individual beneficiaries.

---

88. Stewart King points out that the new non-nationalist proposals also came surprisingly from the committed Catalanist author Xavier Bru de Sala (cited elsewhere in this chapter), for whom this was a "complete reversal" of an earlier stance (King 2010, 239).

Although not explicitly articulated and of doubtful persuasive value, the rationale that seemed to be suggested was that the free market in ideas and literature
would function better if discovery of worthy (Catalan-medium) authors was not
blocked by historical, political, and demographic disparities.

In the first months after the agreement with the fair was established, the
first Catalan minister of culture to touch the third rail to Frankfurt, Caterina
Mieras, announced that there would be affirmative action—"*discriminació positiva*" (*ABC* 2005)—in favor of Catalan. "We shall support those who need it
more" said the new director of IRL the following year, in order to "correct a
European cultural anomaly"[89]: lack of knowledge of a vibrant contemporary
literary tradition with 800 years of history (Amela 2006). At the actual event
in Frankfurt, former president Jordi Pujol lauded the protagonism of Catalan
in similar terms, for resolving an "anomalous and unjust" situation in which a
literature that is equal or superior in quantity and quality to that in many other
European languages is little known (Piñol and Barranco 2007), an injustice that
he asserted goes against Europe's pluralist policies (Geli 2007c). The inequity
was located in a kind of failure of the European and global market imposed
by linguistic constraints in the system, but the rhetoric of injustice obviously
indexed the conflict within Spain.

Similar redressive action in the market was deemed by the Catalan administration among others to be patently unnecessary for authors already visible in
the global Spanish-language market, an expanding market that functioned as
an effective base for securing further markets in translation (Morán 2007c). In
objecting to the first government team's bid to include Castilian-medium literature in the delegation, an ERC legislator rejected efforts to "dilute, mix, and back
the strong to the detriment of the weak"[90] (Alós 2007a).

This redressive goal was in keeping with the Frankfurt Fair's own stand-
ing policy of curbing brute market forces and specifically Anglo-American
media domination at the fair each year. It regularly attempted to equalize
representation and to limit disparities in display space allocated to large and
small producers. The fair's guests of honor were deliberately chosen to focus
the limelight on smaller literatures that were overshadowed in the global marketplace (Weidhaas 2007). The commercial and critical success of Dutch literature after being so featured was repeatedly cited as a model. By 2007, the
new director of the Frankfurt Fair itself, Jürgen Boos, was reported to be in
agreement with the Catalan decision to officially sponsor only the attendance

---

89. "que apoyemos a quien más lo necesita"; "corregir una anomalía cultural europea."

90. "diluir, mesclar i apostar pel fort en detriment del feble."

of Catalan-medium writers, on precisely these grounds: that it would help end the "unjust" international ignorance of a European language and culture (Alós 2007a, 4).

Strong Position in the Market: The Catalan Brand

The second and apparently more effective (in that it was more broadly repeated and less often challenged) official rationale for prioritizing Catalan at Frankfurt cast the language as a strength rather than a weakness within the marketing frame: it would create brand distinction in the marketplace.[91] "We want to show the distinctive aspect,"[92] said an administration representative early in the Frankfurt campaign (Fernández-Santos 2005). This marketing motif was developed, particularly by ERC leaders, in various political venues in addition to the Frankfurt controversy. For example, Jordi Portabella, the chief antagonist to Elvira Lindo in the controversy described in Chapter 5, pursued this theme as ERC candidate for mayor of Barcelona in spring 2007. Of his meeting with an association of business leaders, Portabella said:

> I argued that a sovereigntist approach to our language and our culture, with a strong projection of Barcelona as capital of Catalonia, was a good product to sell. The Catalan language is a unique product that differentiates us, that personalizes us. And instead of seeing this as an obstacle, this has to be seen as an advantage.[93] (Baulenas 2007)[94]

---

91. The discourse of national branding and commodification of culture to compete globally had been introduced earlier, under Pujol and CiU's leadership. Crameri (2008, 120–121) describes this for 1998 and 1999, but points out that in that conceptualization, cultural and linguistic policy were carefully distinguished from each other, and the branding of Catalonia internationally was construed as in spite of, rather than in concert with, the language goals. Josep-Antón Fernàndez also offers a subtle account of the progressive commodification of culture in Catalonia in the 1980s and 90s, and its contradictory pressures on Catalan language and identity (Fernàndez 2008).

92. "nosotros queremos mostrar el aspecto distintivo."

93. "Vaig defensar que un enfocament sobiranista de la nostra llengua i la nostra cultura, amb la projecció forta d'una Barcelona capital de Catalunya, era un bon producte per vendre. La llengua catalana és un producte únic, que ens diferencia, que ens personalitza. I això, en comptes de veure's com un entrebanc, s'ha de veure com un avantatge."

94. The framing of multilingualism as a resource has been documented in the past decade or longer in minority language settings (e.g., Jaffe 2007b, Heller 2013). Explicit ideological orientation to (multiple) languages as a resource rather than or in addition to a (civil) right or a (social or psycholinguistic) problem was advocated earlier by sociologists of language in the United States. Two classic statements of the language as a resource approach were published in the early 1980s (Fishman 1982, Ruiz 1984).

The term systematically deployed to encode this position in the final year of preparations for the Frankfurt Fair was *singular* "singular."[95] The promotional slogan for the exposition of Catalan culture and literature at the fair was "Catalan Culture: Singular and Universal." Rather than Catalan's status as the *llengua pròpia* or the originary language of Catalonia, its singularity or uniqueness was repeatedly stressed by the team that brought the event to completion.[96]

For example, IRL director Bargalló appeared in the Catalan Parliament in early March 2007 to explain the Frankfurt project. Mentioning that he would invite Castilian-medium authors to speak at Frankfurt, he said that their presence would be articulated in relation to "our singularity within a plurilingual culture, the Catalan language and literature"[97] (*La Gaceta de los Negocios* 2007). He further elaborated,

> We want to explain our reality the way it is and singularize what makes us different. We are plurilingual, certainly, but what makes us different from other plurilingualisms is Catalan. Without the Catalan language, Catalan culture would not have been invited to Frankfurt.[98] (Barranco 2007)

The traditional argument is that without the language the culture would not exist, so it is noteworthy to see the formula take a turn here to a role in the marketplace that would not exist without the language. This motif of singularity remained quite consistent for the rest of the preparatory campaign. The Catalan language is "what identifies Catalan culture within the global culture," Bargalló was quoted as saying seven months later in Frankfurt as the event began (Morán 2007b).[99] *Singular* signified both "unitary and unique," according to Bargalló (Ràfols 2007).

---

95. Catalan *singular* can also be translated as "unique," but because singular has related verb forms in English as it does in Catalan and Spanish, while unique does not, I use the cognate term in this discussion.

96. I do not mean to imply that ERC invented the use of the term "singular," only that it led a particularly noteworthy mobilization of it. Crameri (2008, 182) traces it to the cultural policies of the CiU government under Pujol, and we will see that it appeared in important linguistic legislation in that period. Moreover, in the formal debate over his selection as president on November 24, 2006, the Socialist Montilla defended the need for affirmative action to protect Catalan (which had been questioned by Catalan Partido Popular leader Josep Piqué) by saying that Catalan is what "singularizes" the country (Desclot 2006, Fernández 2006).

97. "nuestra singularidad dentro de una cultura plurilingüe, la lengua y la literatura catalana."

98. "Queremos explicar nuestra realidad tal como es y singularizar lo que nos hace diferentes. Somos plurilingües, cierto, pero lo que nos hace diferentes de otros plurilingüismos es el catalán. Sin la lengua catalana, la cultura catalana no habría sido invitada a Frankfurt."

99. "lo que identifica la cultura catalana dentro de la cultura global."

The term *singular* covers some of the same semantic terrain in Catalan as *pròpia*, signifying that a property distinguishes an individual or entity. However, it is different in that *singular* does not have the essentialism or naturalism that *pròpia* does. The second edition of the *Dictionary of the Institute of Catalan Studies* defines *propi/pròpia* as: "of one person or thing to the exclusion of all others; belonging to oneself and not to another; not borrowed, not artificial; especially fitting to the nature, quality, etc. of someone."[100] In contrast, *singular* in the *DIEC 2* definition, beyond its grammatical use, means simply, "distinguished by something unusual; the only one to possess certain qualities."[101] Unlike *pròpia, singular* carries no further qualifications regarding origin, lack of artifice, or intrinsic nature. It just means "unique." Catalan was thus cast as a tool for distinctively identifying a brand, more akin to a Nike swoosh than to a Romantic soul. The nuances of the dictionary definitions provide a suggestion of a subtle nudging of linguistic exclusiveness out of the frame of traditional authenticity, to which *pròpia* pertains, to the frame of cosmopolitan market branding. Even more important than the differential lexical semantics was that pragmatically *singular* did not have the ideological radioactivity from longstanding political and juridical use that we have seen in earlier chapters that *pròpia* did. Also important is the way that singularity was packaged with concepts of modernity and pluralism in an explicit discourse of branding, which we will look at below.

Speaking critically in response to Bargalló's presentation stressing the strategy of singularity, a parliamentary representative from the anti-nationalist Ciutadans party, Antonio Robles, complained, "He has wrapped up this cultural exclusion perfectly so that it's not noticeable"[102] (*La Gaceta de los Negocios* 2007). Robles's chagrin further suggests that the theme of singularity did not carry the same obvious national essentialism, interpreted as exclusionary, that made the *llengua pròpia* so controversial a concept. In light of this, it is important to remember that in the Catalan Law of Linguistic Policy of 1998, in a section subtitled "La llengua pròpia," three significant terms were explicitly linked: "Catalan is the *llengua pròpia* of Catalonia and singularizes it as a people."[103] For those aware of and attuned to it, the terms "singularize/singularity" would index this collocation and its firm grounding in the ideology of linguistic authenticity that equates a people with an originary language.

---

100. "Que és d'una persona o d'una cosa amb exclusió de tota altra; D'un mateix i no d'altri; No manllevat, no postís; Que convé d'una manera especial a la naturalesa, la qualitat, etc., d'algú."

101. "Que es distingeix per alguna cosa inusitada. Únic a posseir determinades qualitats."

102. "Ha envuelto perfectamente la exclusión cultural sin que se note."

103. "El català és la llengua pròpia de Catalunya i la singularitza com a poble."

Especially in view of this legislative linkage of the *singular* and *pròpia* in relation to language, I do not want to imply that there was a wholehearted abandonment of traditional authenticity rationales and the *llengua pròpia* motif in particular on the part of the administration's team. Within the framework of marketing strategy, IRL director Bargalló more often alluded to the essential and the *pròpia* when speaking of the Frankfurt Fair than did the ERC leadership above him in the government administration.[104] For example, describing the Catalan publishing industry as the most powerful in Spain, he was quoted as saying, "This industry would not have its own [*pròpia*] identification if it weren't for the Catalan language"[105] (Ramis 2007). Bargalló also explained in an interview with a Catalanist newspaper that all cultures are singular and that language is "essential" to make them identifiable:

> what we want to say is that ours is also a distinctive, identifying, and consequently singular culture, like the rest. We want to emphasize that universal culture would lose out without singular cultures, including the Catalan culture. Language is an essential element of this identification.[106] (Ràfols 2007)

There is an obvious irony in the fact that what Catalan leaders wanted was for Catalonia to be recognized as unique like all the rest. To be one of a set of equally distinct and recognizable entities would be to be normal, and normalization has long been a goal of Catalan linguistic and cultural policy. "This would never happen in a normal country" was the familiar refrain of complaints about denigrating treatments of Catalan and Catalonia, including the fuss over Frankfurt (*El Periódico* 2007b). In this sense, Catalonia's leaders did not in fact want it to be different from other countries, but only by distinguishing itself could it become the same. The opportunity to use the discourse of market branding in a global market venue was an opportunity to be normal.

The choice of *singular* as a key term for the campaign was successful in that it was not challenged publicly in the way that *llengua pròpia* had long been. It seemed to fit disarmingly well in the market discourse embraced by opponents of Catalanism. The term circulated and was used approvingly from a number of different positions.

---

104. Albert Branchadell wrote that Bargalló appeared to be trying to undo the position that the vice president Carod-Rovira and his culture minister Tresserras had staked out publicly (Branchadell 2007b).

105. "esta industria no tendría una identificación propia si no fuera por la lengua catalana."

106. "El que volem dir és que la nostra també és una cultura distintiva, identificadora, i en conseqüència singular com la resta. Volem remarcar que la cultura universal hi perdria sense les cultures singulars, i també la catalana. La llengua és element essencial d'aquesta identificació."

For example, a Catalan author said she would have supported the inclusion of Castilian-medium authors but was content to be part of an international promotional strategy to "singularize the presence of Catalan culture"[107] (J.B. 2007a). We saw in Chapter 5 that the center-right, Castilian-medium newspaper *La Vanguardia* defended the Catalan-Castilian bilingual character of Catalonia and repudiated what it saw as a Catalanist attempt to exclude Castilian in the controversy over la Mercè. Nonetheless, the director of the newspaper wrote approvingly of the exhibition at Frankfurt as highlighting Catalan "singularity" without confronting anyone (Antich 2007a). From a much more Catalanist stance, the writer Xavier Bru de Sala used the same term yoked to an authenticating discourse of historicity, writing that the invitation of honor owed to the publishing strength of Barcelona but also to the "singularity and antiquity of our culture" (Bru de Sala 2007).[108]

Singularity was paired with pluralism in the official promotion strategy, and together they were placed explicitly in the frame of branding. Bargalló reportedly sought to project an image of dialogue (between languages and between authors) as "the Catalan cultural brand"[109] (Barranco 2007). This too, echoed positively in the press. An editorial in *El Periódico* quoted approvingly an organizer's claim that the exhibition at Frankfurt represented "the plurality of voices, generations, languages and artistic idioms of Catalonia today." The editorial concluded that as "a diverse and integrative country, the Catalonia of the 21st century has in Catalan its distinctive brand" and yet still "embraces, day to day, cultural phenomena in Castilian with the most complete normalcy"[110] (*El Periódico* 2007a).

Along with its singularity and pluralism, Catalonia's 21st century modernity was a key element of this branding activity at Frankfurt. Visually, there were cultural motifs to suit all tastes, but the publicity tended to minimize the kind of folkloric images commodified as national authenticity in other cases that have been studied (and indeed associated with the earlier cultural policies of the nationalist party CiU; see Crameri 2008). This was not provincial cultural heritage and identity packaged as a vicarious experience of authenticity for a global audience hungry for its own lost sense of it. For example, the signature poster for the exposition featured none of the traditional Catalan tropes. Instead, the internationally known Mallorquin artist Miquel Barceló represented the "singular and

---

107. "la presència de la cultura catalana a la Fira del Llibre s'ha volgut singularitzar."

108. "la singularidad y antigüedad de nuestra cultura."

109. "marca de la cultura catalana."

110. "la pluralitat de veus, generacions, llengües i llenguatges artístics de la Catalunya d'avui"; "un país divers i integrador, la Catalunya del segle XXI, que té en el català la seva marca distintiva, i que acull, dia a dia, les manifestacions culturals en castellà amb la més absoluta normalitat."

universal Catalan culture" in a fresh calligraphy and an expressionist sketch of a ballerina in a tutu, hoisting a barbell above her head (Fig. 6.1). The charming image suggested an apparently fragile culture lifting well above its weight class.

There was less of the traditional *barretina* (that stereotypical red Phrygian cap) than of Catalan molecular cuisine and contemporary design in the exposition.[111] Nor were the Catalan linguistic products marketed at Frankfurt intended as ineffable emblems of identity rather than referentially communicative, as has been found in many situations of minority-language linguistic commodification.[112] Quite the opposite, the point of the turn of honor at the fair was to get Catalan-medium texts recognized as referential and expressive vehicles fully communicative to international audiences, albeit in translation. As Stewart King documents, despite continuing carping from Castilianist critics, Frankfurt was a notable success for Catalonia in terms of sales of rights for international publication and commissions of translations, as well as in positive attention from German media, reviewers, and booksellers (King 2010).[113]

In further commentary about the emphasis on modernity in the brand, Sergio Vila-Sanjuán, who followed the evolution of the event as both a participant and a cultural journalist, praised several parts of the exposition that "sell a fresh aesthetic, a contemporary 'look' [English in original] ....that makes up one of the most exportable elements of current Catalan culture." These "vanguard" exhibitions emphasized Catalonia's reputation for design, "which is precisely what marks its difference, especially if we compare it with the stale aesthetic or kitsch that some invited countries featured in past years"[114] (Vila-Sanjuán 2007). An ERC political

---

111. But see Crameri (2008) for examples of the commodification and exportation of traditional Catalan culture as spectacle in other settings.

112. For examples, see among others Jaffe and Oliva 2013, McLaughlin 2013, Pietikäinen 2010, Pietikäinen and Kelly-Holmes 2013. For further discussion of this contrast in the Catalan case, see Pujolar and Jones 2012.

113. A reviewer for another discussion of this material sensibly asked how audiences would recognize this distinctive Catalan linguistic brand once it was translated, a question that was never raised that I know of in the controversy. This is in part precisely the task of marketing, and one can imagine various ways to retain the mark, some as simple as "translated from the Catalan." (Consider the success of Swedish noir novels as a recognizably distinct genre, albeit in translation.) It is also the case that the target audience for the marketing strategy at this stage were professionals at the fair, not the ultimate reading audience. Catching the eye of the industry and those who could create a buzz for Catalan literary products in the mad rush of the fair was the goal. It seems likely that such industry agents already had strong impressions of the more familiar Spanish language. And these may have been primarily influenced by Latin American literature (whose stunning international boom had been promoted from Barcelona), so the idea of distinguishing the brand does not seem ill-founded.

114. "venden una estética fresca, un look contemporáneo que compone uno de los núcleos más ... exportables de la cultura catalana actual"; "en ocasiones como ésta el diseño es precisamente

FIGURE 6.1 "Catalan Culture, Singular and Universal." Poster for Catalonia as guest of honor at the Frankfurt Book Fair, 2007. Miquel Barceló: © 2015 Artists Rights Society (ARS), New York/ADAGP, Paris.

Reproduced by permission of ARS.

leader spoke of Catalonia as one of the "motors of the new Europe"[115] (Cuadrado 2007a). In a truly striking statement that left the history of domination as well as nostalgia for a monolingual heartland behind to make linguistic pluralism the

lo que marca la diferencia, sobre todo si lo comparamos con la estética rancia o kitsch que algunos paises invitaron aportaron en años anteriores."

115. "motores de la nueva Europa." This refers to an actual program of the European Union, the "Four Motors" (Crameri 2008).

very criterion of (late) modernity, Bargalló was reported to characterize Catalan as "the most modern medium-sized language of Europe" because "there is no monolingual zone in Catalonia"[116] (Vives 2007). Rather than the strategic essentialism of the Ethnicity Inc. model, here was a kind of strategic anti-essentialism.

Among the former Catalan political leaders and rivals who collaborated in promoting the brand of Catalonia in press conferences at the Frankfurt Fair was Pasqual Maragall, former Socialist president of the Catalan government and also the mayor of Barcelona who had led its very successful Olympics with its vanguard "look." Maragall asserted that the exposition showed that Catalonia is "European in a very authentic, umbilical way"[117] (Cuadrado 2007e). He deftly linked the authenticity of Catalonia not to ancient traditions but to qualities diametrically opposed to the stereotyped traits of close-minded, xenophobic provincialism with which Catalanism, like minority authenticities in general, was tarred by critics. The claim to a modern European character was indeed not new to the construction of authentic Catalan identity (in contrast to Spain's), but rather part of earlier eras of Catalanism to which Pasqual Maragall himself could literally claim an umbilical link. He spoke not only as the Socialist former mayor of Barcelona and president of Catalonia, but as the grandson of Joan Maragall, de facto Catalan national poet and part of the vanguard Catalan modernist movement in the late 19th and early 20th century. The grandfather had translated Goethe and Nietzsche into Catalan, a relevant enough credential for Frankfurt. In his *Ode to Spain*, he had also written some of the most famous lines of Catalan poetry, in as he put it "a son's voice speaking a language that isn't Spanish." "Where are you Spain? Don't you hear my voice resounding? . . . Have you unlearned your children's words?" (Translation given in Puppo 2011). The ode ended with "*Adéu Espanya*" "Goodbye, Spain," a line now frequently echoed in the contemporary sovereignty movement.

Pasqual Maragall had argued for the European cosmopolitanism of Catalonia in an op-ed piece published just days before the opening of the Frankfurt Fair, a piece in which he endorsed the policies of the current Catalan minister of culture. He asserted that "Catalonia could become an active center in the defense of diversity" in linguistic terrain, or better, "the promotion of diversity." "Catalonia has to make its cultural specificity count as a European value," he wrote, arguing

---

116. "'La llengua mitjana d'Europa més moderna' perquè 'no hi ha cap zona monolingüe a Catalunya.'" For English speakers the term "medium-sized language" may be reminiscent of automobile marketing, but it has been made popular by Catalan sociolinguists and language planners who reject identification of the language with endangered languages and seek to class it with those of small independent states (Soler 2013, Vila i Moreno and Bretxa i Riera 2014).

117. "europeos de una manera muy auténtica, umbilical."

that multilingual Europe is in a better position to understand the world than is the United States. "Let us be Europeans," he concluded, "starting from the beginning, which is to erase borders. Culture can do a lot in this effort, more than politics"[118] (Maragall 2007). Singular, European, cosmopolitan, pluralistic, vanguard, modern, and in Catalan: this was the Catalan brand marketed for and at the Frankfurt Fair.

The Return of the Llengua Pròpia

And yet: the motif of the *llengua pròpia* popped back up as the Frankfurt event became a fait accompli. A pamphlet prepared by IRL and released under its director Bargalló's authorship in multiple languages, to be distributed to Frankfurt attendees to explain the Catalan culture and the point of the exposition, used the term *llengua pròpia* repeatedly in relation to Catalan (Bargalló 2007). On the eve of the grand opening, Bargalló incorporated the term *pròpia* into the rhetoric of singularity when asked yet again by an interviewer why only Catalan-medium writers were present at the fair. Bargalló responded that the point of the exposition was "to display the literature that singularizes us as Catalans, that is *pròpia* to us, and that unites the various Catalan language territories" (Geli 2007b).[119] Most notably, in the ritual opening of the exposition at Frankfurt in October 2007, President Montilla declared in an otherwise entirely anodyne speech that "Catalan is the *llengua pròpia* of our country,"[120] and that term was reported in the headline in a disapproving Spanish newspaper (Cuadrado 2007b). In keeping with his own earlier pronouncements, Montilla quickly added that Castilian "is also a patrimony of Catalan society" and that the two languages "live together without any conflict except that which some people try to create artificially"[121] (Cuadrado 2007b).

Montilla's statement in particular suggests that the concept of *llengua pròpia*, although politically vulnerable, was also still viewed as essential in the delicate political maneuvering of the period. The ideological contest over foundations of linguistic authority was not settled even among allies. Nonetheless, the dominant

---

118. "Catalunya pot esdevenir un centre actiu de la defensa de la diversitat"; "promoció de la diversitat"; "Catalunya ha de fer valer la seva especificitat cultural com a valor europeu"; "Siguem europeus, començant pel començament, que és esborrar les fronteres. La cultura hi pot fer molt, en això. Més que la política."

119. "mostrar la literatura que nos singulariza como catalanes, la que nos es propia y que une los diversos territorios de lengua catalana."

120. "el catalán es la lengua propia de nuestro país."

121. "convive, sin más conflicto que el que artificiosamente algunos pretenden crear."

trend in the rhetoric around this controversy, just as in those discussed in earlier chapters, suggested that the political power and moral authority of traditional authenticity discourse had waned. The market offered a fresh and robust alternative.

Conclusion: Branding Like a State

As Constantine Nakassis has observed, "the brand concept increasingly functions as the measure of the state, its 'value' and its legitimacy, its ability to 'participate' in the global economy and 'develop' itself" (Nakassis 2013, 119). Nation branding ostensibly targeted to an audience of foreign capital also opens up possibilities for new forms of politics directed to internal audiences and for the management of internal challenges to authority, as Andrew Graan has shown in Macedonia (Graan 2013). In her work on Basque language management, Jacqueline Urla has urged that we should see language activists as strategically motivated and active participants who bend circulating discourses and tropes of neoliberal rationality to their own purposes (Urla 2012b, 74–75). We can apply these ideas taken together to the debate over Catalonia at the Frankfurt Book Fair.

In its guise as Catalonia S.A., the Catalan administration capitalized (so to speak) on the international currency of the discourses of marketing and nation branding to legitimate itself and the Frankfurt project not as hidebound nationalists engaged in the exclusionary traditional "sterile identitarian debate" (Soler 2006), but rather as corporate leadership doing the approved work of contemporary state actors moving in a global market. This alternative position from which to speak developed only with considerable stumbling across several administrations and did not persuade the steadfast critics, but it allowed the Catalan government to emphasize the Catalan linguistic profile while attenuating its dependence on the increasingly problematic and constraining framework of ethnolinguistic authenticity. What its opponents criticized as clientelist-corporatist political interference that violated free market principles, the Catalan administration defended as a strategy for modern global marketing that eschewed essentialist identitarian politics. Whether to see this as a sincere new stance, as Urla saw the new strategy of Basque activists, or as rhetorical tactics of realpolitik is less clear, though surely as politics it inevitably combined a mix of motives.

Michael Silverstein's dynamic model of the indexical order, which I used in Chapter 4 to characterize Montilla's semiotic reprocessing of his poor command of Catalan, also allows us to summarize nation branding as it functioned semiotically and politically in the Frankfurt case (Silverstein 1995). The traditional Romantic ideology typifies a language as an indexical icon of a community imagined as a nation. That is to say, the language is at once a sign associated with a community, indexing it, and at the same time taken as the very image or icon of that community. If we understand this indexical relationship as occurring at what we'll take as a first order of meaning, then we can see nation branding in general as mobilizing that indexical relationship itself at a second order.[122] The nation branding process turns the typified language variety together with its first-order meaning of national community into another sign indexing authenticated value at a second order. In nation branding, this authenticated value or value of authenticity attaches to a national(ized) commodity or even to nation as commodity. This is the process that has been described for many polities recently.

If nation branding in general is a form of second-order indexicality, then the nation branding seen in the struggle over the Frankfurt Fair also operated at a third order. The act of nation branding in itself was mobilized as a sign of the contemporary character of Catalonia and of this Catalan government administration. In short, at this third order of indexicality, nation branding itself became a brand or trademark. By engaging in the expected branding practices, the administration could strategically present itself as a state-like actor of the cosmopolitan, rational, and forward-looking type. These were not to be seen as just 19th century nationalists nor even 20th century liberal free-marketeers but rather 21st century global marketeers. Because so much of global marketing had become ethnicized and nationalized, Catalonia could be less so. In and through the very act of engaging in branding like a state, in just the way that other contemporary nations from Argentina to Switzerland do, Catalan leaders parried accusations lobbed from classically liberal and neoliberal positions. They performatively enacted their project not as a rancid nationalism but as the now-normal practices of normal polities.[123]

---

122. Since such typifications of language varieties themselves involve ideological operations on indexicality, it would be more fitting to term these n and $n+1$ order indexicalities, but it seems useful to simplify here.

123. King (2010) argues that there were similar liberalizing effects of the Frankfurt strategy on the conception of Catalan literature itself, breaking it from its moorings in the national project and perhaps allowing a reimagining of it.

III | CHANGING DISCOURSES OF LANGUAGE IN PERSONAL LIFE

7 BACK TO THE FUTURE

HIGH SCHOOL REVISITED

Introduction

In Parts I and II we have looked at public and mediatized discourses and debates about language in Catalonia. In this third part of the book, we move to the level of the individual and the interpersonal. We will look at how groups of young people from two different generations have responded in their own lives and in their own estimation to the institutional recuperation of Catalan, and how they participate in new discourses about language. Schools are a useful place to gauge change over time, because education has been a central domain in language policies, young people are most often the leaders in new sociolinguistic patterns, and institutionalized age grading allows us to compare generations. For these reasons, I used classroom ethnographies in two different decades, not to evaluate pedagogical practice, but rather to get a view of the sociolinguistic life of young people in interaction.

Language policy in Catalan education has changed remarkably over the last three decades.[1] At the beginning of autonomy when I first did research on language attitudes in Catalan high schools, most school instruction was still in Castilian, although there was study of Catalan as a subject. Throughout the 1980s, the language of instruction was variable across and within schools, and the students I worked with in 1987 had had a spectrum of different experiences. The percentage of officially required Catalan-medium instruction in the curriculum increased over the decade after the institution of linguistic normalization policies in 1983. Catalan immersion programs for Castilian-majority schools were introduced in 1983, widely promoted by the

---

1. For an overview in English of these educational policy changes, see among others Arnau 2014, Artigal 1991, Cots and Nussbaum 1999, Strubell i Trueta 1996, Vila i Moreno 2004a, 2011.

Catalan government, and progressively adopted as the main educational model. By 1990, 90% of primary schools reportedly taught mostly in Catalan (Arnau and Vila 2013, 4; Arnau 2014), although what that meant in practice was variable. The Language Policy Law of 1998 consolidated Catalan as the "vehicle of normal expression" for instruction as well as school administration in all primary and secondary schools for students of all linguistic backgrounds in Catalonia, with some few exceptions.[2] The explicit goal of educational linguistic policy has been for all students to achieve proficiency in both Catalan and Castilian by the time they finish their compulsory education. As F. Xavier Vila wrote,

> A transformation of this magnitude—change of linguistic medium in twenty years in a fully functioning education system—has no precedent anywhere in the world, and less still in democratic regimes and in national communities that are not independent.[3] (Vila i Moreno 2004b, 161)

Language in education has emerged in recent years as the policy terrain most fiercely contested between Catalonia and the central Spanish government, especially under the conservative Partido Popular. Efforts to require Castilian as a medium of instruction, as well as to expand the number of hours required as a subject of instruction (which it already is), at this writing continue to be pressed in the courts and by the Spanish administration, and resisted by the Catalan government. The education battle has helped fuel the sovereignty movement.[4]

The (now former) Spanish minister of education, José Ignacio Wert, infamously said in 2012 that it is necessary to change Catalan schooling in order to *"españolizar"* "Hispanicize" Catalan students and counterbalance school indoctrination in support of Catalan independence (García 2012). Wert added that the goal was for students to feel as proud of being Spanish as Catalan, and to equilibrate the two identities, but it was the Hispanicizing mission that was quoted repeatedly by indignant Catalanists and the Catalan government. There was overwhelming support in Catalonia for Catalan-medium instruction and a

---

2. Legally parents can request early education in Castilian for their children. Whether such a policy has been adequate and adequately fulfilled has been the subject of vehement contestation and intervention by the Spanish government in recent years.

3. "una transformació d'aquesta magnitud—canvi de llengua vehicular en vint anys en un sistema educatiu en ple funcionament—no té cap precedent enlloc del món, i menys encara en règims democràtics i en comunitats nacionals no independents."

4. A series of high-level Spanish court decisions since 2010 have ruled that Castilian must be reintroduced as a medium of instruction. The decisions have been turgid and internally contradictory (Woolard and Frekko 2013), but the gist has been consistently to demand a change in the established Catalan model, and it has been resisted by the Catalan government.

rejection of the policies Wert advocated. In a poll by *La Vanguardia* in 2013, 81% approved of the current immersion program, and 77% rejected the Wert proposal (C. Castro 2013). Groups such as Somescola "We are School" mobilized large demonstrations to resist the unpopular education reforms that Wert led for the Spanish state, and to defend Catalan-medium instruction as a successful policy to help create a fully bilingual population. The mobilization to defend Catalan and Catalan-medium education built on the momentum that had begun in 2010 in response to the judicial curtailment of key clauses in the Statute of Autonomy and that developed into the popular movement for sovereignty.

Before these renewed challenges under the Partido Popular, Catalan may have seemed to be well-established in the school system. However, its relative success was always set within a larger framework in which Castilian is hegemonic at the level of the Spanish state as well as in the commercial marketplace and popular culture. In such conditions, the actual effects that changes in educational linguistic policy have on language and identity have not been entirely predictable or obvious. Survey studies show impressive gains among younger generations in reported ability to use Catalan, but much lower rates of actual use of the language (Bastardas i Boada 2012, Pradilla Cardona and Torres-Pla 2012). To gain a qualitative grasp of this situation ethnographically, in 2007 I returned to a public secondary school where I had done a case study in 1987, in a satellite city of the Barcelona area.[5]

This chapter describes the dynamics of language consciousness among a classroom of young people in 2007, touching on many different facets of the question. The next chapter takes a different tack to the question of changes at the individual scale through interviews with a small cohort of the former students from the 1987 study, to see how their experiences with language choices had changed over the intervening twenty years.

Effects of an educational linguistic policy include many dimensions, from educational achievement through language mastery and use to linguistic consciousness, social identity, and cohesion.[6] The ethnographic and interview-based case study approach that I used in this research is not meant to arbitrate the

---

5. My first return visits to the school were actually made in December 2006, but since most of the study took place in 2007, I simplify in referring to it. For the earlier study, see Woolard 1992, 1997a, 1997b, 2003.

6. Controversies have been raised at the Spanish state level over Catalan-medium instruction and educational failure rates in recent years. Statistics show that students in Catalan schools perform at or above the level of other communities, even on Castilian language tests. This is too large and complex an issue to be addressed in this chapter. For evaluations of various dimensions of Catalan-medium education, see among others Bretxa i Riera 2009, 2014; Bretxa i Riera and Parera Espelt 2012; Strubell i Trueta, Barrachina, and Sintes Pascual 2013; Vila i Mendiburu 2010; Vila i Moreno 2012; Vila i Moreno and Galindo Solé 2010; Cardús 2000.

pedagogical and achievement issues. My goal has been to gain some insight into participants' linguistic consciousness and the play of language in social cohesion and identity formation. What social value do young people attribute to the use of Catalan, or lack thereof, by their peers? How do they hear Catalan, and what images do they hold of the language? Over the decades I have focused particularly on the position of working-class Castilian speakers, and I retain that focus here.

The School and the Case Study Class

IES Joan Cérvola (IES JC or JC) (the pseudonym I have adopted for the school in this book) is considered one of the better public high schools in its city.[7] This is an outlying city in the Barcelona area with an independent identity and local administration, where large numbers of immigrants from the south of Spain had come to work in factories (many now closed) surrounding the city's Catalan core. Most of the participants in my studies were the children or grandchildren of such Spanish immigrant workers. IES JC draws its students from middle-class as well as working-class backgrounds from a number of neighborhoods. The majority are from Castilian-speaking homes, but the school has ample representation of first-language (L1) Catalan speakers and a reputation for a more Catalan orientation than other public schools in the area. IES JC cannot be taken as a representative school, but it allowed me to see what can happen to language use when young people are in regular close contact with peers from both language backgrounds.

Compulsory secondary education in Spain has undergone extensive reform since my 1987 research, and by 2007 the move from primary to high school came two years earlier (at age twelve) than it had for my first case study group, while the minimum school-leaving age was two years later (age sixteen). However, IES JC and most of the kinds of students who attended it were still familiar and recognizable to me. Several teachers from 1987 continued on the staff in 2007. Among the most significant differences, besides the locked gates of the campus and a coat of paint on some classrooms, were the two pull-out alternative classes that had been created. One was an *aula oberta* "open classroom" for students who didn't do well in traditional classroom structures. The other was an *aula d'acollida* "reception class" for new immigrant students who

---

7. In other publications I have used different pseudonyms for this school, and each one has turned out to be the name of an actual school in the area or an institution I discuss elsewhere in the book (Institut Ramon Llull). To avoid this, I now adopt an entirely improbable name, "Secondary Education Institute John Doe," which I will often abbreviate to IES JC or JC.

need to gain competence in Catalan before being mainstreamed to classrooms where that is the medium of instruction.[8] By 2007 transnational immigration made up about 10% of the student body. The education of such new immigrants in Catalonia and in Spain generally is an important topic in its own right and is beyond the scope of this study.[9] The social relations between the Catalan and Castilian languages and between L1 Catalan and L1 Castilian speakers continued to be my primary focus in 2007, as it had been in 1987, and will be the subject of these chapters.[10]

In 1987 students had a mix of classes taught in Catalan and Castilian. By 2007, instruction throughout the school (apart from language classes) was supposedly normally Catalan-medium, and all local students had come through at least nominally Catalan-medium elementary schooling. Except in Castilian class, all the teachers of the case study group began instruction in Catalan, regardless of their own habitual language. However, Castilian continued to be present not only in the hallways but in the classroom. Students pointed out that some of their teachers repeated instructions in Castilian, and at least one routinely switched to Castilian not far into the class. Some teachers conducted side-talk regularly in Castilian. Emotionally fraught or otherwise marked exchanges that fell outside the usual classroom routine also could lead them to switch to that language. (On continuing mixed-language practices within Catalan-medium education, see also Bretxa and Vila i Moreno 2014).

Students in each grade were redistributed annually across three different homeroom groups of thirty to thirty-five with a mix from Catalan-speaking, Castilian-speaking, and immigrant backgrounds, and mixed performance levels. Only a fourth homeroom was academically tracked, as remedial. In 2007 as in 1987, each homeroom group remained together or split into two lab sections throughout the day. After preliminary observations in a number of different classrooms in each year, I selected one homeroom group as the case study to be followed closely for several months.

---

8. In the case study class, the least successful immigrant students had moved on from *aula d'acollida* to *aula oberta*. Several mainstream students conflated the two pull-out classes and talked of them as one, a somewhat mysterious place where their less socially/educationally integrated classmates spent their time.

9. On education of school-age immigrants in Catalonia, see among others Corona, Nussbaum, and Unamuno 2013; Ferrer 2000; Newman, Patiño-Santos, and Trenchs-Parera 2013; Trenchs-Parera and Newman 2009; Vila, Siqués, and Roig 2006.

10. The presence of new immigrants undoubtedly affects these linguistic relations in various ways, but I only touch occasionally on that aspect here.

In 2007 I chose a third-year class, since that was most similar in age to the first-year group studied in 1987.[11] Students came and went, but through most of the six-month observation period there were thirty-three students in the class, sixteen girls and seventeen boys, most of them fourteen or fifteen years old.[12] The group was well distributed across working-class and middle-class backgrounds based on parents' reported occupations. Of those ascertained, nine fathers were skilled laborers, seven white collar or professionals, and six were small business owners or independent artisans. In contrast to 1987, almost all mothers worked outside the home, the majority in clerical jobs, although others were housecleaners, waitresses, and small business owners.

There were several students in the class who had been born outside of Spain. All those born within the Spanish state had been born and raised in Catalonia, in the immediate local area, but mostly of parents or grandparents who were not.[13] Sixteen students in the class were L1 speakers of Castilian (in some cases Latin American varieties), twelve were L1 speakers of Catalan, three reported that they were Catalan-Castilian home bilinguals, and two had other first languages.[14]

All but one of the local students I was able to interview had Spanish immigrants among their parental, grandparental, or in the one most remote case, the great-grandparental generation. The two students most strongly identified as Catalan speakers had at least one Castilian-speaking grandparent. There were very few

---

11. In 1987 the students were in their first year of secondary school. I sacrificed comparability in stage of life, i.e., the transition to secondary school, in order to maintain comparable age.

12. As my ethnographic observations progressed, it turned out that this was a relatively well-behaved group with a number of good students, a chance occurrence given the lack of academic tracking in the school. The hyper-masculine styles and aggressive physicality often seen among young working-class males in the Barcelona area (Pujolar 2001) were relatively absent in this group. This is not to say these were quiet or subdued students. Boisterous behavior was still the norm, and the noise level in the classroom was often deafening, but the rowdiness had a relatively childlike quality.

13. There were seven foreign-born (one of them from a Catalan family and completely Catalan-identified) in this class, an unusually high percentage for the school. Two Latin American girls had immigrated in primary school and were not only fully integrated academically and socially but actually belonged to the dominant social group in the classroom, one of them at its very core. They are included among study participants and interviewees. Only four transnational immigrants were in the pull-out classes to accommodate their special needs, in line with the average for the school. Two of these were socially very well-integrated in the class, and two were rarely present and very marginal socially, but none of these four returned parental consent forms and so they are not included in the study. One was only a member of the class for about three months.

14. Although the fairly balanced proportions of the first languages in this case study were probably not typical of public high schools in Catalonia, they were a surprisingly close approximation of their representation in the population of high school students in Catalonia as a whole (Consell Superior d'Avaluació del Sistema Educatiu 2008).

Catalan-origin surnames (particularly the paternal surname) among the class. Both the maternal and paternal family names of even the two most Catalan-identified girls in the class were of Castilian origin (as all the most common surnames in Catalonia are, a point discussed in Chapter 1). Most seemed only dimly aware of their family immigration history and few if any had a strong sense of roots outside of Catalonia.

The students' reports on their families showed a trend toward Catalan across generations. Four students who reported that Catalan was their first language had one parent who used only Castilian in the home. Two interviewees who reported Castilian as their first and parental language reported their own habitual language to be both Catalan and Castilian. All changes between the two generations or across the students' lifetime were toward Catalan or the addition of Catalan, a trend that is similar to findings of other studies (Boix-Fuster 2015, 153).

In my first meeting with the class, I explained that I was interested in the linguistic situation at their school compared to the way it had been in 1987. The teacher commented that this school was probably not typical, in that more Catalan was heard there than in other public schools. This set off a free-for-all class discussion, with multiple students clamoring to talk at once about their own experiences. The teacher and I followed the students' lead as they developed this theme for the rest of the class period.[15] Some reported that there was more Catalan used socially in this school than the primary school they had come from; for others there was less. The students themselves soon raised the question of how the languages sounded to them, which will be discussed in detail below.

Through my participant observation across the school day two to four times a week over the next six months, I was able to contextualize that vociferous initial discussion in the day-to-day linguistic practice in the classroom, on the school patio, and in field trips, which I recorded as well as observing.[16] To explore further

---

15. I was introduced to the students in their Catalan language class, and this lively debate took place there. This was not a well-considered choice and may have biased matters, but fortunately it was the same bias in both years, and in fact the same Catalan teacher who introduced me. That the classroom discussion was so clamorous and involved considerable controversy suggests that the students did not feel as constrained by the context as might be imagined. My participant observation and recordings throughout all their classes across many months as well as private interviews months later in the study broadened the context and nuanced but did not disconfirm any of what I heard and saw in that initial encounter.

16. Recordings of classroom interactions throughout the day included whispered conversations and decidedly non-academic activities at students' desks or worktables. I have chosen not to give transcriptions of the multi-party interactions here because they were so context-specific and apparently chaotic that without the onsite observer perspective I had and sometimes even with this, and more explanation than there is space for, they are just bewildering to the reader. Nonetheless, I have used them to verify the descriptions of language patterns.

the linguistic views the students expressed, I carried out the same matched guise test of language attitudes that I had done in earlier decades.

Finally, I interviewed the twenty-four students for whom I was able to obtain permission.[17] Those who did not return signed parental consent forms included five boys who attended pull-out classes, four of them new immigrants. A Castilian speaker who was openly critical of some Catalanist policies told me apologetically that his parents did not want him interviewed. Thus the summary presented here lacks the perspective of the most marginal students and the most critical of Catalan policy, and it underrepresents boys.[18] It is a paradox of research ethics that I could not nag students to return their consent forms in order to make sure that their social groups were fairly represented in the study.

Despite flaws in the sample, the ethnographic summary of this classroom presented in this chapter includes the entire spectrum of linguistic backgrounds and habits among the girls, from the most monolingually Castilian to the most monolingually Catalan, and a broad if incomplete spectrum of the boys. I interviewed and recorded L1 Castilian as well as L1 Catalan speakers, immigrants as well as Barcelona-born, working-class and middle-class, disengaged and unsuccessful as well as high-performing students. Although they cannot be taken as representative of the population of Catalonia, these were real kids in a real school. I draw together my multiple sources of data to present as much as possible in just one chapter a rounded overview focused on their own linguistic consciousness, with an eye toward the way they resembled and differed from their counterparts of 1987.[19]

---

17. Interviews of 45–90 minutes each were carried out with fifteen of the girls and nine of the boys.

18. The reluctance of those least supportive of Catalanist policies—or at least their parents—to participate in a school-based study of what was described in the consent form as "the language situation in the Barcelona metropolitan area" suggests that the issue itself is associated with a Catalanist viewpoint and raises the fears about Catalanist institutional hegemony discussed in Chapter 3. However, all the self-selection bias did not trend in this same direction; a very shy L1 Castilian girl who spoke Catalan habitually and whose closest friend was a Catalan speaker also did not return the consent form and did not participate in the study.

19. Both Catalan and Castilian were used in recorded classroom interaction and interviews. In the transcript extracts in this chapter I represent Catalan in regular roman type as the unmarked language, because it was the vehicular language of the classroom in which the open discussion was held, and as the normal medium of schooling it was chosen by students in more interviews than Castilian was. In transcript extracts Castilian originals are represented in *italics*. English glosses use roman type for the unmarked language and italics for switches to the marked language. Within the body of the text, citations of single words in either language are given in italics; if both appear, the Catalan form comes first. See front matter for other transcription conventions.

A Measure of Language Attitudes

As a basic gauge of differences in students' views of the Catalan and Castilian languages across the years, I carried out the same experiment about language attitudes with the case study class that I had done with larger samples of students in 1980 and 1987 (Woolard 1989a, Woolard and Gahng 1990). It is a version of the matched guise test, a well-known design developed in Quebec many decades ago, which asks listeners to evaluate the personal qualities of a series of recorded speakers (Lambert 1972). Each speaker is heard once in each language, but listeners are not told this until after the experiment is completed. When they are debriefed, they are usually very surprised to learn that there were repetitions, and this was the case with this group of students. By holding context, text, and speaker constant and varying only the language used, the test gauges the effect of language choice on the impression a speaker makes.[20] The speakers, all young adult females, represented a range of accents from Andalusian and provincial Catalan phonology to very standard Castilian and Catalan varieties. The personality traits that listeners rated clustered along two principal dimensions, which beginning with my first study in 1980 I dubbed Status (e.g., intelligent, cultured) and Solidarity (e.g., likeable, attractive, has a sense of humor).[21] In all three years that I conducted the experiment, results differed significantly for the two dimensions.

On the Status measure, the group in 2007 followed the same pattern as those in 1980 and 1987. They gave the speakers significantly higher Status ratings when they spoke in Catalan than when they spoke in Castilian. This pattern held regardless of the first language of the speaker or the listener. The statistical effect of higher Status value for Catalan than Castilian is not only undiminished but even, at least speaking loosely, strengthened across the years (Table 7.1).[22]

This might seem to be an unsurprising outcome. Catalan is now normally the language of schooling, which reinforces its association with the relatively higher social class of Catalan speakers, to which I attributed the high Status value

---

20. The same recordings of adult female speakers reading an academically oriented text were used with this group as with students in multiple schools in 1980 and 1987. See Woolard 1989a for details. I now find the design imperfect, but keeping it the same over time allows useful comparison. In addition to the small size of the 2007 sample (restricted to the case study class), an important difference from earlier years is that these students had been told earlier for informed consent purposes of my general interest in the language situation, whereas earlier subjects were not. It's not possible to tell if this affected the ratings.

21. Solidarity might better be considered a measure of general "likeability," but for consistency with the literature on linguistic status and solidarity and my own practice since 1980, I label it Solidarity.

22. Technically it is not statistically appropriate to compare directly the strength of the effect across the different years, given the different samples of listening subjects.

Table 7.1 Mean Status Scores by Language Guise and Year

Year	Catalan	Castilian	Difference
1980	.0415	−.0415	.0830*
1987	.0951	−.0941	.1892*
2007	.1659	−.1576	.3226**

* significant at α level of .05.

** significant at α level of .01.

of the language in the earlier years. However, it is a useful confirmation of the continuing prestige value of the language, given the persistent doubts and pessimism many Catalan advocates express. Such doubts are fueled by both the overwhelming dominance of Castilian in the media and commercial culture, and by the continual dismissals we have seen in Part I and II of this book, of Catalan as a provincial "local" language of limited value and little cultural weight. That is not how students responded to it in this experiment any time over three decades.

On the Solidarity measure, in contrast, there was no statistically significant difference at all between the speakers' scores in Catalan and Castilian in 2007. A speaker's Solidarity ratings neither rose nor fell significantly with her use of one language or the other.[23] This was a notable change from earlier years, when there were complex patterns of significant effects of language choice on Solidarity.

The 1980 results had shown that listeners rewarded co-members of their own ethnolinguistic group for using their own language, and penalized them when they used the out-group language.[24] However, they were indifferent to the use of one language or the other by speakers who were not co-members of their primary linguistic group; there was no reward of increased Solidarity for the out-group. This pattern of ingroup Solidarity rewards and penalties amounted to a patrolling of ethnolinguistic boundaries that encouraged each group to stick to its own language in informal social interactions, and that would specifically discourage new users of Catalan.

---

23. The Solidarity finding is in keeping with the overall results of another matched guise experiment from the same period with a larger sample (Newman, Trenchs-Parera, and Ng 2008). However, that study's results on Status are very different, with no significant language effect. Its subject sample, in which there was quite high representation of transnational immigrants, differed importantly from my series of studies.

24. This interpretation assumes that ethnolinguistic background is—or was in the past—identifiable by accent. In pilot studies, adult listeners made such identifications reliably for most of the speakers.

By 1987, linguistic solidarity values had begun to change. Teenaged listeners still favored their own language, but L1 Catalan listeners had come to extend the reward of increased Solidarity not just to the L1 speakers but to all of the speakers when they used Catalan.[25] This was a fitting development given that linguistic and social changes, such as the spread of *xava* discussed earlier, were making it difficult for young people to diagnose who was a native speaker on the basis of speech style. This new pattern of rewards suggested that the social boundaries associated with language choice were beginning to break down.

With the 2007 group, the experiment suggests that the value of one language over the other for conditioning social solidarity had disappeared. Listeners from the different linguistic backgrounds did not judge speakers differently in their different language guises; that is, speakers were not rewarded or penalized on the Solidarity measure for using one language or the other. The choice between speaking Catalan or Castilian in itself appeared to do nothing to enhance or lower a speaker's social desirability in these young people's ears.

To summarize what my repeated studies with the matched guise measure suggested about changes in 2007 as compared to 1980 and 1987: In 2007 as in earlier years, Catalan endowed a speaker with higher Status—that is, more prestigious personal characteristics—than did speaking in Castilian. The prestige value of Catalan appeared to be even stronger in 2007 than before. In contrast, differences in Solidarity—that is, the attribution of personal characteristics valued in warm affective relations—were no longer conditioned by language choice or by people's linguistic background. The informal social value of linguistic identity and language choice had been neutralized.

Any experimental measure is by definition artificial, and this test was constrained by design choices I had made over thirty-five years earlier in the very first round. The classroom discussion, observation, and individual interviews that I draw on in the next sections gave me indispensable opportunities to expand on the experimental findings and hear how students talked about languages and speakers in their own terms.

Discourses about Languages: Elegance and Coarseness

In the boisterous class discussion that developed in my first visit, stereotyped images of the Catalan and Castilian languages quickly emerged that were later elaborated and occasionally contested in individual interviews.[26] The

---

25. Castilian-speaking listeners in 1987 in turn did not penalize their co-members for using Catalan, the way their counterparts had done in 1980.

26. Transcription and translation errors in an earlier report (Woolard 2009) have been corrected here.

students' own words made vivid the differential status value of the languages revealed in the matched guise test. Regardless of their linguistic background or practice, most of them described Catalan as elegant in contrast to Castilian as typically coarse. These consistent images illustrate the ideological processes of linguistic iconization and erasure, in which schematic contrasts are drawn between linguistic forms (Irvine and Gal 2000). Maintenance of the iconic contrast necessitates selective attention to particular linguistic features, kinds of speakers, and instances of speaking while ignoring evidence that does not fit.

The image of Catalan emerged quickly when the class discussion heated up after one student asserted that there should be more use of Castilian in addition to Catalan in schooling. In response Victoria, child of a linguistically mixed marriage and a Castilian-dominant working-class home, set out succinctly the status value that Catalan had in her ears. She also emphasized the limited effect of that value on her own linguistic practice, as seen in Ex. 7.1. In Victoria's view, this made it all the more important to use Catalan in school.

Ex. 7.1 Victoria: Elegance of Catalan

A mi, per exemple, m'agrada més parlar el català perquè el veig més elegant, vale, de llengua, ((Ss riuen)) però parlo més el castellà. Em sembla que m'agrada més (x) català però parlo més castellà.	I like to speak Catalan more because I see it as more elegant, ok, as a language, ((students laugh)) but I speak more Castilian. It seems as if I like Catalan more but I speak Castilian more.

Asked whether they agreed with Victoria's feeling that Catalan is more elegant, two-thirds of the students raised their hands in agreement, many of them also calling out enthusiastically. In private interviews beginning about two months later, the elegance of Catalan was affirmed repeatedly, with fourteen of the twenty-four students interviewed either offering this term themselves or confirming it when I inquired. Some students, both L1 Catalan and L1 Castilian, told me in their interviews that neither language sounded more elegant than the other. Only one, a Catalan speaker, said that Castilian sounded more elegant than Catalan. Even he added that Catalan sounded "more cultured,"[27] in a nuanced distinction that his classmates did not share.

---

27. "més cult."

Other terms emerged in individual interviews to develop closely related images of Catalan, usually cast explicitly as "more so" than Castilian. Twelve students characterized Catalan as sounding "refined" (CT *fi, finet*), six as more "cultured" (CT *cult/* CS *culto*), and four as "intelligent" (CT *intel·ligent/*CS *inteligente*) or "wise" (CT *savi*). Individual elaborations of this theme included descriptions of Catalan as "less vulgar" (CT *menys vulgar*), "more polished" (CT *més polit*), "more well-spoken" (CT *més ben parlat*), "prettier" (CT *més bonic*), "more beautiful" (CT *més maco*), "much better" (CS *mucho mejor*), and simply "better!" (CT *millor!*), as one student had called out when I tried to sum up the class discussion. L1 Castilian students were just as likely as L1 Catalan students to endorse this vision of Catalan as elegant, refined, and superior. "I see it as a, I don't know, a better language," said Victoria's close friend Teresa, an L1 Castilian speaker.[28]

After I counted hands for the elegance of Catalan, I asked the class how many thought Castilian sounded more elegant. No hands went up. Asked more explicitly if there was no one who thought Castilian sounded more elegant, several students chorused "No."[29] One Castilian speaker called out—in Castilian—in a pithy display of linguistic iconization: "It doesn't sound elegant. It sounds Castilian!"[30]

"We use Castilian more when we're mad" explained one student, to agreement from others.[31] Arnau, a strongly Catalan-identified classroom provocateur asserted with a bit of coy hesitation at his punch line, "The people who speak Castilian are people who don't have much culture, let's say."[32] This shift of focus from the quality of the language to the quality of people associated with it brought shocked protests from several classmates and laughter and applause from others (probably responding more to Arnau's prized ability to rile the class than to approval of his claim). Classmates moved to mitigate Arnau's bald assertion

---

28. "El veig com una llengua- no sé, millor."

29. It is conceivable that this shows the biasing effect of conducting this discussion in a Catalan class, of a reluctance to disagree with classmates, or of intimidation about publicly defending Castilian. The shouting, open disputes among classmates, explicit defense of Castilian, and direct contradiction of the teacher by students that were all recorded in this class session (as in others) show that these biasing effects did not entirely constrain the discussion.

30. *"No suena elegante . . . ¡Suena castellano!"*

31. "El castellà l'utilitzem més quan estem:: cabrejats."

32. "La gent que parla castellà, és gent que no té gaire:: cultura, diguem."

and restore the focus on language.[33] Camila was drowned out by others before she could finish her thought:

Ex. 7.2 Camila: Spoken the way it is

El català sona més elegant perquè es parla tal i com és, però, per exemple, el castellà, hi ha molta gent que en comptes de dir 'he acabado', diu 'he acabao', i coses així. Però no perquè siguin-

Catalan sounds more elegant because it's spoken the way it really is, but in Castilian, for example, there are a lot of people who instead of saying "he acabado" (("I've finished")) say "he acabao", and things like that. But it's not because they're-

Camila contrasted what she and others perceived as consistent exact pronunciation in Catalan with a widespread but stigmatized elision of sound segments in varieties of Castilian that is stereotypically Andalusian. Her premise that there is one way that a language really "is," along with the assertion that Catalan is always spoken that way, is a succinct example of the rigidly standard language ideology that Susan Frekko has shown is frequently applied to contemporary spoken Catalan (Frekko 2009a). Supporting Camila's line of argument, her classmate Katia explained that Castilian lacks elegance only because "no one speaks it in a sophisticated way."[34]

Blunt pejorative terms to describe Castilian were used by Castilian speakers as well as Catalan speakers in private interviews. The most common were "coarse" (CT *bast*/CS *basto*; six mentions) and "vulgar" (*vulgar*/*vulgar*; three mentions), and there were also several assertions that it was spoken in a careless manner (CT *deixat*/CS *dejado*). Individual students said that Castilian "sounds more poorly-spoken" (CT *sona més mal parlat*), "cruder" (CT *més barroer*), "brusque" (CS *brusco*), "loutish" (CS *de garrulo*), and, most picturesquely, "more 'fuck, dude'" (*més "joder tio"*, with the obscenity in Castilian). In a tacit repudiation of the easy assumption we have seen in earlier chapters of the superior suitability of Castilian to be a public language, it was described as sounding "more for being around the house" (*més d'estar per casa*). This last came from an L1 Catalan speaker whose family did not use Castilian around the house.

---

33. The invisibility or deniability of the social structural underpinning of linguistic value is crucial to the process of misrecognition and the linguistic authority of anonymity, as discussed in Chapter 2.

34. "Ningú el parla sofisticadament."

There was nothing very new about these descriptors in this school. However, in 1987, when they arose in interviews they were often attached directly to the contrasting ethnolinguistic groups: "Catalans are more refined," "Castilians are less cultured," "ruder," "more coarse," were among the comments from JC students twenty years before (Woolard 2003, 96). These consistent stereotypes date from before Catalan-medium education and are based in social class associations of linguistic forms with personae, not the educational language policy that has since then made Catalan the usual medium of instruction. In contrast to 1987, Arnau's bald assertion about personal qualities was a relatively rare and controversial moment in 2007 (although we will see more nuanced accounts below that echo Arnau). It appears that the linguistic images were becoming detached from personae and their essential ideological belonging transferred to the languages themselves. If so, it is not clear whether this may owe to the changed policies or to the increased sensitivity to ethnic comments in public that had emerged in Catalonia and Spain by this time.

Interviews also brought confirmations of the assertion that for Catalan speakers, Castilian is associated with anger. "At my house we use Castilian more when we're mad," so Catalan in contrast sounds "sweeter" said one home bilingual.[35] A Catalan speaker acknowledged that she had always understood that "Castilian is more for telling someone off,"[36] since that is how it is used in her home. Another Catalan-speaking girl similarly asserted that "when I'm really, really really mad, I say it in Castilian, because Castilian sounds stronger, I mean, it's involuntary, it just comes out in Castilian."[37] Yet another asserted that when people say swear words or are "angry" and "they want to insult someone, normally they say it in Castilian."[38] Castilian was also said to be best "if you tell a dirty joke,"[39] and for "joking around" in general.[40]

Interviewees accounted for such pragmatic suitability in terms of what have recently been discussed as the "qualia" (putatively perceptible qualities) of languages (Gal 2014). Castilian feels/sounds stronger. It makes insults sound "more powerful, they're felt more," whereas Catalan would make them sound "weaker"

---

35. "A casa meva utilitzem el castellà quan estem enfadats"; "més dolç."

36. "el castellà era més per fotre la bronca."

37. "Quan estic molt, molt molt enfadada ho dic en castellà, perquè el castellà sona més fort; o sigui és involuntari, em surt en castellà."

38. "enfadats"; "volen insultar, normalment ho diuen en castellà."

39. "si tu expliques un *chiste* verd."

40. "fer bromes."

said one Catalan-speaking girl.[41] Victoria, the home bilingual student who first asserted the elegance of Catalan, also volunteered that "swear words in Castilian sound like stronger" while Catalan "seems like weaker than Castilian, it softens more the words you say."[42] A boy said that Castilian was more useful "when you have to give someone orders; it's more, like it's more imposing."[43] For another, Castilian is "more direct, harder."[44] With a different evaluative spin, Castilian-speakers said that Catalan "sounds weaker, more subtle, you know?"[45] and is "more distant, as if it were a language for speaking formally, seriously."[46] A Catalan speaker felt that Castilian "has more force" and Catalan is "higher-pitched and softer."[47] These characterizations evidence a trend that has been observed earlier to associate Castilian with hegemonic masculinity and Catalan with normative femininity, at least among youth (Pujolar 1997, 2001, Woolard 1997a, Bastardas i Boada 1985).[48]

In this stereotypic imagery we have clear examples not only of Irvine and Gal's concept of linguistic iconization, but also of the associated ideological process of erasure that they call "register stripping" (Irvine and Gal 2000).[49] That is, recognition or even actual use of the language for particular functions has been lost. Register stripping is occurring in both languages, but in complementary domains, in accordance with their complementary iconic value.

For Catalan, the lost registers are those of forceful and rough everyday uses. For Castilian, it is formal and refined registers that are lost from sight. However, the erasure lies more in practice for Catalan and only in ideology for Castilian. Most of these students really are less likely to tell or hear rude jokes or insults in Catalan, and one found it impossible to accept popular music

---

41. "més potents, que es fan sentir més" vs. "més fluixes."

42. "Les paraulotes en castellà sonen com més fortes" vs. "pareix com més fluix que el castellà, suavitza més les paraules que diu."

43. "quan has de donar ordres a algú; queda més, com si imposessis més."

44. "més directe, més dur."

45. *"suena (.) más débil, más sutil, ¿no?"*

46. *"más distante, como si fuese una lengua para hablar formalmente, serio."*

47. "té més força"; "més agut i més suau."

48. Surprisingly, there were only two mentions that associated Catalan with older people, and then the connection was indirect, passing through wisdom. Nor was there conscious association of Castilian with youth.

49. In this use, "registers" are recognizably distinct varieties of a given language associated with particular functions and domains of use, a more traditional linguistic understanding of the term than that involved in the current concept of enregisterment introduced by Asif Agha (2007a).

in Catalan. (La Queta's first lesson on how to insult in Catalan, discussed in Chapter 3, was not mistaken in its priorities.) In contrast, they actually do encounter (and need to exercise) formal registers of Castilian in their school studies, as Teresa pointed out in the discussion. They would also hear it on the majority of television channels if they watch. Despite their widely shared vision of Castilian as careless and vulgar, several of the students mentioned that they had a model of Castilian eloquence in their language teacher. They lauded him for his "elegant" Castilian style and his "prestigious voice."[50] Yet when students conjured images of the language itself, ideological erasure made that exemplary speaker invisible, in a process all too familiar in language ideology. Even while acknowledging the prestigious voice of her articulate Castilian teacher, Katia was able to assert, as we have seen, that "no one speaks it in a sophisticated way." (This may tell us as much about whether teachers count as "someone" in the teenagers' view of the social world as it does about the languages.)

When questioned further in interviews, students could recognize variable and high forms of Castilian and recall refined speakers with cultivated styles, such as this teacher. But almost none of them could bring to awareness (in the interview context) variable forms of Catalan. They insisted that there was only one form that counted as Catalan. The nearly monolingual Castilian-speaking Pilar said: "I don't know any careless way to speak Catalan."[51] Lola, also a nearly monolingual Castilian speaker in practice, similarly asserted, "Catalan sounds very refined always—always."[52] This view was not just outsiders' inability to discern variation within a language they don't speak or meet only in school; it was shared by L1 Catalan speakers. Susanna, practically monolingual in Catalan, independently affirmed that even "when you speak normally" Catalan "sounds elegant, sounds good."[53] "There isn't any careless way"[54] of speaking Catalan, said a Catalan-dominant bilingual, exactly as did the Castilian speaker Pilar. Again, we see evidence that these students hold the same view that Susan Frekko has identified in discussing language experts' view of Catalan: a standard register is now taken to be the whole language (Frekko 2009a).

---

50. "veu de prestigi."

51. *"Yo no conozco una manera dejada de hablar catalán."*

52. *"El catalán suena muy fino siempre—siempre."*

53. "Quan parles normal, queda elegant, queda bé."

54. "No hi ha una manera deixada."

The belief that Catalan has no register or stylistic variation accompanied highly purist attitudes about that language among these students. The only other form of Catalan they could think of was that mixed with Castilian. In their purist view, these were not different ways to speak Catalan for different purposes, they were real Catalan versus a false Catalan that is "in reality" Castilian. As one interviewee put it, "people say a lot of Castilianisms, words converted to Catalan that are in reality Castilian."[55] "There are a lot of people who say '*buenu*' (('okay')) and it's not *buenu*," said another.[56] None of these young people celebrated linguistic hybridity, and some flatly rejected language mixing: "The Catalan that I don't like is Catalan that, that mixes words with Castilian. It sounds really bad."[57]

Where did these young people think the different qualities of the languages came from? As seen above, some of them spoke as if these were intrinsic to the language variety itself. Often, however, frequency of use was suggested as the source, as Teresa said in the class discussion: "Castilian, we all speak it. It's very used, no? It's seen a lot, spoken a lot."[58] Later she expanded on this: "It's not that they speak badly, it's . . . that from speaking it so much it even changes the way of saying things. It's become a little more vulgar, no?"[59] Another observed months later in an interview that "Castilian has been heard a lot, too much, and it's gotten worn out."[60] In contrast, because Catalan is spoken "in few places" it is "like newer."[61]

These comments suggest a belief that languages wear down through use, and specifically that pronunciation changes with frequent use for everyday purposes (an idea that finds some support in traditional linguistics). Catalan was

---

55. *"La gente dice muchas castellanadas, palabras convertidas al catalán pero que son de castellano en realidad."*

56. "Hi ha molta gent que diu 'buenu,' i 'buenu' no és.'" The form criticized here is a discourse marker widely incorporated into vernacular Catalan. It is based on the Castilian form *bueno* "good, well, ok", which has been partially Catalanized through the emblematic change of the final vowel that we saw parodied in Chapter 4. The prescriptively correct corresponding Catalan discourse marker would be *bé* "well," but it is not as widely used for this discourse function.

57. "El català que no m'agrada és el català que, que barreja paraules amb castellà. Sona molt malament."

58. "El castellà, ho parlem tots. És molt usat, no? Està molt vist, molt parlat."

59. "no és que parlin malament, és . . . que ia de tant parlar-lo ia es canvia i tot de:: de manera de dir les coses. Ia s'ha tornat una mica més vulgar, no?"

60. "El castellà ja s'ha sentit molt i massa s'ha anat desgastant."

61. "a pocs llocs, com més nou."

paradoxically protected by its less frequent use. Some students, however, seemed to be giving a version of the sociolinguistic conceptualization of markedness, in which the less frequent form in a linguistic contrast pair adds specialized or "marked" meanings to that of the more basic or "unmarked" counterpart (see Woolard 2004 for discussion). Supporting this interpretation, one interviewee explained that Castilian is viewed as coarse "because we use Castilian a lot to say, I don't know, whatever stupid thing, you know?"[62] Teresa showed a similar awareness of markedness when she suggested that although those who like her speak Castilian at home hear Catalan as more elegant, those who speak Catalan routinely at home might not.[63]

No student mentioned school in relation to the refined image of Catalan, or any other domains of use (in contrast to expressive pragmatic functions discussed above) to account for linguistic stereotypes. Instead, they pointed to associations of the languages with people typed by social class, iconic social styles, and the different urban spaces they inhabited. Putting the matter most baldly, one student called out in the class discussion, "Catalan is the language of the rich."[64] Anton, an L1 Castilian speaker very favorably disposed toward use of Catalan, put this thought cheerfully and picturesquely:

Ex. 7.3 Anton: Language of the rich

sembla més mm elegant . . . .És com a Inglaterra que abans els rics i els (.) feudals feien servir el francès perquè era més (.) més elegant.	It seems more mmm, elegant . . . It's like in England in the past, the rich and the (.) feudal lords used French because it was more (.) more elegant.

The bilingual Victoria explained that Castilian is seen as coarser because it is associated with "the neighborhoods that are a little shabby,"[65] like her own, where "more Castilian is spoken."[66] Katia explained the logic by which

---

62. "Es que el castellà el fem servir molt per dir jo què sé qualsevol <u>tonteria</u>, no?"

63. Indeed, her Catalan-speaking classmate Xavier said in interview that he didn't hear Catalan as more elegant, or more anything at all, he just hears it as "normal," encapsulating the idea that the language is unmarked for him. However, not all Catalan speakers heard it this way, as shown by Susanna's remark reported earlier about the elegance of Catalan even in "normal" speech.

64. "El català és la llengua dels rics."

65. "els barris així una mica deixats."

66. "es parla més castellà."

sociolinguistic stereotyping and enregisterment work. She gave as an example a preferentially monolingual Castilian-speaking classmate who attended the alternative class and was disengaged and disruptive in the little time he spent in the regular classroom. His track suits, buzz-cut hair, and stud earrings were icons of the street-tough style that classmates called *quillo* and she labeled *gitano* "gypsy" (by which she made clear that she meant a style, not a descent group).

Ex. 7.4 Katia: Gypsy style and bad Castilian

Él se podría considerar así, gitano, y él habla mal el castellano. Entonces mucha gente asocia eso, y tú dices va esto es castellano malo, y la gente se le pega hablar así a todo el mundo.	He could be considered like that, gypsy, and he speaks Castilian badly. So then a lot of people associate that, and you say, well that's bad Castilian, and people pin speaking like that on everyone.

In exact counterpoint, the relatively *quilla*-identified Jenifer pointed to another stylized persona to explain why Catalan had a refined image:

Ex. 7.5 Jenifer: Catalan-speaking *pijos*

com que les persones que parlen català son més bé pijos i gent aixi que son més refinats.	because people who speak Catalan are more likely to be *pijos* (("preppies")) and people like that, who are more refined. [67]

Catalans and Castilians

These students' explanations of the social derivation of images of the languages take us to the question of adolescent social identities and styles. In keeping with trends we have seen throughout this book, they preferred to think of language use and social identities as choices, as matters of personal style rather than of ethnolinguistic origins.

In my 1987 study in this school, almost all students had discussed the social landscape of their classroom, school, and city in terms of two groups defined by language background and habitual use: "Catalans" and "Castilians." Even

---

67. This generalization may surprise people of older generations, for whom *pijos* preferentially speak Castilian, but this Catalan image of *pijos* dominates among young people in working-class areas.

students who endorsed the well-known slogan that "all those who were born and live here are Catalan" quickly resorted to a distinction between Catalans and Castilians as ethnolinguistic identities when discussing their social relations in the school.

When asked what social groups and types of people could be found around the school in 2007, no one volunteered the categories "Catalans" and "Castilians." Several interviewees explicitly rejected their relevance when I suggested these terms. Most importantly, most of these students did not use these terms in the course of describing their own social worlds. Only two out of the twenty-four interviewed drew on Catalan/Castilian as a contrast set in explaining social relations to me.[68]

For most of this younger set, there was not a significant group in Catalonia that they thought of as Castilians, and most of their classmates who were not foreign-born were Catalan in their eyes. The category of Catalans had expanded well beyond its use in 1987. Whether from Catalan-speaking, Castilian-speaking, or bilingual homes, and regardless of their preference for speaking Castilian among friends, if young people were raised in Catalonia and used Catalan in some school activities, all of them were "Catalans" in these students' view. Even bilinguals who continued to use Castilian preferentially in peer relations were likely to be viewed as "Catalan," especially if they used the Catalan language routinely at school.

Anton was from a Castilian-speaking family but had a strong Catalan identity himself. When I asked him who was Catalan, he thought only of foreign immigrants as potentially excluded:

Ex. 7.6 Anton: Who is Catalan?

KW: "Bé, qui és català? Tothom a la classe és català o?"

A: "Ah, si hi ha algú de fora?"

KW: Ok, who is Catalan? Is everyone in the class Catalan, or?

A: Oh, you mean if there is anyone from outside?

Other interviewees also struggled to make sense of what I meant when I pressed them by asking, "Twenty years ago people here often talked about

---

68. The most extensive use of this pair of terms came from Susanna, the most strongly Catalan-identified girl in the class. Even she had two Castilian-origin surnames and a grandmother who had been brought to Catalonia from southern Spain as an infant. This school, like its city, is demographically dominated by people of immigrant origin, whether one or two generations removed. These students' expansive understanding of who is Catalan may not be shared by residents of less immigration-influenced areas and with deeper family roots in Catalonia.

Catalans and Castilians. Are groups talked about in this way now?" Several proposed the terms *espanyol* or *espanyolista* as a more relevant contrast to Catalan, including these very straightforward comments from the L1 Castilian-speaking Jenifer and the Catalan-speaking Roser.[69]

Ex. 7.7a Jenifer: Catalans and *espanyols*

És que hi ha gent que diu que-que no és català, o sigui són catalans però diuen que no són catalans són espanyols.	It's that there are people who say- who aren't Catalan, I mean they're Catalan but they say that they're not Catalan, they're *espanyols*.

Ex. 7.7b Roser: Independentists and *espanyolistes*

Ara més que catalans i castellans es parla més d'independentistes i espanyolistes.	Now more than Catalans and Castilians, independentists and *espanyolistes* are talked about more.

These and similar comments from other interviewees represent a significant change in the interpretive frame, rather than just a relabeling of the previously existing category "Castilian." Castilian had been a language-based ethnic identity (as we will see in the next chapter it still is for at least one of those earlier informants twenty years later). But *espanyol* was taken by several of the students who commented on it more as an ideological category and an anti-Catalan political stance. Unlike Castilian in the 1980s, *espanyol* identity was usually associated not only with Castilian monolingualism but also with overt political talk and display of symbols such as the Spanish flag and the Osborne bull, the muscular brand image of a large commercial alcohol producer that has come to be used widely as a Spanish nationalist sign in popular culture (Brandes 2008). (See Lola's invocation in Ex. 7.9 of the socio-political meaning of the bull emblem.)[70]

The key terms of social identity at this school had moved away from Castilian and Catalan defined as two contrasting ethnolinguistic identities. Instead, many of these students conceptualized *espanyol* as a marked identity that was a voluntary choice signaling a political orientation, against an unmarked Catalan

---

69. I retain the Catalan forms *espanyol* and *espanyolista* in this discussion because the political connotation is lost in the translation "Spaniard" or even "Hispanicist," which I use elsewhere in the book when I am not quoting someone directly.

70. The image adopted by Catalanists in response is a small, decidedly less imposing and muscular Catalan burro.

identity that was broadly shared. Comments from other interviewees such as the Catalanist Arnau showed that it is not use of the Castilian language as such that is associated with *espanyol* identity, but rather the rejection of Catalan and a choice to use Castilian almost exclusively. Castilian-dominant language choices did not disqualify a young person from being seen as Catalan, but a functionally monolingual Castilian speaker who avoided use of Catalan even in school was more likely to be seen as *espanyol*. Since students had to go out of their way not to use Catalan in the classroom under the existing educational linguistic policies, such functional monolingualism on the part of those raised in Catalonia suggested to peers that they were *espanyol* by deliberate orientation.

Youth Subcultural Identities

Instead of the ethnolinguistic categories of Catalan and Castilian that predominated in this school in 1987, social identities relevant to high school life were more readily defined in 2007 in terms of youth subcultural styles. Many of these are globally familiar categories that had emerged in Spain since the 1980s. Those represented in this school included the *skater* (skateboarder), the *rapero* (hiphop style), and Latino style under various names. The most significant identities for this group were the *pijo/pija* "preppie" and the *quillo/quilla* (also known as *gitano/gitana*, as discussed above, *choni*, as mentioned in Chapter 4, *cani*, and other more pejorative terms).[71] These are the local instantiations of the contrast widely found in youth culture between the preppie on the one hand and the burnout or chav/ette on the other. The styles associated with all these groups were predictable from familiar international patterns (e.g. Eckert, 2000).

In 1987, language had been used to peg people, and then manners and styles of dress were discussed as predictably associated with these ethnolinguistic identities. In the interviews with students in 2007, the ordered relation between linguistic identity and style was reversed. Young people (in the abstract and concretely) were identified first by style. Language entered into talk about social differences secondarily, on my prompting and as a corollary to the stylistic diagnostics of identity. This does not mean that language preference was not correlated with social identity and relations in 2007. Rather, the students did not themselves explicitly construe—or were no longer comfortable talking openly about—their social status and relations in ethnolinguistic terms, the way their

---

71. These terms for social groups are the same in Catalan and Castilian, and are almost always pronounced as in Castilian.

counterparts did a generation earlier.[72] In keeping with the social and ideological trends proposed in Part I, this younger cohort cast identities as matters of individual choice among stylistic options rather than of origins and ascription.

Pijo is a long-recognized social type in Catalonia associated with the wealthy (particularly nouveau riche) and the culturally shallow. By 2007, a *pijo/a* was defined by all these young people as someone who "va de marques," that is, who dresses in (expensive) brand-name clothing. *Pijo* was originally seen as a social class position expressed in stylistic differences (as in Bourdieu's model of class cultural distinction), and the style was strongly associated linguistically with use of Castilian. But that had changed, as the Catalan speaker Miquel observed. Miquel was himself identified as a skater, which he recognized was a style that male *pijos* had adopted.

Ex. 7.8 Miquel: *Pijos* and social class

Abans un pijo era la gent que tenia diners . . . que anava amb la roba més cara . . . Ara, s'ha confós tot.	Before, a *pijo* was someone who had money . . . who went around in the most expensive clothing . . . Now, everything has gotten confused.

As other styles adopted expensive brands as emblems (Billabong and Vans for skaters, Nike for *quillos*), *pijo* had come to be simply another stylistic choice, open to kids like Teresa and Victoria from poor and shabby neighborhoods. Miquel named Victoria the "*pija* par excellence" of the class. This is not an insult; it is "just a way of dressing," as another said.[73] As Eckert found for suburban Detroit, the width of the pant leg is key, as the kids told me repeatedly and I was able to observe myself. In 2007, *pijas*, the girls, wore skinny jeans pegged at the ankle, skaters and male *pijos* wore baggy skate pants, male *quillos* wore track suits, and female *quillas* wore wide bellbottoms dragging on the ground. *Pijas* as well as *quillas* wore low-riding pants, but *pijas* nervously tugged their pants up toward the waist while *quillas* repeatedly smoothed them lower on the pelvic bones. *Pijo* boys wore branded polo shirts; *pijas* were known for their pink and other pastel-colored clothes, ballet shoes, soft sweaters, and fluffy knit scarves. One girl told

---

72. We might surmise that, as Bucholtz describes for race in a US school, students have become uncomfortable talking openly in terms of ethnic differences, rather than that ethnic differences don't matter (Bucholtz 2011). Catalonia like the rest of Spain has in recent years begun to be more circumspect than in the past about public commentary on race—and possibly ethnicity, I am not certain—although there still have been scandalous occurrences, particularly in sports events.

73. Emili: "és una manera de vestir."

me that she was recognizable as a *pija* because she stood with her left foot turned out (and as I looked around, I saw what she meant).

The *quillo/a*, in contrast, is a working-class style that is equivalent to the chav/ette in England, and what has recently become nationally known in the United States as the Jersey Shore "guido/ette" style. *Quillas* were identified with shiny synthetic materials, tight tops, exposed flesh ("showing everything"), heavy eye liner extending beyond the corner of the eye, hoop earrings, quilted parkas with fur-trimmed hoods, and the bellbottoms already mentioned. Lola, the iconic *quilla*-style figure in the class, understood these styles as classed. She pointed out that *quillas* systematically wear outmoded styles (and the *pija* Katia independently observed this) and asserted that this was because they didn't have the money that *pijos* have to buy the latest fashions. *Quillo* males wore the ubiquitous track suit, earrings, and most often buzz cut hair (there was only one male identified as *quillo* in this classroom, and he did not participate in the study). Like Eckert's burnouts, *quillos* smoked tobacco; *pijos* did not. *Quillos* were demonstratively not oriented to school culture or academic success, again a familiar pattern internationally.

Linguistically, at this school the *pijo* was often stereotyped as Catalan-speaking, as Jenifer said, but it was recognized that this did not always hold. The girls most identified as *pijas* in this classroom spoke primarily Castilian at home and socially, although almost all also used Catalan and were not seen as anti-Catalan.

In contrast, most of the students saw *quillos* as exclusively Castilian speaking.[74] Although born and raised in Catalonia, *quillos* are indexed by the stylized Andalusian accent whose emblematic icon is the aspirated "s" as described by Joan Pujolar (2001).[75] For example, plural nouns are commonly pronounced with a final [h] rather than an [s]: *quillas* is pronounced "quillah," as in the next extract. In keeping with the image of the Castilian language as more vulgar than Catalan, the *quillo* style is considered coarse and vulgar. That is, the *quillo* type is the personification—and in fact the source—of the negative linguistic stereotype enregistered as Castilian by these students. It is also the social persona that is the source of the parody of "Montillan" discussed in Chapter 4.

Moreover, *quillo* identity is frequently understood to entail the political stance of the *espanyol*: *quillos* are identified with Castilian because they are pro-Spain

---

74. The L1 Castilian but fluently bilingual Alex demurred from such an association, saying this kind of identity "doesn't have a language."

75. Students informed me that the label *quillo* itself derived from an Andalusian-origin diminutive, *chiquillo* 'little boy.'

and anti-Catalan. (Not all *espanyols*, however, are *quillos*). The *quillo* takes up much of the social space formerly captured by the term *xarnego* (a term these students did not even know). But the pejorative *xarnego* was framed in terms of origins, as we saw in Chapter 4 in comments about Montilla. The *quillo* identity, in contrast, is understood by these young people as a stylistic choice, even if it is ethnically coded.

Using the aspirated /s/ herself, Lola, the iconic *quilla* of the class, asserted that her style was entirely a matter of personal choice and that it ran against the grain of the social and political stereotype. Speaking of the group of clandestine smokers she joins in a far corner of the patio every day, Lola confirmed the *quilla* stereotype while claiming that she defies it in her own self-aware and cosmopolitan being:

Ex. 7.9 Lola: Defying the *quilla* stereotype

L: *somos nosotras, que somos las de-, lah quillah, como nos llaman.*

L: We are the, the *quillah* as they call us.

KW: *¿Sí? Te consideras quilla?*

KW: Yes? Do you consider yourself *quilla*?

L: *De manera de vestir, sí. Pero de manera de ser no.*

L: In my way of dressing, yes. But in my way of being, no.

KW: *Ah no? [¿por qué?]*

KW: Ah no? [why?]

L: *[Porque:] las quillas es España. España, España, España y Cataluña es lo peor.*

L: [Because] with *quillas* it's Spain. Spain, Spain, Spain, and Catalonia is the worst.

KW: *Ah.*

KW: Ah.

L: *Y España, España, España.*

L: And Spain, Spain, Spain.

KW: *Sí.*

KW: Yes.

L: *Entonces yo no, yo me considero catalana.*

L: And not me, I consider myself Catalan.

KW: *Ah vale.*

KW: Ah, ok.

L: *Es que si yo me considerara española yo en Cataluña no estaría viviendo, para qué voy a vivir en una tierra que no quiero?*

L: If I considered myself Spanish I wouldn't be living in Catalonia, why would I want to live in a land that I don't love?

KW: *Sí, sí.*

KW: Yes, yes.

L: *Entonces yo me considero catalana, lo que pasa es que me gusta la manera de vestir (.) de las quillah.*

L: So I consider myself Catalan, it's just that I like the *quillahs'* style of dressing.

KW: *Sí.*

KW: Yes.

L: *Entonces yo me visto así.*

L: So I dress like this.

KW: *Ah vale, vale.*

L: *Pero yo no tengo el toro y España ahí como de origen ¿sabes?*

KW: *¿Y normalmente todo eso va juntado con ser quillo o quilla?*

L: *Sí.*

KW: *Ah, ah, veo, curioso* ((quiet voice)). *¿Pero tú puedes escoger lo que te guste [(xx)]?*

L: *[Sí, yo por] ejemplo yo me hablo con todah las quillas. Y yo digo que aquí Cataluña pues yo la quiero. Al igual que España y al igual que Europa ¿me entiendes? Y al igual que el mundo, o sea. Es que una cosa está dentro de otra.*

KW: Ah, ok, ok.

L: But I don't have the bull and Spain there like it's ((my)) origin, you know?

KW: And normally all this goes together with being *quillo* or *quilla*?

L: Yes.

KW: Uh huh, I see, curious ((quiet voice)). But you can choose what you like [(xx)]?

L: [Yes, I for] example I talk with all the *quillah.* And I say that here, Catalonia, well I love it. The same as Spain and the same as Europe, you understand? The same as the world, I mean. One thing is inside the other.

Although it might seem to be self-conscious rhetoric generated for the interview, Lola apparently really did talk to peers about her sense of identity. When interviewed six weeks earlier the Catalan Miquel had approvingly described the independence of her spirit and the disconnect between her political identity and her outward style. Miquel had used almost the same words that Lola herself used a month and a half later[76]:

Ex. 7.10 Miquel: Style and political identity

M: La Lola m'encanta la-, la-, la opinió que té la Lola, perquè la Lola

KW: [Hmm]

M: [Vesteix] així perquè a ella li agrada vestir així.

KW: Sí?

M: Ella no se sent ni més espanyola ni més catalana.

KW: Ah sí?=

M: I love Lola, the, the, the opinion Lola has, because Lola

KW: [Hmmm]

M: dresses like that because she likes to dress like that.

KW: Yes?

M: She doesn't feel either more Spanish or more Catalan.

KW: Ah, yes?=

---

76. Collusion among the students in constructing interview responses is very plausible, but in this particular case it seems unlikely just in the practicalities of the chronological order and time between the interviews.

M: =Ella se sent, ha nascut a ((city name)) se sent ((city name)).

KW: Sí, sí.

M: I ella vesteix aixi perquè vale, li agrada, fuma perquè li agrada fumar.

KW: Sí.

M: No eh, no vesteix aixi perquè és més espanyola ni és més espanyola per ser com els altres

KW: Ah sí.

M: Ella vesteix aixi, va amb la gent que li cau bé, i ja està.

KW: Ja, ja, ja, sí, sí, [ella és]

M: [I m'agrada] aquesta opinió perquè a veure, és el seu punt de vista.

KW: Sí, sí.

. . . .

M: Clar, i, i té, i té una personalitat.

M: =She feels, she was born in ((this city)) and she feels like she's ((from here)).

KW: Yes, yes.

M: She dresses like that because, ok, she likes it. She smokes because she likes to smoke.

KW: Yes.

M: She, eh, doesn't dress like that because she's more *espanyola* nor is she more *espanyola* in order to be like the others.

KW: Ah, yes.

M: She dresses like that, she goes around with the people that she likes, and that's it.

KW: yeh, yeh, yeh, yes, yes, [she is]

M: [And I like] this opinion because, see, it's her point of view.

KW: Yes, yes.

. . .

M: Sure, and she has, she has individuality.

Both informants asserted the simultaneous predictable iconizing linkage of youth culture style, linguistic identity, and sociopolitical stance on the one hand, and Lola's willful defiance of such stereotypes on the other. Lola gave an account of personal style and language as an unpredictable act of bricolage, in which an individual can cobble together varying emblems and stances, uncannily similar to Penelope Eckert's and Norma Mendoza-Denton's descriptions of agentive self-styling among American teenagers (Eckert 2000, Mendoza-Denton 2008). The ideological construction of self and belonging had changed noticeably over twenty years from a framework of origins, ascription, and ethnolinguistic groups to one of style, choice, and individual self-construction. Lola's particular linguistic and stylistic choices were certainly not those espoused by the blogger from Veu Pròpia who defended his right to choose to speak Catalan (Chapter 3), but her claim to Catalan identity was similar. Her stance was also like the blogger's, which can roughly be paraphrased as "I do what I feel like, because I feel like it." For both, identity was not a matter of origins or social fate, but a personal project of self-construction: "I choose." School policy had not altered Lola's choice, but she imagined other circumstances would. Asked if she thought she would ever launch herself into speaking Catalan, Lola replied that it would happen when she began work, where "it is what it is"[77] and she imagined that linguistic choice would no longer be left to her.

Working-Class Castilian Speakers and Language Choice

In 1987, some of the case study students from Castilian-speaking backgrounds did feel they had a choice of language and identity when they moved to IES JC. Those whom I called "Catalan converts" chose a Catalan identity and Catalan as a habitual language. Others whom I called New Catalans constructed a bilingual public identity. What they had in common was that they came from middle-class homes. Working-class Castilian speakers then didn't find those options open to them, mostly because they had not had as much exposure to the language in their primary schools. As we will hear from some of them in the next chapter, they could not use the language comfortably in social relations, and Catalan identity was rarely claimed or accorded to them.

In 2007, more linguistic options were open to and exercised by working-class as well as middle-class students. I will illustrate the spectrum here with a few quick sketches of individual working-class L1 Castilian speakers who made different choices in linguistic and personal styles.

We have heard from Lola, the iconic and yet iconoclastic working-class Castilian speaker, about her *quilla* style and her Catalanist political sentiments. Lola was a poor student who frequently skipped school and had repeated a year. Older than her classmates, she had a sexualized image and a transgressive stance symbolized by her clandestine cigarettes on the patio. By her own account and that of peers, Lola rarely spoke Catalan. The reason Lola gave for not speaking Catalan was not political but personal: "I don't like the voice that it gives me. I sound really like a little girl . . . It's like my vocal cords change to when I was six years old."[78] Despite her linguistic and stylistic choices, Lola professed a love of Catalonia, and volunteered that she supported independence. (This was before the sovereignty movement had started to grow.) Asked if she would call herself Catalanist, as I reported in Chapter 1, Lola said "No, because I don't speak it . . . But I want Catalonia to be free."[79]

---

77. "*Es lo que hay.*"

78. "*es que no me gusta la voz que se me pone. . .Se me ve como muy niña. . .las cuerdas vocales es como si me cambiaran de cuando tenía seis años.*"

79. "*No, porque tampoco lo hablo. . .Pero . . . yo quiero que Ehpa- que Cataluña esté libre.*"

Teresa was a contrast to Lola in many ways. A good student from a very poor, Castilian-dominant neighborhood, she was a core member of the popular crowd. Attractive and wishing to become a film actress, she was cited by classmates as exemplifying *pija* style along with her best friend Victoria. Teresa used Catalan conscientiously in school, appreciated its elegance, claimed to wish to learn it better, and argued for its use in instruction. She was predominantly Castilian-speaking socially, preferring to use that language with close friends, but she spoke Catalan regularly in the classroom and with some Catalan-speaking peers. Teresa claimed a Catalan identity but with noticeable markers of hesitation, as seen in the following extract. Despite that hesitation, she was firmer in rejecting a Spanish identity. Already at age fifteen this working-class girl, who had seen little of the world beyond the metropolitan fringe of Barcelona, opted for the term whose value we are familiar with from Chapter 5: "cosmopolitan."

Ex. 7.11 Teresa: Cosmopolitan identity

KW: mira tu et consideres emm de nacionalitat et consideres catalana, espanyola:?

R: jo em considero (.) No sé. Sí, em considero (.) catalana.

. . .

KW: ets [espanyola] o?

R: [no] és que jo veig espanyola com una mica de (.) eh fran:quisme.

. . .

R: i no. Llavors a mi això del franquisme no m'agrada, llavors no no dic que sóc.

KW: Sí sí.

R: A veure que sí que jo sé, sóc catal- (.) Bueno primer sóc de ((birth town)) després de ((this town)) després de és que jo (.) jo sóc com cosmopolita. ((laughs)) . . . Del món. Ja està.((laughing))

KW: Look, in umm nationality, do you consider yourself Catalan, Spa:nish?

R: I consider myself (.) I don't know. Yes, I consider myself (.) Catalan.

. . .

KW: are you [Spanish] or?

R: [no] I see Spanish like a little from (.) uh Fran:coism.

. . .

R: and no. So for me, I don't like this stuff of Francoism, so no, I don't say that I am ((Spanish)).

KW: Yes yes.

R: Let's see, yes, I know that I'm Catal- (.) Well, first I'm from ((birth town)), then I'm from ((this town)), then it's that I (.) I am like cosmopolitan. ((laughs)). . . From the world. That's all.((laughing))

Alex was a working-class Castilian speaker from the same poor neighborhood as Teresa and one of the top students in the class. He moved in the same large popular crowd. Alex spoke Catalan very well and usually used it in classwork, but like Teresa he used Castilian socially with any peers who addressed him in that language. Alex explained to me that precisely because Catalan was not his familiar home language, he enjoyed speaking it.[80]

Ex. 7.12 Alex: Speaking Catalan as enjoyable change

R: *me siento mejor en ca-, catalán que en castellano no sé.*

R: I feel better in Ca-Catalan than in Castilian, I don't know.

KW: *¿Mejor en catalán que en castellano?*

KW: Better in Catalan than in Castilian?

R: *Sí, y- y creo que me sale mal igualmente el catalán cuando lo hablo*

R: Yes, a-and I think that Catalan likely comes out badly when I speak it

KW: *Hmm*

KW: Hmm

R: *Pero no sé, me gusta hablar el catalán.*

R: But I don't know, I like to speak Catalan.

. . .

. . .

R: *Más que nada es porque eh, no sé, porque soy de aquí y no sé, no-, no me gusta que se perdiese el catalán*

R: More than anything it's because uh, I don't know, because I'm from here and I don't know, I wouldn't like Catalan to be lost.

. . .

. . .

R: *O sea que, mm, si tengo oportunidad de hablar el catalán, lo hablo, porque a mi me gusta y ya está, es que no sé cómo explicarlo*

R: I mean, mm, if I have an opportunity to speak Catalan, I speak it, because me, I like it, and that's all, it's like I don't know how to explain

KW: *No, no, está bien*

KW: No, no, that's okay

R: *Igual que- como el caste- como estoy, supongo que es porque ya estoy bastante harto de hablar castellano, pues pa(ra) cambiar un poco.*

R: It's as likely that-since Cast- since I am, I suppose that it's because I'm already pretty tired of speaking Castilian, so for a little change.

This was an idiosyncratic account, but it is of special interest as an expression of the idea I developed in Chapter 2 that *not* speaking one's "own" language can be attractive and prized by speakers.

Asked what he identified as, Alex said "I'm everything. Catalan, Castilian, Spanish."[81] When he spoke of Catalans, he used the pronouns "we" and "ours."

---

80. Readers may observe that Alex was speaking in Castilian. After over fifty minutes in Catalan, he had switched to Castilian shortly before this question came up to explain the typical attributes of the social type *quillo*, saying it would be easier to do it in that language (even though he asserted the identity had no linguistic belonging). This triggered a change in the medium of the rest of the interview.

81. *"Yo soy todo . . . soy catalán, castellano y español."*

For example, he objected to the Partido Popular's efforts "to make it so that we Catalans don't have our Statute of Autonomy."[82] As seen in the extract above, he said that he liked to speak Catalan because "I'm from here, and I don't want Catalan to be lost."

Anton completes the Catalan end of this spectrum of working-class Castilian speakers' responses to the possibilities of Catalan language and identity.[83] Grandchild of Andalusian immigrants, from a monolingual Castilian-speaking home, Anton speaks Catalan fluently and well, as his Catalan teacher confirms. He uses Catalan in class as well as preferentially with Catalan-speaking peers and friends like Victoria who are also habitually bilingual. He identifies both as habitual languages but says he prefers Catalan over Castilian. Although his network of closest friends at the school was Castilian-medium, Anton identified as Catalanist and chose to come to JC for its Catalan atmosphere. He spoke of Catalan as "our *llengua pròpia*" and Catalonia as "my land." For example, speaking critically of a Spanish government policy initiative, he said, "I think that they should respect that we have a—a language of our own, no?"[84] Anton's Catalan identity is much stronger than the Spanish identity he also acknowledges:

Ex. 7.13 Anton: Claiming Catalan identity

KW: Parlant de nacionalitats, tu diries quina identitat eh sents que tens?	KW: Speaking of nationalities, what identity would you say uh you feel you have?
R: Jo català.	R: Me, Catalan.
KW: Català, sí? Sí?	KW: Catalan, yes? Yes?
R: Sí.	R: Yes.
KW: I també et sents espanyol o no?	KW: And do you also feel Spanish or not?
R: Sí, també.	R: Yes, also.
KW: També?	KW: Also?
R: Sí, però la gent i la meva terra és-, és ((long pause, implying it's simply Catalan))	R: Yes, but the people and my land is, is ((long pause, implying it's simply Catalan))

---

82. *"que los catalanes no tengamos nuestro Estatuto."*

83. Readers should recall that the male students identified as *espanyolista* by peers did not have parental permission to participate in the study, so this sample is biased. However, those boys were of middle-class rather than working-class backgrounds like these students who were my focus.

84. "em sembla que haurien de respectar que nosaltres tenim una-, un idioma propi, no?"

Of this spectrum, Lola's language habits were basically identical to those students I labeled "Castilians" in 1987. Unlike those earlier counterparts, Lola (and others such as Pilar, whose voice we will hear below) could and did lay claim, sometimes vociferously, to Catalan identity. Teresa, Alex, and Anton (and others like them) all fit the profile of what in the 1987 study I called "New Catalans": L1 Castilian speakers who publicly showed bilingual profiles through bilingual practices in the classroom and with peers, and who claimed and were accorded Catalan identity. As in 1987, New Catalans in 2007 were distinct not only from functionally monolingual Castilians (like Lola and Pilar) but also from what I called "Catalan converts," students from Castilian-speaking homes who had adopted Catalan-dominant linguistic practices and often downplayed their Castilian-speaking origins.[85] The difference was that there were more New Catalans in 2007 than in 1987, and there were New Catalans who came from working-class families and neighborhoods.

In 1987, I had also found bilingual competence and strong Catalan identification among children of Castilian-speaking backgrounds in this school, but in that period they were from middle-class families. Working-class kids of Castilian origin remained Castilian in identification—by self and other—as well as in language habits, for the most part. In 1987 this was in part because their access to Catalan in primary school had been limited, as we will see in the next chapter.

In 2007, it was no longer mostly middle-class students who used Catalan as a second language, as it had been in 1987. Anton, Alex, and Teresa were all grandchildren of Andalusian immigrants and children of transport and factory workers, but they used Catalan fluently and regularly. Alex and Teresa came from a lower-class neighborhood that they and others described not only as Castilian-dominant but as poor, dangerous, and stigmatized. Unlike their counterparts from twenty years earlier, these young people who were from relatively disadvantaged backgrounds felt prepared by their preschool and elementary school experience to take up Catalan if they chose to do so in the classroom and in peer relations. At least in this case study comparison, immersion education had extended the competence in Catalan that allowed young people a bilingual identity and reduced social class difference in such access. Moreover, the distinction between Catalan and Castilian origins, which had been significant socially in 1987, was of little conscious relevance to these students. They saw themselves and were viewed by their peers as Catalans.

---

85. There was at least one "Catalan convert" in 2007, a girl of mixed Latin American and Spanish immigrant heritage who was strongly identified socially as Catalan and Catalan-speaking. However, she was from a middle-class family, so I do not include her in this spectrum.

Language and School Work

Although Catalan was the official medium of instruction, students' actual language use in this classroom was mixed, as the student profiles above suggest. Most but not all spoke at least some Catalan in classroom activities, many with Castilian or *xava* accents (see Chapter 4 for discussion of *xava*). An academically and socially very successful girl of middle-class Latin American origins did not speak any Catalan except the minimum required in Catalan class. Lola and her friend Jenifer also spoke minimal Catalan for classwork, as did Pilar, from whom we will hear more below. When they did they almost always codeswitched quickly and frequently to Castilian, even in Catalan class. Nonetheless, Lola and Jenifer prepared and presented, or at least initiated, their end-of-year social studies oral report in Catalan. These and several other students spoke directly to teachers in Castilian. All teachers except in the Catalan class accepted Castilian from them without comment or interactional disruption. Many teachers switched to Castilian to answer students who put questions to them in that language. Only the Catalan teacher reminded students to speak in Catalan when they lapsed into Castilian during class discussions.

In 2007, even those who did not use Catalan orally in class wrote assignments and tests in Catalan, because that was usually the language of the textual materials and they found it easier to do so. All the interviewees professed to think it fine—both in principle and for them personally—that Catalan was the medium of instruction (but recall that the most politically *espanyolista* members of the class did not participate in the study). Regardless of their use or nonuse of the language, they claimed to have absolutely no problem understanding written or oral Catalan, even when like Jenifer they admitted to trouble in producing vocabulary while speaking or diacritics in writing. Even Lola and Pilar, who always preferred to speak Castilian, insisted that it was appropriate for Catalan to be the language of instruction.

Some L1 Castilian speakers argued in the class debate that because they spoke Castilian at home, it was all the more important for them to have the opportunity to develop proficiency in Catalan at school. In exchange, some Castilian speakers affirmed in interview that more school hours should be devoted to learning Castilian, since there were Catalan speakers who they felt could not speak Castilian well. In fact Susanna, one of the most monolingual Catalan speakers in the class, acknowledged she had some difficulty speaking Castilian because she did it so little. Susanna would not object to studying as many hours of Castilian language as Catalan as a subject, but she felt firmly that Catalan should remain the medium of instruction.

In my interviews with low-achieving Castilian-speaking students, I explored whether school might have been easier for them if instruction were in Castilian. They rejected the idea. For example, when Lola described herself as a poor student, I proposed she might be more successful in Castilian. "No, that's not it, I know that that's not it. I'm not going to blame the language," she replied. I persisted in pointing out that some people believe Catalan-medium instruction creates problems for Castilian speakers. "They're just trying to make excuses in some way," Lola replied.[86]

The educational consequences of non-mother tongue instruction in early education and particularly for working-class children remain a deeply controversial question with a large research literature. I do not want to imply that these young people are arbiters of this question. We might analyze their interpretation of their own experience as distorted by misrecognition, following Bourdieu. However, if we are tempted to see Lola, Jenifer, and Pilar's failure to use Catalan as a comment on school language policy, these students do not themselves see the issues as aligning this way. They presented their own language practices as a personal choice about comfort and self-image that bore no relation to educational language policy or political allegiance. Whether they did use Catalan in the classroom or not, all students claimed that they felt adequately prepared to do so if they so chose. This had not been true in 1987.

Still probing the links between linguistic practice and school success, I asked teachers as well as interviewees to identify the best students in the class. Students converged on two girls and four boys whom teachers independently confirmed were the highest-achieving students on the basis of their grades. Of these six, two were from Catalan-speaking homes, three were from bilingual homes (two more Castilian oriented, one more Catalan), and one was from a monolingual Castilian-speaking home. Three were children of white collar professionals or small business owners; three were from working-class homes. A Castilian-dominant or monolingual Castilian-speaking background did not exclude even working-class students from performing well, as was the case for Victoria and Alex, among the top achievers. Others from working-class and Castilian-speaking homes like Teresa and Anton were very solid students.

---

86. *L: No, no es eso, yo sé que no es eso.*

KW: No es eso, sí.

L: Porque yo no le voy a dar la culpa a la lengua o sea=

KW: =Bueno pero, hay- hay alguna gente que dice eso, ¿no?, que=

L: =Tsk. Porque yo creo que se intentan excusar de alguna manera.

In many other respects, language use in the classroom remained the same as decades before. Teachers did not always use Catalan, even though it was allegedly the medium of instruction. Some students basically never used Catalan, regardless of their assertion that they could if they wanted to. Castilian was commonly heard not only on the patio and in the hallways but also in the classroom. Although some working-class kids from Castilian-speaking backgrounds used Catalan comfortably, it was still almost exclusively working-class students like Lola and Jenifer (and now transnational immigrants) who did not.[87] Working-class Barcelona-born Castilian speakers such as Lola also joined working-class transnational immigrants in failing sometimes spectacularly, just as Lola's Castilian counterparts had in 1987.

Language and Peer Social Relations

Various interviewing tactics I used showed the same apparent indifference to language in the students' own peer relations that the experimental measure had revealed. For example, I asked interviewees to name the most "likeable" (CT *simpàtic, -a*/CS *simpático, -a*) among their classmates. This was one of the traits that contributed strongly to the Solidarity factor in the experimental results. The boys singled out most often as *simpàtic* by Castilian speakers as well as Catalan-speaking classmates were Catalan speakers and home bilinguals, known by some as class clowns (with the Catalanist provocateur Arnau leading the group). There was less consensus about the girls, but Castilian speakers and home bilinguals were most frequently named as the most likeable, again by both Castilian speakers and Catalan speakers. The socially monolingual Castilian speaker Pilar was the girl most often named among the most likeable, and she was identified as such even by the most Catalan-identified boy (Arnau) and girl in the class.

I am not certain I grasp these young people's understanding of what I translate as "likeable," but it obviously does not entail a shared linguistic identity. (To at least some it appeared to mean mostly "entertaining.") Their choices also seem at first look to disconfirm the incipient feminization of Catalan and the heteronormative masculinity associated with Castilian, but perhaps not; the relationship may be indirect. These were mostly fourteen

---

87. Although some middle-class students questioned Catalanist politics and were identified as strongly Spanish-oriented, they used Catalan fluently in the classroom and in some cases in peer relations. One middle-class Latin American immigrant did not speak Catalan but did well in school.

year olds, an age at which androgynous males are more likely to be considered attractive, at least in American and British popular culture. The choice of physically slight, wisecracking, Catalan-speaking boys as most likeable may simply be evidence of a sort of Justin Bieber or boy-band effect, rather than counter-evidence to the feminization of Catalan and masculinization of Castilian.

Almost all students, even those who had basically monolingual social relations, insisted that language background and language choice were not important issues for them. "Now we don't fight over who speaks Catalan and who speaks Castilian. Now it doesn't matter," said Lola.[88] The Catalan-dominant Montse developed the same idea:

Ex. 7.14 Montse: Bilingual friendships

es pot ajuntar una que parla castellà amb una altra català i s'entenen entre elles i tot. Per exemple l'Aida i la Sonia. Són molt amigues i la Sonia és-, jo crec que parla més castellà i l'Aida molt català, molt català. I són molt amigues de tota la vida- però diferències entre elles no ah, mmm, no hi han diferències.	one who speaks Castilian can get together with one who speaks Catalan and they understand each other and everything. For example Aida and Sonia. They are very good friends and Sonia is, I think that she speaks Castilian more and Aida a lot of Catalan, a lot of Catalan. And they've been good friends all their lives—but differences between them, no, uh, umm, there aren't any differences.

This claim to nonchalance about language affiliation in judging peers and forming friendships fits with the results of the matched guise experiment. It has also been a common thread in young people's discourse for much of the period of autonomy (Boix-Fuster 1993). It is in fact part of what has preoccupied Catalan activists, who fear that such indifference will lead to language loss (Larreula 2002). What was changed in 2007 compared to my earlier studies was not the overt discourse of linguistic laissez-faire so much as the limited extent to which these students actually drew on ethnolinguistic categories as they discussed their own social world in detail, as we saw earlier. There was also some difference in actual language use in peer relations.

---

88. *"Ya no nos peleamos para ver quién habla catalán y a ver quién habla castellano. Ahora ya da igual."*

In schoolwork, Catalan predominated with plenty of room for even monolingual Castilian. In exchange, in peer relations Castilian predominated, again with much leeway for extensive and even monolingual use of Catalan.

In the class discussion, the provocative Catalanist Arnau summarized language choice, describing a pattern recognizable as the traditional convergence to Castilian that in my earliest work I called the Accommodation Norm (Woolard 1989a). "No!" classmates called out. Several gave themselves as counterexamples, describing their use of what in that earlier work I labeled the Bilingual Norm.

Ex. 7.15 Class discussion: Accommodation vs. bilingual norm

Arnau: Els que parlen castellà, no parlen català a una persona que parla català. Parlen castellà. I els que parlen català, parlen castellà amb les persones que parlen castellà.

Ss: No::!

. . .

Susanna: a mi, si em parlen en castellà, io parlo en català perquè sempre he parlat el català.

T: Tu ets un cas bastant aïllat. ((Ss riuen))

Pilar: *No, yo también.*

Aida: Tu, a *que, a mí* ma *madre* sempre m'ha parlat en castellà, i io mai he parlat en castellà amb la meva família.

T: Tu li parles català a la teva mare?

Pilar: Io parlo castellà amb tothom, em parli en català o em parli en castellà.

. . .

Male S: *todo s'entiende* (xx)

Arnau: Those who speak Castilian don't speak Catalan to a person who speaks Catalan. They speak Castilian. And those who speak Catalan, speak Castilian with people who speak Castilian.

Ss: No::!

. . .

Susanna: If they speak to me in Castilian, I speak in Catalan because I've always spoken Catalan.

T: You're a pretty isolated case. ((ss laugh))

Pilar: *No, me too.*

Aida: You, *it's that to me,* my *mother* always has spoken to me in Castilian, and I have never spoken in Castilian with my family.

T: You speak Catalan to your mother?

Pilar: I speak in Castilian with everyone, whether they speak to me in Catalan or in Castilian.

. . .

Male S: *Everything is* underst*ood* (xx)

KW: I això és comode? Si una persona et parla en català i tu segueixes en castellà, és còmode?

KW: And is this comfortable? If a person speaks to you in Catalan and you follow in Castilian, is that comfortable?

Pilar: Sí, si io l'entenc a ella, i ella m'entén a mi.

Pilar: Yes, if I understand her and she understands me.

My classroom observations and recordings generally confirmed all of these students' claims. Arnau was right about the most frequent pattern. As in past decades, most but not all Catalan speakers in this class accommodated to Castilian speakers when addressing them directly, although they would happily converse across them in Catalan. For example, while taking a lead in a group project at the end of the school year, Miquel switched between Castilian and Catalan as he addressed first Lola and Jenifer and then Emili and Roser; his comments to the whole group were often in Castilian. The Catalan speakers Emili and Roser followed the same pattern. Lola and Jenifer addressed all of them in Castilian most of the time.

However, there was no single language etiquette in the interaction I observed and recorded. Susanna and Pilar had each fairly accurately described their own pattern of using the Bilingual Norm with peers. (Pilar actually used Catalan in this exchange with the teacher.)[89] The one time I heard Susanna use Castilian was with a new Brazilian student who she thought didn't understand Catalan, but in interview she claimed that sometimes when speaking to Pilar or others who use only Castilian she would find herself switching to that language. Recordings also showed workgroup and other classroom accommodation to Catalan by L1 Castilian speakers like Teresa, Alex, and Anton, and some codeswitching and instability of code choice within interactions. And, as their male classmate had said, everything was understood. In the next section I will briefly profile the distinctive language patterns of several friendship networks.

---

89. Ironically, Pilar made her assertions that she speaks Castilian "with everyone" in Catalan. "Everyone" here is likely to have meant peers, as well as being hyperbolic ideological erasure of cases that don't fit the claim. Pilar said in interview that out of respect she would use Catalan in response if addressed in that language by people she didn't know. As discussed in footnote 15, this discussion broke out in Catalan class, and Pilar was directly addressing the teacher, who generally insisted on Catalan from everyone. In this context, it is equally noteworthy that in her first turn Pilar used Castilian to contradict the teacher.

Language in Social Cliques

As had been true in 1987, there were distinct Castilian-medium, Catalan-medium, and mixed-language friendship networks identifiable in this class. These were especially visible on the patio during recess, and they were also confirmed in interviews by students' naming of best friends.[90]

The biggest of the cliques, with seven core and several peripheral members, used Castilian as its medium of general interaction. This was a mixed-gender group that included the *pija* social leaders of the classroom—Victoria, Teresa—and some of the most gregarious, such as Anton. It was similar to the "popular" crowds described in American high schools, holding the most visible central territory on the patio, where its principal activity was talking, with little engagement in physical activity (Bucholtz 2011). There were no students from monolingual Catalan homes among the focal members, but Victoria and Anton both identified their habitual language as "both" and addressed each other directly in Catalan. This clique included the most Spanish-oriented student politically as well as one of the most Catalanist, Anton. It owed its size and diversity to the linking of two networks through the romance of one central pair. As Eckert had found for American middle schools, the leaders in heterosexual pairing were also the leaders in setting the linguistic style for this group that appeared self-consciously advanced into being teenagers (Eckert 2011). The girl in this romantic pair, Cristina, was a socially monolingual Latin American, and friends felt that her language preference may have swung first the linguistic choice of her partner and then of the larger group with whom he had spoken Catalan earlier. Romantic pairing and mixed-gender cliques had not been visible on the patio in this age group in 1987.

Many from this popular crowd had gone to elementary school together. They reported that they had mostly spoken Catalan with each other then, regardless of their home language. Some seemed surprised to reflect on how much they had shifted to Castilian with each other since moving to high school and particularly in the past year. In addition to the influence of the romantic leaders, some suggested it was because there were more Castilian speakers and immigrants who learned Castilian first in the larger population of the high school. The ambient language and accommodation to new relationships reset the medium of their individual interactions, they suggested. Perhaps demography and the traditional Accommodation Norm were enough to account for the changes. However, the

---

90. In the distinct networks, most members reciprocated mentions of each other as best friends, although the networks were also loosely linked by single individuals who were named by fewer or even only one member of a group. Apart from those who went to the pull-out alternative classes, few students were not integrated into some network in the class.

forthright Lola had attended the same elementary school as the core of the popular crowd, and as mentioned earlier, she was reluctant to speak Catalan because she felt it made her sound childish. It seems plausible that others were also motivated to leave Catalan behind as a language associated with preschool and primary school, as they were staking out adolescent identities in secondary school.[91]

The Catalan-dominant cliques were more gender segregated than the popular Castilian-dominant group and less advanced in teenaged positioning. A network of L1 Catalan boys, mostly skaters in style, spent their recess time on the back of the playground, playing sports; Lola referred to them as *niños* "(little) boys."[92] This group included those identified by peers as the most likeable in the classroom, such as Miquel and Arnau, who dependably provided laughs. Members of this network sometimes circulated into the popular Castilian-medium crowd at the front of the patio.

Members of exclusively Catalan-medium networks were not necessarily L1 speakers of the language. Susanna and two studious, high-achieving friends were tightly identified by self and peers (they wore identical costumes for the *carnestoltes* "Carnival" party). Although one of them was of Castilian-speaking Latin American background, they used Catalan exclusively. In another case, a Catalan-speaking and a Castilian-speaking girl formed a close, isolated pair using exclusively Catalan together. These Catalan-oriented female groups were not visible at all on the patio, spending recess in the library or tucked into other quiet corners.

In an inversion of school standards of integration and marginalization, the transgressive Lola characterized these academically successful but reclusive Catalan-identified girls as "self marginalized" and not well integrated into the class. Lola herself hung out in a different margin, in a far corner of the patio with the smokers, all Castilian speakers and many of them older, as she was. Her *quilla*-styled classmate Jenifer spent recesses with Latina-identified immigrants in a distinct marginal territory of the patio.

There were several notable differences in peer language use and friendship networks in this class compared to what I had observed in this school in the

---

91. In a thorough study of the school population of one city in this same period, Vanessa Bretxa found a similar shift away from Catalan and toward Castilian among students from bilingual and L1 Castilian backgrounds that accompanied the move to secondary school (Bretxa i Riera 2014).

92. As in 1987, the Catalan-medium networks were smaller than the Castilian-medium network, among the boys as well as the girls. This may reflect culture differences between Castilian and Catalan styles of sociability, as I speculated in 1987. Or it may simply again be the result of the statistical tendencies to default to Castilian as new members are incorporated in a group in this Castilian-dominant community; the more members, the higher such a probability.

earlier generation. First was the presence and social centrality of a heterosexual pairing, already discussed.

Secondly, social class influence on language patterns appeared to have been diluted in peer interactions just as it had in academic language use. Unlike 1987, several working-class L1 Castilian-speaking kids used Catalan with Catalan-speaking peers. For example, the gregarious Anton, whose father was a truckdriver, used it preferentially even though he was part of the large Castilian-medium popular group.

Third and most interesting, there was a girls' network (too loose to be called a clique), with members from both ethnolinguistic backgrounds who used mixed language practices with each other. There had been an ethnolinguistically mixed boys' network in 1987, but girls' friendships had been strikingly homogeneous linguistically then. All girls in the class had matched their language choice to that of their friends in interactions, and this had affected how they were identified by classmates. Moreover, in the language attitudes experiment in 1987, Catalan girls had differed significantly from boys in attaching more solidarity value to the Catalan language. I interpreted this as suggesting a gendering of the semiotic display of identity that fit with patterns described in other parts of the world (Woolard 1997a).

In 2007 in contrast, a linguistically mixed group of girls, which included Aida and Pilar, espoused and practiced linguistic non-accommodation with their friends, as they had claimed in the class debate. These girls also maintained clearly distinct linguistic identities from each other in their peers' eyes. This was captured in recordings of them playing around together in the classroom and confirmed by the girls themselves and by others' descriptions of them. For example, L1 Catalan speaker Montse commented, "When the four of us talk, Aida, Camila, Pilar and me, of course, Pilar in Castilian, Camila and Aida and me in Catalan."[93]

In her interview, Pilar gave the same account of her pattern of non-accommodation with Montse:

Ex. 7.16 Pilar: Non-accommodation

P: *con la compañera de al lado me comunico en castellano. Ella me habla a mi catalán y yo a ella castellano.*	P: With the classmate next to me I communicate in Castilian. She speaks to me in Catalan and I to her in Castilian.
KW: *Ah, ¿sí? Eh, ¿quién, quién tienes al lado?*	KW: Ah, yes? Who, who do you have next to you?

93. "Quan parlem les quatre, que es l'Aida, la Camila, la Pilar i io . . . clar, la Pilar en castellà, . . . la Camila, l'Aida i io en català."

P: *Montse.*

KW: *Tienes a Montse sí, ¿y ella te habla en catalán?*

P: *Sí.*

KW: *¿Y tú a ella en castellano?*

P: *Sí, pero le pregunté que si le importaba pues que yo hablara castellano y me dijo que no, que le daba igual*

. . .

P: *como a ninguna nos importa y nos entendemos igual, pues siguen ellas en catalán y nosotras en castellano.*

KW: *¿Y va bien* això? *Esto, no. ¿no estás incómoda con? ¿Es fácil ir cambiando de-, o sea que?*

P: *Sí, porque yo lo veo- yo es como si fuera castellano también ej que no sé y como es una lengua que me han enseñado desde pequeña pues no me cuesta nada entenderlo.*

P: Montse.

KW: You have Montse, yes, and she speaks to you in Catalan?

P: Yes.

KW: And you to her in Castilian?

P: Yes, but I asked her if she cared if I spoke to her in Castilian and she said no, it didn't matter to her.

. . .

P: So since it doesn't matter to any of us and we understand each other anyway, well they continue in Catalan and we do in Castilian.

KW: And that works? That's not, you're not uncomfortable with? It's easy to switch- or I mean, what?

P: Yes, because I see it-it's as if it were Castilian too, it's like, I don't know, since it's a language that they've taught me since I was little, well it doesn't take anything for me to understand it.

From the earliest years of Catalan autonomy, language policymakers had advocated this pattern of passive bilingualism as a step in the normalization of Catalan. However, in past decades most speakers found it hard to put into practice. Mismatch of language could be maintained in large groups, but in dyadic interaction many speakers felt it was awkward, distancing, or downright hostile. Convergence to Castilian was the most common solution, as it continues to be, although less uniformly than before. In my earlier case study in this school, girls had been especially unlikely to apply or speak in favor of using this Bilingual Norm with their friends. Now several of these teenaged girls, including the socially central Teresa, told me that it was acceptable for people who are close to express themselves in their own languages.

The girls that I've quoted who actually put the Bilingual Norm into practice in this classroom were not part of very tight or influential networks. In those, even among friends from distinct backgrounds the matching of interlocutors' languages persisted, although accommodations could be found in both directions. Nonetheless, Pilar was reported as well-liked by a wide spectrum of classmates, and in her own words she highlighted what I think is the most striking effect of Catalan immersion education. It was schooling in Catalan from the earliest age, she said, that had made this working-class Castilian speaker so comfortable hearing the language that to her, "it's as if it were Castilian." The effects of such comfortable familiarity for use of Catalan are ambivalent.[94] Pilar was equally comfortable being addressed in Catalan and maintaining her own preference for Castilian with her Catalan friends.

Summary and Conclusion

Political controversy over language policy has focused intensely on Catalan-medium education in recent years. The ethnographic approach of this case study of two generations of students did not evaluate the pedagogical aspects of the question. Instead, my goal has been to give a glimpse of the ways that language policy played out in young people's own linguistic consciousness, in their every-day linguistic and social practice, and in the positions they stake out and are accorded in their social world.

In one sense, Catalan has been "normalized" as a public language for these students who came up through Catalan immersion in comparison to the cohort that had sat in the same classrooms a generation before. It had given them the linguistic competence and social permission to use the language themselves. Even some of the most monolingually Castilian-speaking among the younger generation took Catalan-medium schooling for granted as transparent, unremarkable, and appropriate. The familiar refrain "we don't have a problem here" captured the stance of most (again, not all) of this group. However, while Catalan was a familiar and accepted institutional voice, it was still not an anonymous one in their ears. A stereotype of Catalan as a high-status language of refinement had become nearly absolute, but it had not become hegemonic in the sense of saturating consciousness and obscuring its social roots from their view. This high status was accompanied by a narrowing vision of what the Catalan language is and what social purposes it serves. Playful, forceful, and transgressive registers and resonances were largely unrecognized and certainly not normalized for many of these young people.

Overall, there was increased use of Catalan in the classroom, across a broader spectrum of speakers, in more kinds of activities, and more frequently than in

---

94. Pilar's comment resonates with the observation of Vanessa Bretxa (2014, 50), following Salvador Cardús (2000), that with preschool now beginning at age three or earlier, the distinction between primary socialization and schooling has been diluted.

the earlier study. However, continuity as well as change over the twenty years between the studies was audible. Catalan educational policy was far from purging Castilian from public schools, even this relatively Catalan-oriented one. In 1987, Castilian could be heard everywhere in the school; in 2007, Castilian was still used and heard everywhere, from the classroom to the hallways to the patio. In 1987, teachers who taught in Catalan questioned and responded in Castilian to those students they identified as Castilian speakers. In 2007, some teachers also responded in Castilian to questions put to them in Castilian, although they were less likely to switch to Castilian in order to initiate exchanges with individual students and thus tag them with a personal linguistic identity.

The most important consequence of the change in educational linguistic policy that I saw was the weakening of social class barriers to acquisition and use of Catalan. In 1987, the L1 Castilian speakers in the case study who used Catalan fluently for classroom and social purposes had all been from middle-class homes and central neighborhoods. In 2007 in contrast, a number of Castilian speakers from working-class families and peripheral, lower-class neighborhoods used Catalan fluently in class and informally with peers. These same working-class kids figured among the solid academic performers and social leaders. A greater proportion of students than before had access to competence in Catalan and also to school achievement in that medium. In 2007 as in 1987, several of the highest-achieving kids were Catalan speakers, but in 2007 other high achievers were from working-class bilingual or Castilian-speaking homes. In turn, more than one student from a Catalan-speaking home struggled in classwork and had been held back for remediation, in 2007 just as in 1987. It was still the case, however, that those who were failing most visibly in school were more likely both to be working class—now often transnational immigrants—and to speak Catalan rarely at most.

Informal social uses of language among peers showed continuity as well as sparks of change. In 2007 as in 1987, most closely identified friends used the same language with each other. In some cases this meant that those from Castilian-speaking backgrounds adopted Catalan as a habitual language. In other cases, it meant students who would otherwise prefer to use Catalan used Castilian. Because more young people were now functionally bilingual, the direction of accommodation in casual interactions had become a somewhat more open question. A new development was that in 2007, more students, and especially girls, did not accommodate their friends linguistically, but instead followed the Bilingual Norm of each using her own language.

In social categorization, a major change was that there was little evidence of a conceptualization of Castilians in contrast to Catalans within Catalonia for most of these young people. Catalan identity was extended to more diverse backgrounds and more diverse linguistic habits compared to their counterparts of twenty years before. It may be the case that Catalan education has been a nation-building tool in that more young people who have been educated in the Catalan-medium system think of themselves as Catalan, as some larger-scale studies have found (Clots-Figueras and Masella 2013). But that does not automatically imply the nation of Catalan activists that the Spanish minister of education and other critics feared, because that same process also changed what it means to be and feel Catalan. As Manuel Castells and his research team found just a few years before this case study, speaking Catalan and claiming Catalan identity had become an unmarked, normal practice for young people, an accepted fact of life that no longer implicated a resistance-based political or social agenda (Castells et al. 2004). Still, even before the court's curtailment of the revised Statute of Autonomy ignited the sovereignty movement in 2010, there were signs from even the more complacent young people in this study that their routine Catalan identity could be mobilized politically if they perceived attacks on Catalan education and autonomy, much as Castells cautioned and as María José Hierro Hernández found after the court ruling (Hierro Hernández 2013, 349–350). Conservative Spanish politicians such as former minister of education Wert attribute the growth of independentist sentiment to indoctrination by the Catalan school system, but Hierro Hernández found that the influence of the schools on identity has been overestimated (Hierro Hernández 2013, 395). In my case study group it was actually Lola, one of the most transgressive against school norms and the least linguistically Catalanized, who espoused the most Catalanist political position. Given their exasperation with her school behavior and academic performance, Lola's teachers would surely have been wryly amused by the proposition that they had been able to recruit her into any educational project at all.

Finally and in keeping with the developments discussed in Part I of this book, language affiliations and practices were less likely to be seen by these young people in 2007 than those in 1987 as a reflex of origins and enduring ethnolinguistic group belonging. Ideological change pointed toward both of the two directions we have seen in public discourse, linguistic anonymity and individual self-construction. On one hand, institutional use of Catalan was taken by most of these students as a matter of course that was not "about" them or their personal identity and did not need to be tailored to their home language as some critics of Catalan education urged. On the other hand, they saw their own language patterns in interaction more than the earlier generation did as an individual's exercise of options, as choices among personal styles that people can and do make, rather than as enduring essential characteristics. We will pursue these themes in the next chapter as we look at how the linguistic biographies of some of the 1987 cohort developed over the following twenty years.

8 IS THE PERSONAL POLITICAL? LINGUISTIC ITINERARIES ACROSS TIME

Who is considered Catalan in 21st-century Catalonia, at the personal and interpersonal level? What does it mean for individuals to speak or not to speak Catalan, after roughly three decades of policies aimed at normalizing the language in a wider society? The last chapter approached these questions through the experiences of high school students educated in Catalan, in comparison to students at the same school twenty years earlier who had experienced varying degrees of Castilian-dominant bilingual education. In this chapter I return to talk with some of those earlier students, now adults, to consider the question of change over time in language and identity from their perspective.

Launched in their adult work and social lives, these interviewees, all about 34 years old, reflected on their time in high school and on the changes and continuities they had seen since then in the sociolinguistic environment and in their own linguistic biographies and identities. "I've surely changed a lot!" Elena exclaimed, after hearing that I was interested in their relationships to the two languages.[1] "Yes, me too!," Elena's friend Adela agreed.[2] A third interviewee, Rosario, independently asserted that her stance toward Catalan identity and language was now "totally different" from when she was in high school. I explore such reports of change in this chapter.

Youth and the Stability of Sociolinguistic Identity

Following one set of individuals over time allows us to gauge the changing ethnolinguistic climate of Catalonia from a different angle than the comparison of cohorts. Such a longitudinal view also permits

---

1. "¡Yo seguro que he cambiado mucho!"

2. "¡Sí, yo también!"

us to consider a question of more general interest to the study of sociolinguistic variation and difference: Do the linguistic identities formed in the crucible of adolescence remain with individuals throughout their lives? Penelope Eckert has aptly called high school "a hothouse for the construction of identities" (Eckert 1997, 163), and this is one of the reasons that sociolinguistic studies have so often been carried out with this age group.[3] The high school years in the industrial and postindustrial West are a period of specialization in the dramatized semiotics of social identity, including linguistic signs of identity. But how durable are the linguistic identities constructed in, and so crucial to, that stage of life?

This question is especially significant for minority-language communities, where young people's practices are taken as a harbinger of societal-level language maintenance or shift. Reading age-differentiated linguistic patterns at a given moment as representing sociolinguistic change over time, sociolinguists and activists often think of teenagers' language use as diagnostic of the community's sociolinguistic future. Catalan language activists have been particularly concerned about a documented turn away from Catalan toward Castilian dominance in peer relations and popular culture consumption that appears in secondary school (Bretxa i Riera 2009, Larreula 2002, Pujolar i Cos et al. 2010). We saw a glimpse of such a shift in some students' reports of their own linguistic practices in the last chapter. Language planning efforts such as the "Wind up Catalan" (*Dóna corda al català*) campaign discussed in Chapter 3 primarily aim to foment what is called "social use" of Catalan among youth and preadolescents for this reason. "As our teenagers go, so goes the language" is a common belief. But is this always true, and to what degree? Might adolescent choices in language and identity sometimes be as much age-graded processes specific to a particular life stage as they are signs of change in progress across time in a community? This is a question of the relation of social phenomena occurring at different time scales (Blommaert 2010, Wortham 2005).

In studies of bilingualism and sociolinguistic variation, early adolescence is often cast implicitly or explicitly as the end of a critical period that fairly decisively establishes the individual's linguistic habitus (Labov 1972, Bourdieu 1991). Yet there is now also considerable agreement among experts that linguistic identities are fluid and can be variably constructed through choices among stylistic practices in interaction (Bucholtz and Hall 2004, Rampton 1999). This is a linguistic facet of the project identity and project authenticity that I discussed in Chapter 2. The research emphasis on the interactional fluidity of individual linguistic identity in

---

3. The convenience of institutional access and sampling no doubt also has influenced this focus. In Catalonia, schools were the main locus for linguistic normalization policies after Franco and they were thus an important site for sociolinguistic studies.

synchronic perspective has not been so firmly translated recently to the question of diachronic change across biographical time. There has been less consideration of the extent to which a speaker's language can change over the post-adolescent life course, and how such changes are embedded in socially constructed, culturally specific life stages and life events (Eckert 1997, 152).[4] This chapter develops this line of inquiry by bringing evidence from a small cohort of individuals whose life stories I was able to follow after twenty years.

The 1987 Cohort

In my 1987 study at the school I now call IES Joan Cérvola, there were thirty-six students, thirteen of them first-language (L1) speakers of Castilian. Among these thirteen, I identified three types on the basis of their different relationships to the Catalan language: "Catalan converts" who adopted Catalan-dominant language habits, sometimes passing as native Catalan speakers; "New Catalans" who saw themselves as Catalan and spoke Catalan but who also publicly presented Castilian-based bilingual personae in interactions; and "Castilians," as they were known among their peers, who retained monolingual identities and fundamentally monolingual social practices. The Catalan converts and New Catalans in this classroom were all from middle-class families, while those who remained Castilians were from working-class backgrounds. (In this book I have retained my earlier use of the term "New Catalans" for consistency, but readers should be aware that it is now used in public discourse in Catalonia to refer to transnational immigrants.)

I tacitly assumed that the young Castilians' reluctance to speak Catalan in this first year of secondary school would carry into the future. If they didn't take up the language in adolescence, when immersed in a Catalan-dominant school environment, when would they? At a conference at a US university I drew out the implications of these different linguistic patterns for the possible hardening of ethnolinguistic differentiation along social class lines over time in Catalonia. After my talk, a young man in the front row said, "You have just described my high school." Startled, I peered closely to see if I should have recognized him. No, no, he reassured me, he was from a neighboring city in the Barcelona area, where he had attended a very similar public school. He recognized his own experience in what I had presented (to my considerable relief). But, he continued, I had only captured the early years of high school.

---

4. For work that bears on this question, see Lieberson 1970; Grosjean 2010; Pedraza, Attinasi, and Hoffman 1980; Zentella 1997; Keim 2007; Sankoff 2004, 2005, 2006; Mendoza-Denton 2008; and further discussion in Woolard 2011.

Language use changes, and he offered himself as an example of a Castilian speaker who had later come to use Catalan comfortably. I should try to find out what happened, he suggested, as the young people in my study moved through and beyond high school. Twenty years after the first study, I was finally able to set out to do so.

Working from old addresses and through social networks, I found one-third of the original participants, despite the fact that some resided as far away as England and Australia. I interviewed eleven of them.[5] Eight of the re-interviewees were L1 Castilian speakers: two Catalan converts, one New Catalan, and five Castilians, in my original classification of them. This last group of five is the main focus of this chapter. All five of them had incorporated Catalan into their active linguistic lives at some level by the time they were young adults. With one important exception, they also had come to claim a Catalan identity and a positive orientation toward the language. A caveat, again: if the thirty or so individuals in the last chapter cannot be taken as representative of the larger population, this is even truer of this small panel of less than a dozen re-interviewees. However, this small longitudinal study allows us to see real individuals' changing understandings of their social environment and of their own responses to it, in real time.[6]

The 1987 study had shown that the move to secondary school was a juncture that offered the potential to remake oneself linguistically. (For similar findings, see Bretxa i Riera 2009, 2014, Bretxa and Vila i Moreno 2012.) This was the decisive moment for two boys in my study, who had become Catalan converts (Víctor and Rafael, quoted in Chapters 3 and 4). They told me they had agreed to transform themselves linguistically and speak only Catalan at their new school, and they succeeded. Despite a dawning awareness of its social significance, not all Castilian speakers were positioned or willing to adopt Catalan as part of their

---

5. I re-contacted participants by means of a bilingual Catalan-Castilian letter sent to the address where they had resided in high school. The response rate was higher for native Castilian speakers than for the full sample, with responses from three of the six who had acquired Catalan by high school, and five of the seven I had classed as functionally monolingual in Castilian. This is a high rate for a long-term follow-up study, but the sample is nonetheless tiny.

The dominance of Castilian in the extracts owes less to informants' choices than to my own lead as interviewer, in an impulse not to bias the interaction toward Catalan with people I remembered as teenaged Castilian speakers. Nonetheless, Catalan was used in some portion of all interviews, confirming to some degree informants' claims to speak the language. Elena and Adela, close friends, were interviewed together. All others were interviewed singly, in their homes or cafes, in informal meetings of one to two and a half hours. As throughout this book, all informant names are pseudonyms.

6. Late acquisition of Catalan among similarly positioned informants was also found in the studies of Pujolar and González (2013).

repertoire at that time. However, their paths over the following twenty years showed that the opportunity for significant linguistic development didn't end with high school.

Various later social junctures had proven to be as significant linguistically for these Castilians as high school had been for some of their peers. Specifically, entrance into higher education (as the students I quoted in Chapter 3 had predicted), the labor market (as Lola predicted for herself, Chapter 7), romance, and experience living abroad all proved to be consequential for use of Catalan. This is not necessarily because these contexts brought linguistic exposure that informants had not experienced before. Rather, they altered speakers' social environments and views of themselves in ways that allowed or motivated them to mobilize the linguistic resources that had been theoretically available to them earlier. Joan Pujolar and colleagues have coined the Catalan term *muda*, which translates as both "move" and "molting," as in a bird's seasonal change of plumage, for this kind of potentially reversible change in linguistic repertoire across an individual's life (Pujolar and Puigdevall 2015, Pujolar and Gonzàlez 2013, Pujolar i Cos et al. 2010).

I could not have predicted from their high school incarnations where these young people would arrive linguistically, socially, and professionally two decades later; nor would many of them have guessed themselves.[7] For this reason I refer to their linguistic "itineraries" rather than "trajectories," although the latter term has recently become popular (Alarcón and Garzón 2011, Pujolar and Gonzàlez 2013). "Trajectory" is useful to capture the dynamism of the linguistic repertoire over the lifespan, but in physics, trajectories are mathematically predictable from the start and uniformly directional. The term may inadvertently imply that once launched, individuals follow a set linguistic direction into the future. In contrast, the linguistic paths of some of the individuals I re-interviewed had taken turns since high school. "Itineraries" is an alternate term that has been used to encompass such turns and detours (Bucholtz et al. 2012, Bretxa i Riera and Parera Espelt 2012), so I adopt it here. I mean it as a record of a route actually taken, a journey with all its twists and turns, not the well-plotted plan with which an optimistic traveler might set out.

In the rest of this chapter I explore these linguistic itineraries through the reflections of these thoughtful interviewees, drawing primarily on extracts

---

7. I was very impressed by the insightful adults who had bloomed from the perennial teenagers of my memory. This points up the self-selection bias in the re-interview sample. From the reports they gave, not all their classmates had such successful and happy lives, but I did not get responses from those who may have found themselves less fortunate.

taken from the adult interviews, with some complementary material from the same informants' high school interviews.[8] I organize the material to highlight the several distinct junctures that led to their linguistic transformations. Taken together their accounts also reveal a shared explanation held by most of them of late language acquisition: a narrative of maturation into adult flexibility in contrast to rigid adolescent preoccupations with the social semiotics of distinction and shame.[9]

Reluctance to Speak: Shame

To begin, why had the Castilians been so reluctant to use Catalan when they were younger, given that they had opted, or their parents had opted for them, to attend a relatively Catalan-identified school? The linguistic situation was more painful and explicitly socially fraught for students in the 1980s that for those in the later study reported in Chapter 7. As adults they told stories that showed how they ran afoul of the binary opposition between linguistically defined "Catalans" and "Castilians." This contrast set no longer explicitly organized social life at JC by 2007, but it still did for these older informants.

Elena and Rosario were both the locally born children of workers who had immigrated from Andalusia to immigrant-dominated peripheral neighborhoods of this city. In high school the girls were fans of the Real Madrid soccer team, belonged to Andalusian flamenco dance groups (which were widely popular at the time), and said they felt more Spanish than Catalan. They were perceived by peers as the "Castilian girls," and they in turn felt marginalized by the class. In Ex.8.1, Rosario recalled herself as speaking little Catalan and being "hurt" (*dolida*) by Catalan peers who insulted her as a Castilian speaker.

---

8. All extracts are from interviews I conducted in December 2006–June 2007 unless dated 1987 in the extract heading. In this chapter (unlike Chapter 7), unmarked roman font in the original transcript is Castilian, and italic font is Catalan, because Castilian was the language predominantly used in this interview set. English glosses in this chapter use roman font for the unmarked language of the particular interview or interview segment, and italics for switches to the marked language. See front matter for other transcription conventions.

9. These accounts were co-constructed with me as interviewer, and in one case with a fellow interviewee. As noted above, I contributed strongly to the medium of the conversations, and thus no doubt to the substance as well. However, the broad scope of this book allows only abbreviated extracts that are not adequate for the close interactional analysis needed to display the mechanisms of co-construction, so this observation remains cautionary. Reminders of my role in several of these short extracts include the positive affirmations I often gave as receipt tokens, and my garbled, often ungrammatical prompts.

Ex. 8.1 Rosario: Hurt and insulted

KW: Y el catalán, qué? Hablas catalán (x)?

KW: And what about Catalan? Do
you speak Catalan (x)?

R: Pues (.) cuando tú me entrevistaste
seguramente que poco verdad?

R: Well (.) when you interviewed me
I'm sure it was little, right?

KW: Poco, poco.

KW: little, little.

R: Y seguramente que estaba un
poquillo como (.) dolida no? con
los catalanes.

R: And I'm sure I was a little, like
(.) hurt, no? By the Catalans.

KW: Un poco sí.

KW: A little, yes.

R: Sí. Me parece que te explicaría a
lo mejor que: sufrí un poquillo
de: (.) de: (.) la gente me insult-
porque yo jugaba a balonmano en
el club de al lado de: (.) de JC.

R: Yes. I think that I would explain
it to you probably tha:t I suffered
a little fro:m (.) fro:m (.) people
insulted m- because I played hand-
ball in a club next to: (.) to JC.

R: y era la única niña que hablaba
castellano.

R: and I was the only girl who spoke
Castilian.

KW: Ah.

KW: Ah.

R: Yo venía de otro sitio. Y me habían
insulta:do mucho y tal. Entonces
yo tenía como un poco de (.)

R: I came from another place. And
they had insu:lted me a lot and so
forth. So I had like a little (.)

KW: Pero insultado com- de?

KW: But insulted ho- about?

R: Llamarme cos- llamarme me acuerdo que me llamaban gita:na:

R: Calling me thin- I remember that
they called me gy:psy:

KW: Ah sí?

KW: Oh, really?

R: cosas así porque no hablaba
catalán.

R: things like that because I didn't
speak Catalan.

Later in the interview (Ex. 8.2) Rosario also recalled the shame that she felt about being called *xarnega/charnega*, the insulting epithet for immigrants much used at the time but almost unknown among young people now (see discussion in Chapter 4).

Ex. 8.2 Rosario: Shame

R: Es que antes (.) Yo me acuerdo
que nos daba mucha vergüenza.

R: It's that before (.) I remember that
it made us feel very ashamed.

KW: Sí?

KW: Yes?

R: Hablarlo.

R: To speak it.

KW: Sí.

R: Por miedo a: al error, la gente enseguida se reía de ti:. Qué catalán más malo hablas, charnega, te llamaba co:sa::s.

. . .

R: Mi madre también lo habla mal e y (.) y entonces le daba mucha vergüenza porque la gente se reía de ella incluso nosotras que al ser pequeñitas.

KW: Yes.

R: For fear o:f of a mistake, right away people would laugh at you:. What terrible Catalan you speak, *charnega*, they called you thi::ngs.

. . .

R: My mother also speaks it badly and and (.) and at that time she was very embarrassed because people laughed at her, including us, because we were just little.

Both as a teenager and as an adult another interviewee, Elena, also focused on the shame of being laughed at when speaking Catalan. Ex. 8.3 is taken from her 1987 interview, when I asked her whether the change in medium of instruction between her primary and secondary schools caused her difficulty.

Ex. 8.3 Elena (1987): Laughed at

KW: Cuando empezaste aquí a JC, tuviste problemas con el cambio de lengua?

E: Sí, bastante. Me ha costado adaptarme. Es que a mi me molestaba mucho porque empezaba a hablar catalán, y algunas palabras no me salen, no? Y la gente se ríe, me da un poco de vergüenza hablarlo.

KW: When you started here at JC, did you have problems with the change in language?

E: Yes, quite a bit. It's been hard to adjust. It bothered me a lot because I would start to speak Catalan, and some words won't come out, right? And people laugh, it makes me feel a little ashamed to speak it.

Twenty years later, Elena provided more details (Ex. 8.4). She still remembered vividly the name of the boy who laughed at her in class because she didn't distinguish lax and tense vowels (called open and closed in Catalan) when reading aloud in Catalan.[10] Her indignation resonates with Josep-Lluís Carod-Rovira's warning in the Catalan parliament against ridiculing President Montilla's Catalan pronunciation (Chapter 4).

---

10. His clearly Catalan surname and first name are represented in the transcript by a pseudonym. Note that when I ask in terms of "Catalan speaking," Elena answers in terms of "Catalan" as an identity category.

Ex. 8.4 Elena (2007): Laughed at

((Did anyone ever laugh at you?)) [11]

E: A mí en JC sí. . . . me acuerdo perfectamente de una (.) en clase hablando yo leyendo yo (.) un trocito de discurso en catalán (.) que dije varias palabras (.) mm el acento va cerrado o abierto y yo no lo dec- no lo pronunciaba bien, y la persona que estaba detrás de mí se estaba riendo.

KW: . . . Y era catalanohabl- porque a veces son los [castellanohablantes que se ríen].

E: [Era catalán era] catalán,

KW: Pero no, éste era catalán.

E: Prat. Es que me acuerdo de él. Jordi Prat.

KW: Ahhh. Ah. . . .

E: Era catalán de toda la vida. Sí, porque yo para mí estaba haciendo un esfuerzo (.) y (no entiendo cómo) una persona (.) que yo considero que la gente que está estudiando es gente que tiene que tener la mente abierta que se esté:: riendo de una persona que está intentando aprender.

((Did anyone ever laugh at you?))

E: At me, at JC, yes . . . I remember perfectly one (.) class, I was speaking, I was reading (.) a piece of Catalan discourse (.) and I said a few words (.) m-m the accent is closed or open and I didn't say- I didn't pronounce it well, and the person behind me was laughing at me.

KW: . . . And was it a Catalan speak- because sometimes it's the [Castilian speakers who laugh]

E: [He was Catalan, he was] Catalan.

KW: But no, this one was Catalan.

E: Prat. I remember him. Jordi Prat.

KW: Ahhh. Ah. . . .

E: He was a lifelong Catalan. Yes, because I, for me I was making an effort (.) and (I don't understand how) anyone, because I think that people who are studying should be people with an open mind, could be:: laughing at someone who is trying to learn.

In Ex. 8.5, Elena (with the collaboration of Adela) explained that such experiences were a shock to young people like her who came to high school from entirely Castilian-speaking environments (and schools, despite mandatory teaching of Catalan at the time). Humiliating encounters with Catalans could easily turn them against Catalan, as Elena said happened with her sister.

---

11. This question was not posed verbatim, so it is not given in Castilian here and is paraphrased from a composite of my earlier turns.

Ex. 8.5 Elena and Adela: The shock of Catalan

E: A ver en el núcleo en el que nos movíamos en e:l colegio

KW: Sí.

A: era un núcleo totalmente castellano.

KW: Sí.

E: Eh absolutamente castellano es decir (.) tanto amista:de:s como: familia etcétera. Entonces el salto a JC, durante los primeros años en JC la adaptación fue difícil, porque salíamos de un núcleo muy castellanizado, a empezar a a entenderte con gente en catalán, que no habíamos estado acostumbrados. Entonces el choque es difícil. Es difícil porque tú entiendes la lengua pero no la hablas.

KW: Sí.

E: Y te encuentras con opiniones de todas las clases. Con gente que te entiende y gente que no te entiende. Si tienes un carácter más o menos adaptable como me considero yo, no te afecta. Pero si tienes un carácter un poco:: duro, te plantas te: y te te vuelves c- en contra del catalán.

E: See, in the nucleus that we moved in during primary school

KW: Yes.

A: it was a totally Castilian nucleus.

KW: Yes.

E: Uh, absolutely Castilian, I mean (.) frie:ndships a:s much as family, etc. So in the jump to JC, during those first years at JC adaptation was difficult, because we came out of a very castilianized nucleus, to begin to to come to an understanding with people in Catalan, that we weren't accustomed to. So the shock is difficult. It's difficult because you understand the language but you don't speak it.

KW: Yes.

E: And you encounter all kinds of opinions. People who understand you and people who don't understand you. If you have a more or less flexible personality, like I think I have, it doesn't bother you. But if you have a somewhat::t difficult personality, you take a stand and you: you you turn ag- against Catalan.

As an adult, even Josefina, who had already become a bilingual New Catalan by high school, recalled a school incident with Catalans that had upset her. But for Josefina—a step ahead of Elena in the Catalanization process throughout her life—the incident came earlier, in primary school, and she suggested in Ex. 8.6 that it motivated her to make the transition to Catalan when the opportunity came with the move to high school.

Ex. 8.6 Josefina: Upset and a little hurt

J: *a l'EGB també. Una de les coses que jo tinc és de que: m- a mi em costava molt la: adreçar-me amb tothom en català.*

J: in EGB ((primary school)) too. One of the things that I have is tha:t m- for me it was very hard for me to speak to everyone in Catalan.

KW: *Sí*

KW: Yes.

J: *I quan havia de fer català treia bones notes i tot però després, l:a- el hàbit, de parlar-lo, em costava molt, no trobava tot el vocabulari. Llavons emm crec que hi havien unes nenes a la meva classe ara ja no m'en recordo ben bé eh? però (.) allò que tens mm a la ment?*

J: And when I had to do Catalan I got good grades and all, but then the: the habit of speaking it was hard for me, I couldn't find all the vocabulary. So then umm I think that there were some girls in my class, now I don't remember well, you know, but (.) that kind of thing that you keep in your head?

KW: *Sí.*

KW: Yes.

J: *Eh (.) que alomillor pot ser que van dir "clar és que no sap parlar perquè és castellana."*

J: Uh (.) so it could be that they said, "of course she doesn't know how to speak because she's Castilian."

KW: *Ah.*

KW: Ah.

J: *I va ser una d'aquelles coses que em va mm em va molestar perquè jo els hi vaig dir "jo no sóc castellana jo sóc catalana igual (.) que vosaltres, però els meus pares són: castellans. Però jo sóc catalana igual que vosaltres." I suposo que això alomillor em va ferir una mica, i va ser el que em va fer um (.) fer un canvi i sobretot després a l'institut no? Que l'institut és una (.) és un món molt més gran.*

J: And it was one of those things that made me mm made me upset because I said to them, "I'm not Castilian I'm Catalan the same (.) as you, but my parents are Castilians. But I'm Catalan just like you." And I suppose that probably hurt me a little, and was what made me um (.) make a change, most of all later at the high school, no? Because high school is a (.) is a much bigger world.

The insults, ridicule, and rejection that these three women recalled were linked in their accounts to their own feeling of vulnerability about speaking incorrectly. The term that most use for this feeling was *vergüenza* (CT *vergonya*), which translates in English as both "shame" and "embarrassment," but more commonly as the former. *Vergüenza* was also the term that José Luis used as a teenager in his 1987 interview (Ex. 8.7). Just the anticipation of being shamed by laughter at a mistake was enough to keep him from speaking Catalan. The interviews confirm that the slogan of the "*Dóna corda al català*" ("Wind up Catalan!") campaign directed at young people was on target: "Speak without shame!" (See Chapter 3). All these informants pointed to the same constraining linkage of shame and linguistic purity that James Wilce (2009) has suggested sociolinguists need to explore. This linguistic shame complex is a form of symbolic violence, in Bourdieu's (1991) term.

Ex. 8.7 José Luis (1987): Shame

KW: Dirías que hablas catalán muy a menudo o

KW: Would you say you speak Catalan very often or

JL: No, poco.

JL: No, little.

KW: Hablas catalán con alguien más que Toni y Emili?

KW: Do you speak Catalan with anyone besides Toni and Emili?

JL: No, nunca. Porque tal vez me dé vergüenza, si digo alguna cosa mal dicha o algo, a lo mejor se ríen.

JL: No, never. Maybe because it would make me ashamed, if I say something wrong or something, they might laugh.

KW: Lo han hecho alguna vez?

KW: Have they ever done that?

JL: No, nunca, como que nunca hablo.

JL: No, never, since I never speak ((it)).

Outgrowing Shame and Intolerance

Losing this fear of linguistic shame allowed these several informants to launch themselves into speaking Catalan, as Rosario explained in Ex. 8.8.

Ex. 8.8 Rosario: Loss of shame

R: y ahora pues (.) Si- ahora si voy a sitios hablo catalán. Al- algunos (.) fallos me salen pero bueno. Ahora sí.

R: And now well (.) If- now if I go places I speak Catalan. I make s- some (.) mistakes but okay. Now, yes.

KW: Más que antes de irte a:: Inglaterra dirías que usas (.) catalán?

KW: More than before you went to:: England, would you say you use (.) Catalan?

R: Sí, con menos vergüenza.

R: Yes, with less shame.

What allowed these former nonspeakers to overcome their *vergüenza* and begin to speak Catalan? They offered a common narrative of outgrowing shame and concern about what others think, on one hand, and of encountering greater tolerance of difference after adolescence, on the other. They saw young people as more susceptible to shame than adults: very vulnerable and sensitive, as Elena, Adela, and Rosario variously said.

Ex. 8.9 Elena: Outgrowing shame

E: Yo lo veo mejor ahora pero lo veo mejor desde mi mi edad.

. . .

KW: (x) tu vida, no?

E: Desde mi vida, exacto. No le no: (.) A mí ahora no no me importa que me digan o no me afecta que me digan nada (.) y en aquel entonces pues sí.

KW: Sí.

E: Porque eres más joven eres más vulnerable. Te afecta que digas por ejemplo: eh *la tassa* con un tono o con otro (.) si lleva una ese o no lleva

E: I see it as better now but I see it as better from my my age.

. . .

KW: (x) your life, no?

E: From my life, exactly. Not no:t (.) To me now it's not not important to me whether they say something to me or it doesn't matter to me if they say something (.) and back them, well yes ((it did)).

KW: Yes.

E: Because you're younger and you're more vulnerable. It matters to you that you say, for example, uh *la tassa* ((the cup)) with one tone or another (.) whether it has or doesn't have one "s". [12]

With age comes security to accept your own mistakes, Adela explained in Ex. 8.10.

Ex. 8.10 Adela: Accepting mistakes

A: Me costó pero bueno. Anteriormente: emm me daba más como más vergüenza o algo no sé. Supongo que por la edad.

. . .

A: It was hard for me but, okay. Befo:re umm it made me more ashamed or something, I don't know. I suppose because of the age ((I was)).

. . .

---

12. With this example, Elena indicates the same voicing contrast in intervocalic sibilants that we saw in Chapter 4 creates the iconic shibboleth of "Level S Catalan" for which José Montilla was criticized. It stereotypically bedevils Castilian speakers as they write or read Catalan aloud or try to translate from Castilian cognates (in this case, *taza*, with a voiceless interdental fricative).

A: Y entonces en ese momento dije
   bueno mm si me equivoco pues
   me he equivocado, me da igual.
   Supongo que la seguridad de la
   edad o a (.) no sé, no sé.

A: And then at that moment I said
   well ok, mm if I make a mistake
   well I made a mistake, I don't care.
   I suppose the security of age or at
   (.) I don't know, I don't know.

KW: Sí.

KW: Yes.

A: Pero: intenté intenté a empezar a
   hablar el catalán.

A: Bu:t I tried I tried to start speaking Catalan.

These informants spoke of age positively, and repeatedly characterized the adolescent preoccupation with shame as foolishness or stupidity (*tonterías*), as shown in Ex. 8.11 below. We will see the term *tonterías*, like *vergüenza*, recur in other extracts.

Ex. 8.11 Rosario: Foolishness

Yo te digo. Hmm (.) En e:: antes
de irme yo hablaba catalán en en
el trabajo pero (.) ya está. Pero
aquello: con amigos y eso, jamás.
A veces me juntaba con amigos
que hablan catalán ellos hablaban
catalán y yo castellano y me sentía
más cómoda. Ahora me da igual,
ahora se le me han quitado las
tonterías de la cabeza yo creo.

I'll tell you. Umm (.) In uh:: before
leaving ((the country)) I spoke Catalan
at work but (.) that was it. But tha:t,
with friends and that, never. Sometimes
I'd get together with friends who
speak Catalan they would be speaking
Catalan and me, Castilian, and I felt
more comfortable. Now I don't care,
now I've gotten all that foolishness out
of my head I believe.

Rosario characterized her younger self and her high school group as "closed-minded" (Ex. 8.12). This explanation was also implicit in Adela's account in Ex. 8.13 of how her ex-husband opened his mind and "changed the chip" after high school to become proud of speaking and being Catalan. "Changing the chip," as in changing the microchip card in a cellphone, is a popular phrase to refer to a change in mindset. It aptly captures the kind of gestalt change that is involved in a linguistic *muda*. It was also used by José Luis (see Ex. 8.16) to capture the turn-about in his own attitude toward the Catalan language.

Ex. 8.12 Rosario: Closed-minded youth

R: Es que también sabes qué pasa?
   que cuando nosotras empezamos
   (.) íbamos este grupo.

R: It's also, you know what happens?
   When we started ((high school))
   (.) we went as a group.

KW: Sí.

R: Margarita, Adela (.) y éramos todas muy: m (.) un grupo muy cerrado y: y mu- muy cerradas también de mente. Me parece.

KW: Tú crees?

R: Hmm. Yo creo que sí. Entonces con 14 y 15 años sí, la verdad es que.

KW: Yes.

R: Margarita, Adela (.) and we were all very, m (.) a very closed group a:nd and ver- very closed-minded, too. It seems to me.

KW: You think so?

R: Hmm. I think so. Back then, at 14 or 15, yes, the truth is.

Ex. 8.13 Adela: Changing the chip

A: *A l'escola rebutjava el català per-què: emm se sentia com se sentia com imposat.*

KW: *Aha sí sí.*

A: *i el rebutjava. Però després és lo que diem que canvies el xip t'obres la ment i i no tenia cap problema en parlar el català.*

KW: *Ahh.*

A: *A més se sentia molt català i: súper orgu- orgullós de ser català i de parlar-lo.*

A: At school he rejected Catalan becau:se um he felt he felt like imposed on.

KW: Aha, yes yes.

A: and he rejected it. But later it's what we were saying, that you change the chip, you open your mind and and he had no problem speaking Catalan.

KW: Ahh.

A: And what's more he felt very Catalan a:nd super prou- proud to be Catalan and to speak it.

These informants asserted that with age people generally become not only less vulnerable themselves but also more tolerant and less invested in patrolling linguistic boundaries. With age comes a sense of proportion, said Elena in Ex. 8.14, and Adela added that prejudices disappear.

Ex. 8.14 Elena and Adela: Age relativizes

E: hay gente muy (.) castellana cas-tellana que también ataca contra el catalán y gente muy catalana muy catalana que ataca contra el castellano, cuando (.) tendría que la gente tendría que neutralizar un poco más los los no sé

. . .

E: There are people who are very Castilian Castilian who also attack against Catalan, and people who are very Catalan very Catalan who attack against Castilian, when, it should be that people should neutralize a little more the, the, I don't know

. . .

A: Sí.

E: Es que es más el núcleo de gente
de gente de entre los quince: y
los veinte:: que es (.) eres como
más revolucionario eres como
que que te crees que vas a cambiar
algo, no es que no entiendo. En
esas edades sí sé que se ve más la
diferencia. Pero yo creo que una
vez pasas ya la barrera de los vein-
ticinco, veintiséis, todo es mucho
más relativo, lo ves diferente
[(xxx)].

A: [(xx)] los prejuicios se acaban y
ya miras

E: Sí.

A: las cosas realmente importantes
en la vida.

A: Yes.

E: It's that, it's more that core of
people people between fiftee:n and
twenty:: that is (.) you're more like
revolutionary you're like you think
that you're going to change something, it's not that I don't understand. At those ages yes, I know that
you notice differences more. But
I think that once you're past the
barrier of twenty-five, twenty-six,
everything is much more relative,
you see it differently [(xxx)].

A: [(xx)] your prejudices disappear
and you look at

E: Yes.

A: the things that really matter in life.

We see in these several extracts that these informants presented a develop-
mentalist model in which aging out of teenaged self-consciousness and foolish
youthful preoccupations with difference and sameness opens the individual's
mind to the possibilities of speaking Catalan. In this model, shame is a powerful motivator, but what they see as the commonsense world that shapes the consciousness of the normal adult is less threatening and is more tolerant than that
of the adolescent. Adults are held to be—or should be—more open-minded
and less dogmatic about language politics than teenagers, as a matter of social-
psychological development and personal growth. This liberates individuals like
them to take up new linguistic practices and broaden their identities.

Environments for Change in the Linguistic Repertoire

In addition to the shared view of the effects of maturity on language practices and identities, each of these informants' accounts also pointed to specific
changes in environment or experience that led to new stances toward linguistic
practice and a new sense of self. In this section I briefly identify these significant
changes in social environment and give an extract to illustrate each of them.

Elena: High School and University

Elena had indeed changed a lot, in my perception as in hers. She completed university training in a liberal profession and now has a practice with a Catalan-speaking associate. She reported that she uses Catalan daily and as her habitual choice in work and commercial exchanges. As a teenager she had claimed Castilian identity and Spanish nationality, and only reluctantly acknowledged after questioning, "I ought to say I'm Catalan … because I was born in Catalonia." As an adult, she considered herself proud to be both Catalan and Spanish.

For Elena, simply continuing in high school when her friends dropped out after reaching school-leaving age was a prime factor affecting her relationship to Catalan (Ex. 8.15). As Adela, Rosario, and others left school, Elena's Castilian-speaking circle "evaporated," as she phrases it here. Persevering on her own with high school, Elena came to make friends with people she refers to as "Catalans," including some I have labeled as bilingual New Catalans, such as Josefina. As she adapted to new friends, she says, "little by little I broke the barrier of shame, and I learned it [Catalan] easily."

Ex. 8.15 Elena and Adela: Continuing education and university

E: Para mí fue determinante (.) a ver (.) nosotras empezamos el insituto todas juntas. Ella, Rosario, Margarita, varias compañeras del colegio.

KW: Sí.

E: Qué sucedió? Que a medida que avanzábamos me iban dejando sola. Todas me dejaban. ((laughs)) Ellas dejo- dejaron de estudiar.

KW: Ah sí? porque ya Adela=

E: =Ella dejó de estudiar. Margarita dejó de estudia:r. Rosario dejó de estudia:r. Entonces yo me hice el camino sola. Es decir yo mi núcleo se me fue evaporando. Entonces yo me hice de nuevas amistades. Y las nuevas amistades que yo iba conociendo todas eran catalanas.

E: For me the deciding factor was (.) let's see (.) we all started high school together. Her ((Adela)), Rosario, Margarita, several class-mates from primary school.

KW: Yes.

E: And what happened? As we advanced, they left me there alone. They all left me. ((laughs)) They qui- quit school.

KW: Oh, yes? Because Adela already=

E: =She quit school. Margarita quit schoo:l. Rosario quit schoo:l. And so I traveled that road alone. That is, me, my core group evaporated on me. So I made new friends. And the new friends that I was meeting were all Catalan.

KW: Ahh (.) vale vale.

E: Claro.

A: Lo de ella fue más progresivo.

E: Lo mío (.) lo mío fue:: que yo seguí estudiando, y me fui haciendo de otro grupo de gente de amistades me fui adaptando. Y poco a poco fui rompiendo la barrera esta de la vergüenza y: y me fui haciendo entender y: (.) y y lo aprendí fácil y ya está y luego la universidad ya era todo mucho má:s fácil. Ya en la universidad, es diferente porque ya: del instituto ya sales con las (.) con las bases y ya no tienes tanta vergüenza: y es diferente.

. . .

E: Pues estuve aquí los cinco años de universidad. Y ahí (.) ehh pues eso. A ver. En la universidad notas que es más (.) hay má::s ehh mezcla de culturas en general. Es decir hablas el castellano igual que hablas el catalán, y ya la gente (.) les da igual, no te miran tan mal como en el JC, en el instituto.

KW: Ah (.) ok, ok.

E: Of course.

A: Her experience was more gradual.

E: My experience (.) my experience wa::s that I continued studying, and I went along making another group of people of friends, I went on adapting. And little by little I was breaking this barrier of shame a:nd and I was making myself understood a:nd (.) and and I learned it easily and that's it, and then later at university, everything was much easier. At the university it's different because you already: come out of high school with the (.) with the foundation and you don't feel so much sha:me and it's different.

. . .

E: So I was there the five years of university. And there (.) uhh well, that. Let's see. At university you notice that it's more (.) there's mo::re uh mixture of cultures in general. I mean you speak Castilian same as you speak Catalan, and people (.) they don't care, they don't look at you badly like they did at JC, in high school.

As some of my earlier informants had predicted for themselves (Chapter 3), university life was a linchpin in Elena's linguistic transformation. Linguistically, she found "everything much easier" at the university because, having gained a foundation in Catalan in high school and breaking into a new social setting, she no longer felt shame. Moreover, at the university, she felt that people mixed across linguistic lines and were more accepting than in high school. For Elena, then, the move from high school to university functioned the way the move from primary school to high school had for Josefina (see Ex. 8.6 above). Those like Josefina who had acquired basic knowledge of Catalan in primary school could make the social leap to speaking Catalan regularly in high school, which they found to be a more ethnolinguistically mixed place that gave them the opportunity to speak it. This same experience came one stage later for Elena at university, after acquiring the linguistic base in high school.

José Luis: Work

In high school José Luis had Catalan-speaking friends, but as we saw earlier he asserted, and my observations confirmed, that he basically never spoke the language. At that time José Luis did see himself as Catalan by virtue of birthplace, but culturally and linguistically he identified as Castilian. This is the label he used in high school to describe himself when talking about peer groups, adding at one point, "I'd like to be Catalan."

When I re-interviewed him, José Luis had a white-collar job in which the work was almost exclusively in Castilian. However, he reported that he used Catalan in his daily life and had exclusively Catalan-medium relations with some friends. He spoke Catalan comfortably to me in part of our interview. He too had come to see himself as Catalan as well as Spanish and asserted that he found being bilingual enriching and personally satisfying.

When did he make the change? José Luis worked a low-level job in social services after high school in order to pay for his later university studies. It was entry into the workforce that led him to "change the chip" linguistically (Ex. 8.16) and to gain what he characterizes as linguistic consciousness (Ex. 8.17 and 8.18). He expressed with considerable hedging but then also with satisfaction the experience that in Chapter 7 young Lola anticipated for her own future self, in which work necessitates speaking Catalan in a way that school never had. He came to see himself as having foolishly passed up earlier linguistic opportunities (Ex. 8.18).

Ex. 8.16 José Luis: Work

El trabajo un poco pues te (.) te fuerza, te fuerza entre comillas no? Pero (.) es un poco donde cambias un poco el chip y y te diriges, la gente se dirige a ti en catalán. Tú pues te diriges en catalán es un poco.	Work, well, it sort of forces you (.), "forces you" in quotes, no? But (.) it's sort of where you sort of change the chip and you talk, people talk to you in Catalan. So you talk to them in Catalan, sort of.

Ex. 8.17 José Luis: Becoming conscious

JL: *Estava pensant en quan vaig començar a parlar català.*

JL: I was thinking about when I started to speak Catalan.

KW: *Mm. Sí.*

KW: Mm. Yes.

JL: *No. Més que res és una consciençiació no? de la terra, i de que vius a Catalunya això fa que parlis en català*

JL: No. More than anything it was becoming conscious, no? Of the land, and that you live in Catalonia, and that makes you speak Catalan.

. . .

. . .

JL: *Sí (.) Et prens una miqueta les coses més en sèrio, te te n'adones collons, estic a Catalunya no? Per què no parlo en català? Si (.) si estic a Catalunya.*[13]

JL: Yes (.) You take things a little more seriously, you you realize, hell, I'm in Catalonia, no? Why don't I speak Catalan? If (.) if I'm in Catalonia.

Ex. 8.18 José Luis: Giving up foolishness

JL: *Sí. Sí sí que prens una miqueta més consciència no? la gent que t'envolta, de (.) de lo que tens o deixes de tenir, de lo important que són algunes coses que tu (.) que tu et negaves a poder a parlar català o algo i dius hòstia però si és si és una tonteria.*

JL: Yes. Yes yes you gain a little more consciousness, no? Of the people around you, of (.) of what you have or what you're letting go, of how important some things are that you (.) that you refused to be able to speak Catalan or something and you say damn, but this is this is foolishness.

KW: *Molt bé, molt bé.*

KW: Very well, very well.

JL: *És una tonteria.*

JL: It's just foolishness.

Like Elena, Adela, and Rosario, José Luis depicted the transformation as a matter of maturation, an opening of the mind against the closed-minded preoccupations of adolescence. But in his case it was the new environment of the workplace that triggered the moment of recognition and the opportunity for change.

---

13. José Luis uses the verb form *estic* "I am" twice in this excerpt, from the Catalan verb *estar* rather than *ésser*, which prescriptively and normally is used in Catalan to indicate location. Paradoxically, this could be either a very common transfer from Castilian or evidence of mastery of a fine point of Catalan. Prescriptively *estar* is used rather than *ésser* in Catalan when the emphasis is on an extended period in the same location, which may be the point José Luis is emphasizing here; he lives in Catalonia and isn't going anywhere else.

Adela: Social Networks and Romance

Having left high school without graduating, Adela worked in a factory for over seventeen years. She basically spoke no Catalan when last interviewed at fourteen and did not begin until after she divorced at age twenty-eight. Restarting her social life, she joined a recreational group with a young relative and found herself in the midst of Catalan speakers. And there, having outgrown her teenaged shame, she began to speak Catalan. By thirty-four, she had a Catalan-speaking domestic partner and a Catalan-medium relationship with him. She planned to speak Catalan with their baby, due in a few months. Adela enjoyed watching "The Word Hunters" (*Caçadors de paraules*), a popular show about the Catalan language on the Catalan public television channel, and she gave her partner a book based on the program to celebrate Sant Jordi, the Catalan patron saint's day, when books are exchanged. From a monolingual Castilian speaker with an Andalusian accent who left high school early, Adela had become a proud and eager learner and even a fan of Catalan.

It was the relationship with her new romantic partner that set Adela's new stance toward the Catalan language. Adela and her co-interviewee Elena asserted with a laugh "Love has to break down the foolishness; if love can't, nothing can" (Ex. 8.19).

Ex. 8.19 Adela and Elena: Love overcomes foolishness

A: Yo con mi pareja hablo, pero por- es una opción que yo escogí. Él no me obligó a decir háblame en catalán.

A: Me, with my partner I speak ((Catalan)) but bec- it's an option that I chose. He didn't make me say "speak to me in Catalan."

KW: Sí.

KW: Yes.

A: Evidentemente.

A: Obviously.

KW: Sí sí.

KW: Yes yes.

A: De hecho él: en principio me preguntó si quería que:: que yo- que él me hablara en castellano. Y yo le dije que no.

A: In fact he: in the beginning he asked me if I wanted him to:: to speak to me in Castilian. And I told him no.

KW: Ah no? O sea que ya:

KW: Ah no? That is, that already:

A: Yo preferí. Claro. Porque (.) eh t- (x) tengo más facilidad con el castellano para expresarme incluso a veces voy a decirle algo y le pregunto esto cómo se dice? Porque aún hay palabras, o en el momento que no

A: I preferred. Sure. Because (.) uh (x) I have more ability to express myself in Castilian, in fact at times I go to say something to him and I ask him how do you say this? Because there are still words, or in the moment that don't

KW: Sí.

E: Claro.

A: Pero yo hablo con él en catalán.

KW: Sí. Pero él estaba dis- dispuesto en principio a hablarte [en]

A: [en] castellano. Pero (x) yo dije que no.

KW: Ah muy bien muy bien.

E: Es que el amor tiene que romper esas (tonterías). ((laughs)) No me digas, es que si el amor no puede con eso [((all laugh))]

A: [con eso ya no puede con nada.]

KW: Yes.

E: Of course.

A: But I speak with him in Catalan.

KW: Yes. But he was will- willing in the beginning to speak to you [in]

A: [in] Castilian. But (x) I said no.

KW: Ah, very well, very well.

E: It's like love has to break down this (foolishness). ((laughs)) Don't tell me, it's like if love can't do it [((all laugh))]

A: [with that then it can't with anything].

Josefina: Parenthood

Entry into parenthood can also motivate changes in the linguistic repertoire (cf. Boix-Fuster 2009). For example, Pujolar and colleagues (2010, 22) reported that 40% of Castilian-speaking couples use Catalan with their children as much or more than they use Castilian. A 2008 survey shows that approximately 41% of parents in Catalonia speak Catalan to their children, yet only 32% speak it to their own parents (Generalitat de Catalunya 2009). Josefina belongs to this 9% who have shifted the intergenerational language.

Hurt at what she perceived as exclusion by Catalan speakers in primary school (see Ex. 8.6 above), by high school Josefina was a "New Catalan" who had already made the change to bilingual practice and persona. As an adult she reported that she shifted increasingly to Catalan when she joined the workforce. But her Catalan identity was reformulated and moved to a new stage when she became a mother and decided to speak only Catalan to her children, believing that would help them gain native-speaker linguistic control and native-speaker advantages. (Even the household answering-machine message was in monolingual Catalan.) This rupture of intergenerational transmission of the mother tongue is significant for the expansion of Catalan, and it is also significant for Josefina's own social identity. She considers herself wholly Catalan and believes she sometimes now passes for a first-language speaker of Catalan. Her husband, with whom she continues to speak directly in Castilian, was carried along toward Catalan willy-nilly by her linguistic practices with the children (Ex. 8.20).

Ex. 8.20 Josefina: Parenthood

J: *Ell quan vam tenir els nens, va decidir (.) que: que s'expressava molt millor en castellà i que ho faria aixins als nens i aixins els nens també (.) aprendrien el castellà des de petitons.*

J: He, when we had the kids, he decided (.) tha:t that he could express himself much better in Castilian and that he would do it with the kids and that way the kids could also (.) learn Castilian from when they were very little.

KW: *Sí.*

KW: Yes.

J: *Però després va veure que no, que(.) els nens tiraven en català, i que clar, que ell es quedava una mica (.) com en (.) no com: fora de la conversa però clar, si els nens parlaven sempre:(.) amb mi i m'explicaven tot en català, tots els seus amics eren catalans, totes les seves mestres eren catalans (.) pues ell es va sentir una mica com dir (.) què raro no? que jo li parli en castellà? I llavons es va: va fer el canvi i va dir no no pues jo(.) també parlaré en català.*

J: But then he saw that no, that (.) the kids turned toward Catalan, and that of course, that he was left a little (.) like in (.) not like: out of the conversation but sure, if the kids always: spoke (.) to me and told me everything in Catalan, all of their friends were Catalans, all their teachers were Catalans (.) *well* then he felt a little, like (.) how weird, no? That I speak to them in Castilian? And so he: he made the change and said no no *well* then I'll (.) speak in Catalan, too.

KW: *Ahhhm.*

KW: Mmm.

J: *Llavorens des de que tenim els nens que res això ho va decidir: el primer mes.* [14]

J: So then since we have had the kids then nothing, he decided: this the first month.

KW: *Ah sí? (.) Sí sí sí.*

KW: Oh yes? (.) Yes yes yes.

J: *Doncs llavorens ell ho diu que s'ha: mm que s'ha estirat molt més no?*

J: So then he says that that he ha:s mm that he's stretched a lot more, no?

In a hint of the changes possible even later in the lifespan, Josefina pointed to her own immigrant mother, who never spoke Catalan while Josefina was

---

14. If the decision Josefina mentions here refers to the husband's decision to speak Catalan rather than Castilian, then there are apparent internal inconsistencies in the timeline of this report, since all of the Catalan-speaking circumstances detailed could not have occurred "in the first month" of having children. This is a reminder that these informants' reports must be taken as narratives with their own rhetorical purposes and conventions, rather than as some kind of direct access to actual past events.

growing up because—in the familiar pattern—someone had ridiculed her early on. As a grandmother she too was influenced by the Catalan dominance of her young grandchildren. She had begun to use some Catalan with them and even attempted to read to them in that language.

Ex. 8.21 Josefina: Grandparenting

J: *En canvi la mare (.) umm per el que:: mm va ser no sé, ehh quan va venir (.) algú la va ridiculitzar parlant en català.*

KW: *Ah sí?*

J: *I llavorens va dir que ella no parlaria català.*

KW: *I:?*

J: *Una posició molt tonta però (.) la va—ho va fer. I ara sí que (en) va parlant amb els nens, sempre parla alguna cosa en català però ((laughs)) no tota una frase.*

KW: *Ah sí? O sigui que els nens estan canviant els hàbits=*

J: *=Sí sí=.*

KW: *=lingüístics de=*

J: *Inclús per exemple ((laughing voice)) l'altre dia es van quedar ells amb els nens, (clar) sempre els (si-) hi expliquen un conte. Els hi expliquen molts llegint. I clar tots els contes estan en català. I deia ma mare diu, "és que me costa molt llegir en català" i li va llegir ((laughing voice)).*

KW: *Ahh.*

J: *I clar feia gràcia perquè li llegia, i ((laughs)) li deia el meu home diu, "pues inventi-s'ho si no: ho sap llegir, pues eso, <u>inventa i ja està.</u>"*

KW: *Està bé. ((laughs))*

J: *I deia diu "no no. Si jo ja llegeixo, ves?"*

J: In contrast my mother (.) umm for wha::t mm was I don't know, uhh when she came (.) someone ridiculed her speaking in Catalan.

KW: Oh yes?

J: And so she said she wouldn't speak Catalan.

KW: A:nd?

J: A very foolish position but (.) she did—she did it. And now yes, she's speaking it with the kids, she always says something in Catalan but ((laughs)) not a whole sentence.

KW: Oh yes? So the kids are changing the habits=

J: =Yes yes=

KW: = linguistic ((habits)) of=

J: =Including for example ((laughing voice)) the other day they were staying with the kids, (sure) they always (te-) tell them a story. They read to them a lot. And of course all the stories are in Catalan. And my mother said, she says "It's hard for *me* to read in Catalan" and she read to them ((laughing voice)).

KW: Ahh.

J: And of course it was funny because she read to them and ((laughs)) my husband said to her, he says "*Well* make one up, if you don't know how to read it, *well then,* <u>make it up and</u> there you are."

KW: That's good. ((laughs))

J: And she said she says "No no. I'm reading already ((in Catalan)), *see?*"

Rosario: Cosmopolitan Travel

The juncture that significantly altered Elena and Adela's high school friend Rosario's linguistic life was a period living abroad. Her experience illustrates the claim discussed in Chapter 5 that there are forms of cosmopolitanism that are not only compatible with but can actually generate a greater interest in and involvement with Catalan.

After switching from JC to another high school that she hoped to find more hospitable, Rosario finally finished her diploma in night school. She then left for London, where she found a good job in retailing and married a Northern European. Rosario returned to Barcelona seven years later a multilingual cosmopolitan. English was her household language with her husband, and she spoke Catalan comfortably. Remembering her high school days Rosario said "surely I didn't feel Catalan back then," and acknowledged with a laugh that in fact she now felt "quite Catalan."[15]

Rosario's newfound comfort in speaking Catalan was in her view partly a matter of the seemingly natural process of maturing and leaving behind foolishness as described by her peers, and partly a response to what she saw as a more relaxed attitude among contemporary Catalans about linguistic correctness. Principally, though, she attributed her change of linguistic stance to her cosmopolitan experience. Movement through new linguistic environments not only added a new language, English, to her repertoire; it also afforded her a different orientation to her old linguistic environment, a kind of gestalt change.

Ex. 8.22 Rosario: Cosmopolitan experience

R: Yo, es que también, yo he cambiado mucho ((laughs)). Es que bueno. Primero que era muy tonta de joven, creo. Y luego (.) es que (una vez) que viajas te das cuenta de- es que, qué más d- y qué más da de dónde seas. Es que da igual! Realmente (.) da igual. Yo ahora soy más feliz y tengo amigos de todos sitios de (.) Tsk. Y (.) y ves que es es im-es importante aprender las lenguas pero no es tan importante hablarlas perfecto. (.) A no ser que las necesites para (.)

R: I, it's also that, I've changed a lot ((laughs)). It's, well. First, I was very foolish when I was young, I think. And then (.) it's that (once) you travel you realize that-, it's like, who care- and who cares where you're from. It doesn't matter! It really (.) doesn't matter. Me, now I'm happier and I have friends from all over from (.) Tsk. And (.) and you see that it's it's im- it's important to learn languages but it's not so important to speak them perfectly. Unless you need them for (.)

KW: Sí.

KW: Yes.

---

15. "bastante catalana."

R: Para el trabajo no?

KW: Sí. Tienes razón. Pero esto

R: Y es (xx) que vas allí y todos hablamos inglés y todos somos de fuera, no?

KW: Ah ya.

R: Un italiano un uno de Lituania uno de (.) yo qué sé. Y es (.) pues ves (.) que es super (.) útil el inglés (.) en ese sentido no?

KW: Sí sí.

R: De tantos sitios y que todos llegan a poder comunicarse.

R: For work, right?

KW: Yes. You're right. But that

R: And it's (xx) you go there and we all speak English and we're all from someplace else, no?

KW: Ah, ok.

R: An Italian, a one from Lithuania one from (.) I don't know where. And it's (.) you see (.) that English (.) is super (.) useful in that way, right?

KW: Yes, yes.

R: From so may places and everyone manages to be able to communicate.

Travel and the experience of learning English imperfectly in an international social milieu diminished the tension between Catalan and Castilian for Rosario. It led her to see her earlier alienation from Catalan as foolish and freed her to take up both the language and Catalan identity on her return to Barcelona. Rosario's perspective on the language had become that of a cosmopolitan, one who embraces but is not preoccupied by multiple linguistic demands. Not only did she range across a broader geographical and social landscape, she relativized the meaning of Catalan and Castilian ethnolinguistic identities to that broader scale, which reduced the formerly great weight of Catalan to something personally manageable for her. As was suggested in the public debate about Catalan cosmopolitanism discussed in Chapter 5, cosmopolitanism motivated Rosario to adopt rather than reject or dismiss Catalan.[16]

Reacting against Catalanism

Not all of the Castilian speakers that I re-interviewed depicted such a positive relationship to the Catalan language and identity as those I have discussed so

16. In their work among low- to middle-class secondary school students in Barcelona, Newman, Trenchs-Parera, and colleagues also found that participants who expressed cosmopolitan orientations showed attitudes favoring bilingualism and diversity (Trenchs-Parera and Newman 2009, 509; see also Newman, Trenchs-Parera, and Ng 2008; Trenchs-Parera, Larrea Mendizabal, and Newman 2014).

far. The stance that their classmate Josep took had become both more negative and more politicized than that of the others. In high school he had actually been ahead of the others in mastering Catalan, although he recognized that his Catalan peers had him pegged as a "Castilian" and thus didn't speak it with him (that experience is discussed in Woolard 2007a). As an adult Josep had come to use Catalan fluently in his professional life, and was proud of his proficiency, but he had not incorporated it into his sense of self.[17] Josep is the informant whom I quoted in Chapter 4 on the impossibility of nonnative speakers' learning the weak pronouns and the "archaic" sound patterns of Catalan.

Recounting his linguistic experiences, Josep focused on his discomfort speaking in Catalan and the awkwardness of a continual need to translate from Castilian. In Ex. 8.23 he framed that experience squarely within the ideology of linguistic authenticity by drawing on the *lengua propia* motif (see Chapter 3) to describe how he had not naturalized or internalized the language as his own. Instead, for him it was a language of the local place, and that locality entailed alienation rather than identification, because he did not feel himself to be truly of the place, and in fact he contemplated leaving it. Josep said he did not express his inner emotions in Catalan, since it was not his own.

Ex. 8.23 Josep: Own language

Yo no considero el catalán una lengua propia mía. . . . No la considero una lengua propia. La considero una lengua del lugar pero yo no- ni lloro ((en catalán)).	I don't consider Catalan a language of my own . . . I don't think of it as my own language. I think of it as a language of the place but I don't—I don't even cry ((in Catalan)).

Although he was proud that he has good friendships with Catalans, Josep cast himself as part of a Castilian and sometimes Andalusian "us" that he contrasted "totally" and enduringly to a Catalan "them." In Ex. 8.24, he drew on a deeply gendered conception of the domestic sphere as the heart of these groups' cultural differences:

---

17. Although Josep identified as Castilian as an adult, he continued to use preferentially the Catalan form of his name. This is reflected in the pseudonym assigned him in the 1987 study, which is preserved here.

Ex. 8.24 Josep: They're different

R: Totalmente. Ni la forma de lim-
piar de las mujeres, ni la forma de
cocinar, ni la forma de vestir, de
tratar al hombre, a los hijos edu-
carlos, no tiene nada que ver entre
las personas de tradición catalana
y las personas de tradición
andaluza: castellana: eh:

R: Totally. Not the way women clean,
not the way of cooking, nor the
way of dressing, of talking to the
husband/man, of teaching the
children, there's no similarity at all
between people from the Catalan
tradition and people from the
Andalusian, Castilian tradition, eh:

KW: Todavía?

KW: Still?

R: Todavía, todavía . . . . Yo he ido a la
casa de un catalán, muy amigo mío,
y es que son diferentes- cojones. Es
que son-son-son son diferentes.

R: Still, still . . . I've been to the home
of a Catalan, a good friend of mine,
and they're different, hell. It's just
that they're, they're, they're different.

Josep came from the same neighborhood, the same school, and the same immigrant-descent origin as his classmates already discussed, and attended the same university as Elena had. Politically conservative, he experienced that university as a place that politicized and exacerbated rather than diminished ethnolinguistic lines of difference. The contrast between their perspectives illustrates how individuals who share ethnolinguistic background, social location, and many life experiences can nonetheless live in different sociolinguistic worlds, interpreting linguistic tensions and possibilities differently.

Chronotopes in Life Stories

These differing accounts of changes or continuity in language and identity derive from interviews, not from direct observation. Therefore my analysis is of necessity as much about informants' narratives (to which as interviewer I contributed) as it is about their actual linguistic transformations. Given this, I have found the literary theorist Mikhail Bakhtin's (1981) notion of the chronotope useful to capture differences that are of interest. In this concept, Bakhtin cast time and space as interconnected in a frame that formally constitutes and distinguishes different literary genres of narrative. For example, Ancient Greek romances take place in a significantly different chronotope or time-space than do 19th century European novels, with characters ranging across very different kinds of geographical and social landscapes.

Bakhtin's resonant concept of the chronotope has been deployed to a variety of ends in linguistic anthropology in recent years (see Lempert and Perrino 2007).

It is related to the notion of "scale" that is now being used in discourse analysis to theorize alternative discursive constructions and representations of social life; see, e.g. Blommaert (2010). For my purposes, the most important point in Bakhtin's formulation is that distinctive chronotopes determine not just distinct literary genres, but also the different "images of man" that occur in these different genres (Bakhtin 1981, 85). For Bakhtin, different scales of time and locale are not just linked to different specific forms of personhood (Agha 2007b), but they actually *enable* different kinds of character development. Bakhtin's template allows us to see how informants' accounts give different meanings to personal experiences, charter different potential for personal transformation and action in the worlds they live in, and, specifically, allow different stances toward use of the Catalan language.

Elena, Adela, José Luis, and to some extent Rosario all constructed a story of their linguistic evolution within what I will call a *biographical chronotope*.[18] They told their stories in the form of a Bildungsroman, the coming-of-age literary genre in which character development is primarily a matter of self-actualization, of individual maturation and self-realization in which characters come to terms with a social environment that is less susceptible to change. In these interviews as in the Bildungsroman, the social context offers the challenges, but developments and changes occur in the individual, who adapts to those challenging structures.

In contrast, Josep framed his account within what I call a *socio-historical chronotope*, which places the individual's life in a larger social scale. These two different frames differentially facilitate a psychological and apolitical reading of personal experience on the one hand vs. a sociological and politicized understanding on the other. They also enable different roles for the interviewees as protagonists of their own stories, and different possibilities for the development of their own character. The biographical chronotope corresponds with a project-oriented sense of personal identity that does not rest on a traditional view of linguistic authenticity, while Josep's socio-historical chronotope somewhat counterintuitively incorporates a sense of identity and an ideology of linguistic authority

---

18. Rosario is similar to Elena and Adela in her adult stance toward Catalan language and identity, and her account of her linguistic transformation also emphasized shedding the sense of shame that hampered her second-language acquisition when young. However, from a Bakhtinian perspective, much of the story she told of her transformation featured a different chronotope. She recounted a metamorphosis derived from travel across contrasting landscapes in a cosmopolitan chronotope that I have analyzed in detail elsewhere as uncannily akin to what Bakhtin called "adventure time in everyday life" (Woolard 2013). I set aside that difference here and instead highlight the ways that Rosario's account fits with the others.

based in naturalistic, originary sources of authenticity.[19] I will develop these points further in the next sections.

The Biographical Chronotope

Within the frame of the biographical chronotope, new speakers of Catalan were "super-proud," in Adela's term, to claim competence in the language as adults, and they interpreted their own linguistic growth in apolitical terms of individual growth. They rejected the politicization of language, insisting that bilingualism was an individual choice they made to enlarge their personal world, and they did not tie their choices closely to changing language policies. As we have seen, they presented themselves as growing and changing, gaining perspective and consciousness, unfolding and opening as individuals. Elena and Adela's co-constructed account in particular depicted developing individuals who were relatively unaffected by, and for Adela didn't even really register, changes in a political landscape, despite the considerable social and policy changes in Catalonia in their lifetimes. (Rosario, however, felt that there had been a relaxation of linguistic purity among Catalan speakers generally.)

After a discussion of mixed-language classes at Elena's fitness club that proceed "without any problem," I attempted to ask what Elena and Adela thought about the situation of the languages compared to twenty years earlier. Elena resolved the ambiguous level of my halting prompt by answering explicitly in biographical terms that contrasted her childhood sensitivity about criticism to her adult invulnerability, as we saw in Ex. 8.9. In Ex. 8.25, I provide more of the context of that comment to show how she chose to respond in personal terms.

Ex. 8.25 Elena: From my life

KW: Eso de problemas. Estabamos hablando de la crispación un poco antes entre (.) bueno Rajoy y Carod=

KW: Concerning problems. We were talking a little earlier about the tension between, well, Rajoy and Carod=

E: =Sí=

E: =Yes=

KW =por ejemplo. Pero cómo veis . . . el ambiente y la situación de las lenguas ahora? Comparado (sic) a ((laughs)) hace veinte años? En total=

KW: =for example. How do you (pl.) . . . see the environment and the situation of the languages now compared to ((laughs)) twenty years ago? Overall=

---

19. Because I mostly give examples from women of the biographical chronotope and from a man for the socio-historical chronotope, readers may think that this is a gendered difference. These interview accounts are certainly gendered in many ways, but there is not a straightforward male/female difference in either the chronotopic frames or the orientation to Catalan.

A: =A nivel:: ciudadano o a nivel [político]?

A: =At the level:: of the citizen or the level of the [political]?

KW: [Sí:::], no. A nivel ciu-dadano. Público. La vida, la vida normal. La vida mm::

KW: [Yes:::], no. At the level of the citizen. Public. Life, normal life. Life, ummm

A: Aquella época no me acuerdo.

A: That period, I don't remember.

E: Yo lo veo mejor ahora pero lo veo mejor desde mi mi edad.

E: I see it as better now but I see it as bet-ter from my my age.

8 A: [(xxx)]

A: [(xxx)]

KW: [x] tu vida, no?

KW: [x] your life, no?

E: Desde mi vida exacto (.) no le no: (.) a mí ahora no no me importa que me digan o no me afecta que me digan nada (.) y en aquel entonces pues sí.

E: From my life, exactly. (.) Not no:t (.) To me now it's not not important to me whether they say something to me or it doesn't matter to me if they say something (.) and back them, well yes ((it did)).

We also saw in Ex. 8.13 above that Adela insisted on an individual, psycholog-ical explanation of her former husband's alienation from Catalan in high school. She went on to reject explicitly my attempt at an institutional explanation and insist again on the individual explanation, as seen in Ex. 8.26.

Ex. 8.26 Adela: Not the school

KW: *O sigui que l'escola a vegades provoca els problemes diguéssim,* <u>bueno</u>

KW: So sometimes the school creates the problems, let's say, <u>okay</u>

A: *No, estava parlant del Manuel, que a l'escola rebutjava el català. Ell tenia problemes. A EGB no, a l'institut. Però després va canviar. És lo que diem que quan se t'obre la ment doncs ell no tenia cap problema en parlar el català.*

A: No, I was talking about Manuel, that at school he rejected Catalan. He had problems. Not in primary school, in high school. But after that he changed. It's what we said, that when your mind opens, then he had no problem about speaking Catalan.

As seen briefly here, Josep's friend José Luis places himself in the biographical chronotope and maturational model used by the women. Other male informants who were re-interviewed but whose stories are not discussed here include Rafael, who has a more complicated position than any outlined here. One of the "Catalan converts" in high school, Rafael is now cosmopolitan like Rosario, socially and politically very aware like Josep, but progressive, Catalanist, and ori-ented to a project identity.

In the chronotope in which these informants place themselves, a kind of universal human nature that evolves from childhood to adulthood is the prime motivational force of language behavior—theirs and others'. Neither timeless ethnolinguistic traits nor politico-historical and institutional forces enter into this evolution.

I will take a short detour here to follow out implications of this stance that are somewhat tangential to this biographical chronotope, but central to the topic of the chapter and the book. In these informants' accounts, the implication is that those who remain preoccupied about language, as nationalists do, are not fully mature adults. Elena, for example, specifically contrasted the linguistic maturity of which she was proud not only with her own adolescent self, as Rosario did for herself, but also with the immaturity of some adult others, saying: "I think that thirty year old people who limit themselves because of language, for me I see that as absurd."[20] It was her bilingualism, not Catalan as such, that she valued. Elena was most explicitly scornful of Catalan professionals who she found could not speak Castilian fluently (Ex. 8.27).

Ex. 8.27 Elena: Ridiculous not to know Castilian

encuentro patético . . . que el ((professional)) que tengo enfrente no sepa hacer dos frases en castellano. Y me parece ridículo.	I find it pathetic . . . that ((a professional)) standing in front of me should not know how to put two sentences together in Castilian. And I find it ridiculous.
. . .	. . .
Considero que no saber hablar el castellano es un atraso. Por qué? Pues porque es la segunda lengua más hablada del mundo y hay que saber hablarla.	I think it's a step backward not to know how to speak Castilian. Why? Well because it's the second most spoken language in the world and it's necessary to know how to speak it.

This is a familiar Castilianist discourse we saw in Chapter 3. It was a position from which Adela demurred, in part because she heard it as a criticism of her own partner. Throughout the interview Elena criticized nationalists and endorsed bilingualism, in phrases that resembled the discourse of bilingualism that is espoused by conservative forces and the anti-Catalanist Ciutadans party.

---

20. "Pienso que la gente con treinte años que se limite por culpa del idioma, yo para mí lo veo un absurdo."

Recognizing this resonance, I asked Elena and Adela how they viewed that party. To my surprise, Elena flatly rejected Ciutadans as Spanish nationalists, just as she rejected Catalan nationalism.

Ex. 8.28 Elena: Ciutadans as rightwing nationalists

KW: habéis oído del partido nuevo eh Ciutadans?

. . .

E: Sí hombre sí, es que:: son de derechas absolutamente.

. . .

E: yo yo lo veo clarísimo que es bastante facha. Que es un gru- es un partido muy de ide-de ideas nacionalistas, pero de derechas.

KW: bueno, tienen un discurso un poco parecido de esto de bilingüismo, somos abiertos, estamos a favor de todo.

E: Plurales.

KW: Plurales, sí. Todo eso. Pero tú no lo tienes claro?

E: A mí no, a mí no. Yo no los he visto plurales. Yo los he visto muy nacionales. Muy de derechas.

KW: Have you heard of the new Ciutadans party?

. . .

E: Yes, man, yes, it's tha::t, they're absolutely rightwing.

. . .

E: I see it very clearly that it is pretty fascist. That it's a grou- it's a party with nationalist ideas, but from the rightwing.

KW: Well, they have a discourse that's a little similar to this one of bilingualism, we're open, we're in favor of everything.

E: Pluralist.

KW: Pluralist, yes. All that. But you have doubts?

E: To me, no, to me, no. I haven't seem them as pluralist. I've seen them as very nationalist. Very rightwing.

Elena's response in Ex. 8.28 does not fit the traditional template of endorsements of bilingualism that leads Catalans activists to interpret them skeptically. It is consistent with her view that language choice is a matter of personal evolution that is only mistakenly politicized.

The Socio-historical Chronotope

In contrast to the biographical narrative scale, Josep, who had become more anti-Catalanist since early high school, framed his personal experience in a socio-historical chronotope that highlighted developments at the level of the Catalan political community and the Spanish state. Josep drew on a chronotope in which there had been socio-historical change in the Catalan context, but he himself was a relatively unchanging protagonist living in this transformed time-place. He was constrained but not formed by his social environment, and presents himself as rooted in what Bakhtin calls ancestral time, drawing his character from his descent, not from the synchronic horizontal community of his contemporary surroundings, with which he felt at odds. Unlike Elena, Adela, and even his friend José Luis, Josep was very aware of his changing socio-historical environment, which he perceived as degenerating in response to parochial Catalan traditionalism on the one hand and the chaos induced by transnational immigration on the other. To be fully realized as the protagonist of the complete life that he believed he is capable of, Josep contemplated moving to a more hospitable part of Spain.

As we saw earlier, when I asked Elena and Adela about the social context, they answered in terms of individual psychology. In noteworthy contrast, when I (in equally stumbling prompts) asked Josep questions about his personal development and his own linguistic biography, he often responded with commentary about socio-historical and political change, as for example in Ex. 8.29:

Ex. 8.29 Josep: Political changes

KW: Pues me interesaba eso, a ver eh: que-dónde has ido desde entonces

KW: Well I was interested in that, let's see, eh, what-where you (sing.) have gone since then.

J: Sí. Ha-ha-ha habido una serie de problemas, bueno problemas no, cambios políticos importantes. Cuando yo:: eh: estudiaba en mi instituto, JC, digamos que la mayoría de las clases se daban en castellano, pocas-pocas clases se daban en-en catalán, estaba todavía introduciéndose. Había un porcentaje elevado de clases, que eran en castellano y el catalán digamos que todavía se estaba introduciendo. Eh:: sucede que esto ha cambiado totalmente, con *la llei de normalització lingüística.*

J: Yes. There has-has-has been a series of problems, well, not problems, important political changes. When I:: uh: was studying in my high school, JC, let's say the majority of the classes were in Castilian, few-few classes were given in Catalan, it was still being introduced. There was a high percentage of classes that were in Castilian and let's say Catalan was still being introduced. Uh:: so it happens that this changed completely, with *the Law of Linguistic Normalization.*

In a similar example, Josep turned the activity of pointing out different relatives in a family photo into a general social commentary:

Ex. 8.30 Josep: The red belt

Ésta es mi familia . . . Han cambiado, eh? . . . Es que aquí: bueno, como tú bien sabes ha:y: una división bastante . . . Aquí: estamos la mitad castellanoparlantes: y: catalanoparlantes:. En la zona del cinturón rojo que le llaman, cinturón industrial de Barcelona, eh: por qué le llaman cinturón rojo? porque ahí-siempre-ganan- lo:s: socialistas	This is my family . . . They've changed, eh? . . . It's that here: well, as you well know, there is a division rather . . . He:re we're half Castilian-speakers a:nd Catalan-speakers. In the zone of the red belt, as they call it, the industrial belt of Barcelona, eh: why do they call it the red belt? Because there the Socialists always win

Josep combined a sociological consciousness of class differences and historical change with categorical thinking about cultural contrasts between Catalans and Castilians (Ex. 8.31), as well as between the Iberian-born population and new transnational immigrants (Ex. 8.32). (Notice how the linguistic descriptors function as ethnic as well as class categorizations in his usage; Joan Pujolar has analyzed this usage among more Catalanist sectors (Pujolar 2007b).)

Ex. 8.31 Josep: Consciousness

Si en Cataluña hay seis millones de personas y tres son castellanoparlantes y tres son catalanoparlantes, la gran diferencia es que los castellanoparlantes n::o tienen la formación académica que tienen los catalanoparlantes, no tienen la conciencia política, ni la conciencia de nación que tienen los catalanoparlantes. La mayoría de puestos en los cuales eh: se trabaja con las manos y no se reflexiona mucho sobre ideología política, corresponde a los castellanoparlantes, gente de Andalucía, de Extremadura, de Murcia y demás. En cambio los catalanoparlantes, siempre, de: porque es su idiosincrasia, su forma de ser, el *tarannà* que dicen ellos eh:: es de estudiar y de tener las ideas muy claras.	If in Catalonia there are six million people and three are Castilian speakers and three are Catalan speakers, the great difference is that the Castilian speakers do no::t have the academic training that the Catalan speakers have, they don't have the political consciousness, nor the national consciousness that Catalan speakers have. The majority of positions in which uh: one works with one's hands and doesn't reflect much on political ideology go to the Castilian speakers, people from Andalusia, from Extremadura, from Murcia and so forth. In contrast the Catalan speakers always, because it's their idiosyncrasy, their way of being, their *way* as they say, is to study and to have very clear ideas.

Ex. 8.32 Josep: Immigration explosion

J: Luego: hace: seis años, si tu- no
sé si has estado por aquí, pero
desde hace seis años, e: ha
habido un boom inmigratorio
importantísimo

J: So, six years ago, if you- I don't know
whether you have been around here,
but since about six years ago, there's
been a very important explosion of
immigration

KW: De fuera, no?

KW: from outside, no?

J: Pero muy importante, y ahora
empezamos a tener los primeros
problemas serios.

J: But very important, and now we're
starting to have the first serious
problems.

Within his sociological and historical analysis of a changing context, Josep saw himself as set apart, a unique individual, distinguished from others with similar backgrounds:

Ex. 8.33 Josep: Self-made man

Yo ya había acabado la carrera y ya
tenía clientela . . . Ya es un poco
el "self-made man," que dicen los
americanos, no?

I had finished my degree and I already
had a a clientele . . . It's a little bit the
((story of the)) "self-made man", as the
Americans say, right?

Josep saw himself as unchanging in his basic character and attitudes and always an anomaly in his social milieu. He insisted that he had been politically conservative his whole life, despite his working-class background (and despite my incomprehension, as I missed Josep's desire not to be viewed as normal).

Ex. 8.34 Josep: Spanish pride

J: Yo soy conservador y de derechas . . .
yo, el concepto de España, como
unidad de nación, el cast- es-es-es que
lo siento, a mi me sale. Yo-yo-yo de
pequeño, de bien pequeñín, yo cogía
el libro::, el atlas de historia, y:: miraba
el imperio español, con orgullo.

J: I'm conservative and from the right . . .
for me, the concept of Spain, as a unified nation, the Cast- it's it's it's what
I feel, what comes from me. I-I-I, when
I was little, really little, I picked up a
book, a historical atlas a::nd I looked
at the Spanish empire, with pride.

KW: Sí.

KW: Yes.

J: Tú crees que esto es normal?

J: Do you think that's normal?

KW: Sí, perfecto.

KW: Yes, perfectly.

J: Pero yo es que:: Yo nunca me han
dicho que si España, que nunca
ha habido una foto de Franco en
mi casa. Jamás ... O sea nada. ...
me-me ha venido solo.

J: But it's that I:: Me, they never told
me that Spain is this, there was never
a photo of Franco in my house.
Never ... I mean nothing. ... it
came to m-me on my own.

In contrast to Elena and Adela's pride in having become Catalan-speaking Catalans and adapted to their environment, Josep expressed an unchanged pride, from his earliest age, in being part of the enduring legacy of the Spanish empire. His story was about the stable essence of an already completed character who does not "become" as he experiences historical time. Historical reality in Josep's telling was an important arena for disclosing individual character, but not for determining it, much as Bakhtin observed of a similar genre (Bakhtin 1981, 140–141).

Josep's relationship to Catalan was mediated by a strong sense of the historical, the political, and the sociological. In his representation, Josep himself has not changed, but the world he lives in had, and for the worse. He did not see his predicament as a self-identified Andalusian Spaniard in Catalonia, attached to his native Castilian language, as simply personal. For Josep, the solution was not to reconcile his relationship to language and identity in his context, as his classmates Elena, Adela, José Luis, and Rosario did, but rather to take a political stance against changes in his environment that he viewed as unjust to a whole group.[21] Josep envisioned that relief would come only in moving to another landscape in Spain where his biographical roots would fit with the roots of the contemporary community.

Summary and Conclusion

In this chapter, we have heard from several people who had participated in my original high school study in 1987, as they presented themselves to me in interviews twenty years later. All those from Castilian-speaking backgrounds that I was able to re-interview reported and showed noteworthy development of their command and use of Catalan since adolescence. They narrated linguistic changes, which Pujolar and colleagues would call *mudes*, that coalesced around some specific social juncture such as university, a first job, a romantic relationship, living abroad, or parenthood. For all but one of those interviewed, not only had the use

---

21. Elena also asserted that some Catalan linguistic policies could be viewed as unjust, but distinguished her personal situation—"it's not unjust for me, I'm not affected," she said—from that of a hypothetical Spaniard wishing to move to Catalonia for a job.

of Catalan grown considerably since they were teenagers, their self-identification as Catalan had developed as well.

Beyond these crystallizing events, several of these informants offered a shared understanding of an underlying cause of such linguistic transformations or *mudes*. They posited qualitative differences in the way that adolescents and adults normally orient to identity and in the role of language choice in establishing such identity. They viewed linguistic shame and intolerance of difference as immature traits that inhibit second-language learning. They argued that these are foolish inhibitions that are normally shed with age and experience, allowing new linguistic forms to be taken up more freely and mistakes to be tolerated better by others.

This upbeat account of linguistic expansiveness and flexible identification across the lifespan needs to be modulated. First, the dissenting position expressed by their classmate Josep surely represents a significant segment of the Castilian-speaking population in the Barcelona area. Second, these are self-representations of linguistic changes that I confirmed only superficially in the course of our interviews, not in the kind of in-depth observation I was able to do in the school ethnographies. In a similarly interview-based study, Emili Boix reminds us that there are social reasons why some interviewees might present themselves as more "Catalan" than they actually are in daily practice (Boix-Fuster 2009, 126). Then, even those who had taken up Catalan language and identity had not forgotten the pain and snubs they had experienced as youngsters because of their ethnolinguistic identification. Moreover, their primary identities as Castilian speakers remained with them as the foundation on which the pride in their transformation was built. Unlike their young counterparts, they still thought and talked in terms of "Catalans" and "Castilians" as ethnolinguistic identities that gave meaning to their social worlds but did not prevent them from claiming Catalan as well as Spanish identity.

In relation to the Catalan language, there were limits to the late linguistic growth that these informants showed and claimed, a point that Adela remarked with some regret, wishing she had had the opportunity to benefit from Catalan immersion education. The interviews showed that to a greater or lesser degree, the Catalan they spoke was marked by linguistic transfers from Castilian beyond those often found among first-language Catalan speakers, in a pattern also seen by Boix and Sanz (2008). Many Catalan language activists would find such linguistic patterns to confirm their fears about the state of the language and their predictions for its further deterioration.

These informants' active use of Catalan in no way brought a disavowal of Castilian. Except for Josefina, who had converted to a primarily Catalan identity, what these new speakers claimed was a bilingual, or in Rosario's case multilingual, identity. Nor does it follow that those who embraced Catalan as part of their identity embraced the Catalan nationalist project. Josefina now sees herself as fully Catalan in some essential way, but for others the incorporation of this identity into the adult sense of self is more akin to a civic, residential identity than an ethnic or nationalistic one. "I'm from here, I live here," said Rosario in claiming her Catalan identity. The Catalan language and Catalan identity had become relatively de-ethnicized and depoliticized facets of Elena and Adela's personal landscape, and they strongly objected to their politicization by others, of either persuasion.[22] Elena, in particular, spoke vociferously against Catalan nationalism, but she was also vociferous in her disdain for anti-Catalanist Spanish nationalists and the Ciutadans party. Adela was enamored and proud of Catalan and things Catalan and less censorious about Catalan-dominant speakers than Elena, but she nevertheless echoed her friend in speaking against all nationalist sentiments and politicians who try to "sell" a language. Rosario, in contrast, found a bit to her own surprise that she had begun to favor political parties that focused on the interests of Catalonia.

Different informants in this re-study structured their autobiographical narratives within fundamentally different chronotopes, or space-time frames, which charter different visions of personal as opposed to social responsibility for their current linguistic situations and selves. Most presented themselves in a kind of biographical chronotope, as successfully maturing individuals in a relatively unchanging social world. Josep in contrast appeared as an unchanging, steadfast, and politically aware protagonist in a deteriorating world framed in a socio-historical chronotope. Most importantly for the theme of this book, these different chronotopes provide narrative ground for different stances toward bilingualism and specifically toward the use of Catalan. These stances are legitimated by different ideologies of language that accompany these different chronotopic frames.

For Josep, the authority and legitimacy of a language was based primarily in the ideology of authenticity that is traditional to ethnonationalist discourse. As explored in Section I of this book, a traditionally "authentic" language is one that is taken to correspond to the true nature of the self, and that self is defined by origins. Despite claiming considerable linguistic mastery, Josep rejected Catalan's power over him as an imposition because it was not his own language. Catalan felt foreign to him; he did not cry in it, as he said. To insist that he speak Catalan was then to hamper his personal freedom, and freedom is a central concept in his neoliberal politics. On the surface it may seem paradoxical, given Josep's alertness to socio-historical change, that he drew on a traditional linguistic ideology. However, within his account of social history, distinct ethnolinguistic groups

---

22. Such sentiments were also found by Pujolar i Cos et al. (2010, 33, 38).

with fixed cultural traits were significant social actors. The traditional ideology of authenticity was coherent with his interpretation of the historical and political drama of Catalonia as a conflict between contrasting and competing ethnolinguistic groups.[23]

The interviewees who embraced identities as speakers of Catalan did not represent their adult view of language choice within the traditional rhetoric of authenticity, although that had informed their outlook when they were younger. They had become neither Castilian holdouts nor Catalan converts, but instead were new New Catalans, to use the term I coined for their 1987 cohort. They depicted themselves as having shed adolescent concerns about linguistic authenticity almost entirely—"who cares!," as Rosario exclaimed. Only immature people care, Elena and Adela strongly implied.

Elena, Adela, José Luis, Josefina, and Rosario all broke the tie of linguistic origins to identity that Josep maintained. In its place they mobilized a rhetoric that was newer in the Catalan setting, more resonant with the ideological complex of "anonymity" that casts a language as owned by no one in particular and thus available to all with the will to take it up. Further, these informants took not a politicized stance toward language choice but rather a personalistic one. They cultivated a personal coherence based in a both-and rather than either-or model of being, and they had achieved their own alternatives to the "possessive investment in monolingualism" I discussed in Chapter 3. As in the Javanese example sketched in Chapter 2, the self they especially valued actually depended on having multiple languages in place of a single one. It was precisely the ability to move between languages in daily life that gave these informants so much satisfaction.

For Elena and Adela, José Luis, and Rosario—unlike Josep—the use of the Catalan language had come to be and should be about communication among individuals, not group identity or political divisions; about adult rationality, not youthful emotional vulnerability; and about possibilities and becoming, not origins. Their stance was consonant with the late modern cultivation of the self and with project authenticity as proposed in Chapter 2. One could see in it the neoliberal ideology of the self-governing entrepreneurial individual, but labels such as neoliberalism are too broad to distinguish informatively the contrasting

---

23. It is perhaps not surprising that those who present themselves as most comfortable with their situation tell their story in a way that emphasizes their own individual role in creating it, while one who is less satisfied expresses unhappiness with the circumstances. This patterning of personal vs. generalizing accounts resembles that found by Reichman (2011) in relation to Honduran migrants' decisions to emigrate. Those who left gave socially generalizing accounts of their actions, while those who remained behind gave personalistic interpretations of their neighbors' decisions.

perspectives presented in this chapter. Although Elena and Adela may seem to have drawn on a neoliberal model of the freely choosing self, it was Josep who cast himself as an enterprising individual actively aligned with neoliberal politics and economics of freedom. The discourses of neoliberal subjectivity circulate and are redistributed across different linguistic and identity stances and political positions. They are taken up and put to use in different ways by different individuals, even those who share closely related class and cultural backgrounds. Each appropriates and mobilizes bits of the ascendant discourse in circulation in their own ways toward different ends. The irony is that Elena and Adela's experience of personal linguistic flexibility, just like Josep's experience of linguistic constraint and injured Castilian identity, was underpinned by political structures that granted linguistic legitimacy. The difference lies in the scale of perception and explanation on which their accounts operate. The chronotopic differences create different experiences, making the personal political for some, and the political personal for others.

9 CONCLUSION

The difficulty lies, not in the new ideas, but in escaping from the old ones, which ramify, for those brought up as most of us have been, into every corner of our minds.

—JOHN MAYNARD KEYNES

Preface to The General Theory of Employment, Interest and Money (1935)

This book has taken stock of changes in the politics of language in Catalonia over the more than three decades since the return to autonomy, across several domains of public and private social life. My focus has been on explicit discourses about language as well as the linguistic ideological ground that is shifting under them, particularly in the 21st century. To represent these changes, I have made two simultaneous analytic moves that are in tension in a way that I hope is not unproductive.

On the one hand, I have drawn a broad-stroke, highly idealized contrast between two ideological foundations of linguistic authority and legitimacy in the modern period that derive from Enlightenment and Romantic conceptions of language and society. The reader who has started anywhere other than this last chapter is now very familiar with these two ideological constellations as linguistic anonymity and authenticity.

On the other hand, in examining evidence from several domains of public discourse and from two generations of young people, I have tried to complicate simplistic stereotypes that are widely purveyed by political forces and the media, of Catalan linguistic policies and activism as forms of primordialist and exclusionary ethnic nationalism. I have explored changing, multiple, and sometimes internally conflicted conceptualizations of language among private individuals and public figures. These conceptualizations appear in the rhetoric of electoral campaigns, in the ambiguities of linguistic parody, in discourses of urban and national branding, and in individuals' own accounts of themselves, their peers, and their linguistic practices.

The main argument throughout this book has been that Catalan linguistic authority is no longer firmly grounded in the authenticity value that sustained its legitimacy during the return to political autonomy. This is true of both the public authority of the Catalan language and the interpersonal authority of its speakers. Although the transition has been uneasy and subject to continuing contestation, in all the domains I studied I have found the development of alternatives to the primordialist, traditionalist, and naturalistic visions of linguistic authenticity. The moves have been variously toward an alternate foundation of legitimacy in anonymity, toward an escape from the binary logic of authenticity vs. anonymity altogether into forms of rooted cosmopolitanism, and toward a post-natural, goal-oriented sense of authenticity as project rather than origin.

When Catalonia regained autonomy in 1979–1980, the polity took up the agenda of making Catalan a "normal" public language. Catalan enjoyed great strengths not often associated with minoritized languages that facilitated this project: a long-established standardized form, high rates of maintenance among the autochthonous population, habitual everyday use by well-educated middle-class speakers among others, and a consequent prestigious resonance across the community, regardless of linguistic background. Still, establishing Catalan as a widely used public language would prove to be no simple task. Its continued position in the official and commercial shade of the globally powerful Castilian language, the scale of demographic and linguistic changes created through labor migration from southern Spain under the repressive Franco regime, and the logics of linguistic ideologies all militated against the transformation.

At the advent of autonomy, Catalan figured focally in Catalanist discourse as the territory's "own" language, its *llengua pròpia*, with primordial roots that conferred on it a rightful place as the true language of Catalonia, seen as a moral and socio-cultural status that had been violated by the state for many decades, even centuries. As well, in everyday communicative practice in the eyes and ears of community members, first-language speakers of Catalan were the true "Catalan Catalans" to whom the language belonged. This authenticity value held sway despite many Catalan activists' and politicians' efforts to cultivate a voluntarist civic nationalism that eschewed descent- and heritage-based calculations of ethnic identity and encouraged acquisition of Catalan as an assumable, inhabitable index of belonging to the Catalan community. In practice for most ordinary speakers in the early days of autonomy, Catalan social identity was reserved to those who spoke Catalan as a first and habitual language (as if these were the same thing, which most of the time they were), and the language was heard as the property of such speakers.

Such a fundamental association of the language with a valued identity had contributed to the high rate of linguistic maintenance among autochthonous Catalans despite political repression and institutional marginalization, but the renewed project of making Catalan a public language was hampered as much as it was supported by this ideology of authenticity, for two reasons. First, opposing interests claimed public value for Castilian by casting it as an anonymous "common" language belonging to anyone and everyone, and denigrated Catalan in contrast as a merely local language with limited communicative utility, restricted to marking an exclusionary identity. Equally or more important, the connotations of linguistic authenticity in everyday life worked against the adoption of Catalan by the large population of working-class Spanish immigrant origin or descent, who felt (as some still feel) that the language could not be theirs, particularly if they wished to retain their own sense of authentic personal identity. Catalan in the newly autonomous Catalonia was caught between an ideological rock and a hard place. Catalan was neither the "naturally" taken-for-granted language of public communication, nor the "naturally" true language of the private heart and home throughout the community.

In response to these dual limitations on Catalan linguistic authority, one discursive turn taken by Catalan policymakers and activists was toward the kind of ideological anonymity characteristic of dominant public languages that are so ubiquitous that they appear to come from no social position and belong to no one in particular. This appears in advocates' efforts to depict and thus establish Catalan as the common language of all in Catalonia and to dissociate it from both ethnic and political belonging. However, politics and demography have not allowed any easy naturalization of Catalan linguistic authority as anonymous. As Albert Branchadell has observed, it is not possible for two languages to be anonymous within the same space (Branchadell 2012, 7).

From the perspective of critical sociolinguistics, this is not necessarily a bad situation. Although many in the classroom of young people I worked with took Catalan for granted as the medium of instruction in their schools, their self-aware reflections showed that most did not misrecognize the source of its value and take it as invisible or anonymous. Catalan schooling did, however, give the younger generation of working-class Castilian speakers in this study actual linguistic options that their earlier counterparts did not have. Rather than falling into linguistic lockstep because of their Catalan-medium schooling, they exercised varying linguistic choices in their personal relations and even in schoolwork, but one can meaningfully choose whether to use a language only if one has access to its forms. The younger cohort did not speak of the sense of linguistic shame expressed by the older generation, which is a key to the silencing of the marginalized in Bourdieu's model of linguistic domination. Catalan-medium education is no pedagogical utopia, and working-class students from non-Catalan-speaking backgrounds are still the strong majority of those who lose their way or turn away from school, in a class-driven pattern still to be confronted effectively. Nonetheless, legitimate ownership of Catalan was more widely distributed among the younger than it had been among the older group in my study when they were students. For better or worse in the eyes of Catalan linguistic activists, young people had become less likely (and able) to socially distinguish first- from second-language speakers, as the formerly stigmatized *xava* variety was shared by both. Even someone like Pilar who chose to speak as little Catalan as possible could feel that because of her schooling from earliest days, Catalan sounded like her own language when friends spoke it to her; "It's as if it were Castilian."

An alternative to the sociolinguistic naturalism that underpins both anonymity and authenticity has also been expressed increasingly in a post-natural, goal-oriented understanding of personal and community authenticity as project rather than origin. Such a conceptualization of linguistic community had been present in Catalan politics throughout the 20th century and especially the post-Franco period. Various language campaigns of the autonomous period had operated on the principle that a language, like a nation, is a daily plebiscite, to paraphrase Ernest Renan.[1] This view has taken on new dimensions in the new millennium in politics, media, and private life. Across these different domains, I have traced weakening and breaking threads of sociolinguistic naturalism and identified emerging efforts by participants to weave different accounts of the legitimate linguistic foundations of society and self. A similarly anti-essentialist, post-naturalist discourse of project-based Catalan identity and of cosmopolitan nationalism has also been woven into the sovereignty movement. As Súmate, an immigrant-oriented organization advocating the right to decide on independence, describes its hope of "constructing a new and collective project" in its Castilian-medium slogan, "It's not the origin but the destination that matters"[2] (Súmate n.d.).

These newer conceptualizations of Catalan language and identity are part of strategic political rhetoric, certainly, as seen in electoral campaigns and nation branding for the global market, but they are not only that. They inform the views expressed by two generations of young individuals from Castilian- as well as Catalan-speaking background with whom I worked. To be sure, the broad circulation of such ideas and discourses does not mean that everyone embraces

---

1. Renan would surely have objected. The 19th century French philologist and theorist of nationalism thought that languages, unlike nations, were natural entities, and held racist views of their significance.

2. "la ilusión por construir un proyecto nuevo y colectivo"; "no importa el origen sino el destino."

them, and those who do so may find it difficult to sustain them and not fall into contradictions and more familiar logics. There are many Joseps who feel the Catalanist project is hostile to their ethnolinguistic identity and tradition. Not everyone who embraces Catalan identity has embraced the language, or vice versa. Certainly not everyone who claims that identity or uses that language supports independence, for myriad reasons. Although there are relationships among these phenomena, they are not straightforwardly predictable, and that is one of the points of this book.

In the past three decades, there has been a progressive acquisition of knowledge of Catalan among the Castilian-speaking population of Catalonia, as was reflected among both my older and younger cohorts of informants. Although active use is often a different matter, Catalonia has broken the mold for minoritized languages, and the direction of second-language acquisition implied in bilingualism has mutated, as Rudolf Ortega put it. It is not only first-language Catalan speakers who routinely gain bilingual skills now, and the majority of those who claim knowledge of Catalan are first-language speakers of Castilian (Ortega 2015). The conditions that made earlier Catalan sociolinguists understand bilingualism to be an insidious stage in predictable language shift and loss do not so clearly hold in Catalonia now.

It is tempting to see the return of political autonomy in 1979–1980 as creating a kind of natural experiment in the effects of policymaking and formal institutions on language values and linguistic practices, but it is a wildly uncontrolled experiment. On the one hand, the developments I have documented here are historically specific to Catalonia and respond to conjunctural political, social, and demographic conditions that are not commonly found in language contact settings around the world. On the other hand, beyond the political structures and linguistic policies of Catalonia, much more has changed during the same period. Spain entered the European Union, and Catalonia, like the rest of Spain, enjoyed and then suffered enormous economic changes. It participated in the trends of economic and cultural globalization, rapid growth in transnational migration, and the increasing hegemony of the market-based political and social philosophy of neoliberalism that have affected national identity and language situations around the world.

All these circumstances mean that changes in discourses about language in Catalonia did not develop only in response to changes in internal political structures. The new discourses of language and identity in Catalonia are not entirely peculiar to it and share features found elsewhere in the world, in domains from youth culture to nation branding, although they are taken up and refashioned to the Catalan context by active participants. The twin monoliths of Enlightenment anonymity and Romantic authenticity that characterize linguistic modernity have both been buffeted in the current global dispensation. Intellectual elites, community activists, and ordinary speakers in more than one setting around the world now show a "strategic desire to locate resources for a cosmopolitan future in vernacular ways of being themselves" (Pollock 2000, 623), and to refuse the ideological dichotomy that has sustained language hierarchies in the modern period.

Catalan activists deeply regretted that its double denaturalization, through political domination in combination with demography, prevented Catalan from being a "normal language," but in the last decades multiple forces have made sociolinguistic naturalism itself increasingly and openly subject to question. Around the world, people are no longer so certain just what a normal language is. This uncertainty is as much an opportunity as a challenge for Catalonia.

EPILOGUE

It is impossible to write a conclusion to a book about a process that is so obviously not concluded. As I write this last comment at the end of summer 2015, Catalonia prepares for parliamentary elections that are presented by the independentist coalition as a plebiscite on sovereignty, but that are also framed by a rising populist movement as an opportunity for a new leftist grassroots politics. Whatever the outcome of these elections, it will not be the last word on Catalan sovereignty and the form of Catalonia as a nation.

It is almost as hard to know where my role as observer begins and ends. Long-term anthropological work (what my colleague Joan Pujolar wryly called "life-long ethnography") on a public issue in a cosmopolitan community of engaged readers is a hall of mirrors. I have been writing and talking at least since the early 1990s about the need for the Catalan language to be de-ethnicized if it is to become a widely available public language, and talking about authenticity and anonymity as competing foundations of linguistic authority since the early 2000s, to the point that as Albert Branchadell (2012) commented, I've become personally identified with that contrast. Across the decades I have always felt fortunate to enjoy a thoughtful, positive reception of my work in Catalonia. As I wrote in the acknowledgments, I share mutual influences with many Catalan colleagues whom I meet on the stairs of the Escher-like edifice I have been working on for so long.

Sociolinguists are well aware of the problem that William Labov called the observer's paradox, and I have tried to acknowledge in Part III of this book the degree to which my role as interviewer and interlocutor may have shaped the accounts of individuals whom I observed and interviewed. It has been brought home to me more recently that the dimensions of the observer's paradox may be greater than that. Among my Catalan readers and interlocutors are not just academics but also activists and policymakers. Am I observing or contributing to the change in public and political discourses about language in Catalonia? Some Catalan colleagues have suggested to me that the answer is both.

When Josep-Lluís Carod-Rovira adopted the rhetoric of de-ethnicization of language and nation in the 2006 campaign that I discussed in Chapter 3, one sociolinguist jokingly asked me if I had been doing some political consulting. Or at least I assumed he was joking. I had not been consulted, and as an American academic I don't easily imagine that researchers' ideas about language might willy-nilly influence public discourse. In the United States, academic sociolinguists and linguistic anthropologists are used to crying in the wilderness of public panics about Ebonics, bilingual education, or the perils of Spanish in the public sphere. They are rarely heard and even more rarely see their ideas taken up in the public sector, even when they work hard to make that happen. But it's different in places like Catalonia, where a vice president might be trained in philology.

In the summer of 2014, Maria Rosa Garrido Sardà, who had worked with me on this research from its early days, was surprised to see some familiar phrases in a campaign flyer in support of sovereignty that she had been handed on the street. I was equally struck when she passed it on to me. Clearly addressed to immigrants and children of immigrants, the flyer echoed Manuel Castells' concept of "project identity": "The hour has come to consolidate your personal project." It urged the reader to do that by supporting independence for Catalonia. The flyer went on in what to Maria Rosa and me were uncannily resonant words:

> What do those who oppose this project want? . . . To make citizens who are deracinated from the land, traditions and culture. That is, citizens of the world who belong to nowhere.[1]

Had I correctly characterized the "voice from nowhere" that would be in contention, or might I have intervened in some small way in that contention, or both? If my work has had any effect it is through indirect links, and I would like to think it is positive. Whatever else it may represent, that flyer is a good reminder to me that this book is the product of a long dialogue with and within a self-aware, reflexive community. That dialogue has taken place and will continue to take place within multiple frames. As happens on the set of *Polònia*, it's time for a director to step through the fourth wall and move this conversation to another stage. *Talleu, és bona!* Cut, it's a wrap!

---

1. "Ha arribat l'hora de consolidar el teu projecte personal . . . .Què volen les persones que s'oposen a aquest projecte? . . . Aconseguir ciutadans desarrelats de la terra, de les tradicions i de la cultura. És a dir, ciutadans del món que no pertanyin a enlloc." Source: Assemblea.cat Sabadell/Sabadell per la Independència.

REFERENCES CITED

A.V. and J.B. 2007. Arriba el "dia D" de Frankfurt. *El Punt*, June 12, 2007, p. 34.

ABC. 2005. Caterina Mieras afirma que la literatura catalana es la que se hace en catalán. *ABC*, May 5, 2005, p. 32.

Abril, Joan. 2006. Tribuna: ¿Una Mercè sense pregó? *El Punt*, September 23, 2006, p. 12.

Ackerman, Bruce. 1994. Rooted cosmopolitanism. *Ethics* 104:516–535.

Agencias. 2007. El PP presenta la campaña "Somos España" para defender la nación ante el "órdago independentista" de Ibarretxe. *Público*, October 1, 2007. http://www.publico.es/espana/3315/el-pp-presenta-la-campana-somos-espana-para-defender-la-nacion-ante-el-ordago-independentista-de-ibarretxe.

Agha, Asif. 2007a. *Language and Social Relations*. Cambridge, UK: Cambridge University Press.

Agha, Asif. 2007b. Recombinant selves in mass mediated spacetime. *Language & Communication* 27:320–335.

Aguilar, Isabel. 2005. "Lenguas en guerra," de Irene Lozano, premio Espasa de Ensayo. *ABC*, September 28, 2005. http://www.abc.es/hemeroteca/historico-28-09-2005/abc/Cultura/lenguas-en-guerra-de-irene-lozano-premio-espasa-de-ensayo_611171078622.html.

Alarcón, Amado, and Luis Garzón, eds. 2011. *Language, Migration and Social Mobility in Catalonia*. Leiden, The Netherlands: Brill.

Albiñana, Marta. 2006. José Montilla, una persona "normal." *El País*, October 10, 2006, p. 37.

Alexandre, Víctor. 2014. L'aprenentatge del català malgrat els catalans. *Racó Català*, July 15, 2014. http://www.racocatala.cat/opinio/article/34318/laprenentatge-catala-malgrat-catalans.

Alós, Ernest. 2006. La noche en catalán. *El Periódico*, March 21, 2006, p. 44.

Alós, Ernest. 2007a. Frankfurt, aparador i laberint. *El Periódico*, October 7, 2007, pp. 2–4.

Alós, Ernest. 2007b. La gran exposició de Frankfurt mostra una Catalunya mestissa. *El Periódico*, October 9, 2007.

Alós, Ernest. 2007c. Montilla i Monzó treuen tensió a l'inici de la Fira de Frankfurt. *El Periódico*, October 10, 2007. http://www.elperiodico.cat/ca/print.asp?idpublicacio_PK=46&idnoticia_PK=448812&idioma=CAT&h=071010.

Alsedo, Quico. 2007. Carmen Calvo "cree" que "habrá" autores en español en la embajada catalana en Fráncfort. *El Mundo*, June 21, 2007, p. 63.

Alzamora, Sebastià. 2006. El president postcatalà. *Avui*, November 24, 2006, p. 11.

Amela, Victor M. 2006. Frankfurt corregirá una anomalía cultural. *La Vanguardia*, Ocober 4, 2006, p. 76.

Ammon, Ulrich. 2013. World languages: Trends and futures. In *The Handbook of Language and Globalization*, ed. Nikolas Coupland, pp. 101–122. Oxford, UK: Wiley-Blackwell.

Anderson, Benedict. 1991. [1983]. *Imagined Communities: Reflections on the Origin and Spread of Nationalism*, 2nd ed. London: Verso.

Andreu, Marc. 2006. Impulsores y diputados de C-PC desconocían el pasado de su líder. *El Periódico*, November 23, 2006.

Andreu, Marc. 2008. Carod quiere una secesión unilateral y amistosa en el año 2014. *El Periódico*, May 8, 2008. http://www.elperiodico.com/print.asp?idpublicacio_PK=46&idnoticia_PK=507423&idioma=CAS&h=080508.

Antich, José. 2007a. El éxito de Frankfurt. *La Vanguardia*, October 11, 2007, p. 2.

Antich, José. 2007b. La feria de Frankfurt. *La Vanguardia*, October 9, 2007, p. 2.

Appadurai, Arjun. 1996. *Modernity at Large*. Minneapolis: University of Minnesota Press.

Appiah, Kwame Anthony. 1997. Cosmopolitan patriots. *Critical Inquiry* 23 (3): 617–639.

Appiah, Kwame Anthony. 2005. *The Ethics of Identity*. Princeton, NJ: Princeton University Press.

Appiah, Kwame Anthony. 2007. *Cosmopolitanism: Ethics in a World of Strangers*. New York: Norton.

Aracil, Lluís V. 1966. Bilingualism as a myth. *Interamerican Review* 2–4:521–533.

Aracil, Lluís V. 1982. *Papers de sociolingüística*, Vol. 9. Barcelona: Edicions La Magrana.

Arasa, Daniel. 2006. Portabella o "Portalletja." *La Vanguardia*, September 29, 2006, p. 7.

Argemí, Aureli. 1981. Presentació: Som una nació. In *Quan cal, hi som: Llibre col·lectiu d'urgència en defensa de la nostra llengua*, ed. Manuel de Pedrolo, pp. 8–10. Barcelona: Diàfora.

Argenter, Joan A. 2007. Els discursos sobre la situació lingüística a Catalunya. Diagnosi i prospectiva: De la monotonia a la polifonia. In *El discurs sociolingüístic actual català i occità | Lo discors sociolingüistic actual catalan e occitan*, ed. Barbara Czernilofsky, Bàrbara Roviró, Peter Cichon, et al., pp. 135–147. Vienna: Praesens Verlag.

Arnau, Joaquim, ed. 2014. *Reviving Catalan at School: Challenges and Instructional Approaches*. Bristol/Barcelona: Multilingual Matters/Institut d'Estudis Catalans.

Arnau, Joaquim, and F. Xavier Vila. 2013. Language-in-education policies in the Catalan language area. In *Reviving Catalan at School: Challenges and Instructional Approaches*, ed. Joaquim Arnau, pp. 1–28. Bristol/Barcelona: Multilingual Matters/ Institut d'Estudis Catalans.

Artigal, Josep Maria. 1991. *The Catalan Immersion Program: A European Point of View*. Norwood, NJ: Ablex.

Associated Press. 2014. Catalonia votes to ask Spain for secession ballot. *New York Times*, January 16, 2014.

Atkinson, David. 2000. Minoritisation, identity and ethnolinguistic vitality in Catalonia. *Journal of Multilingual and Multicultural Development* 21 (3):185–197.

Avui. 2006a. Ciutadans justifica el no pel continuisme de Montilla. *Avui*, November 25, 2006.

Avui. 2006b. L'ha dita grossa. *Avui*, October 16, 2006, p. 3.

Avui. 2006c. Montilla, tercer president amb arrels andaluses. *Avui*, November 8, 2006, p. 12.

Avui. 2006d. Pujol creu que la immersió lingüística perilla amb ERC. *Avui*, December 18, 2006, p. 7.

Avui. 2006e. Tots els cognoms són catalans. *Avui*, November 15, 2006.

Avui. 2007. Catalunya, potència editorial europea. *Avui*, October 9, 2007, p. 46.

Babunski. 2006. Patriotisme social . . . i què? *Des de Lleida*. November 26, 2006. http:// lo-lleidata.blogspot.com/2006/11/patriotisme-social-i-qu.html.

Bakhtin, Mikhail M. 1981. *The Dialogic Imagination*. Translated by C. Emerson and M. Holquist. Austin: University of Texas Press.

Ballart, Jordi. 2002. Saying Catalan words in Spanish: Social representations of xava Catalan. *Hispanic Research Journal* 3 (3):191–208.

Ballart, Jordi. 2013. Variació fònica al català de Barcelona: L'accent xava. *Treballs de Sociolingüística Catalana* 23:133–151.

Barbeta, Jordi, and Francesc Bracero. 2006. Entrevista Josep Lluís Carod-Rovira, Presidente de Esquerra Republicana; "Catalunya puede tener un president andaluz, pero España no uno catalán." *La Vanguardia*, November 19, 2006, pp. 18–19.

Bargalló, Josep. 2007. Què fem a Frankfurt? La cultura catalana convidada d'honor a la Fira del Llibre 2007. http://www.slideshare.net/JosepBargallo/que-fem-fkt-catala.

Barranco, Justo. 2007. Bargalló recuerda que "sin el catalán la cultura catalana no estaría en Frankfurt." *La Vanguardia*, March 8, 2007, p. 44.

Barth, Fredrik. 1969. Introduction. In *Ethnic Groups and Boundaries: The Social Organisation of Culture Difference*, ed. Fredrik Barth, pp. 9–38. Boston, MA: Little, Brown.

Barthes, Roland. 1972. *Mythologies*. New York: Hill and Wang.

Bassets, Marc. 2005a. El debate sobre la literatura catalana en Frankfurt llega a la prensa alemana. *La Vanguardia*, June 11, 2005, p. 51.

Bassets, Marc. 2005b. Frankfurt no quiere exclusiones. *La Vanguardia*, May 28, 2005, pp. 36–37.

Bassets, Marc. 2007. El Llull llevará a Frankfurt a autores en castellano para hablar de la literatura catalana. *La Vanguardia*, March 23, 2007, p. 54.

Bastardas i Boada, Albert. 1985. *La bilingüització de la segona generació immigrant.* Barcelona: Edicions de la Magrana.

Bastardas i Boada, Albert. 2007. *Les polítiques de la llengua i la identitat a l'era "glocal."* Barcelona: Generalitat de Catalunya.

Bastardas i Boada, Albert. 2012. El català i els joves: Propostes de política lingüística del Consell Social de la Llengua Catalana. *Treballs de Sociolingüística Catalana* 22:77–92.

Baulenas, Lluís Anton. 2007. Un cafè amb. . .Jordi Portabella: "Per poc que pugui, exigiré ser alcalde." *Avui*, May 23, 2007, p. 10.

Beck, Ulrich, and Edgar Grande. 2007. Cosmopolitanism: Europe's way out of crisis. *European Journal of Social Theory* 10 (1):67–85.

Benhabib, Seyla. 2006. *Another Cosmopolitanism*. Oxford: Oxford University Press.

Berger, Verena. 2005. Presencia y ausencia del teatro castellano en Barcelona. In *La cultura catalana de expresión castellana*, ed. Stewart King, pp. 123–142. Kassel: Edition Reichenberger.

Bhabha, Homi K. 2001. Unsatisfied: Notes on vernacular cosmopolitanism. In *Postcolonial Discourses: An Anthology*, ed. Gregory Castle, pp. 39–51. Blackwell.

Bibiloni, Gabriel. 2006. El català bleda-xava va amb tu. *El blog de Gabriel Bibiloni*, March 28, 2006. http://bibiloni.cat/blog/?p=162.

Bilbeny, Norbert. 2001. És possible un catalanisme no nacionalista? In *El nou catalanisme*, ed. Norbert Bilbeny and Àngel Pes, pp. 77–94. Barcelona: Editorial Ariel.

Billig, Michael. 1995. *Banal Nationalism*. London: Sage.

Biosca, Marc. 2009. "El català, llengua comuna" torna a sortir al carrer. *La Corbella* 15:4.

Blommaert, Jan. 2010. *The Sociolinguistics of Globalization*. Cambridge, UK: Cambridge University Press.

Blommaert, Jan, and Jef Verschueren. 1998. The role of language in European nationalist ideologies. In *Language Ideologies: Practice and Theory*, ed. B. B Schieffelin, K.A. Woolard, P. Kroskrity, pp. 189–210. New York: Oxford University Press.

Boix-Fuster, Emili. 1993. *Triar no és trair: Identitat i llengua en els joves de Barcelona*. Barcelona: Edicions 62.

Boix-Fuster, Emili. 2008. 25 años de la Constitución española: Las ideologías lingüísticas en la configuración del Estado español. In *Lengua, nación e identidad: La regulación del plurilingüismo en España y América Latina*, ed. Kirsten Süselbeck, Ulrike Mühlschlegel, and Peter Masson, pp. 271–302. Madrid: Iberoamericana Vervuert.

Boix-Fuster, Emili. 2009. *Català o castellà amb els fills? La transmissió de la llengua en famílies bilingües a Barcelona*. Sant Cugat del Vallès: Editorial Rourich.

Boix-Fuster, Emili. 2015. Multilingualism in Barcelona: Towards an asymmetrical multilingualism. In *Urban Diversities and Language Policies in Medium-Sized Linguistic Communities*, ed. Emili Boix-Fuster, pp. 143–167. Bristol, UK: Multilingual Matters.

Boix-Fuster, Emili, Joan Melià, and Brauli Montoya. 2011. Policies promoting the use of Catalan in oral communications and to improve attitudes towards the language. In *Democratic Policies for Language Revitalization: The Case of Catalan*, ed. Miquel Strubell and Emili Boix-Fuster, pp. 150–181. New York: Palgrave Macmillan.

Boix-Fuster, Emili, and Cristina Sanz. 2008. Language and identity in Catalonia. In *Bilingualism and Identity: Spanish at the Crossroads with Other Languages*, ed. Mercedes Niño-Murcia and Jason Rothman, pp. 87–106. Amsterdam: John Benjamins.

Boix-Fuster, Emili, and F. Xavier Vila i Moreno. 1998. *Sociolingüística de la llengua catalana*. Barcelona: Editorial Ariel.

Bosch, Alfred. 2006a. L'imbècil: La Mercè en la llengua. *Avui*, September 7, 2006, p. 2.

Bosch, Xavier. 2006b. Pluja fina. *Avui*, November 27, 2006.

Bourdieu, Pierre. 1977. *Outline of a Theory of Practice*. Cambridge, UK: Cambridge University Press.

Bourdieu, Pierre. 1982. *Ce que parler veut dire: L'économie des échanges linguistiques*. Paris: Fayard.

Bourdieu, Pierre. 1991. *Language and Symbolic Power*. Cambridge, MA: Harvard University Press.

Branchadell, Albert. 1997. *Liberalisme i normalització lingüística*. Barcelona: Editorial Empúries.

Branchadell, Albert. 1999. La política lingüística a Catalunya: Liberals vs nacionalistes. In *La llengua catalana al tombant del mil·leni*, ed. Miquel Àngel Pradilla Cardona, pp. 35–66. Barcelona: Editorial Empúries.

Branchadell, Albert. 2007a. ¿Despolititzar quina llengua? *El Periódico*, February 15, 2007.

Branchadell, Albert. 2007b. Marcant perfil a Frankfurt. *El Periódico*, June 22, 2007, p. 5.

Branchadell, Albert. 2012. One nation, one (common) language? Language and nationalism in 21st century Catalonia. http://www.recode.info/wp-content/uploads/2013/02/Branchadell-Albert-2012-RECODE.pdf.

Brandes, Stanley. 2008. Torophiles and torophobes: The politics of the bullfight in contemporary Spain. Paper presented to the annual meetings of the American Anthropological Association, San Francisco.

Breckenridge, Carol, Sheldon Pollock, Homi K. Bhabha, and Dipesh Chakrabarty, eds. 2002. *Cosmopolitanism*. Durham, NC: Duke University Press.

Brett, Judith, and Anthony Moran. 2011. Cosmopolitan nationalism: Ordinary people making sense of diversity. *Nations and Nationalism* 17 (1):188–206.

Bretxa, Vanessa, and F. Xavier Vila i Moreno. 2012. Els canvis sociolingüístics en el pas de primària a secundària: El projecte RESOL a la ciutat de Mataró. *Treballs de Sociolingüística Catalana* 22:93–118.

Bretxa, Vanessa, and F. Xavier Vila i Moreno. 2014. L'evolució dels usos lingüístics dins l'aula des de sisè de primària fins a quart d'ESO. *Revista de Llengua i Dret* 62:106–123.

Bretxa i Riera, Vanessa. 2009. El salt a secundària: Els preadolescents, consum cultural i llengua. *Zeitschrift für Katalanistik* 22:171–202.

Bretxa i Riera, Vanessa. 2014. El salt a secundària: Els canvis en les tries lingüístiques i culturals dels preadolescents mataronins en la transició educativa. Ph.D. dissertation, Departament de Sociologia i Anàlisi de les Organitzacions, Universitat de Barcelona.

Bretxa i Riera, Vanessa, and M. Àngels Parera Espelt. 2012. "Et dóna la base": Itineraris biogràfics d'adquisició i ús del català del jovent castellanoparlant de Sabadell i Santa Coloma de Gramenet. In *Posar-hi la base: Usos i aprenentatges lingüístics en el domini català*, ed. F. Xavier Vila i Moreno, pp. 47–56. Barcelona: Institut d'Estudis Catalans.

Briggs, Charles L. 2005. Genealogies of race and culture and the failure of vernacular cosmopolitanisms: Rereading Franz Boaz and W.E.B. Du Bois. *Public Culture* 17 (1):75–100.

Briggs, Charles L., and Richard Bauman. 1992. Genre, intertextuality, and social power. *Journal of Linguistic Anthropology* 2 (2):131–172.

Broch, Àlex. 2005. Frankfurt: Manifest contra la confusió. *Avui*, May 31, 2005, p. 21.

Bru de Sala, Xavier. 2007. Aprobando hacia Frankfurt. *La Vanguardia*, June 27, 2007, p. 13.

Brutt-Griffler, Janina. 2002. *World English: A Study of Its Development*. Clevedon: Multilingual Matters.

Bucholtz, Mary. 2003. Sociolinguistic nostalgia and the authentication of identity. *Journal of Sociolinguistics* 7 (3):398–416.

Bucholtz, Mary. 2011. *White Kids: Language, Race, and Styles of Youth Identity*. Cambridge, UK: Cambridge University Press.

Bucholtz, Mary, Brendan Barnwell, Elena Skapoulli, and Jung-Eun Janie Lee. 2012. Itineraries of identity in undergraduate science. *Anthropology & Education Quarterly* 43 (2):157–172.

Bucholtz, Mary, and Kira Hall. 2004. Language and identity. In *A Companion to Linguistic Anthropology*, ed. Alessandro Duranti, pp. 369–394. Malden, MA: Blackwell.

Bueno, Pepa. 2006. Ojú "president" Montilla. *El Periódico*, November 24, 2006, p. 11.

Buxó, Maria Jesús. 2001. El disseny d'identitats a Catalunya. In *El nou catalanisme*, ed. Norbert Bilbeny and Àngel Pes, pp. 47–61. Barcelona: Editorial Ariel.

Cabellos Espiérrez, Miguel Ángel. 2008. La competència en matèria de llengua pròpia en el nou Estatut. *Revista de Llengua i Dret* 49:69–96.

Cabré, Anna. 1999. *El sistema català de reproducció*. Barcelona: Proa.

Cabrera, Lluís, Marta Riera, Juan Miguel Portal, Pedro Morón, Bienve Moya, and Miguel Fernández. 2005. *Els altres andalusos: La qüestió nacional de Catalunya*. Barcelona: L'esfera dels llibres.

Cal, Juan. 2007. La lengua en Francfort. *Segre*, October 10, 2007, p. 5.

Calhoun, Craig. 2002. The class consciousness of frequent travellers: Towards a critique of actually existing cosmopolitanism. In *Conceiving Cosmopolitanism*, ed. Steven Vertovec and Robin Cohen, pp. 86–109. New York: Oxford University Press.

Calhoun, Craig. 2007. *Nations Matter: Culture, History, and the Cosmopolitan Dream*. New York: Routledge.

Candel, Francesc. 1964. *Els altres catalans*. Barcelona: Edicions 62.

Capdevila, Jordi. 2005. El camí cap a Frankfurt 2007; Miquel Alzueata, Editor de Columna: "Els autors en castellà han de fer d'ambaixadors del català." *Avui*, June 6, 2005, p. 36.

Carbó, Ismael. 2006. Carod justifica el tripartit per renovar el catalanisme. *Avui*, November 25, 2006, p. 8.

Carbonell, Jordi, et al. 1977. Escriure en castellà a Catalunya. *Taula de canvi* 6:5–42.

Cardús, Salvador. 2000. *El desconcert de l'educació*. Barcelona: La Campana.

Carod-Rovira, Josep-Lluís. 2007. *El patriotisme social, motor de construcció nacional*. Barcelona. Retrieved from http://www.vilaweb.cat/media/attach/vwedts/docs/carodconferencia.pdf.

Carod-Rovira, Josep-Lluís. 2013. Llengua i Estat. *El Punt Avui*, July 21, 2013. http://www.elpuntavui.cat/noticia/article/7-vista/8-articles/663493-llengua-i-estat.html.

Carol, Màrius. 2006. La lengua. *La Vanguardia*, October 9, 2006, p. 29.

Carretero i Grau, Joan. 2007a. ERC, de planeta a satèl·lit (II). *Avui*, January 21, 2007.

Carretero i Grau, Joan. 2007b. ERC, de planeta a satèl·lit (I). *Avui*, January 20, 2007.

Castán, Patricia. 2006. Hereu defensa la llibertat d'idiomes del pregó de la Mercè. *El Periódico*, September 20, 2006, p. 34.

Castells, Ada. 2007. Ovació a la rauxa. *Avui*, October 10, 2007, pp. 42–43.

Castells, Manuel. 2004. *The Power of Identity*, 2nd ed. Malden, MA: Blackwell.

Castells, Manuel, Imma Tubella, Teresa Sancho, Maria Isabel Díaz de Isla, and Barry Wellman. 2004. Social structure, cultural identity, and personal autonomy in the practice of the internet: The network society in Catalonia. In *The Network Society: A Cross-Cultural Perspective*, ed. Manuel Castells, pp. 233–248. Cheltenham, UK: Edward Edgar Publishing.

Castro, Carles. 2013. El 81% dels catalans dóna suport a la immersió davant l'intent de diluir-la. *La Vanguardia en català*, October 7, 2013. http://www.lavanguardia.com/encatala/20131007/54390622541/81-catalans-defensa-immersio-linguistica.html.

Castro, Liz, ed. 2013. *What's Up with Catalonia?* Ashfield, MA: Catalonia Press.

Cavanaugh, Jillian, and Shalini Shankar. 2014. Producing authenticity in global capitalism: Language, materiality, and value. *American Anthropologist* 116 (1):51–64.

Chun, Elaine. 2004. Ideologies of legitimate mockery: Margaret Cho's revoicings of mock Asian. *Pragmatics* 14:263–289.

Cia, Blanca. 2006. Polémica en Barcelona por Lindo en las fiestas. *El País*, September 22, 2006.

Cirici, David. 2011. L'idioma dels polítics. *Ara*, May 18, 2011. http://www.ara.cat/ara_premium/cultura/Lidioma-dels-politics_0_482951754.html.

Ciutadans-Partido de la Ciudadanía. 2006. Ha nascut el teu partit/Ha nacido tu partido. Electoral campaign flyer. Barcelona.

Clots-Figueras, Irma, and Paolo Masella. 2013. Education, language and identity. *The Economic Journal* 123 (570):F332–F357.

Codó, Eva. 2008. *Immigration and Bureaucratic Control*. Berlin/New York: Mouton de Gruyter.

Colás, Joan. 2006. El pregó de la "Mercedes." *Avui*, September 6, 2006, p. 38.

Comaroff, John L., and Jean Comaroff. 2009. *Ethnicity, Inc*. Chicago, IL: University of Chicago Press.

Consell Superior d'Avaluació del Sistema Educatiu. 2008. *Estudi sociodemogràfic i lingüístic de l'alumnat de 4t d'ESO de Catalunya: Avaluació de l'educació secundària obligatòria 2006*. Barcelona: Generalitat de Catalunya, Departament d'Educació.

Constitución. 1978. Constitución Española. Retrieved from http://www.congreso.es/consti/constitucion/indice/index.htm.

Cònsul, Isidor. 2005. Per què ens fa por la literatura? *Avui*, March 20, 2005, p. 21.

Corona, Víctor, Luci Nussbaum, and Virginia Unamuno. 2013. The emergence of new linguistic repertoires among Barcelona's youth of Latin American origin. *International Journal of Bilingual Education and Bilingualism* 16 (2):182–194.

Corretja i Torrens, Mercè. 1991. Llengua pròpia i Tribunal Constitucional. *Revista de Llengua i Dret* 16:75–83.

Cots, Josep M., and Luci Nussbaum. 1999. Schooling, language and teachers: Language awareness and the discourse of the educational reform in Catalonia. *Language Awareness* 8 (3–4):174–189.

Coupland, Nikolas. 2001. Dialect stylization in radio talk. *Language in Society* 30:345–375.

Coupland, Nikolas. 2003. Sociolinguistic authenticities. *Journal of Sociolinguistics* 7 (3):417–431.

Coupland, Nikolas. 2012. Bilingualism on display: The framing of Welsh and English in public spaces. *Language in Society* 41 (1):1–27.

Coupland, Nikolas. 2014. Language, society and authenticity: Themes and perspectives. In *Indexing Authenticity: Sociolinguistic Perspectives*, ed. Véronique LaCoste, Jakob Leimgruber, and Thiemo Breyer, pp. 14–30. Berlin: Walter de Gruyter.

Crameri, Kathryn. 2000. Banal Catalanism? *National Identities* 2 (2):145–157.

Crameri, Kathryn. 2005. La política cultural catalana (1980–2003) y los escritores catalanes de expresión castellana. In *La cultura catalana de expresión castellana*, ed. Stewart King, pp. 15–30. Kassel: Edition Reichenberger.

Crameri, Kathryn. 2008. *Catalonia: National Identity and Cultural Policy, 1980–2003*. Cardiff, UK: University of Wales Press.

Crameri, Kathryn. 2014. *Goodbye Spain? The Question of Independence for Catalonia*. Brighton, UK: Sussex Academic Press.

Cuadrado, Núria. 2007a. Benach da tono a la "orquesta" política en la víspera de la semana de las letras catalanas. *El Mundo*, October 9, 2007, p. 53.

Cuadrado, Núria. 2007b. "El catalán es la lengua propia de nuestro país y vive sin conflictos con el castellano," dice Montilla. *El Mundo*, October 10, 2007, p. 58.

Cuadrado, Núria. 2007c. Historia e intrigas de una invitación convulsa. *El Mundo*, October 8, 2007, p. 51.

Cuadrado, Núria. 2007d. La cultura catalana inunda Fráncfort con más de 100 autores. *El Mundo*, October 8, 2007, p. 51.

Cuadrado, Núria. 2007e. Maragall recuerda que los escritores en castellano rechazaron acudir a Fráncfort. *El Mundo*, October 8, 2007, p. 29.

Culla i Clarà, Joan B. 2006. Debates, lenguas, televisiones. *El País*, October 13, 2006, p. 32.

Cuyàs, Manuel. 2007. Frankfurt a El Corte Inglés. *El Punt*, June 17, 2007, p. 80.

de Miguel, Amando, et al. 1981. El manifiesto de los 2.300: Por la igualdad de derechos lingüísticos en Cataluña. Manifiesto. (Diario 16-Disidencias, núm. 17, 12-III-1981). In *Quan cal, hi som: Llibre col·lectiu d'urgència en defensa de la nostra llengua*, ed. Manuel de Pedrolo, pp. 109–110. Barcelona: Diàfora.

de Sagarra, Joan. 2006a. El alcalde Hereu y la forastera. *La Vanguardia*, September 24, 2006, p. 6.

de Sagarra, Joan. 2006b. El debate. *La Vanguardia*, November 26, 2006, p. 6.

de Sagarra, Joan. 2006c. El hombre vacuna. *La Vanguardia*, October 14, 2006, p. 17.

del Valle, José. 2005. La lengua, patria común: Política lingüística, política exterior y el post-nacionalismo hispánico. In *Studies on Ibero-Romance Linguistics Dedicated to Ralph Penny*, ed. Roger Wright and Peter Ricketts, pp. 391–416. Newark, DE: Juan de la Cuesta Monographs.

del Valle, José, and Luis Gabriel-Stheeman. 2004. Lengua y mercado: El español en la era de la globalización económica. In *La batalla del idioma*, ed. José del Valle and Luis Gabriel-Stheeman, pp. 253–263. Madrid: Vervuert.

Desclot. 2006. Estupefaccions lingüístiques. *Avui*, November 25, 2006.

Díaz, Rosa. 2006. Elvira Lindo: "La polèmica del català forma part de la vida barcelonina." *El Punt*, September 22, 2006, p. 3.

Díez, Xavier. 2007. "Mobbing" cultural. *El Punt*, August 8, 2007, p. 11.

DiGiacomo, Susan. 1985. The Politics of Identity: Nationalism in Catalonia. Ph.D. dissertation, University of Massachusetts. Ann Arbor, MI: University Microfilms International.

DiGiacomo, Susan. 1999. Language ideological debates in an Olympic city: Barcelona 1992–1996. In *Language Ideological Debates*, ed. Jan Blommaert, pp. 105–142. Berlin/New York: Mouton de Gruyter.

DiGiacomo, Susan. 2001. "Catalan is everyone's thing": Normalizing a nation. In *Language, Ethnicity and the State*. Vol. 1: *Minority Languages in the European Union*, ed. C.C. O'Reilly, pp. 56–77. Hampshire, UK: Palgrave Macmillan.

Duchêne, Alexandre, and Monica Heller, eds. 2012. *Language in Late Capitalism: Pride and Profit*, Routledge Critical Studies in Multilingualism. New York: Routledge.

Eagleton, Terry. 1991. *Ideology: An Introduction*. London: Verso.

Echart, Nazaret. 2007. Cultura exótica. *La Gaceta de los Negocios*, March 8, 2007, p. 14.

Eckert, Penelope. 1997. Age as a sociolinguistic variable. In *The Handbook of Sociolinguistics*, ed. Florian Coulmas, pp. 151–167. Oxford: Blackwell.

Eckert, Penelope. 2000. *Linguistic Variation as Social Practice: The Linguistic Construction of Identity in Belten High*. Malden, MA: Blackwell.

Eckert, Penelope. 2003. Sociolinguistics and authenticity: An elephant in the room. *Journal of Sociolinguistics* 7 (3):392–397.

Eckert, Penelope. 2011. Language and power in the preadolescent heterosexual market. *American Speech* 86 (1):85–97.

EFE. 2006a. 90 asociaciones y ERC se oponen al pregón de la Mercè que Elvira Lindo hará hoy en castellano. *20 Minutos*, September 22, 2006. http://www.20minutos.es/noticia/155240/0/polemica/pregon/barcelona/.

EFE. 2006b. Manifestaciones en Barcelona a favor y en contra del pregón de la Mercè en castellano. *Última Hora*, September 23, 2006.

Ellakuría, Iñaki. 2006. "Ya tienes cara de presidente": Montilla se entrevista con Rodríguez Ibarra y cierra los flecos del Govern el día previo a la toma de posesión. *La Vanguardia*, November 28, 2006, p. 16.

El Mundo. 2005. España plural, Cataluña uniforme. *El Mundo*, May 29, 2005, p. 5.

El Mundo. 2007a. De la Feria del Libro de Fráncfort al debate sobre el nacionalismo. *El Mundo*, June 21, pp. 64–65.

El Mundo. 2007b. Escritores en castellano y catalán debaten juntos los errores cometidos en el camino hacia Fráncfort. *El Mundo*, June 20, 2007, pp. 65–66.

El Mundo. 2007c. Mal ejemplo catalán en Fráncfort. *El Mundo*, October 15, 2007, p. 3.

ElMundo.es/Agencias. 2006. Elvira Lindo leerá esta tarde el pregón de las Fiestas de la Mercé en medio de una fuerte polémica. *El Mundo*, September 22, 2006. http://www.elmundo.es/elmundo/2006/09/22/espana/1158922444.html.

El País. 2006. Aplausos y abucheos en catalán y castellano. *El País*, September 22, 2006.

El País. 2011. La política se mira en el espejo de "Polònia." *El País*, February 17, 2011.

El País. 2014. El 81% de persones voten sí a la independència de Catalunya. *El País*, November 10, 2014. http://cat.elpais.com/cat/2014/11/09/catalunya/1415542400_466311.html.

El Periódico. 2007a. Catalunya a Frankfurt. *El Periódico*, October 10, 2007, p. 6.

El Periódico. 2007b. Espanyol igual a turc. *El Periódico*, October 10, 2007.

El Periódico. 2007c. Juan Carlos ensalza el castellano como instrumento para la paz y la solidaridad. *El Periódico*, October 12, 2007.

El Periódico. 2008a. Felip Puig se queja de que el "president" "destroza" el catalán. *El Periódico*, July 17, 2008.

El Periódico. 2008b. UPD pedirá el apoyo de los catalanes a su manifiesto por el castellano. *El Periódico*, July 1, 2008.

El Periódico. 2010. Ha nascut un artista: José Montilla. *El Periódico*, November 7, 2010.

e-notícies. 2006. Demanen Elvira Lindo que renuncïi al pregó de la Mercè. *e-notícies*, September 16, 2006. http://hemeroteca.e-noticies.com/edicio-1636/actualitat/demanen-elvira-lindo-que-renunci%EF-al-preg%F3-de-la-merc%E8-7853.html.

e-notícies. 2007. Un periodista d'Onda Cero es queixa que Laporta parli català. *e-notícies*, February 14, 2007. http://hemeroteca.e-noticies.com/pop/print/?iddoc=34470&cat=1&subcat=1.

Epps, Brad. 2003. Postnationalism: Supernationalism, *modernisme*, and Catalonia. *Arizona Journal of Hispanic Cultural Studies* 7:133–159.

Erickson, Brad. 2011. Utopian virtues: Muslim neighbors, ritual sociality, and the politics of *convivència*. *American Ethnologist* 38 (1):114–131.

Errington, J. Joseph. 1998. *Shifting Languages: Interaction and Identity in Javanese Indonesia*. Cambridge, UK: Cambridge University Press.

Errington, J. Joseph. 2001. State speech for peripheral publics in Java. In *Languages and Publics: The Making of Authority*, ed. Susan Gal and Kathryn Woolard, pp. 103–118. Manchester, UK: St. Jerome. Reissued 2014, Oxon/NY: Routledge.

Estatut. 1979. Estatut d'Autonomia de Catalunya de 1979. Retrieved from http://www.gencat.cat/generalitat/cas/estatut1979/index.htm.

Europa Press. 2007. Carod-Rovira: Los buenos autores catalanes en castellano son un "potencial propagandístico." *La Vanguardia*, May 31, 2007, p. 43.

Europa Press/San Sebastián. 2013. Aznar acusa a los nacionalistas de perseguir "el desguace del Estado." *El Periódico*, October 14, 2013. http://www.elperiodico.com/es/noticias/politica/aznar-acusa-los-nacionalistas-perseguir-desguace-del-estado-2748729.

Featherstone, Mike, ed. 1990. *Global Culture: Nationalism, Globalization and Modernity*. London: Sage.

Fenigsen, Janina. 1999. "A broke-up mirror": Representing Bajan in print. *Cultural Anthropology* 14 (1):61–87.

Fernàndez, Josep-Anton. 2008. *El malestar en la cultura catalana*. Barcelona: Editorial Empúries.

Fernández, Laura. 2007a. La conspiración del club de los ocho. *El Mundo*, June 14, 2007, p. 61.

Fernández, Laura. 2007b. La cultura catalana se la juega en Fráncfort. *La Razón*, October 8, 2007, p. 43.

Fernández, Mayka. 2006. Montilla defensa el català enfront del PP i Ciutadans. *Avui*, November 25, 2006, p. 7.

Fernández, Víctor. 2005. Los editores no quieren que se politice Fráncfort. *La Razón*, May 28, 2005, p. 33.

Fernández-Santos, Elsa. 2005. El director del Institut Ramon Llull afirma que la polémica de la Feria de Francfort es falsa. *El País*, June 1, 2005, p. 37.

Ferran, Joan, and Daniel Fernández. 2005. Sobre el nacionalismo hiperprotector. *El País*, June 4, 2005, p. 2.

Ferré-Pavia, Carme, and Catalina Gayà-Morlà. 2011. Infotainment and citizens' political perceptions: Who's afraid of *Polònia*? *Catalan Journal of Communication and Cultural Studies* 3 (1):45–61.

Ferrer, Ferran. 2000. Languages, minorities and education in Spain: The case of Catalonia. *Comparative Education* 36 (2):187–197.

Ferro, Lorena. 2006. Guerra lingüística i religiosa per la Mercè. *20 Minutos*, September 21, 2006, p. 31.

Fine, Robert. 2007. *Cosmopolitanism*. London: Routledge.

Fishman, Joshua A. 1965. The status and prospects of bilingualism in the United States. *Modern Language Journal* 49:143–155.

Fishman, Joshua A. 1966. *Language Loyalty in the United States*. The Hague: Mouton.

Fishman, Joshua A. 1982. Whorfianism of the third kind. *Language in Society* 11:1–14.

Fonalleras, Josep Maria. 2007. El "cabreo" de Montilla. *El Periódico*, November 9, 2007.

Fontdevila, Manel. 2006a. El Corral del Seny: Els reptes del govern Montilla [cartoon]. *Regió7*, December 12, 2006, p. 19.

Fontdevila, Manel. 2006b. El Corral del Seny: Llegendes urbanes d'avui [cartoon]. *Regió7*, October 18, 2006, p. 22.

Forn, Iu. 2006a. El català de Montilla. *Avui*, November 27, 2006, p. 3.

Forn, Iu. 2006b. N'hi havia prou amb dijous. *Avui*, November 25, 2006.

FrancescCiuta. 2006. Re: El pregó de les festes de la Mercè de Barcelona es farà en castellà [web comment]. *Racó Català*. September 6, 2006, 00:55. http://www.raco-catala.cat/noticia/11908/prego-festes-merce-barcelona-fara-castella.

Fraser, Nancy. 2000. Rethinking recognition. *New Left Review* 3:107–120.

Frayer, Lauren. 2014. Catalonia's president makes his case for independence from Spain. *NPR*, November 6, 2014. http://www.npr.org/blogs/parallels/2014/11/06/362034832/catalonias-president-makes-his-case-for-independence-from-spain.

Frekko, Susan E. 2006. "Catalan That Doesn't Hurt the Eyes": Linguistic Display and Linguistic Regimentation in Barcelona. Ph.D. dissertation, Department of Anthropology, University of Michigan.

Frekko, Susan E. 2009a. "Normal" in Catalonia. *Language in Society* 38:1–23.

Frekko, Susan E. 2009b. Signs of respect: Neighborhood, public and language in Barcelona. *Journal of Linguistic Anthropology* 19 (2):227–245.

Frekko, Susan E. 2013. Legitimacy and social class in Catalan language education for adults. *International Journal of Bilingual Education and Bilingualism* 16 (2):164–176.

Friedman, Jonathan. 1990. Being in the world: Globalization and localization. In *Global Culture: Nationalism, Globalization and Modernity*, ed. Mike Featherstone, pp. 311–328. London: Sage.

Friedman, Jonathan. 2002. Champagne liberals and the new "dangerous classes." *Social Analysis* 46 (2):33–55.

FUNDACC. 2012. *El baròmetre de la comunicació i la cultura*. http://www.fundacc. org/docroot/fundacc/pdf/Informe_consum_llibres2012.pdf.

Fundació CatDem. 2013. Cosmopolitan nationalism. January 29, 2013. http://www. catdem.org/en/notices/2012/10/cosmopolitan-nationalism-6925.php.

Gabancho, Patricia. 2007. *El preu de ser catalans*. Barcelona: Meteora.

Gal, Susan. 2001. Linguistic theories and national images in nineteenth-century Hungary. In *Languages and Publics*, ed. S. Gal and K.A. Woolard, pp. 30–45. Manchester, UK: St. Jerome. Reissued 2014, Oxon/NY: Routledge.

Gal, Susan. 2012. Sociolinguistic regimes and the management of "diversity." In *Language in Late Capitalism: Pride and Profit*, ed. Alexandre Duchêne and Monica Heller, pp. 22–42. New York: Routledge.

Gal, Susan. 2014. Tastes of talk: Qualia and the moral flavor of signs. *Anthropological Theory* 12 (1–2):31–48.

Gal, Susan, and Kathryn A. Woolard. 2001. Constructing languages and publics: Authority and representation. In *Languages and Publics: The Making of Authority*, ed. Susan Gal and Kathryn A. Woolard, pp. 1–12. Manchester, UK: St. Jerome. Reissued 2014, Oxon/NY: Routledge.

García, Luis B. 2012. Wert admite que el interés del Gobierno es "españolizar a los alumnos catalanes." *La Vanguardia*, October 10, 2012. http://www.lavanguardia.com/politica/20121010/54352442678/wert-admite-interes-espanolizar-alumnos-catalanes.html.

Garcia, N., and T. Padilla. 2011. El greu pecat de parlar en català en una sala de premsa. *Ara*, February 14, 2011.

García Canclini, Néstor. 2005. *Hybrid Cultures: Strategies for Entering and Leaving Modernity*. Minneapolis: University of Minnesota.

Geeraerts, Dirk. 2008. The logic of language models: Rationalist and Romantic ideologies and their avatars. In *Lengua, nación e identidad: La regulación del plurilingüismo en España y América Latina*, ed. Kirsten Süselbeck, Ulrike Mühlschlegel, and Peter Masson, pp. 43–74. Frankfurt am Main/Madrid: Vervuert/Iberoamericana.

Geli, Carles. 2007a. Bargalló acota el papel de los autores en la lengua castellana para Fráncfort. *El País*, March 8, 2007, p. 38.

Geli, Carles. 2007b. Josep Bargalló, Director del Institut Ramon Llull: "A Francfort le va la polémica." *El País*, October 9, 2007, p. 50.

Geli, Carles. 2007c. Pujol apoya que sólo vayan a Francfort autores catalanes. *El País*, October 7, 2007, p. 54.

Generalitat de Catalunya. 1983. *Ley 7/1983, de 18 de abril, de normalización lingüística en Cataluña*. Barcelona: Generalitat de Catalunya.

Generalitat de Catalunya. 1998. *Llei 1/1998, de 7 de gener, de política lingüística*. Barcelona: Generalitat de Catalunya.

Generalitat de Catalunya. 2005a. Dóna corda al català. Barcelona: Generalitat de Catalunya.

Generalitat de Catalunya. 2005b. Es presenta la campanya "Dóna corda al català" per promoure l'ús de la llengua. Gencat, January 24, 2005. http://www6.gencat.net/llengcat/premsa/corda.htm.

Generalitat de Catalunya. 2009. *Enquesta d'usos lingüístics de la població 2008*. Barcelona: Generalitat de Catalunya. Retrieved from http://www20.gencat.cat/docs/Llengcat/Documents/Dades_territori_poblacio/Altres/Arxius/EULP2008.pdf.

Generalitat de Catalunya. 2013. *Informe de política lingüística 2012*. Retrieved from http://www20.gencat.cat/docs/Llengcat/Documents/InformePL/Arxius/IPL2012.pdf.

Generalitat de Catalunya. 2014. 9N 2014: Tu hi participes, tu hi decideixes. http://www.participa2014.cat/resultats/dades/ca/escr-tot.html.

Giddens, Anthony. 1991. *Modernity and Self-Identity: Self and Society in the Late Modern Age*. Stanford, CA: Stanford University Press.

Gilroy, Paul. 2004. *After Empire: Melancholia or Convivial Culture*. Abingdon, UK: Routledge.

Gimeno, Albert. 2006. ¿El idioma es esencial? *La Vanguardia*, September 24, 2006, p. 6.

González, David. 2007. Català sense catalanisme. *Avui*, January 21, 2007, p. 13.

Graan, Andrew. 2013. Counterfeiting the nation? Skopje 2014 and the politics of nation branding in Macedonia. *Cultural Anthropology* 28 (1):161–179.

Graham, Laura. 2011. Quoting Mario Juruna. *American Ethnologist* 38 (1):164–183.

Greenblatt, Stephen. 2005. [1980]. *Renaissance Self-Fashioning from More to Shakespeare*. 2nd ed. Chicago, IL: University of Chicago Press.

Grosjean, François. 2010. *Bilingual: Life and Reality*. Cambridge, MA: Harvard University Press.

Gubern, A. 2006. El pregón en castellano de Elvira Lindo deriva en trifulca preelectoral. *ABC*, September 22, 2006, p. 37.

Güell, Maria. 2005. Juan Marsé: "Iría a Fráncfort escindido, sólo de cintura para arriba o para abajo." *ABC*, May 28, 2005, p. 55.

Guibernau, Montserrat. 2004. *Catalan Nationalism: Francoism, Transition and Democracy*. London: Routledge.

Guibernau, Montserrat. 2013. Nationalism versus cosmopolitanism: A comparative approach. *Journal of Catalan Intellectual History* 5:13–34.

Guillaumet, Francesc. 2007. Reiteran que la literatura catalana es la que se escribe en esta lengua. *La Mañana*, February 15, 2007, p. 57.

Gusfield, Joseph. 1986. *Symbolic Crusade: Status Politics and the American Temperance Movement*. Champaign: University of Illinois.

Habermas, Jürgen. 1989. *The Structural Transformation of the Public Sphere*. Translated by Thomas Burger. Cambridge, MA: MIT Press.

Hale, Charles R. 2005. Neoliberal multiculturalism. *PoLAR* 28 (1):10–28.

Handler, Richard. 1988. *Nationalism and the Politics of Culture in Quebec.* Madison: University of Wisconsin Press.

Handler, Richard. 2001. Anthropology of authenticity. In *International Encyclopedia of the Social & Behavioral Sciences*, ed. Neil J. Smelser and Paul B. Baltes, pp. 963–967. Oxford: Elesevier Science.

Hankins, Joseph D. 2014. *Wrong Skin: Making Leather, Making a Multicultural Japan.* Berkeley: University of California Press.

Hannerz, Ulf. 1990. Cosmopolitans and locals in world culture. In *Global Culture: Nationalism, Globalization and Modernity*, ed. Mike Featherstone, pp. 237–252. London: Sage.

Heller, Monica. 1999. *Linguistic Minorities and Modernity: A Sociolinguistic Ethnography.* London: Longman.

Heller, Monica. 2003. Globalization, the new economy, and the commodification of language and identity. *Journal of Sociolinguistics* 7 (4):473–492.

Heller, Monica. 2010. The commodification of language. *Annual Review of Anthropology* 39:101–114.

Heller, Monica. 2011. *Paths to Post-Nationalism: A Critical Ethnography of Language and Identity.* New York: Oxford.

Heller, Monica, 2013. Language as resource in the globalized new economy. In *The Handbook of Language and Globalization*, ed. Nikolas Coupland, pp. 349–365. Oxford: Wiley-Blackwell.

Heller, Monica, and Alexandre Duchêne. 2012. Pride and profit: Changing discourses of language, capital and nation-state. In *Language in Late Capitalism: Pride and Profit*, ed. A. Duchêne and M. Heller, pp. 1–21. New York: Routledge.

Hernàndez, Enric. 2007. Las razones de Montilla que Zapatero no entiende. *El Periódico*, November 11, 2007.

Hernàndez, Enric. 2008. El desafío catalanista de la ministra de Defensa. *El Periódico*, April 20, 2008.

Hevia, Elena. 2006. La Generalitat encarrila la presència d'escriptors en castellà a Frankfurt. *El Periódico*, August 2, 2006, p. 18.

Hewitt, Roger. 1986. *White Talk Black Talk.* Cambridge, UK: Cambridge University Press.

Hierro Hernández, María José. 2013. *Changes in National Identification: The Case of Catalonia.* Madrid: Centro de Estudios Avanzados en Ciencias Sociales.

Hill, Jane H. 2001. Mock Spanish, covert racism and the (leaky) boundary between public and private spheres. In *Languages and Publics: The Making of Authority*, ed. Susan Gal and Kathryn A. Woolard, pp. 83–102. Manchester, UK: St. Jerome. Reissued 2014, Oxon/NY: Routledge.

Hill, Jane H. 2008. *The Everyday Language of White Racism.* Malden, MA: Wiley-Blackwell.

Hinojosa, Silvia. 2006. Montilla recibirá clases de catalán y abogará porque la nueva ley electoral limite los mandatos. *La Vanguardia*, November 28, 2006, p. 16.

Huertas Claveria, Josep M. 2005. Nacionalismes rancis i nacionalismes de poca volada. *Avui*, June 6, 2005, p. 16.

Hutton, Christopher. 2008. Language as identity in language policy discourse: Reflections on a political ideology. In *Lengua, nación e identidad: La regulación del plurilingüismo en España y América Latina*, ed. Kirsten Süselbeck, Ulrike Mühlschlegel, and Peter Masson, pp. 75–88. Frankfurt am Main/Madrid: Vervuert/Iberoamericana.

IDESCAT. 2013. Catalunya: Estadístiques socials. Retrieved January 4, 2015, from Institut d'Estadistica de Catalunya. http://www.idescat.cat/pub/?id=eulp&n=3566.

IDESCAT. 2014. Apellidos de la población. 2014 Catalunya. Retrieved January 4, 2015, from Institut d'Estadistica de Catalunya. http://www.idescat.cat/cognoms/?lang=es.

In Transit. 2012. Cosmopolitan nationalism. *In Transit*, October 29, 2012. http://www.it-intransit.cat/articles/cosmopolitan-nationalism.

Irvine, Judith T., and Susan Gal. 2000. Language ideology and linguistic differentiation. In *Regimes of Language*, ed. P. Kroskrity, pp. 35–84. Santa Fe: School for American Research.

Izquierdo, Oriol. 2006. Provincianismo. *La Vanguardia*, October 3, 2006, p. 40.

J. 2006. Re: El pregó de les festes de la Mercè de Barcelona es farà en castellà [web comment]. *Racó Català*. September 5, 2006. http://www.racocatala.cat/noticia/11908/prego-festes-merce-barcelona-fara-castella.

J.B. 2005. Mieras anuncia l'any de la Cultura Catalana a Alemanya el 2007. *El Punt*, May 5, 2005, p. 58.

J.B. 2007a. Imma Monsó: "La fira de Frankfurt aportarà visibilitat a la literatura catalana." *Segre*, October 10, 2007, p. 49.

J.B. 2007b. Un debat sobre prestatgeries. *Segre*, February 15, 2007, p. 53.

Jaffe, Alexandra. 1993. Obligation, error, and authenticity: Competing cultural principles in the teaching of Corsican. *Journal of Linguistic Anthropology* 3 (1):99–114.

Jaffe, Alexandra. 2000. Comic performance and the articulation of hybrid identity. *Pragmatics* 10 (1):39–59.

Jaffe, Alexandra. 2001. Authority and authenticity: Corsican discourse on bilingual education. In *Voices of Authority: Education and Linguistic Difference*, ed. Monica Heller and Marilyn Martin-Jones, pp. 269–296. Westport, CT: Ablex.

Jaffe, Alexandra. 2007a. Corsican on the airwaves: Media discourse in a context of minority language shift. In *Language in the Media: Representations, Identities, Ideologies*, ed. Sally Johnson and Astrid Ensslin, pp. 149–172. New York: Continuum.

Jaffe, Alexandra. 2007b. Minority language movements. In *Bilingualism: A Social Approach*, ed. Monica Heller, pp. 50–69. Toronto, ON: Palgrave Macmillan.

Jaffe, Alexandra, and Cedric Oliva. 2013. Linguistic creativity in Corsican tourist context. In *Multilingualism and the Periphery*, ed. Sari Pietikäinen and Helen Kelly-Holmes, pp. 95–117. New York: Oxford University Press.

Jaumot. 2006. Re: El pregó de les festes de la Mercè de Barcelona es farà en castellà [web comment]. *Racó Català*, September 5, 2006. http://www.racocatala.cat/noticia/11908/prego-festes-merce-barcelona-fara-castella.

Johnson, Sally, and Astrid Ensslin. 2007. Language in the media: Theory and practice. In *Language in the Media: Representations, Identities, Ideologies*, ed. Sally Johnson and Astrid Ensslin, pp. 3–22. New York: Continuum.

Jordan, M.J. 2006. Toni Soler s'ha afiliat a Ciutadans? *Avui*, November 25, 2006, p. 49.

Jordi. 2006. Re: Demanen Elvira Lindo que renuncïi al pregó de la Mercè [web comment]. *e-notícies*. September 18, 2006. http://hemeroteca.e-noticies.com/edicio-1636/actualitat/demanen-elvira-lindo-que-renunci%EF-al-preg%F3-de-la-merc%E8-7853.html.

Josep de la Trinxera. 2006. Re: El pregó de les festes de la Mercè de Barcelona es farà en castellà [web comment]. *Racó Català*, September 5, 2006. http://www.racocatala.cat/noticia/11908/prego-festes-merce-barcelona-fara-castella.

Joseph, John E. 2000. *Limiting the Arbitrary: Linguistic Naturalism and Its Opposites in Plato's Cratylus and Modern Theories of Language*. Amsterdam/Philadelphia: John Benjamins.

Jou, Lluís. 1998. Els principis de llengua pròpia i llengües oficials en l'articulat de la Llei 1/1998, de 7 de gener, de política lingüística. *Revista de Llengua i Dret* 29:7–22.

Juliana, Enric. 2006. La rectificación. *La Vanguardia*, November 24, 2006, p. 21.

Keane, Webb. 2003. Public speaking: On Indonesian as the language of the nation. *Public Culture* 15 (3):503–530.

Keim, Inken. 2007. Socio-cultural identity, communicative style, and their change over time: A case study of a group of German-Turkish girls in Mannheim/Germany. In *Style and Social Identities*, ed. Peter Auer, pp. 155–186. Berlin: Mouton de Gruyter.

Kelly-Holmes, Helen, and David Atkinson. 2007. "When Hector met Tom Cruise": Attitudes to Irish in a radio satire. In *Language in the Media: Representations, Identities, Ideologies*, ed. Sally Johnson and Astrid Ensslin, pp. 173–187. London: Continuum.

Kiessling, Roland, and Maarten Mous. 2004. Urban youth languages in Africa. *Anthropological Linguistics* 46 (3):1–39.

King, Stewart, ed. 2005. *La cultura catalana de expresión castellana*. Kassel: Edition Reichenberger.

King, Stewart. 2006. Catalan literature(s) in postcolonial context. *Romance Studies* 24 (3):253–264.

King, Stewart. 2010. From literature to letters: Rethinking Catalan literary history. In *New Spain, New Literatures*, ed. Luis Martín-Estudillo and Nicholas Spadaccini, pp. 233–244. Nashville, TN: Vanderbilt University Press.

Klumbyte, Neringa. 2011. Political intimacy: Power, laughter, and coexistence in late Soviet Lithuania. *East European Politics and Societies* 25 (4):65–677.

Knapp, Margit. 2007. A controversial homage to Catalonia: Commerce replaces politics at the Frankfurt Book Fair. *Spiegel Online International*, October 9, 2007. http://

www.spiegel.de/international/germany/a-controversial-homage-to-catalonia-commerce-replaces-politics-at-the-frankfurt-book-fair-a-510291.html.

Knowles, Sam. 2007. Macrocosm-opolitanism? Gilroy, Appiah, and Bhabha: The unsettling generality of cosmopolitan ideas. *Postcolonial Text* 3 (4):1–11.

Kymlicka, Will. 2001. *Politics in the Vernacular: Nationalism, Multiculturalism and Citizenship*. Oxford: Oxford University Press.

Labov, William. 1972. *Language in the Inner City: Studies in the Black English Vernacular*. Philadelphia: University of Pennsylvania.

La CAL. 2007. La CAL opina: La necessària politització del català. *L'Escletxa* 14:4–5.

La Gaceta de los Negocios. 2007. Cataluña recurre a grandes escritores en castellano para promocionarse en Fráncfort. *La Gaceta de los Negocios*, March 8, 2007, p. 55.

Lambert, W.E. 1972. Evaluational reactions to spoken languages. In *Language Psychology and Culture*, ed. Anwar S. Dil, pp. 80–96. Stanford, CA: Stanford University Press.

Larreula, Enric. 2002. *Dolor de llengua*. València/Barcelona: Eliseu Climent.

Lasalas, Marta. 2006. Patriotisme social. *Avui*, November 24, 2006, p. 5.

La Vanguardia. 2006. Barcelona abierta. *La Vanguardia*, September 24, 2006, p. 28.

La Vanguardia. 2007a. El presidente de IEC quiere autores en castellano en Frankfurt. *La Vanguardia*, June 19, 2007, p. 39.

La Vanguardia. 2007b. La lección de Frankfurt. *La Vanguardia*, October 14, 2007, p. 30.

La Vanguardia. 2007c. Los autores en castellano llamados por Bargalló rechazan su invitación para ir a Frankfurt. *La Vanguardia*, June 13, 2007, p. 43.

Lázaro, Fernando. 2006. Igualdad de las lenguas de España. *La Gaceta de los Negocios*, October 20, 2006, p. 5.

Leguino, Joaquin. 2006. Elvira Lindo. *La Gaceta de los Negocios*, September 28, 2006, p. 5.

Lempert, Michael, and Sabina Perrino, eds. 2007. *Temporalities in Text*. Special issue of *Language & Communication*. 27 (3).

Lieberson, Stanley. 1970. *Language and Ethnic Relations in Canada*. New York: Wiley.

Lindholm, Charles. 2008. *Culture and Authenticity*. Malden, MA: Blackwell.

Lindo, Elvira. 2005. La ceja. *El País*, September 28, 2005.

Lindo, Elvira. 2006a. Los intocables. *El País*, May 24, 2006.

Lindo, Elvira. 2006b. Pregó de la Festa Major de la Mercè 2006. Retrieved October 16, 2013, from Ajuntament de Barcelona. http://merce.bcn.cat/ca/elvira-lindo.

Llansana, Marina. 2005. Frankfurt 2007: L'autoodi institucional. *Racó Català*, October 21, 2005. http://www.racocatala.cat/noticia/9102/frankfurt-2007-lau toodi-institucional.

Lodares, Juan Ramón. 2000. *El paraíso políglota: Historias de lenguas en la España moderna contadas*. Madrid: Taurus.

Lodares, Juan Ramón. 2002. *Lengua y patria: Sobre el nacionalismo lingüístico en España*. Madrid: Taurus.

Lodares, Juan Ramón. 2005. La comunidad lingüística en la España de hoy. (Temas y problemas de diferenciación cultural.) *Bulletin of Hispanic Studies* 82 (1):1–14.

López García, Ángel. 1985. *El rumor de los desarraigados: Conflicto de lenguas en la península ibérica*. Barcelona: Editorial Anagrama.

López García, Ángel. 1988. Respuestas a algunas preguntas no formuladas a propósito del "Vascorrománico." *Verba* 15:375–383.

López García, Ángel. 2004. *Babel airada: Las lenguas en el trasfondo de la supuesta ruptura de España*. Madrid: Biblioteca Nueva.

López García, Ángel. 2009. *La lengua común en la España plurilingüe*. Madrid: Iberoamericana Vervuert.

Loste i Romero, Josep M. 2007. Cal anar-hi amb normalitat. *El Vallenc*, June 29, 2007, p. 46.

madafaka. 2006. Re: El pregó de les festes de la Mercè de Barcelona es farà en castellà [web comment]. *Racó Català*. September 19, 2006. http://www.racocatala.cat/noticia/11908/prego-festes-merce-barcelona-fara-castella.

Maher, John C. 2005. Metroethnicity, language, and the principle of Cool. *International Journal of the Sociology of Language* 175–176:83–102.

Manel. 2006. Re: Demanen Elvira Lindo que renuncïi al pregó de la Mercè [web comment]. *e-notícies*, September 18, 2006. http://hemeroteca.e-noticies.com/edicio-1636/actualitat/demanen-elvira-lindo-que-renunci%EF-al-preg%F3-de-la-merc%E8-7853.html.

Maragall, Pasqual. 2007. Política cultural a Catalunya. *El Periódico*, October 6, 2007.

Marcé, Xavier. 2011. Parlar en català en la intimitat. *Ara*, November 14, 2011, p. 26.

Marcos, P., and E. Company. 2001. La afirmación del Rey de que "nunca se obligó a hablar en castellano" provoca una tormenta política. *El País*, April 25, 2001. http://elpais.com/diario/2001/04/25/cultura/988149601_850215.html.

Marfany, Joan-Lluís. 1996. *La cultura del catalanisme*. Barcelona: Editorial Empúries.

Marhuenda, Francisco. 2006. Jordi Portabella y Elvira Lindo. *La Razón*, September 22, 2006, p. 42.

Mar-Molinero, Clare. 2013. The spread of global Spanish: From Cervantes to reggaetón. In *The Handbook of Language and Globalization*, ed. Nikolas Coupland, pp. 162–181. Sussex, UK: Wiley-Blackwell.

Mars, Amanda. 2006. Ciutadans da la sorpresa al conseguir tres diputados. *El País*, November 2, 2006, p. 24.

Mascarell, Ferran. 1999. *El llibre blanc de la cultura a Catalunya: Un futur per a la cultura catalana*. Barcelona: Edicions 62.

Mascarell, Ferran. 2007. Nuevos y viejos catalanismos. *El País*, June 21, 2007, p. 34.

Massot, Josep. 2006. La cultura que se avecina. *La Vanguardia*, November 22, 2006, p. 39.

Mauri, Luis. 2007. Carod riñe a una España que cree "fracasada" como proyecto plural. *El Periódico*, October 17.

Mauri, Luis. 2008. Ferrusola deplora que un andaluz de nombre castellano sea "president." *El Periódico*, March 15, 2008.

May, Steven. 2012. *Language and Minority Rights: Ethnicity, Nationalism and the Politics of Language*, 2nd ed. New York: Routledge.

McLaughlin, Mireille. 2013. What makes art Acadian? In *Multilingualism and the Periphery*, ed. Sari Pietikäinen and Helen Kelly-Holmes, pp. 35–54. New York: Oxford University Press.

Mel, Miqui. 2006. Hi haurà frankfurts per a tothom. *Racó Català*, August 15, 2006. http://www.racocatala.cat/editorial/11727/hi-haura-frankfurts-per-tothom.

Mendoza-Denton, Norma. 2008. *Homegirls: Language and Cultural Practice among Latina Youth Gangs*. Malden, MA: Blackwell.

Mertz, Elizabeth. 1989. Sociolinguistic creativity: Cape Breton Gaelic's linguistic "tip." In *Investigating Obsolescence: Studies in Language Contraction and Death*, ed. N. Dorian, pp. 103–116. Cambridge, UK: Cambridge University Press.

Miley, Thomas Jeffrey. 2013. Blocked articulation and nationalist hegemony in Catalonia. *Regional and Federal Studies* 23 (1):7–26.

Minder, Raphael. 2013. Catalonia clashes with Madrid over independence vote. *The New York Times*, December 13, 2013. http://www.nytimes.com/2013/12/13/world/europe/catalonia-madrid.html.

Moix, Llàtzer, and Josep Massot. 2006. Entrevista, J.M. Tresserras, conseller de Cultura i Mitjans de Comunicació: "No hay que ir de víctimas ni ser esclavos de los sueños de la generación anterior." *La Vanguardia*, December 21, 2006, pp. 38–39.

Moliner, Empar. 2003. El pacte catalanista i d'esquerdes. *El País*, June 23, 2003. http://www.elpais.com/articulo/paginas/pacte/catalanista/i/d/esquerdes/elpepisupbqc/20031218elpbqcpag_9/Tes.

Montilla, José, and Rafael Jorba. 2013. *Clar i català: Testimoni de quatre anys de presidència*. Barcelona: RBA La Magrana.

Morán, David. 2007a. Fráncfort diagnostica la cultura catalana: "Nacionalismos, regionalismos y vanidades." *ABC*, October 10, 2007, pp. 60–61.

Morán, David. 2007b. Fráncfort y el síndrome de las expectativas. *ABC*, October 7, 2007, pp. 55–56.

Morán, David. 2007c. Montilla en Fráncfort: "La polémica sobre el castellano es pueblerina." *ABC*, October 11, 2007, p. 69.

Moreno Cabrera, Juan Carlos. 2008. *El nacionalismo lingüístico: Una ideología destructiva*. Barcelona: Ediciones Península.

Moreno Cabrera, Juan Carlos. 2010. Lengua/nacionalismo en el contexto español. June 29, 2010. http://bretemas.blogaliza.org/files/2010/06/Texto_Juan_Carlos_Moreno_Cabrera.pdf.

Moreno Cabrera, Juan Carlos. 2014. *Los dominios del español: Guía del imperialismo lingüístico panhispánico*. Madrid: Euphonía Ediciones.

Moritz Schwarcz, Lilia K. 2013. The banana emperor: D. Pedro II in Brazilian caricatures, 1842–89. *American Ethnologist* 40 (2):310–323.

Moyer, Melissa. 2013. Language as a resource. Migrant agency, positioning and resistance in a health care clinic. In *Language, Migration and Social (In)equality: A Critical Sociolinguistic Perspective on Institutions and Work*, ed. Alexandre Duchêne, Melissa Moyer, and Celia Roberts, pp. 196–224. Bristol: Multilingual Matters.

MSerrallonga. 2006. Re: El pregó de les festes de la Mercè de Barcelona es farà en castellà [web comment]. *Racó Català*, September 5, 2006. http://www.racocatala.cat/noticia/11908/prego-festes-merce-barcelona-fara-castella.

Muñoz, Jordi, and Raül Tormos. 2012. *Identitat o càlculs instrumentals? Anàlisi dels factors explicatius del suport a la independència*. Barcelona: Generalitat de Catalunya. Retrieved from http://www.ceo.gencat.cat/ceop/AppJava/export/sites/CEOPortal/estudis/workingPapers/contingut/identitat2.pdf.

Muñoz Molina, Antonio. 2007. Paisajes del idioma. *El País*, March 24, 2007. http://elpais.com/diario/2007/03/24/babelia/1174696761_850215.html.

Nagel, Thomas. 1986. *The View from Nowhere*. New York: Oxford University Press.

Nakassis, Constantine. 2013. Brands and their surfeits. *Cultural Anthropology* 28 (1):111–126.

Navarro, Núria. 2006. Elvira Lindo, Escriptora. Pregonera de la Mercè: "Diré uns mots en català, però no com a defensa." *El Periódico*, September 21, 2006, p. 88.

Neff-van Aertselaer, JoAnne. 2006. Language policies in Spain: Accommodation or alteration? In *"Along the Routes to Power": Explorations of Empowerment through Language*, ed. Martin Pütz, Joshua A. Fishman, and JoAnne Neff-van Aertselaer, pp. 179–197. Berlin/New York: Mouton de Gruyter.

Newman, Michael, Adriana Patiño-Santos, and Mireia Trenchs-Parera. 2013. Linguistic reception of Latin American students in Catalonia and their responses to educational language policies. *International Journal of Bilingual Education and Bilingualism* 16 (2):195–209.

Newman, Michael, Mireia Trenchs-Parera, and Shukhan Ng. 2008. Normalizing bilingualism: The effects of the Catalonian linguistic normalization policy one generation after. *Journal of Sociolinguistics* 12 (3):306–333.

Ninyoles, Rafael Lluís. 1971. *Idioma y conflicto*. Barcelona: Cuadernos Beta.

Noguer, Miquel. 2008. CiU critica el nivel de catalán del presidente Montilla. *El País*, July 18, 2008. http://www.elpais.com/articulo/espana/CiU/critica/nivel/catalan/presidente/Montilla/elpepiesp/20080718elpepinac_9/Tes?print=1.

Nussbaum, Martha Craven, and Joshua Cohen, eds. 1996. *For Love of Country: Debating the Limits of Patriotism*. Boston, MA: Beacon Press.

O'Rourke, Bernadette, Joan Pujolar i Cos, and Fernando Ramallo. 2015. New speakers of minority languages: The challenging opportunity—Forward. *International Journal of the Sociology of Language* 231:1–20.

O'Rourke, Bernadette, and Fernando Ramallo. 2013. Competing ideologies of linguistic authority amongst new speakers in contemporary Galicia. *Language in Society* 42 (3):287–305.

Ortega, Rudolf. 2015. El bilingüisme muta. *El País*, April 5, 2015. http://cat.elpais.com/cat/2015/04/05/cultura/1428264483_338515.html.

Ortega y Gasset, José. 1921. *España invertebrada: Bosquejo de algunos pensamientos históricos*. Madrid: Calpe.

Otsuji, Emi, and Alastair Pennycook. 2010. Metrolingualism: Fixity, fluidity and language in flux. *International Journal of Multilingualism* 7 (3):240–254.

Palol, Miquel de. 2007. Frankfurt a punt. *Avui*, October 2, 2007, p. 24.

Pardos-Prado, Sergi, and Joaquim M. Molins. 2009. The emergence of right-wing radicalism at the local level in Spain: The Catalan case. *International Journal of Iberian Studies* 22:201–218.

Pavlenko, Aneta. 2004. "The making of an American": Negotiation of identities at the turn of the twentieth century. In *Negotiation of Identities in Multilingual Contexts*, ed. Aneta Pavlenko and Adrian Blackledge, pp. 34–67. Clevedon, UK: Multilingual Matters.

Pedraza, Pedro, John Attinasi, and Gerard Hoffman. 1980. Rethinking diglossia. In *Ethnolinguistic Perspectives in Bilingual Education Research: Theory in Bilingual Education*, ed. Raymond B. Padilla, pp. 75–97. Ypsilanti, MI: Department of Foreign Languages and Bilingual Studies, Eastern Michigan University.

Pennycook, Alastair. 2007. Language, localization and the real: Hip-hop and the global spread of authenticity. *Journal of Language, Identity and Education* 6 (2):101–115.

Pericay, Xavier. 2006. Déficits y virtudes de la cultura catalana. *ABC*, August 5, 2006, p. 38.

Pernau, Josep. 2007. De les llengües se n'ha fet bandera. *El Periódico*, June 15, 2007, p. 6.

Phillipson, Robert. 1992. *Linguistic Imperialism*. Oxford: Oxford University Press.

Phillipson, Robert. 2003a. English for the globe, or only for globe-trotters? In *The Politics of English as a World Language*, ed. Christian Mair, pp. 19–30. Amsterdam: Rodopi.

Phillipson, Robert. 2003b. *English-Only Europe? Challenging Language Policy*. London: Routledge.

Pietikäinen, Sari. 2010. Sámi language mobility: Scales and discourses of multilingualism in a polycentric environment. *International Journal of the Sociology of Language* 202:79–101.

Pietikäinen, Sari, and Helen Kelly-Holmes, eds. 2013. *Multilingualism and the Periphery*. New York: Oxford University Press.

Piñol, Rosa Maria. 2006. Montilla: "La cultura catalana no puede entenderse sin la de expresión castellana." *La Vanguardia*, July 4, 2006, p. 47.

Piñol, Rosa Maria, and Justo Barranco. 2007. Frankfurt lee EN CATALÁN. *La Vanguardia*, October 7, 2007, p. 45.

Piquer, Eva. 2005. A Frankfurt, en avió. *Avui*, April 10, 2005, p. 63.

Pi-Sunyer, Oriol. 1985. The 1977 parliamentary elections in Barcelona: Primordial symbols in a time of change. *Anthropological Quarterly* 58 (3):108–119.

Pitarch, Josep L. 2010. El negoci de la llengua. *El Punt*, December 5, 2010.

Pla Nualart, Albert. 2011a. El català d'Alberto Fernández Díaz. *Ara*, May 16, 2011. http://www.ara.cat/premium/opinio/catala-dAlberto-Fernandez-Diaz_0_481751864.html.

Pla Nualart, Albert. 2011b. Trias, el català d'un senyor de Barcelona. *Ara*, May 19, 2011. http://www.ara.cat/ara_premium/debat/Trias-catala-dun-senyor-Barcelona_0_483551671.html.

Plataforma per la Llengua. 2010. *El catalán también es mío/El català també és meu*. Barcelona: Fundació Vincle/Plataforma per la Llengua.

Pol. 2006. Re: Demanen Elvira Lindo que renuncii al pregó de la Mercè [web comment]. *e-notícies*, September 18, 2006. http://hemeroteca.e-noticies.com/edicio-1636/actualitat/demanen-elvira-lindo-que-renunci%EF-al-preg%F3-de-la-merc%E8-7853.html.

Pollock, Sheldon. 2000. Cosmopolitan and vernacular in history. *Public Culture* 12 (3):591–625.

Pontón, Gonzalo. 2007. ¡Es la ciencia, estúpido! *El País*, June 21, 2007, p. 17.

Porcel, Baltasar. 2007. Se acabó el "xarnego." *La Vanguardia*, January 21, 2007, p. 29.

Porta, Jordi. 2005. A Frankfurt sense complexos. *El Periódico*, December 5, 2005, p. 6.

Portabella, Jordi. 2006. D'acord, però hi ha algú més? Esquerra Republicana website, October 3, 2006. http://www.esquerra.cat/opinio/dacord-per-hi-ha-alg-ms.

Povinelli, Elizabeth. 2002. *The Cunning of Recognition: Indigenous Alterities and the Making of Australian Multiculturalism*. Durham, NC: Duke University Press.

Pradilla Cardona, Miquel Àngel, and Joaquim Torres-Pla. 2012. Característiques demolingüístiques dels joves de Catalunya a finals de la primera dècada del segle XXI. *Treballs de Sociolingüística Catalana* 22:119–134.

Puigverd, Antoni. 2006a. Astucia del zorro periférico. *La Vanguardia*, November 24, 2006, p. 18.

Puigverd, Antoni. 2006b. A propósito de Montaigne. *La Vanguardia*, December 11, 2006, p. 22.

Pujolar, Joan. 1997. Masculinities in a multilingual setting. In *Language and Masculinity*, ed. Sally Johnson and Ulrike H. Meinhof, pp. 86–106. Oxford: Blackwell.

Pujolar, Joan. 2001. *Gender, Heteroglossia and Power: A Sociolinguistic Study of Youth Culture*. Berlin: Mouton de Gruyter.

Pujolar, Joan. 2007a. Bilingualism and the nation-state in the post-national era. In *Bilingualism: A Social Approach*, ed. Monica Heller, pp. 71–95. London: Palgrave Macmillan.

Pujolar, Joan. 2007b. The future of Catalan: Language endangerment and nationalist discourses in Catalonia. In *Discourses of Endangerment*, ed. Alexandre Duchêne and Monica Heller, pp. 121–148. London: Continuum.

Pujolar, Joan. 2010. Immigration and language education in Catalonia: Between national and social agendas. *Linguistics and Education* 21:229–243.

Pujolar, Joan, and Isaac Gonzàlez. 2013. Linguistic "mudes" and the de-ethnicization of language choice in Catalonia. *International Journal of Bilingual Education and Bilingualism* 16 (2):138–152.

Pujolar, Joan, and Kathryn Jones. 2012. Literary tourism: New appropriations of landscape and territory in Catalonia. In *Language in Late Capitalism: Pride and Profit*, ed. Alexandre Duchêne and Monica Heller, pp. 93–115. New York: Routledge.

Pujolar, Joan, and Maite Puigdevall. 2015. Linguistic mudes: How to become a new speaker in Catalonia. *International Journal of the Sociology of Language* 231:167–187.

Pujolar i Cos, Joan, Isaac Gonzàlez i Balletbò, Anna Font i Tanyà, and Roger Martínez i Sanmartí. 2010. *Llengua i joves: Usos i percepcions lingüístics de la joventut catalana*. Barcelona: Generalitat de Catalunya, Departament d'Acció Social i Ciutadania, Secretaria de Joventut.

Puppo, Ronald. 2011. The poetry of troubles: Maragall's Els tres cants de la guerra (Three songs of war) and their translation. *Journal of Catalan Studies* 14:217–236.

Què! 2006. Montilla estudiarà català com ja fan 75.000 persones. *Què!*, November 28, 2006, p. 4.

Racó Català. 2006a. CiU i ERC perden una votació decisiva del Parlament sobre Frankfurt 2007 per absències. *Racó Català*, July 14, 2006. http://www.racocatala. cat/noticia/11503/ciu-erc-perden-votacio-decisiva-parlament-sobre-frankfurt-2007-absencies.

Racó Català. 2006b. Es presenta la campanya "A la Fira del Llibre de Frankfurt 2007, en català." *Racó Català*, September 28, 2006. http://www.racocatala.cat/noticia/ 12084/presenta-campanya-fira-llibre-frankfurt-2007-catala.

Racó Català. 2006c. Esquerra Republicana presenta una moció perquè la literatura catalana la representin les obres en català a la Fira de Frankfurt. *Racó Català*, July 4, 2006. http://www.racocatala.cat/noticia/11387/esquerra-republicana-presenta-mocio-perque-literatura-catalana-representin-obres-catala-fi.

Ràfols, Neus. 2007. Cap a Frankfurt. *Avui*, April 23, 2007, pp. 33–34.

Rahola, Pilar. 2006a. Manolito Portabella. *El País*, September 23, 2006.

Rahola, Pilar. 2006b. ¡Qué ciudadana fatiga! *El País*, November 4, 2006, p. 34.

Ramis, Llucia. 2007. Leipzig, despegue catalán entre la nieve. *El Mundo*, March 23, 2007, p. 81.

Rampton, Ben. 1995. *Crossing: Language and Ethnicity among Adolescents*. London: Longman.

Rampton, Ben. 1999. Sociolinguistics and cultural studies: New ethnicities, liminality and interaction. *Social Semiotics* 9 (3):355–373.

Redacción. 2006. Malestar general tras los incidentes del pregón. *La Vanguardia*, September 24, 2006, p. 3.

Reichman, Daniel. 2011. Migration and paraethnography in Honduras. *American Ethnologist* 38 (3):548–558.

ReiDelMam. 2006a. Re: El pregó de les festes de la Mercè de Barcelona es farà en cas-tellà [web comment]. *Racó Català*, September 5, 2006. http://www.racocatala.cat/noticia/11908/prego-festes-merce-barcelona-fara-castella.

ReiDelMam. 2006b. Re: El pregó de les festes de la Mercè de Barcelona es farà en cas-tellà [web comment]. *Racó Català*, September 5, 2006. http://www.racocatala.cat/noticia/11908/prego-festes-merce-barcelona-fara-castella.

Resina, Joan Ramon. 2002. "For their own good": The Spanish identity and its Great Inquisitor, Miguel de Unamuno. In *The Battle over Spanish between 1800 and 2000*, ed. José del Valle and Luis Gabriel-Stheeman, pp. 106–133. London: Routledge.

Ribera, Carles. 2010. Catalunya no és bilingüe. *Avui*, November 5, 2010, p. 3.

Ribot Bencomo, Aida. 2013. Media Representation of Language and Identity in a Catalan TV Comedy: An Approach to Language Ideology and Linguistic Identity. M.A. thesis, Department of Anthropology, University of California, San Diego.

Richards, Greg. 2004. Popular culture, tradition and tourism in the Festes de la Mercè, Barcelona. (Published in Spanish as Cultura popular, tradición y turismo en las Festes de la Mercè de Barcelona.) In *Casos de turismo cultural: De la plani-ficación estratégica a la evaluación de productos*, ed. Joseph Font, pp. 287–306. Barcelona: Ariel.

Richards, Greg. 2007. The festivalization of society or the socialization of festivals? The case of Catalunya. In *Cultural Tourism: Global and Local Perspectives*, ed. Greg Richards, pp. 257–280. New York: Haworth Hospitality Press.

Rico, Jose. 2007. La pedagogía como receta. *El Periódico*, November 21, 2007.

Riera, Miquel. 2006. Cap al "catanyol." *Homo sapiens*. http://hsapiens.blogspot.com/search?q=catanyol.

Riera Gil, Elvira. 2013. Sobre el concepte polític de llengua comuna: Una aproximació teòrica i comparada. *Revista de Llengua i Dret* 60:91–110.

Rodriguez, Richard. 1981. *Hunger of Memory*. Boston: David R. Godine.

Rodríguez Adrados, Francisco. 2006. Respuesta de Rodríguez Adrados. *El País*, March 13, 2006. http://elpais.com/diario/2006/03/13/opinion/1142204410_850215.html.

Rodríguez Pérez, Carlos. 2006. Felicidades, president. *La Vanguardia*, November 24, 2006, p. 30.

Ronkin, Maggie, and Helen E. Karn. 1999. Mock Ebonics: Linguistic racism in paro-dies of Ebonics on the Internet. *Journal of Sociolinguistics* 3 (3):360–380.

Ros, Tito. 2006. Portabella enciende el pregón. *ADN*, September 21, 2006, p. 3.

Royo Arpón, Jesús. 2000. *Arguments per al bilingüisme*. Mataró (Barcelona): Montesinos Assaig.

Ruiz, Richard. 1984. Orientations in language planning. *NABE Journal* 8 (2):15–34.

Rumford, Chris, ed. 2007. *Cosmopolitanism and Europe*. Liverpool: Liverpool University Press.

Sabadellenc. 2006. Re: El pregó de les festes de la Mercè de Barcelona es farà en castellà [web comment]. *Racó Català*, September 5, 2006. http://www.racocatala.cat/noticia/11908/prego-festes-merce-barcelona-fara-castella.

Sabaté i Dalmau, Maria. 2014. *Migrant Communication Enterprises: Regimentation and Resistance*. Bristol: Multilingual Matters.

Sala, Carlos, and Montse Espanyol. 2006. Elvira Lindo abre la Mercè con una lección de cosmopolitismo a sus detractores. *La Razón*, September 23, 2006, p. 39.

Sala i Martín, Xavier 2006. Mis entrevistas: "Sé lo que es trabajar desde los 16 años; empecé de aprendiz doce horas al día." *La Vanguardia*, October 16, 2006, p. 16.

Sàlmon, Álex. 2007. Un Fráncfort inconcluso. *El Mundo*, October 14, 2007, p. 6.

San Agustín, Arturo. 2007. Frankfurt (Article d'Arturo San Agustín en català). *El Periódico*, October 10, 2007.

Sànchez, Cèsar. 2005. Setmana de Sant Jordi a Sabadell. *La Corbella* 8:7.

Sankoff, Gillian. 2004. Adolescents, young adults, and the critical period: Two case studies from "Seven Up." In *Sociolinguistic Variation: Critical Reflections*, ed. Carmen Fought, pp. 121–139. New York: Oxford.

Sankoff, Gillian. 2005. Cross-sectional and longitudinal studies. In *Sociolinguistics/Soziolinguistik: An International Handbook of the Science of Language and Society*, ed. Ulrich Ammon, et al., pp. 1003–1013. Berlin: Walter de Gruyter.

Sankoff, Gillian. 2006. Age: Apparent time and real time. In *Encyclopedia of Language and Linguistics*, ed. Keith Brown, 2nd ed., pp. 110–116. Boston: Elsevier.

Sans, Sara. 2006. Carod receta moderación y "austeridad formal" a Esquerra. *La Vanguardia*, December 17, 2006, p. 21.

Santamaría, Antonio. 1999. Lengua propia, conducta impropia. In *Foro Babel: El nacionalismo y las lenguas de Cataluña*, ed. Antonio Santamaría, pp. 181–197. Barcelona: Ediciones Áltera.

Santos, Pilar. 2006. Montilla es posa com a exemple que el català necessita protecció. *El Periódico*, November 25, 2006, p. 5.

Segarra, Mila. 1985. *Història de la normativa catalana*. Barcelona: Enciclopèdia Catalana.

Segura Girard, Lluís J. 2011. Les llengües oficials en la doctrina recent del tribunal constitucional. *Revista de Llengua i Dret* 56:83–113.

Serra, Màrius. 2006a. Alma bifocal. *La Vanguardia*, November 25, 2006, p. 19.

Serra, Màrius. 2006b. El rancio cosmopolitanismo. *La Vanguardia*, September 26, 2006, p. 24.

Serra, Màrius. 2006c. Pressident del Gover (d'Enteça). *La Vanguardia*, November 24, 2006, p. 22.

Serra i Casals, Enric. 2010. Nogensmenys. *Aprendre llengües*, October 23, 2010. http://enricserrabloc.blogspot.com/2010/10/562-nogensmenys.html.

Sharma, Nitasha Tamar. 2010. *Hip Hop Desis: South Asian Americans, Blackness, and a Global Race Consciousness*. Durham, NC: Duke University Press.

Siegel, James T. 1986. *Solo in the New Order: Language and Hierarchy in an Indonesian City*. Princeton, NJ: Princeton University Press.

Siguan, Miguel. 1988. Bilingual education in Spain. In *International Handbook of Bilingualism and Bilingual Education*, ed. Christina Bratt Paulston, pp. 449–473. New York: Greenwood Press.

Silverstein, Michael. 1995. Indexical order and the dialectics of sociolinguistic life. In *Third Annual Symposium about Language and Society-Austin*, ed. R. Ide, R. Parker, and Y. Sunaoshi, pp. 266–295. Austin: University of Texas, Department of Linguistics.

Silverstein, Michael. 1996. Monoglot "standard" in America. In *The Matrix of Language*, ed. Donald Brenneis and Ronald K.S. Macaulay, pp. 284–306. Boulder, CO: Westview Press.

Silverstein, Michael. 1998. Contemporary transformations of local linguistic communities. *Annual Review in Anthropology* 27:401–426.

Silverstein, Michael. 2003. *Talking Politics: The Substance of Style from Abe to "W."* Chicago, IL: Prickly Paradigm Press.

Simó, Isabel-Clara. 2006. Manifest per a Frankfurt: Literatura catalana és la que s'escriu en català. *Racó Català*, July 9, 2006. http://www.racocatala.cat/noticia/11429/manifest-frankfurt-literatura-catalana-sescriu-catala.

Simó, Isabel-Clara. 2007. Et convé morir. *Avui*, March 31, 2007, p. 25.

Sinner, Carsten, and Katharina Wieland. 2008. El catalán hablado y problemas de la normalización de la lengua catalana: Avances y obstáculos en la normalización. In *Lengua, nación e identidad: La regulación del plurilingüismo en España y América Latina*, ed. Kirsten Süselbeck, Ulrike Mühlschlegel, and Peter Masson, pp. 131–164. Madrid: Iberoamericana Vervuert.

Sintes, Marçal. 2007. Enredado con Fráncfort. *El Mundo*, June 24, 2007, p. 36.

Sintes i Olivella, Marçal. 2010. De la política a la política "polonitzada." *Trípodos* 27:49–58.

Snyder-Frey, Alicia. 2013. He kuleana kō kākou: Hawaiian language learners and the construction of (alter)native identities. *Current Issues in Language Planning* 14 (2):231–243.

Solé i Durany, Joan Ramon. 1996. El concepte de la llengua pròpia en el dret i la normalització de l'idioma a Catalunya. *Revista de Llengua i Dret* 26:95–120.

Soler, Josep. 2013. The anonymity of Catalan and the authenticity of Estonian: Two paths for the development of medium-sized languages. *International Journal of Bilingual Education and Bilingualism* 16 (2):153–163.

Soler, Toni. 2006. El estéril debate identitario. *La Vanguardia*, December 17, 2006, p. 28.

Soler, Toni. 2007. Siete días de elecciones. *La Vanguardia*, June 17, 2007, p. 26.

Soler, Toni. 2008. Y los del "Manifiesto," tronchándose. *La Vanguardia*, July 20, 2008, p. 21.

Strubell i Trueta, Miquel. 1996. Language planning and bilingual education in Catalonia. *Journal of Multilingual and Multicultural Development* 17 (2–4): 262–275.

Strubell i Trueta, Miquel, Llorenç Andreu Barrachina, and Elena Sintes Pascual, eds. 2013. *Resultats del model lingüístic escolar de Catalunya: L'evidència empírica.* Barcelona: Universitat Oberta de Catalunya.

Súmate. n.d. Quiénes somos. Súmate. http://www.sumate.cat/p/quienes-somos.html.

Suñé, Ramon. 2006a. La fiesta sucede a la trifulca. *La Vanguardia,* September 23, 2006, *Vivir* p. 1.

Suñé, Ramon. 2006b. Portabella no asistirá al pregón en castellano de las fiestas de la Mercè. *La Vanguardia,* September 21, 2006, *Vivir,* p. 4.

Süselbeck, Kirsten. 2008. "Lengua," "nación" e "identidad" en el discurso de la política lingüística de Cataluña. In *Lengua, nación e identidad: La regulación del plurilingüísmo en España y América Latina,* ed. Kirsten Süselbeck, Ulrike Mühlschlegel, and Peter Masson, pp. 165–186. Madrid: Iberoamericana Vervuert.

Tapp, Nicholas. 2010. *The Impossibility of Self: An Essay on the Hmong Diaspora.* Berlin: LIT Verlag.

Taylor, Charles. 1991. *The Ethics of Authenticity.* Cambridge, MA: Harvard University Press.

Televisió de Catalunya. 2013a. Catalunya exhibeix al món la seva via independentista. *TV3 Notícies,* September 12, 2013. http://www.ccma.cat/324/1600000-personescom-a-minim/noticia/2170774/.

Televisió de Catalunya. 2013b. Interior xifra en almenys 1.600.000 els participants a la Via Catalana. *TV3 Notícies,* September 12, 2013. http://www.ccma.cat/324/Interiorxifra-en-almenys-1600000-els-participants-a-la-Via-Catalana/noticia/2171062/.

Terricabras, Josep-Maria. 2008a. La lengua, problema político. *El Periódico,* July 9, 2008.

Terricabras, Josep-Maria. 2008b. La mala fe y la fe mala anticatalana. *El Periódico,* January 16, 2008.

The Economist. 2014. Wars of Spanish secession. *The Economist,* May 3, 2014. http://www.economist.com/news/europe/21601570-catalonia-set-independence-votedespite-madrids-hostility-wars-spanish-secession.

Thiers, Ghjacumu. 1993. Language contact and Corsican polynomia. In *Trends in Romance Linguistics and Philology,* ed. R. Posner and J.N. Green, pp. 253–270. Berlin: Mouton de Gruyter.

Torquemada, Blanca. 2006. Irene Lozano: "El español también es la lengua propia de Cataluña y el País Vasco." *ABC,* January 2, 2006. http://www.abc.es/hemeroteca/historico-02-01-2006/abc/Nacional/irene-lozano-el-español-tambien-es-lalengua-propia-de-cataluña-y-el-pais-vasco_1013400180498.html.

Trask, Larry, and Roger Wright. 1988. El "vascorrománico." *Verba* 15:361–373.

Tree, Matthew. 2007. Aftertaste: On a controversial speech. Matthewtree.cat. February 11, 2007. http://www.matthewtree.cat/index.php?seccio=article&articles_id=91&idioma=esp.

Trenchs-Parera, Mireia, Imanol Larrea Mendizabal, and Michael Newman. 2014. La normalització del cosmopolitisme lingüístic entre els joves del segle XXI? Una exploració de les ideologies lingüístiques a Catalunya. *Treballs de Sociolingüística Catalana* 24:281–302.

Trenchs-Parera, Mireia, and Michael Newman. 2009. Diversity of language ideologies in Spanish-speaking youth of different origins in Catalonia. *Journal of Multilingual and Multicultural Development* 30 (6):509–524.

Tribunal Constitucional. 2010. Sentencia del Tribunal Constitucional 31/2010, de 28 de junio de 2010. Recurso de inconstitucionalidad 8045-2006. Retrieved from http://boe.es/diario_boe/txt.php?id=BOE-A-2010-11409.

Trilling, Lionel. 1972. *Sincerity and Authenticity*. Oxford: Oxford University Press.

Trosset, Carol S. 1986. The social identity of Welsh learners. *Language in Society* 15:165–192.

Tubau, Ivan. 1990. *Paraula viva contra llengua normativa*. Barcelona: Editorial Laertes.

Tubau, Ivan. 2007. Nomenklaturas y ficciones. *El Mundo*, June 27, 2007, p. 68.

Tudela, Joan. 2013. Antifranquisme lingüístic. ARA.cat. http://blogspersonals.ara.cat/anysdaprenentatge/2013/09/28/antifranquisme-linguistic/.

Urla, Jacqueline. 2012a. *Reclaiming Basque: Language, Nation, and Cultural Activism*. Reno: University of Nevada Press.

Urla, Jacqueline. 2012b. "Total quality language revival." In *Language in Late Capitalism: Pride and Profit*, ed. Alexandre Duchêne and Monica Heller, pp. 73–92. New York: Routledge.

Urry, John. 2003. *Global Complexity*. Cambridge, UK: Polity Press.

Usó, Vicent. 2007. A frankfurt (o al Frankfurt). *El Periódico Mediterráneo*, June 24, 2007, p. 5.

Vallbona, Rafael. 2007. Yo no voy y ¿qué? *El Mundo*, June 14, 2007, p. 60.

Vallory, Eduard. 2007. El Rasclet: Estratègies, objectius postnacionals. *Avui*, January 21, 2007. Retrieved from http://eduardvallory.blogspot.com/2007/01/estratgies-de-partit-objectius.html.

Vargas Llosa, Mario, et al. 2008. Manifiesto por una lengua común. *El País*, June 23, 2008. http://elpais.com/elpais/2008/06/23/actualidad/1214209045_850215.html.

Vázquez Montalbán, Manuel. 2001. Sobre la nació real dels ciutadans. In *El nou catalanisme*, ed. Norbert Bilbeny and Àngel Pes, pp. 64–76. Barcelona: Editorial Ariel.

Ventura, Jordi, and Pau Escribano. 2007. *El llibre mediàtic de Polònia*. Barcelona: Televisió de Catalunya/Columna Edicions.

Vernet, Jaume, and Eva Pons. 2011. The legal systems of the Catalan language. In *Democratic Policies for Language Revitalisation: The Case of Catalan*, ed. Miquel Strubell and Emili Boix-Fuster, pp. 57–83. Hampshire, UK: Palgrave Macmillan.

Vertovec, Steven, and Robin Cohen, eds. 2002a. *Conceiving Cosmopolitanism: Theory, Context, and Practice*. Oxford: Oxford University Press.

Vertovec, Steven, and Robin Cohen. 2002b. Introduction: Conceiving Cosmopolitanism. In *Conceiving Cosmopolitanism: Theory, Context, and Practice*, ed. Steven Vertovec and Robin Cohen, pp. 1–22. New York: Oxford University Press.

Veu Pròpia Bages. 2008. Per què un immigrant parla català? May 13, 2008. http://bag-esveupropia.blogspot.nl/2008/05/perqu-un-immigrant-parl-catal.html.

Vidal, Pau. 2015. *El bilingüisme mata*. Barcelona: Pòrtic.

Vila, Ignasi, Carina Siqués, and Teresa Roig. 2006. *Llengua, escola i immigració: Un debat obert*. Barcelona: Editorial Graó.

Vila i Mendiburu, Ignasi. 2010. Els programes de canvi de llengua de la llar a l'escola: El repte de la catalanització escolar. *Treballs de Sociolingüística Catalana* 20:229–260.

Vila i Moreno, F. Xavier. 2003. Els usos lingüístics interpersonals no famliars a Catalunya. *Treballs de Sociolingüística Catalana* 17:77–158.

Vila i Moreno, F. Xavier. 2004a. Barcelona (Catalonia): Language, education and ideology in an integrationist society. In *Contactforum: Language, Attitudes & Education in Multilingual Cities*, ed. E. Witte, et al., pp. 53–86. Brussels: Koninklijke Vlaamse Academie Van Belgie Voor Wetenschappen en Kunsten.

Vila i Moreno, F. Xavier. 2004b. De l'ús al coneixement: Algunes reflexions sobre la pro-moció de la llengua al sistema educatiu. In *Jornades de la secció filològica de l'Institut d'Estudis Catalans a Vic*, pp. 149–169. Barcelona/Vic: Institut d'Estudis Catalans/Universitat de Vic/Ajuntament de Vic.

Vila i Moreno, F. Xavier. 2011. Language-in-education policy. In *Democratic Policies for Language Revitalization: The Case of Catalan*, ed. Miquel Strubell and Emili Boix-Fuster, pp. 119–149. New York: Palgrave Macmillan.

Vila i Moreno, F. Xavier, ed. 2012. *Posar-hi la base: Usos i aprenentatges lingüístics en el domini català*. Barcelona: Institut d'Estudis Catalans.

Vila i Moreno, F. Xavier, and Vanessa Bretxa i Riera, eds. 2014. *Language Policy in Higher Education: The Case of Medium-Sized Languages*. Clevedon, UK: Multilingual Matters.

Vila i Moreno, F. Xavier, and Mireia Galindo Solé. 2010. El sistema de conjunció en català en l'educació primària a Catalunya: Impacte sobre els usos. *Treballs de Sociolingüística Catalana* 2010:21–69.

Vila i Ros, David. 2007. La llengua comuna. *Avui*, September 6, 2007, p. 27.

Vilarós, Teresa M. 2003. The passing of the xarnego-immigrant: Post-nationalism and the ideologies of assimilation in Catalonia. *Arizona Journal of Hispanic Cultural Studies* 7:229–246.

Vila-Sanjuán, Sergio. 2007. Catalunya en Frankfurt: Una impresión. *La Vanguardia*, October 14, 2007, p. 55.

VilaWeb. 2015. Carolina Punset escandalitza les Corts amb un insòlit atac contra el català. *VilaWeb*, June 25, 2015. http://www.vilaweb.cat/noticia/4398972/20150625/carolina-punset-escandalitza-corts-insolit-atac-valencia.html.

Villatoro, Vicenç. 2006. ¿Ciutadans o Montilla? *El País*, November 22, 2006. http://www.elpais.com/articulo/cataluna/Ciutadans/Montilla/elpepiespcat/20061122elpcat_5/Tes?print=1.

Villatoro, Vicenç. 2007. Barcelona contra Catalunya. *El Temps*, March 24, 2007.

Vives, Aina. 2007. Frankfurt forçosament català. *El Punt*, June 14, 2007, p. 44.

Wardhaugh, Ronald. 1987. *Languages in Competition: Dominance, Diversity, and Decline*. New York, Oxford: Basil Blackwell.

Webster, Noah. 1967. [1789]. *Dissertations on the English Language*. Menston, UK: Scolar Press Limited.

Weidhaas, Peter. 2007. *A History of the Frankfurt Book Fair*. Translated by C.M. Gossage and W.A. Wright. Toronto, ON: Dundurn Press.

Werbner, Pnina. 2006. Vernacular cosmopolitanism. *Theory, Culture & Society* 23 (2–3):496–498.

Werbner, Pnina, ed. 2008. *Anthropology and the New Cosmopolitanism*. London: Berg.

Wheeler, Max W. 2005. *The Phonology of Catalan*. Oxford: Oxford University Press.

Wheeler, Max W., Alan Yates, and Nicolau Dols. 1999. *Catalan: A Comprehensive Grammar*. London: Routledge.

Wilce, James M. 2009. *Language and Emotion*. Cambridge, UK: Cambridge University Press.

Williams, Raymond. 1973. Base and superstructure in Marxist cultural theory. *New Left Review* 87:3–16.

Woolard, Kathryn A. 1986. The politics of language status planning: "Normalization" in Catalonia. In *Language in the International Perspective*, ed. Nancy Schweda-Nicholson, pp. 91–102. Norwood, MJ: Ablex.

Woolard, Kathryn A. 1987. Codeswitching and comedy in Catalonia. *Pragmatics* 1 (1):106–122.

Woolard, Kathryn A. 1989a. *Double Talk: Bilingualism and the Politics of Ethnicity in Catalonia*. Stanford, CA: Stanford University Press.

Woolard, Kathryn A. 1989b. Sentences in the language prison: The rhetorical structuring of an American language policy debate. *American Ethnologist* 16 (2):268–278.

Woolard, Kathryn A. 1991a. Catalan as a public language. In *Contemporary Catalonia in Spain and Europe*, ed. Milton M. Azevedo, pp. 50–61. Berkeley, CA: Gaspar de Portolà Catalonian Studies Program, University of California at Berkeley.

Woolard, Kathryn A. 1991b. Linkages of language and ethnic identity: Changes in Barcelona, 1980–1987. In *Language and Ethnicity: Focusschrift in Honor of Joshua A. Fishman*, ed. J. Dow, Vol. II, pp. 61–81. Amsterdam/Philadelphia: John Benjamins.

Woolard, Kathryn A. 1992. *Identitat i contacte de llengües a Barcelona*. Barcelona: Edicions de la Magrana.

Woolard, Kathryn A. 1995. Changing forms of codeswitching in Catalan comedy. *Catalan Review* 9 (2):223–252.

Woolard, Kathryn A. 1997a. Between friends: Gender, peer group structure and bilingualism in urban Catalonia. *Language in Society* 26 (4):533–560.

Woolard, Kathryn A. 1997b. Identidades de clase y género en los proyectos lingüísticos nacionales: Alguna evidencia desde Cataluña. *Revista de Antropología Social* 6:193–213.

Woolard, Kathryn A. 1998. Introduction: Language ideology as a field of inquiry. In *Language Ideologies: Practice and Theory*, ed. B.B. Schieffelin, K.A. Woolard, and P. Kroskrity, pp. 3–47. New York: Oxford University Press.

Woolard, Kathryn A. 1999. Simultaneity and bivalency as strategies in bilingualism. *Journal of Linguistic Anthropology* 8 (1):3–29.

Woolard, Kathryn A. 2002. Bernardo de Aldrete and the Morisco problem: A study in early modern Spanish language ideology. *Comparative Studies in Society and History* 44 (3):446–480.

Woolard, Kathryn A. 2003. "We don't speak Catalan because we are marginalized": Ethnic and class connotations of language in Barcelona. In *Language and Social Identity*, ed. Richard Blot, pp. 85–103. Westport, CT: Praeger.

Woolard, Kathryn A. 2004. Codeswitching. In *A Companion to Linguistic Anthropology*, ed. Alessandro Duranti, pp. 73–94. Malden, MA: Blackwell.

Woolard, Kathryn A. 2007a. Bystanders and the linguistic construction of identity in face-to-back communication. In *Style and Social Identities*, ed. Peter Auer, pp. 187–205. Berlin/NY: Mouton de Gruyter.

Woolard, Kathryn A. 2007b. La autoridad lingüística del español y las ideologías de la autenticidad y el anonimato. In *La lengua, ¿patria común?*, ed. José del Valle, pp. 129–142. Madrid: Vervuert Iberoamericana.

Woolard, Kathryn A. 2008. Language and identity choice in Catalonia: The interplay of contrasting ideologies of linguistic authority. In *Lengua, nación e identidad: La regulación del plurilingüismo en España y América Latina*, ed. Kirsten Süselbeck, Ulrike Mühlschlegel, and Peter Masson, pp. 303–323. Madrid/Frankfurt: Iberoamericana/Vervuert.

Woolard, Kathryn A. 2009. Linguistic consciousness among adolescents in Catalonia: A case study from the Barcelona urban area in longitudinal perspective. *Zeitschrift für Katalanistik* 22:125–149.

Woolard, Kathryn A. 2011. Is there linguistic life after high school? Longitudinal changes in the bilingual repertoire in metropolitan Barcelona. *Language in Society* 40 (5):617–648.

Woolard, Kathryn A. 2013. Is the personal political? Chronotopes and changing stances toward Catalan language and identity. *International Journal of Bilingual Education and Bilingualism* 16 (2):210–224.

Woolard, Kathryn A., and Susan E. Frekko. 2013. Introduction: Catalan in the twenty-first century: Romantic publics and cosmopolitan communities. *International Journal of Bilingual Education and Bilingualism* 16 (2):129–137.

Woolard, Kathryn A., and Tae-Joong Gahng. 1990. Changing language policies and attitudes in autonomous Catalonia. *Language in Society* 19:311–330.

Woolard, Kathryn A., Aida Ribot Bencomo, and Josep Soler Carbonell. 2014. What's so funny now? The strength of weak pronouns in Catalonia. *Journal of Linguistic Anthropology* 23 (3):127–141.

Wortham, Stanton. 2005. *Learning Identity: The Joint Emergence of Social Identification and Academic Learning*. Cambridge, UK: Cambridge University Press.

Wurl, Ursula M. 2011. El concepte jurídic de llengua pròpia. *Llengua i Dret* 56:3–64.

Ximénez de Sandoval, Pablo. 2008. ¿Está perseguido el castellano? *El País*, April 21, 2008. http://elpais.com/diario/2008/04/21/sociedad/1208728801_850215.html.

Zentella, Ana Celia. 1997. *Growing Up Bilingual: Puerto Rican Children in New York City*. Oxford: Blackwell.

INDEX

Italicized page numbers indicate illustrations and photographs. Tables are indicated by "t" following the page number.

Made in the USA
San Bernardino, CA
30 April 2018